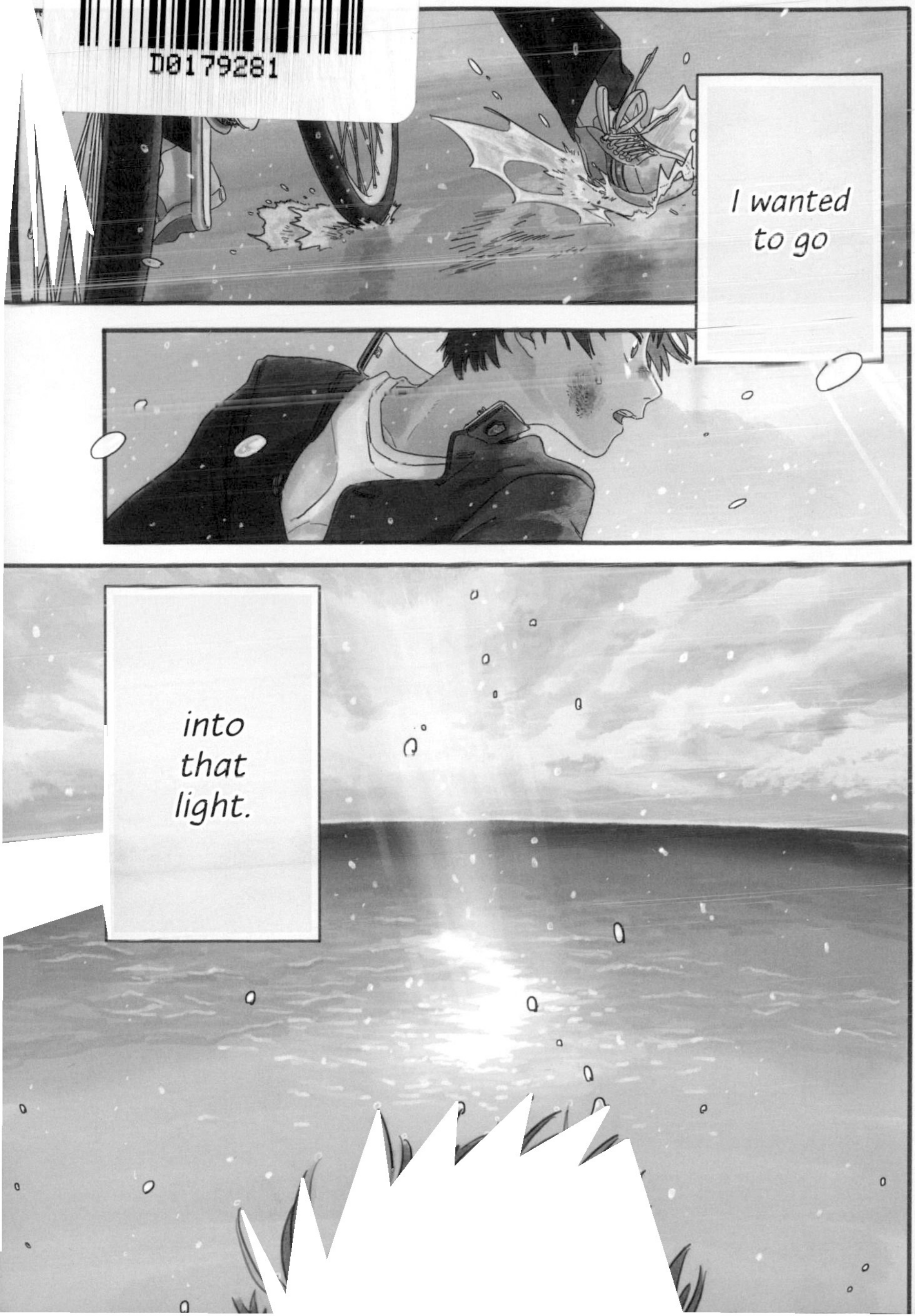
I wanted to go
into that light.

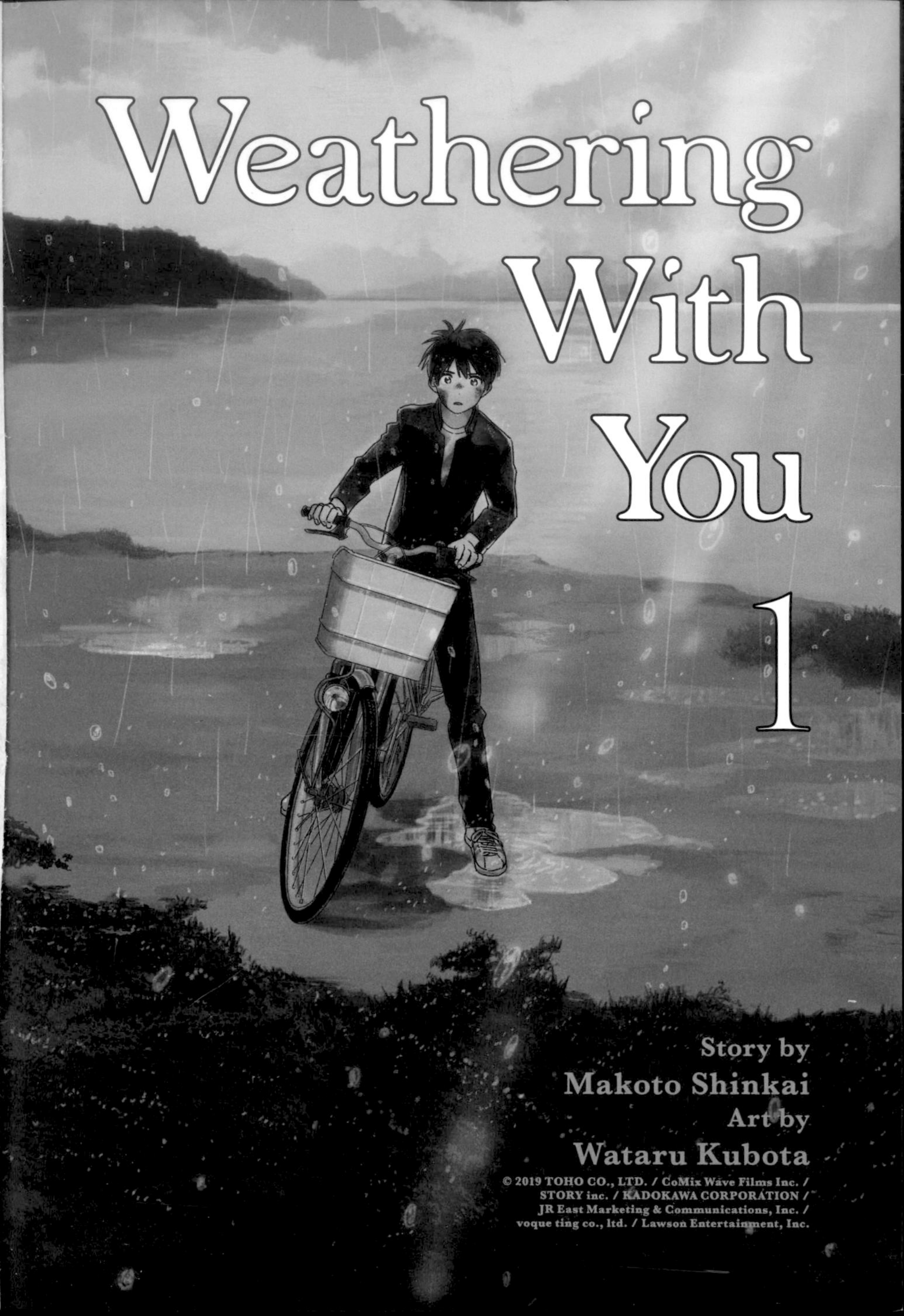
Weathering
With
You
1
Story by
Makoto Shinkai
Art by
Wataru Kubota
© 2019 TOHO CO., LTD. / CoMix Wave Films Inc. / STORY inc. / KADOKAWA CORPORATION / JR East Marketing & Communications, Inc. / voque ting co., ltd. / Lawson Entertainment, Inc.

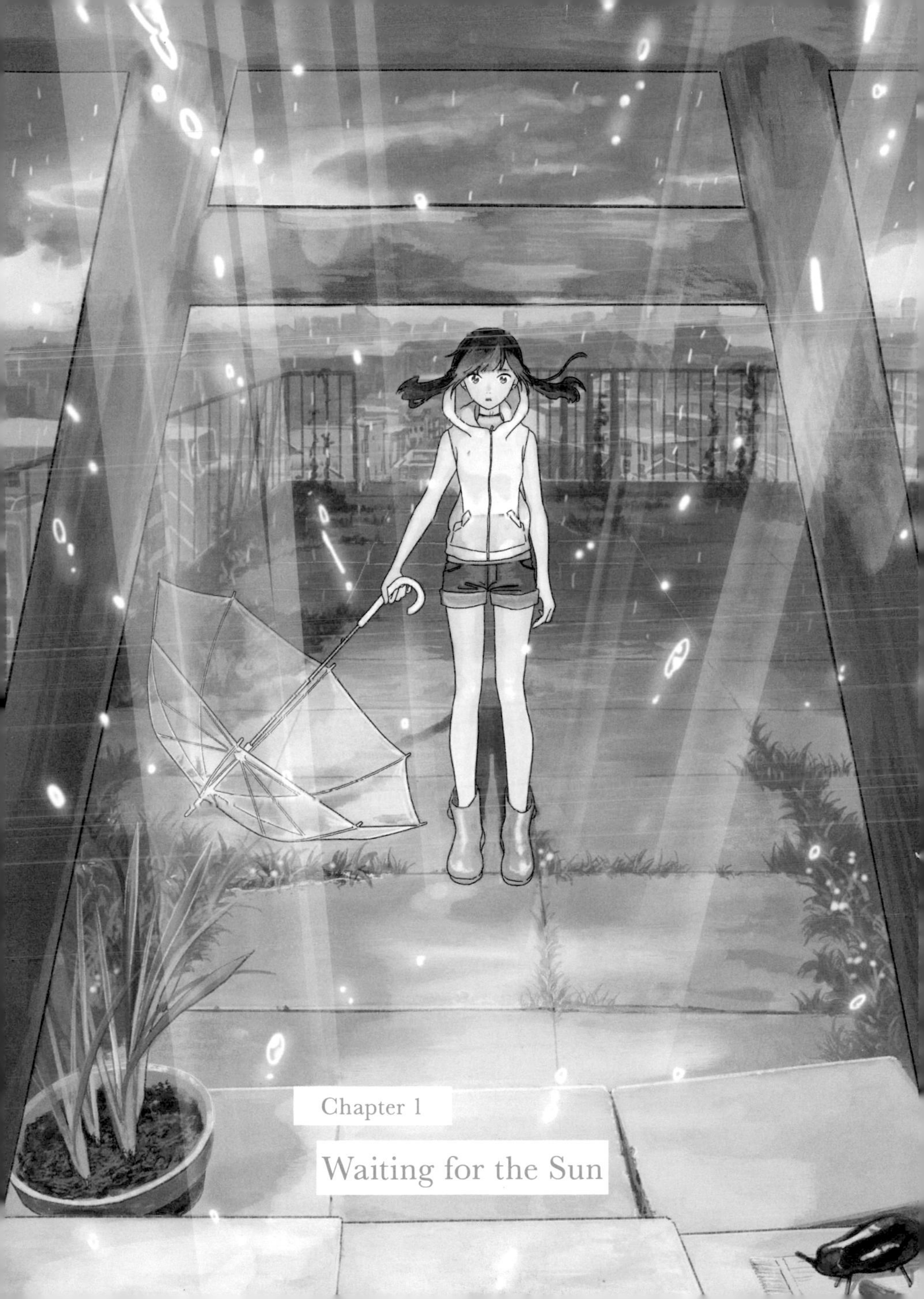

Chapter 1

Waiting for the Sun

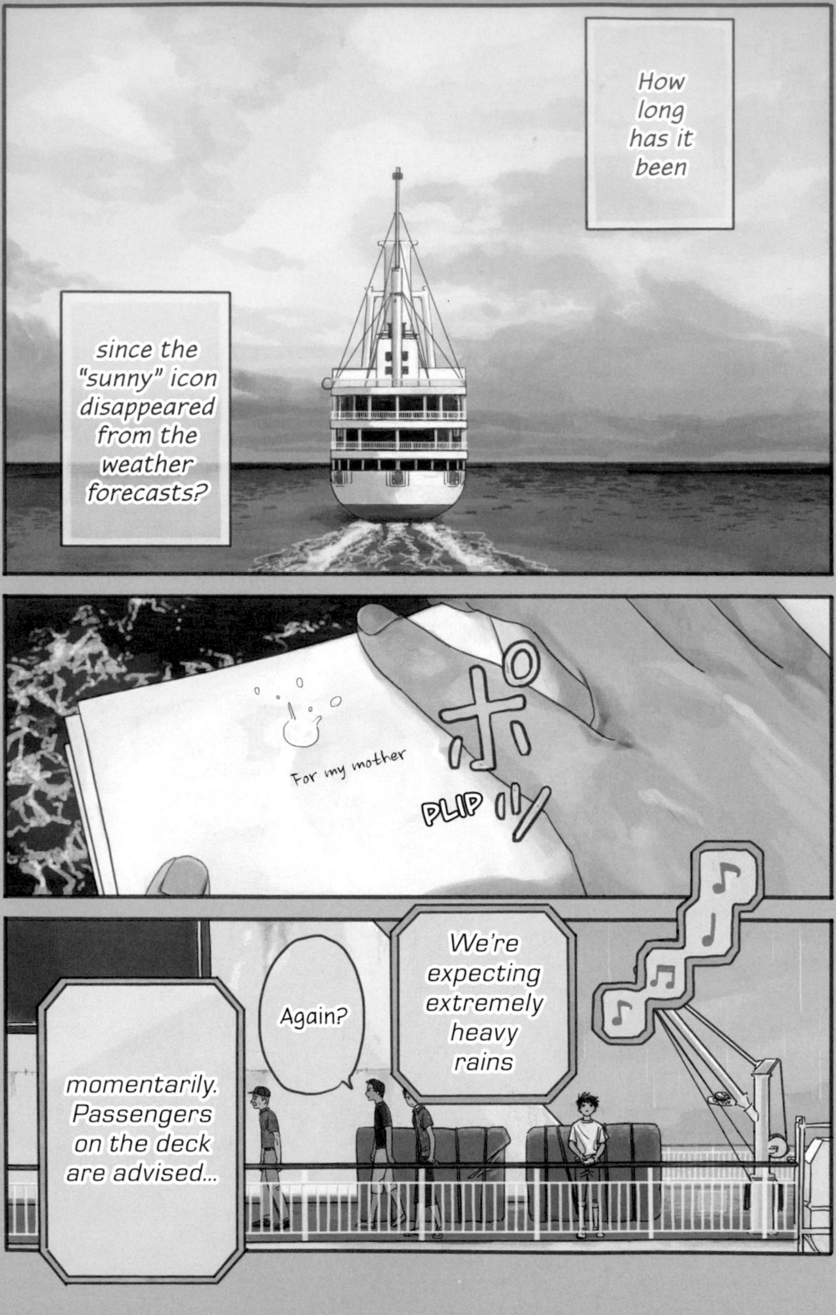
How long has it been
since the "sunny" icon disappeared from the weather forecasts?
For my mother
ポ
PLIP
We're expecting extremely heavy rains
Again?
momentarily. Passengers on the deck are advised...

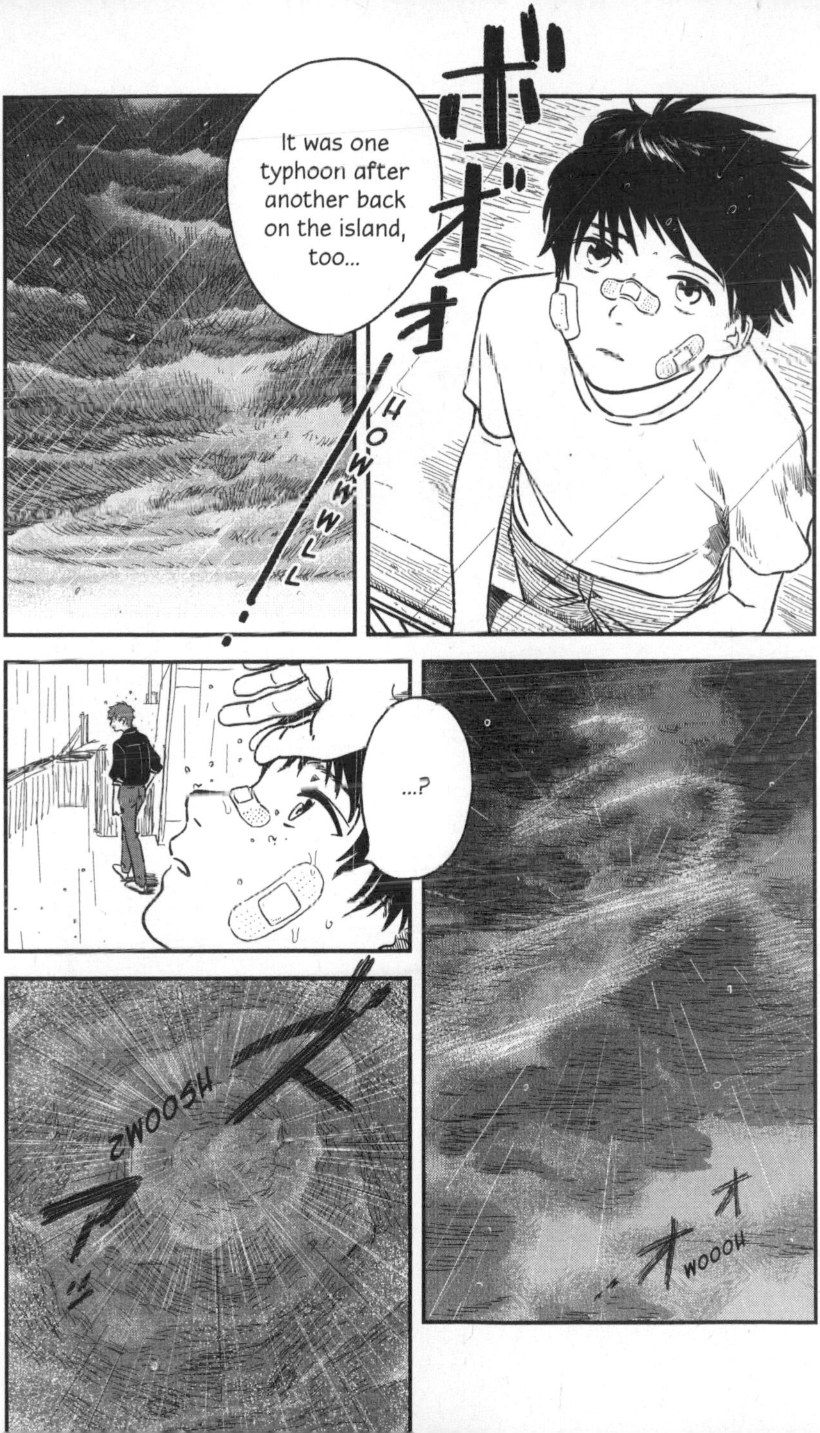

ボゴオォ
It was one typhoon after another back on the island, too...
HOWWWLL
オオ
WOOOH
...?
ZWOOSH

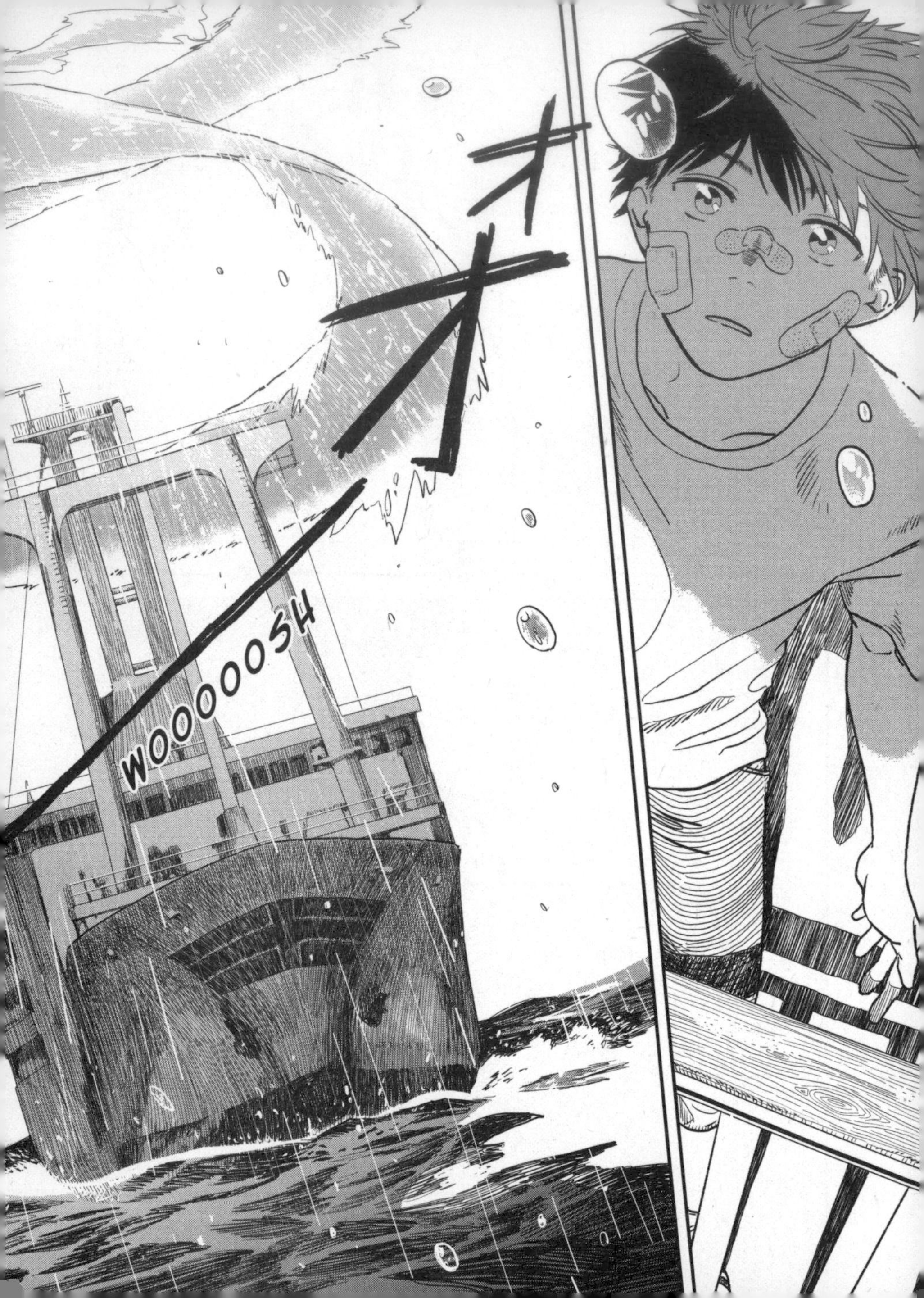
WOOOOOSH

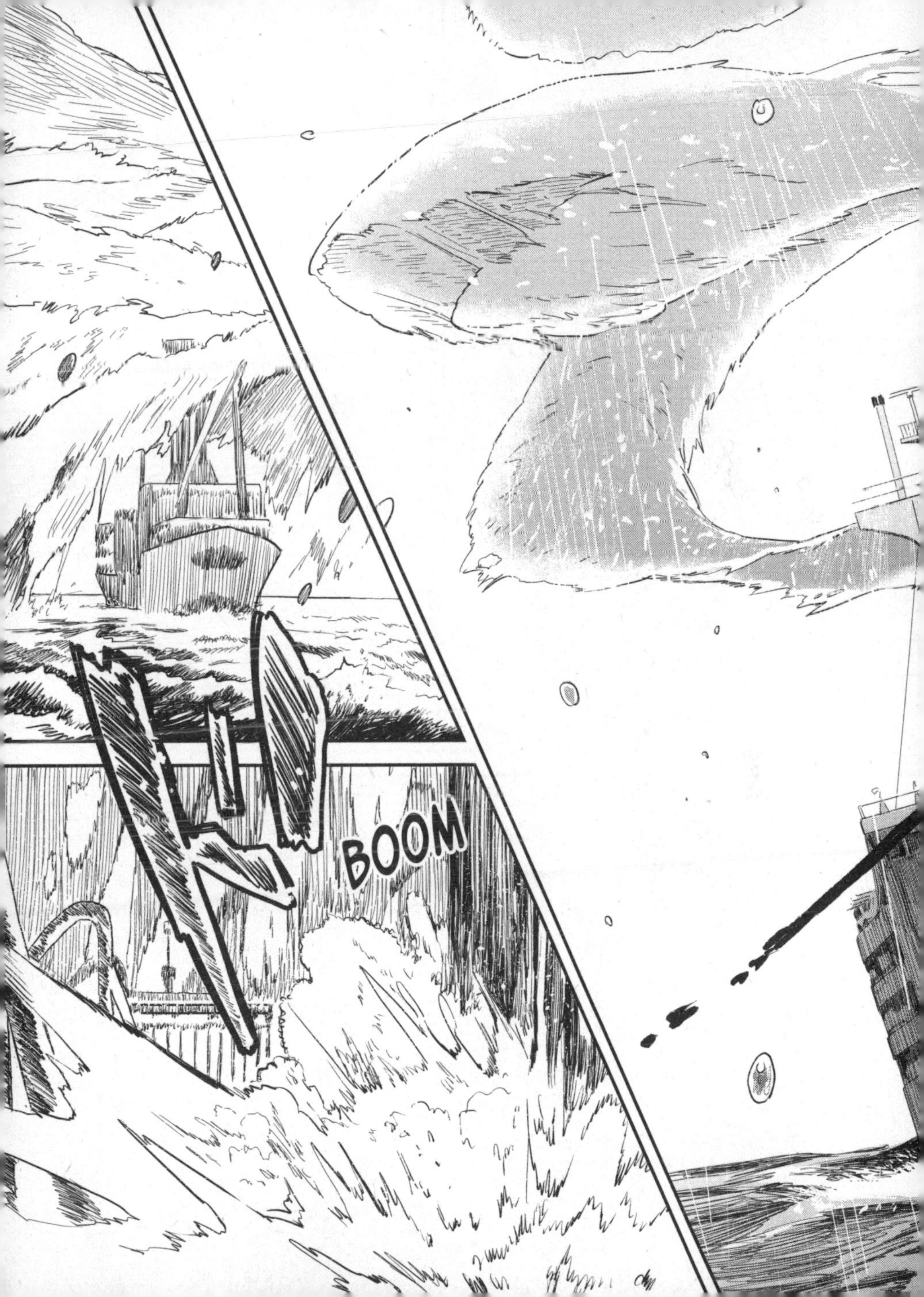
BOOM

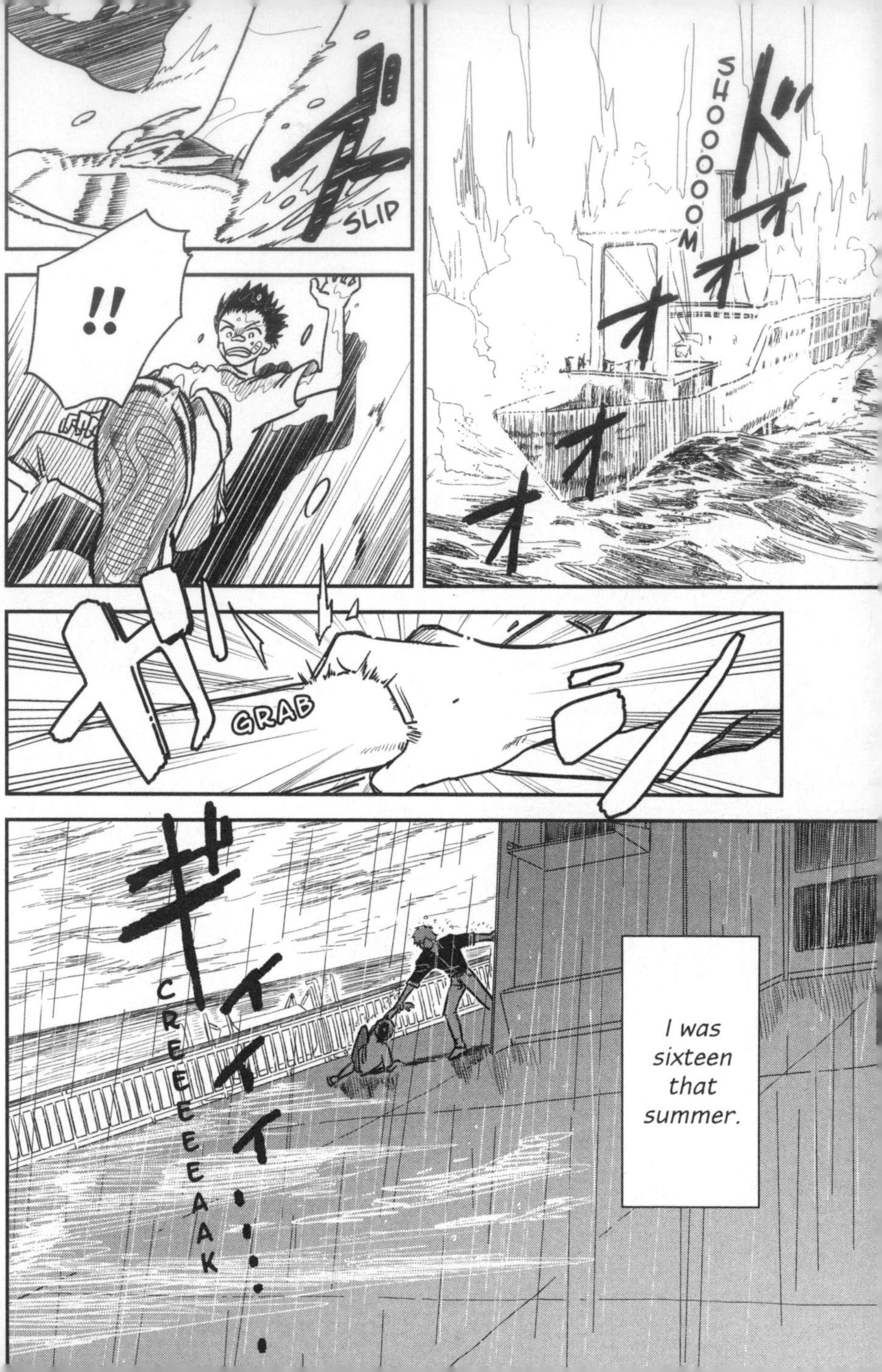
SHOOOOOOOM
SLIP
!!
GRAB
CREEEEEAAK
I was sixteen that summer.

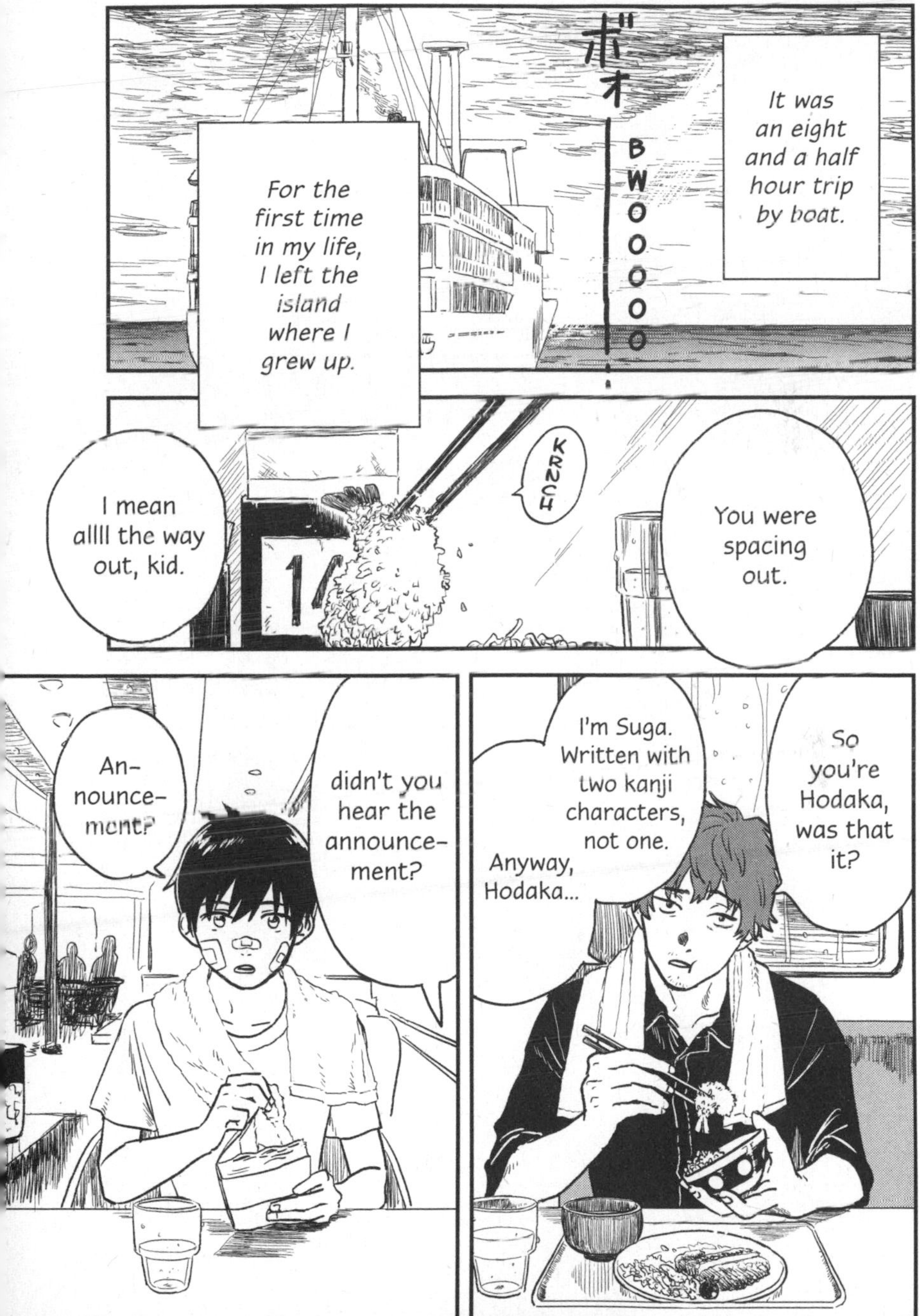
It was an eight and a half hour trip by boat.
ボオ
BWOOOOOO
For the first time in my life, I left the island where I grew up.
You were spacing out.
KRNCH
I mean allll the way out, kid.
So you're Hodaka, was that it?
I'm Suga. Written with two kanji characters, not one.
Anyway, Hodaka...
didn't you hear the announcement?
An-nouncement?

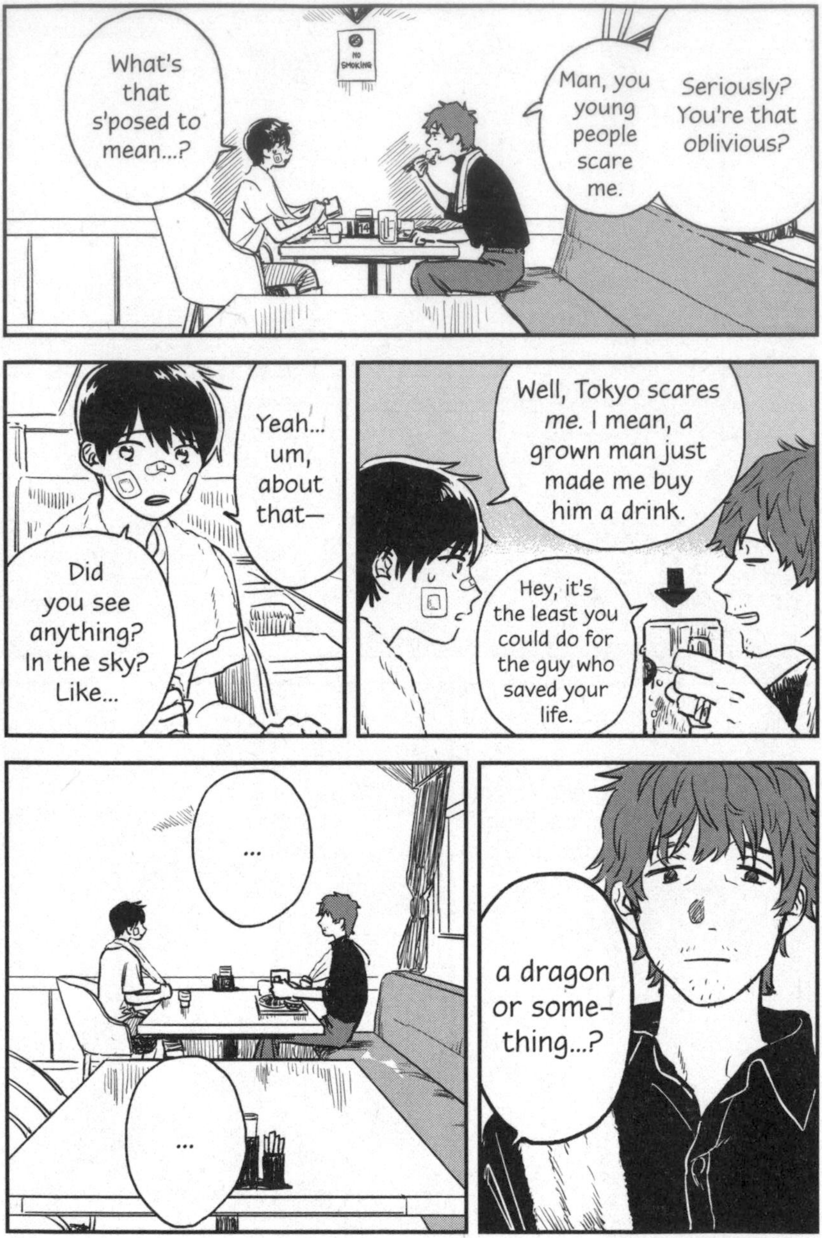
NO SMOKING
Seriously? You're that oblivious?
Man, you young people scare me.
What's that s'posed to mean...?
Well, Tokyo scares *me.* I mean, a grown man just made me buy him a drink.
Hey, it's the least you could do for the guy who saved your life.
Yeah... um, about that—
Did you see anything? In the sky? Like...
a dragon or some-thing...?
...
...

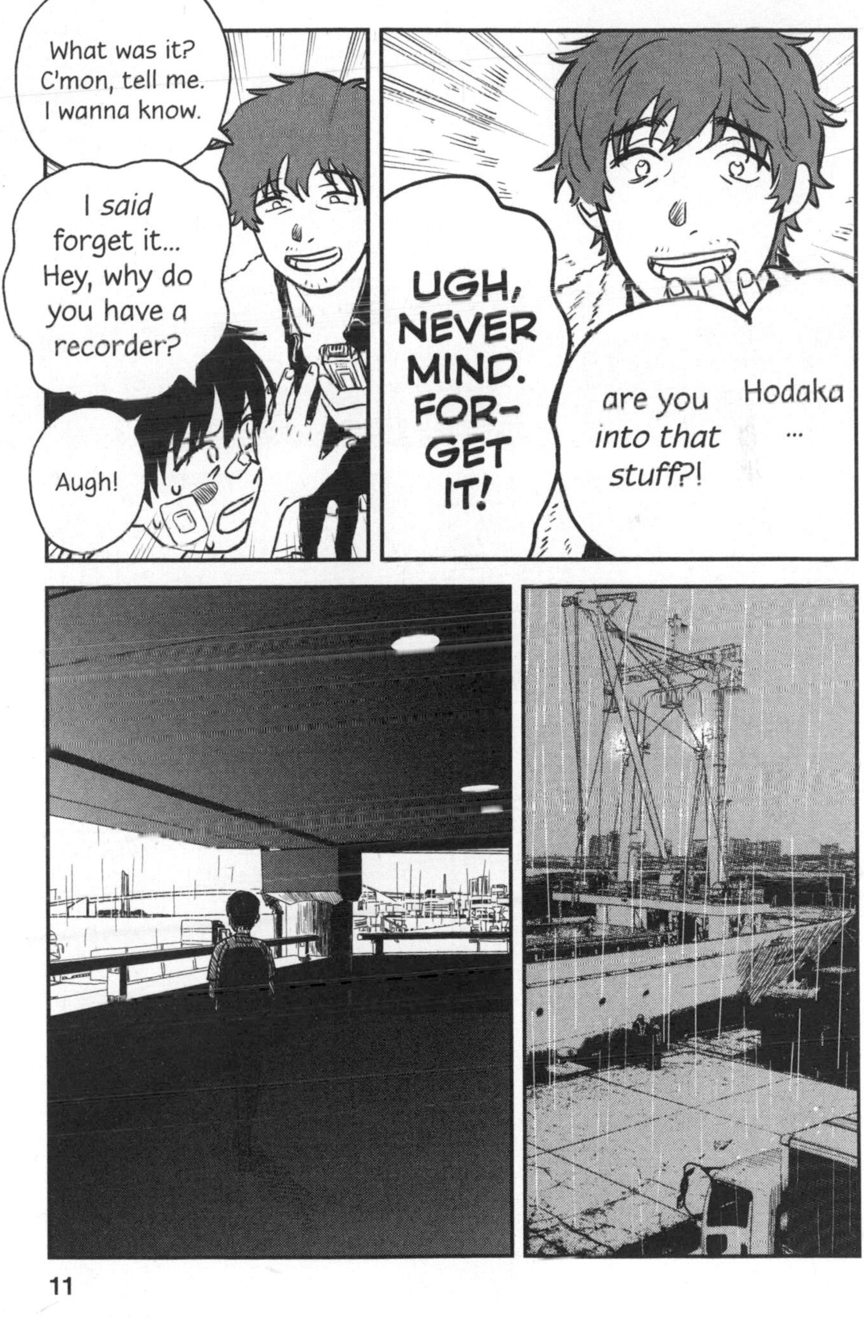
Hodaka ...
are you into that stuff?!
UGH, NEVER MIND. FOR-GET IT!
What was it? C'mon, tell me. I wanna know.
I *said* forget it... Hey, why do you have a recorder?
Augh!

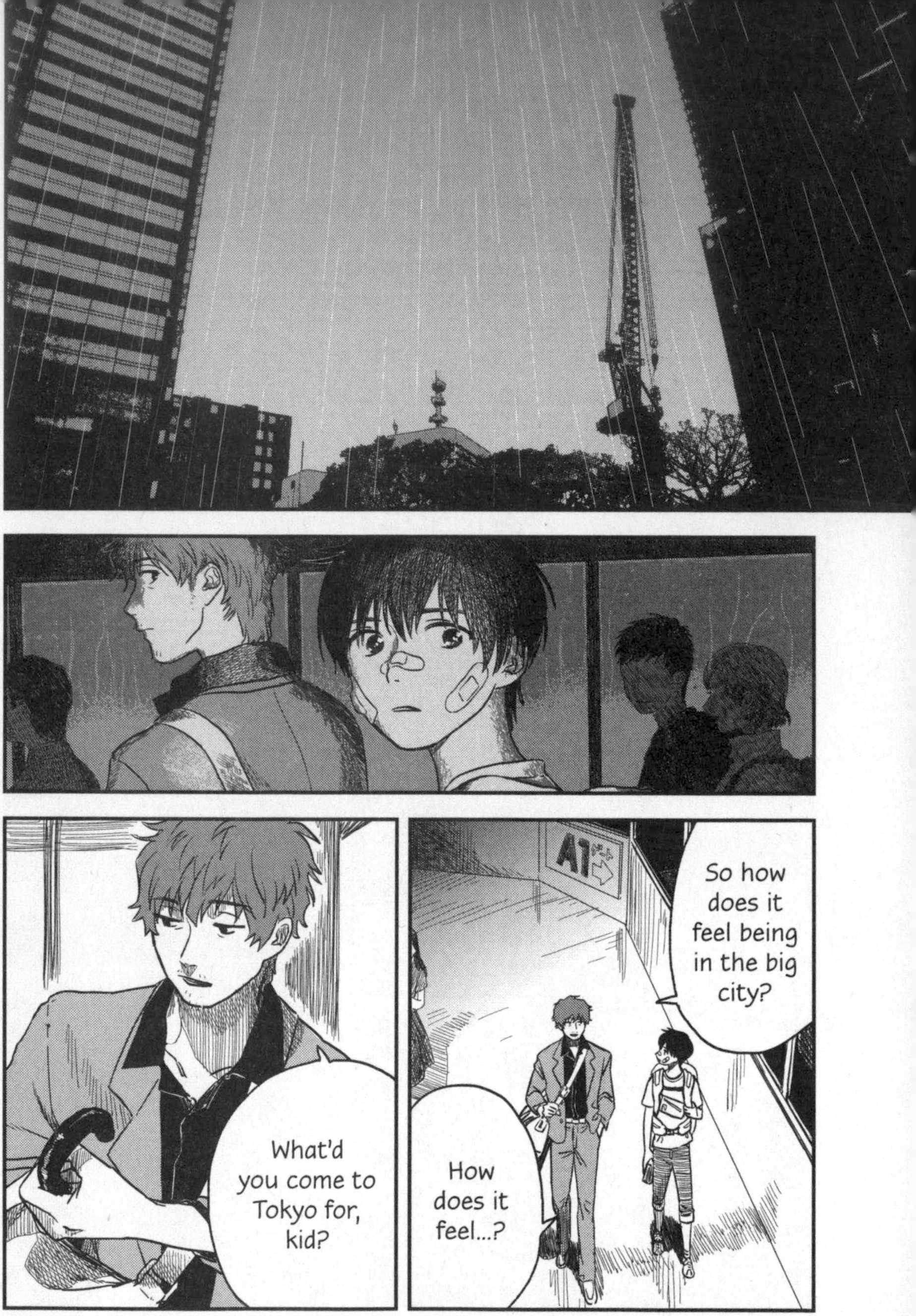
A1
So how does it feel being in the big city?
How does it feel...?
What'd you come to Tokyo for, kid?

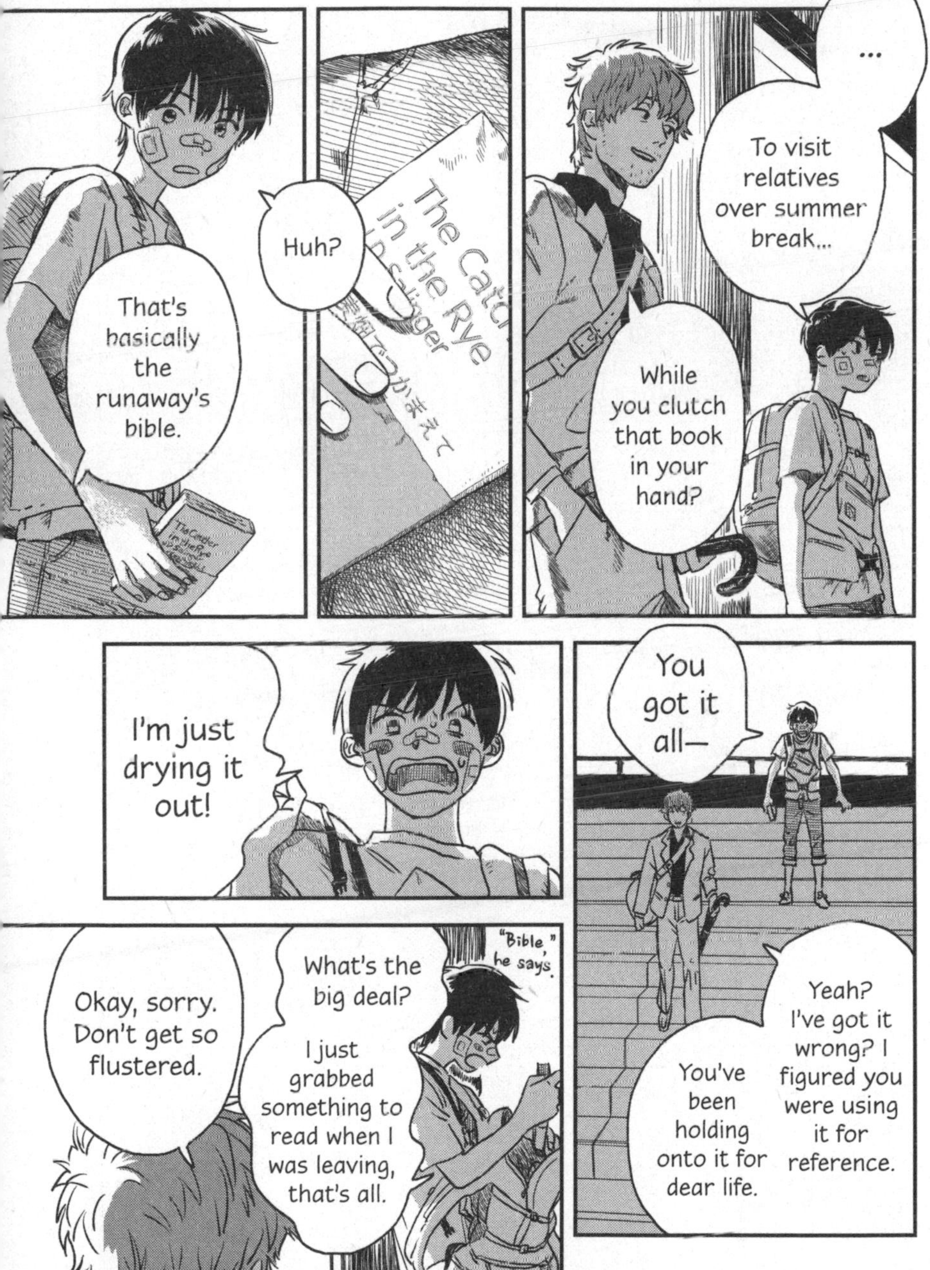
...
To visit relatives over summer break...
While you clutch that book in your hand?
in the Rye
Huh?
That's basically the runaway's bible.
You got it all—
Yeah? I've got it wrong? I figured you were using it for reference.
You've been holding onto it for dear life.
I'm just drying it out!
"Bible," he says.
What's the big deal?
I just grabbed something to read when I was leaving, that's all.
Okay, sorry. Don't get so flustered.

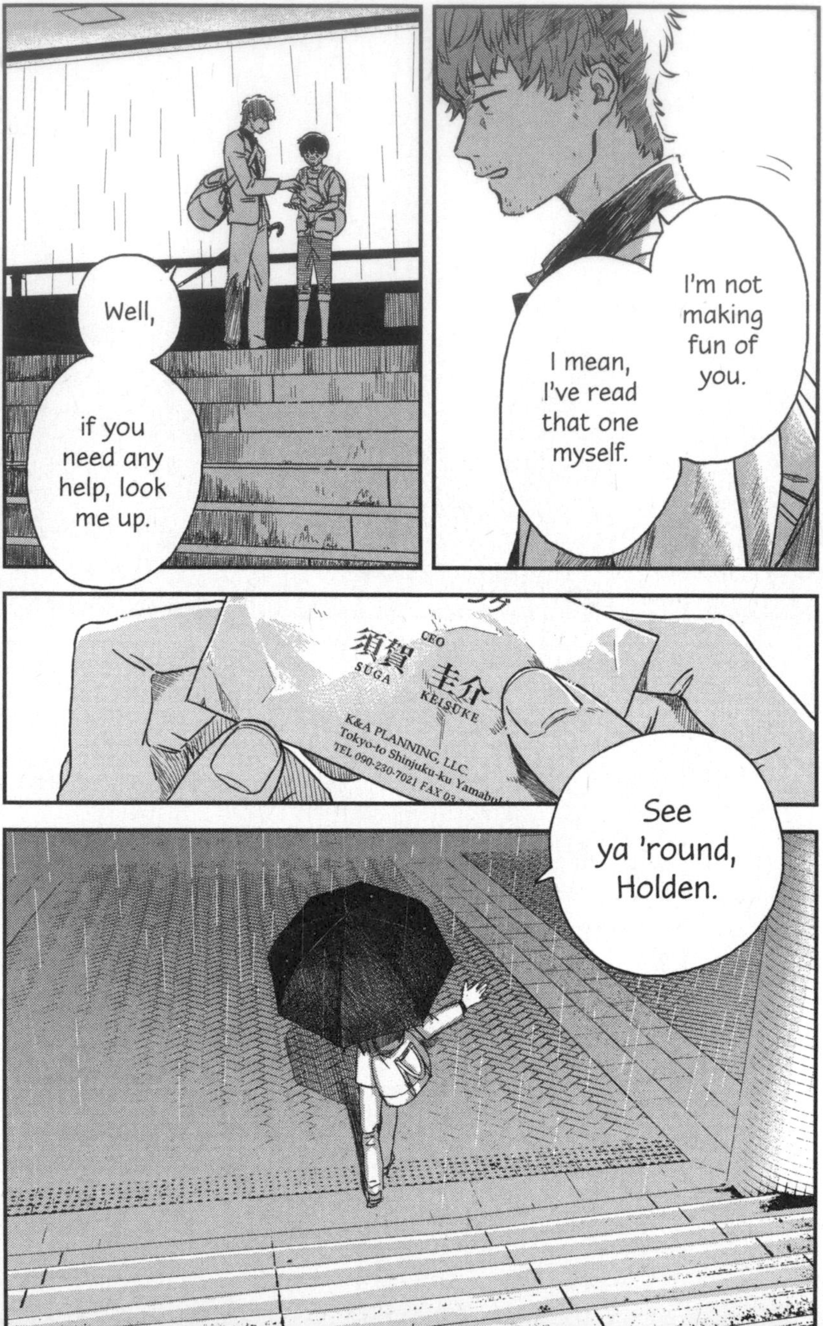
I'm not making fun of you.
I mean, I've read that one myself.
Well,
if you need any help, look me up.
CEO
須賀 圭介
SUGA KEISUKE
K&A PLANNING, LLC
Tokyo-to Shinjuku-ku
TEL 090-230-7021
See ya 'round, Holden.

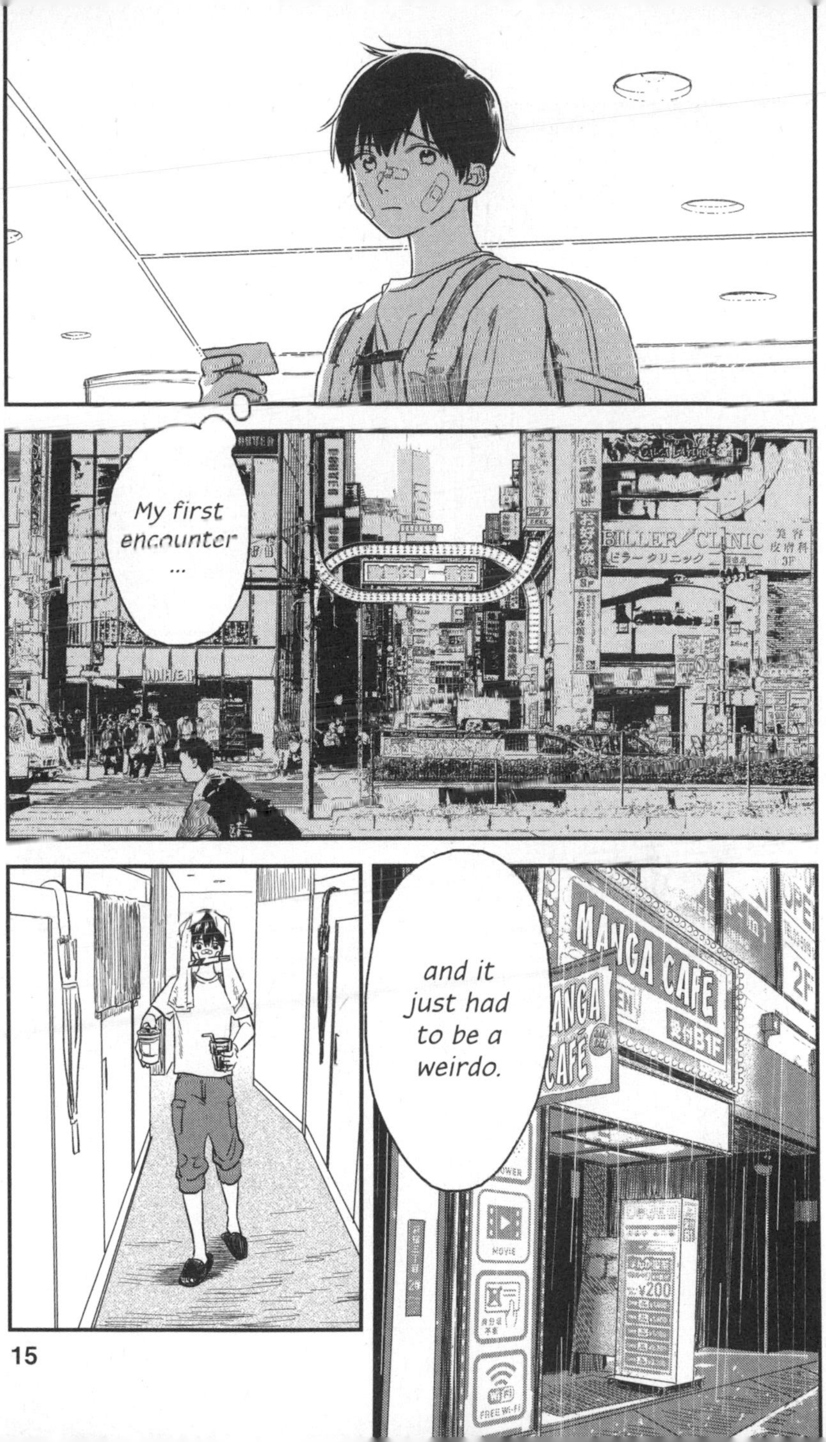
My first encounter ...
BILLER/CLINIC
ビラークリニック
and it just had to be a weirdo.
MANGA CAFÉ
受付B1F
2F
MOVIE
¥200
FREE Wi-Fi

CLICK

The number of localized cloud-bursts

BEEP

has far exceeded that of last year, which was already the greatest on record—

...

let that guy get to me.

I can't

RATE	
HOURS	Part-time
SPECIFICATIONS	☑ No resume required
OTHER TERMS	High school student, No student ID required

MATCHING JOB POSTS: 0

Please edit your search options and try again.

BING

...

I will live in Tokyo.

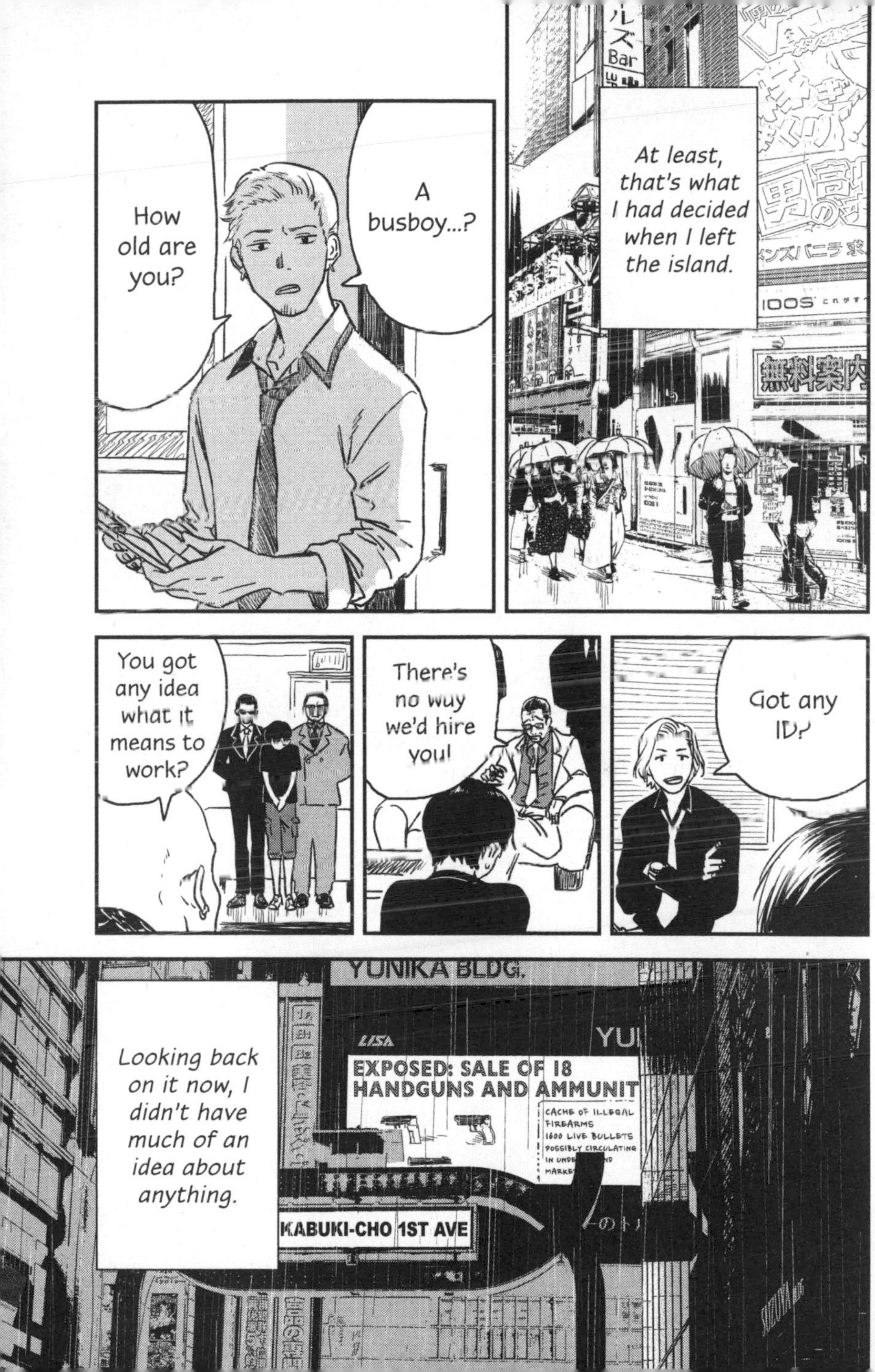
At least, that's what I had decided when I left the island.
A busboy...?
How old are you?
Got any ID?
There's no way we'd hire you!
You got any idea what it means to work?
Looking back on it now, I didn't have much of an idea about anything.
YUNIKA BLDG.
EXPOSED: SALE OF 18 HANDGUNS AND AMMUNIT
CACHE OF ILLEGAL FIREARMS
1600 LIVE BULLETS
KABUKI-CHO 1ST AVE

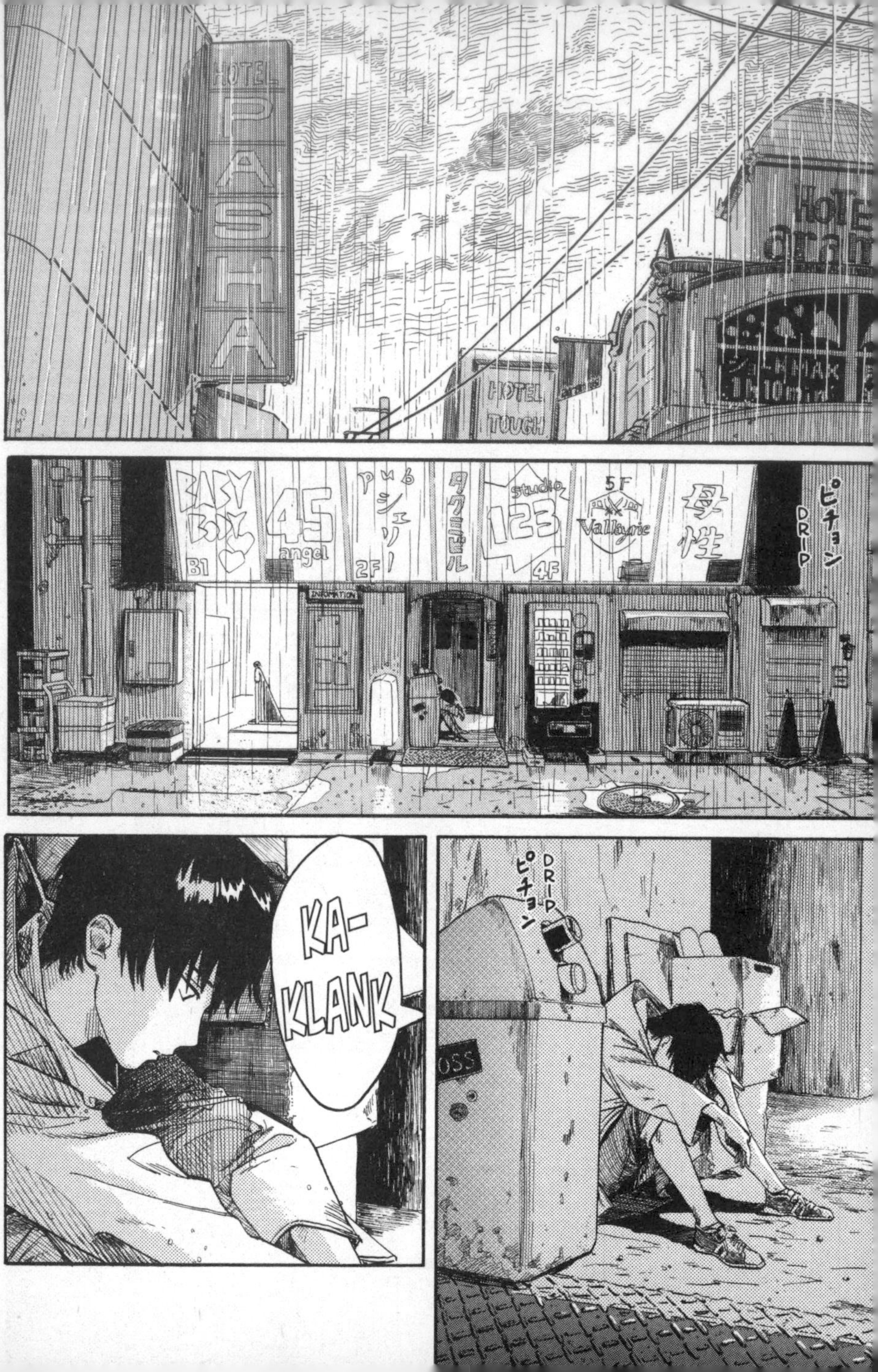
HOTEL
PASHA
HOTEL
TOUGH
ピチョン
DRIP
母性
5F
studio
123
4F
タクミビル
pub
シェリー!
2F
45
angel
B1
INFORMATION
DRIP
ピチョン
KA-KLANK

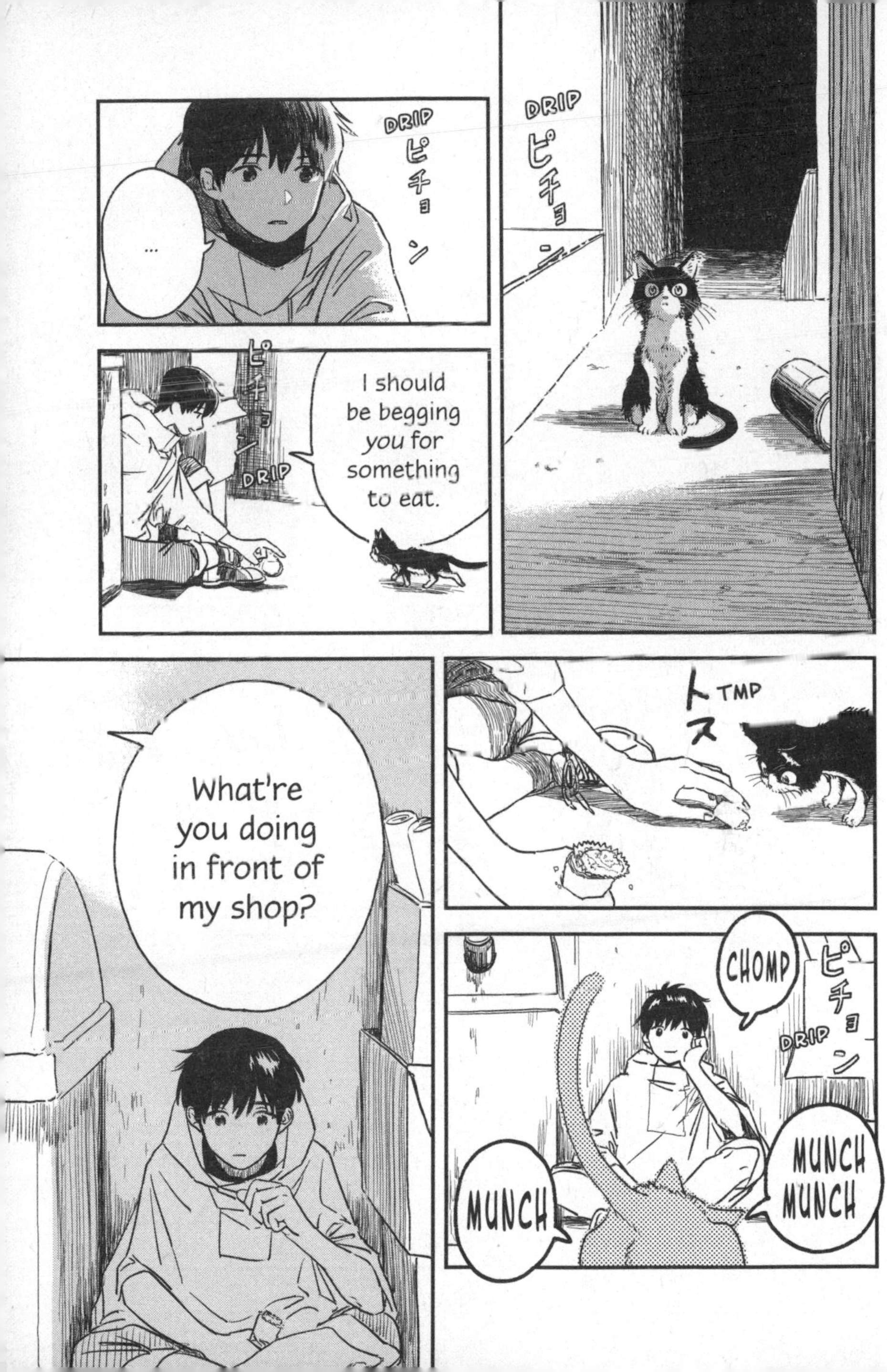
DRIP
ピチョン
DRIP
ピチョン
...
ピチョン
DRIP
I should be begging *you* for something to eat.
トス
TMP
CHOMP
ピチョン
DRIP
MUNCH MUNCH
MUNCH
What're you doing in front of my shop?

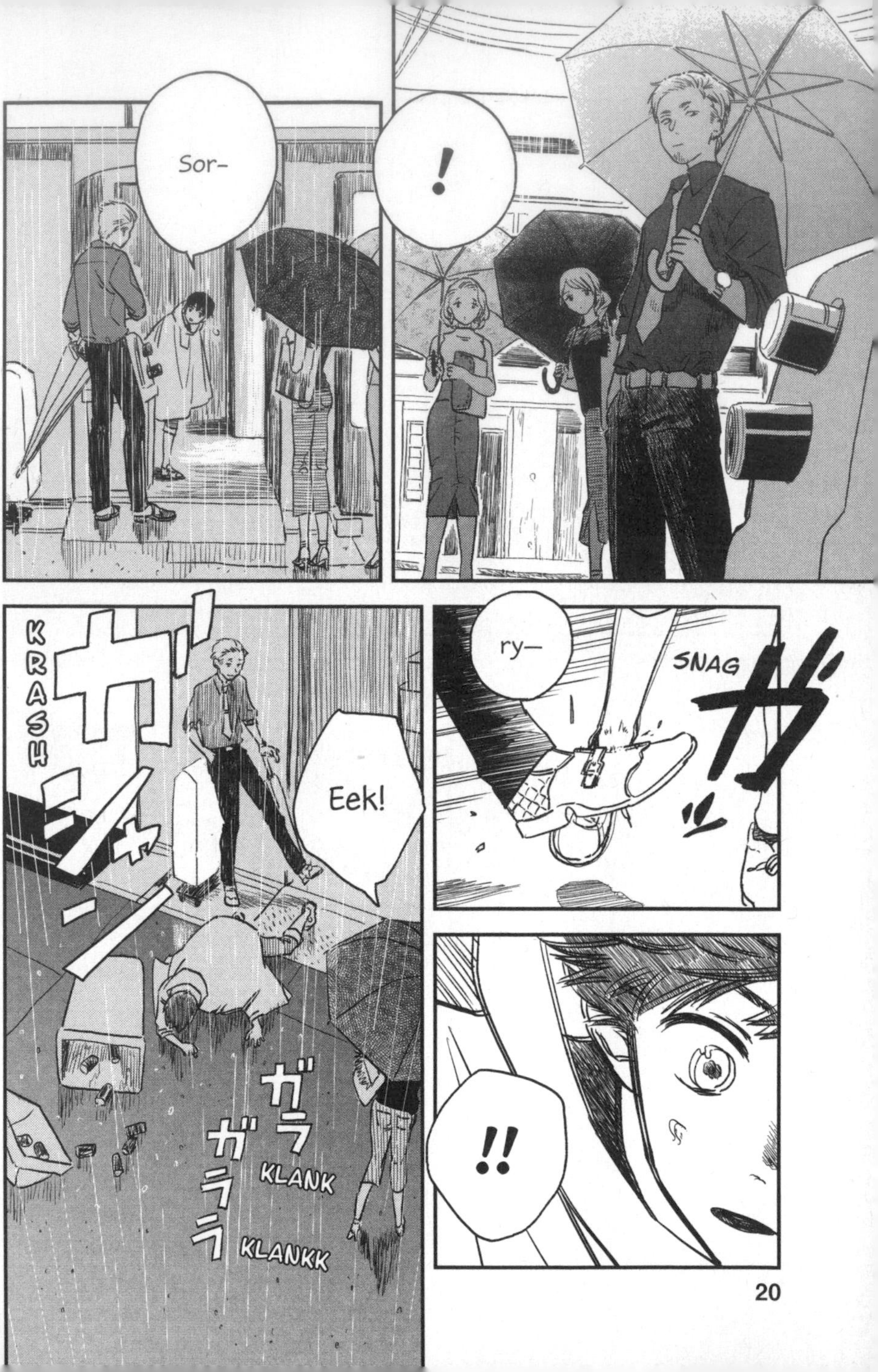
!
Sor-
ry—
SNAG
ガッ
!!
KRASH
ガシャー
Eek!
ガラガラ
KLANK
ガララ
KLANKK

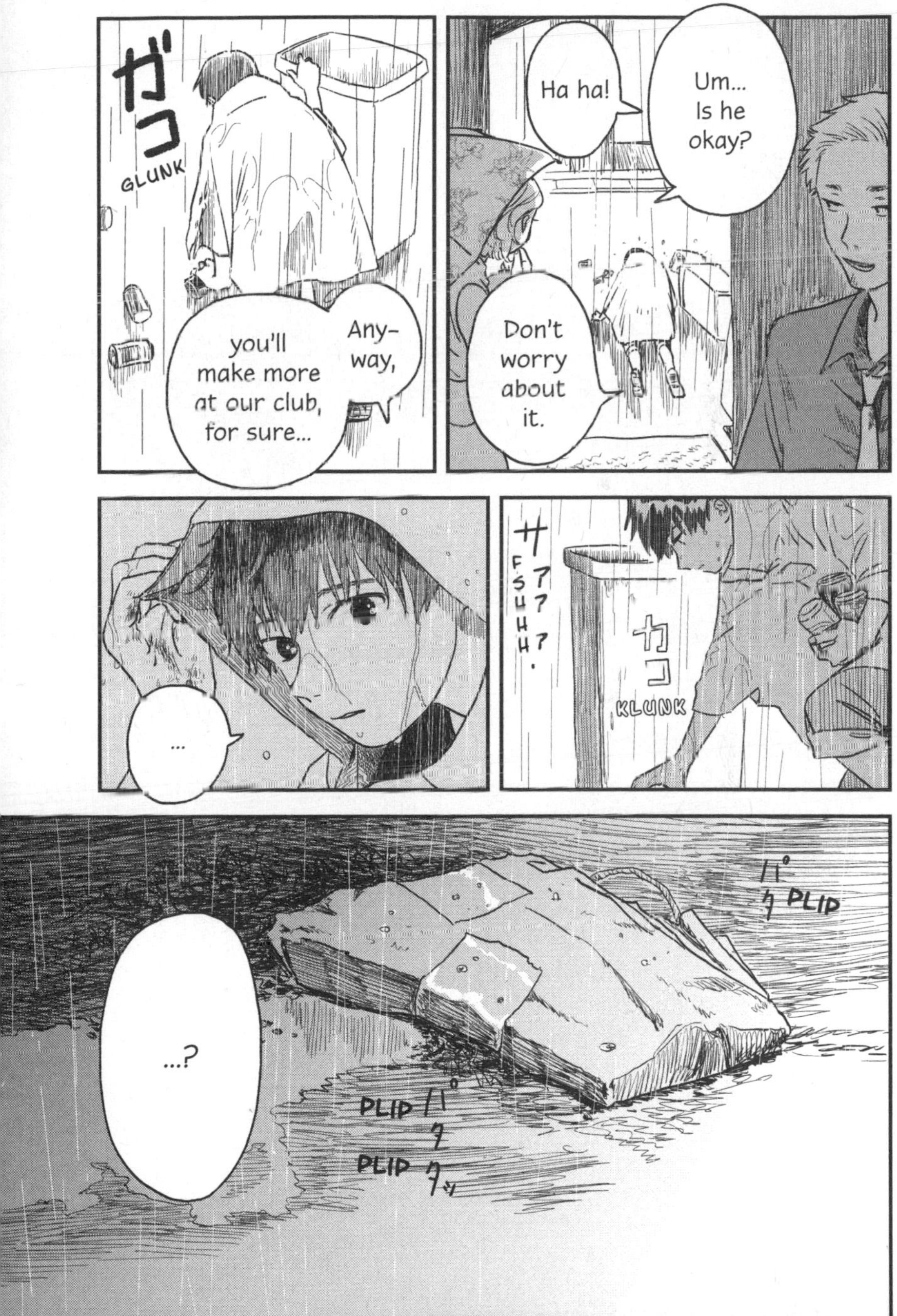
Um... Is he okay?
Ha ha!
Don't worry about it.
ガコ
GLUNK
Any-way,
you'll make more at our club, for sure...
サァァァ
FSHHH.
カコ
KLUNK
...
パッ
PLIP
...?
PLIP パク
PLIP クッ

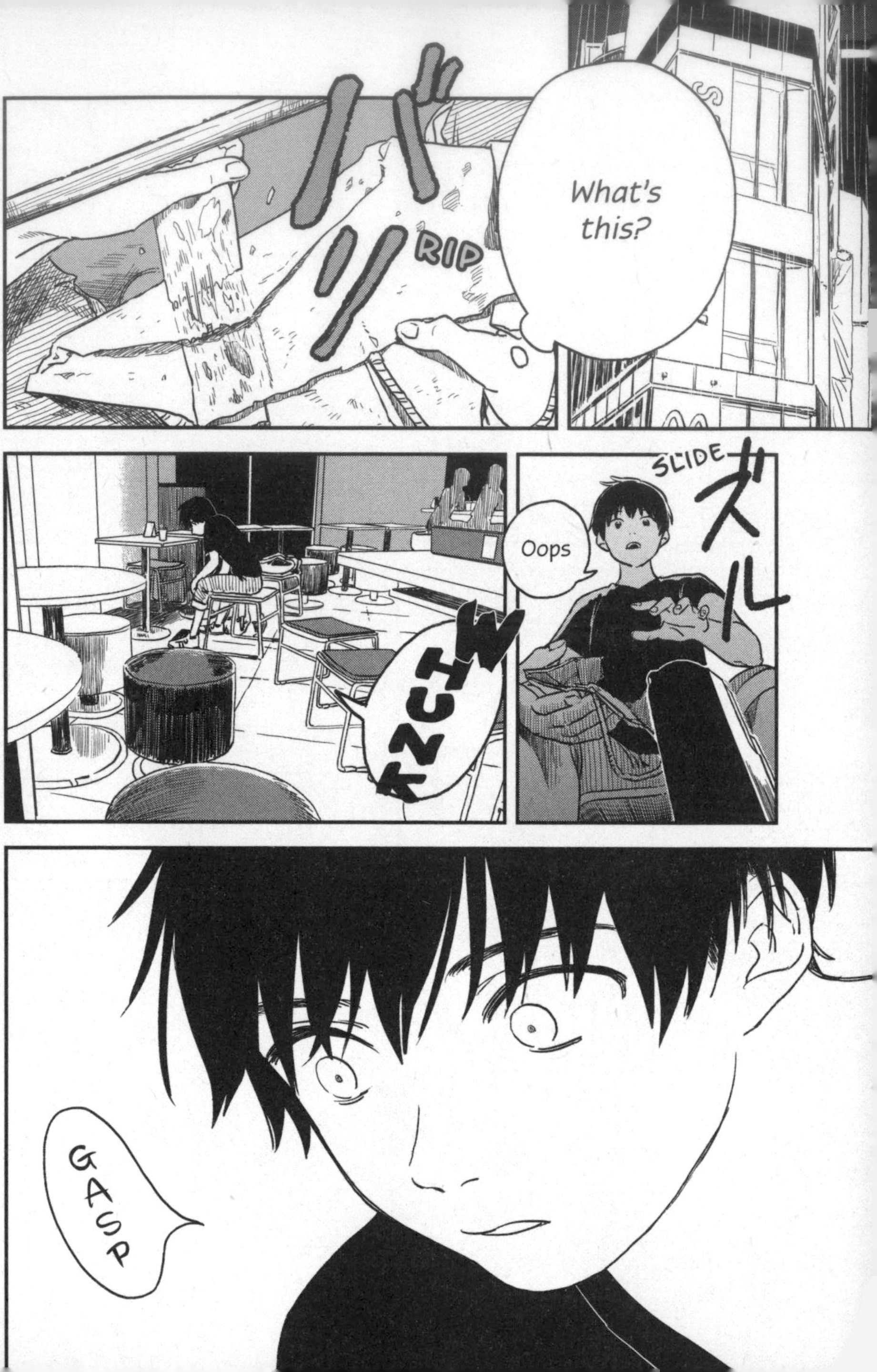
What's this?
バリ
RIP
SLIDE
ズル
Oops
WHUNK
GASP

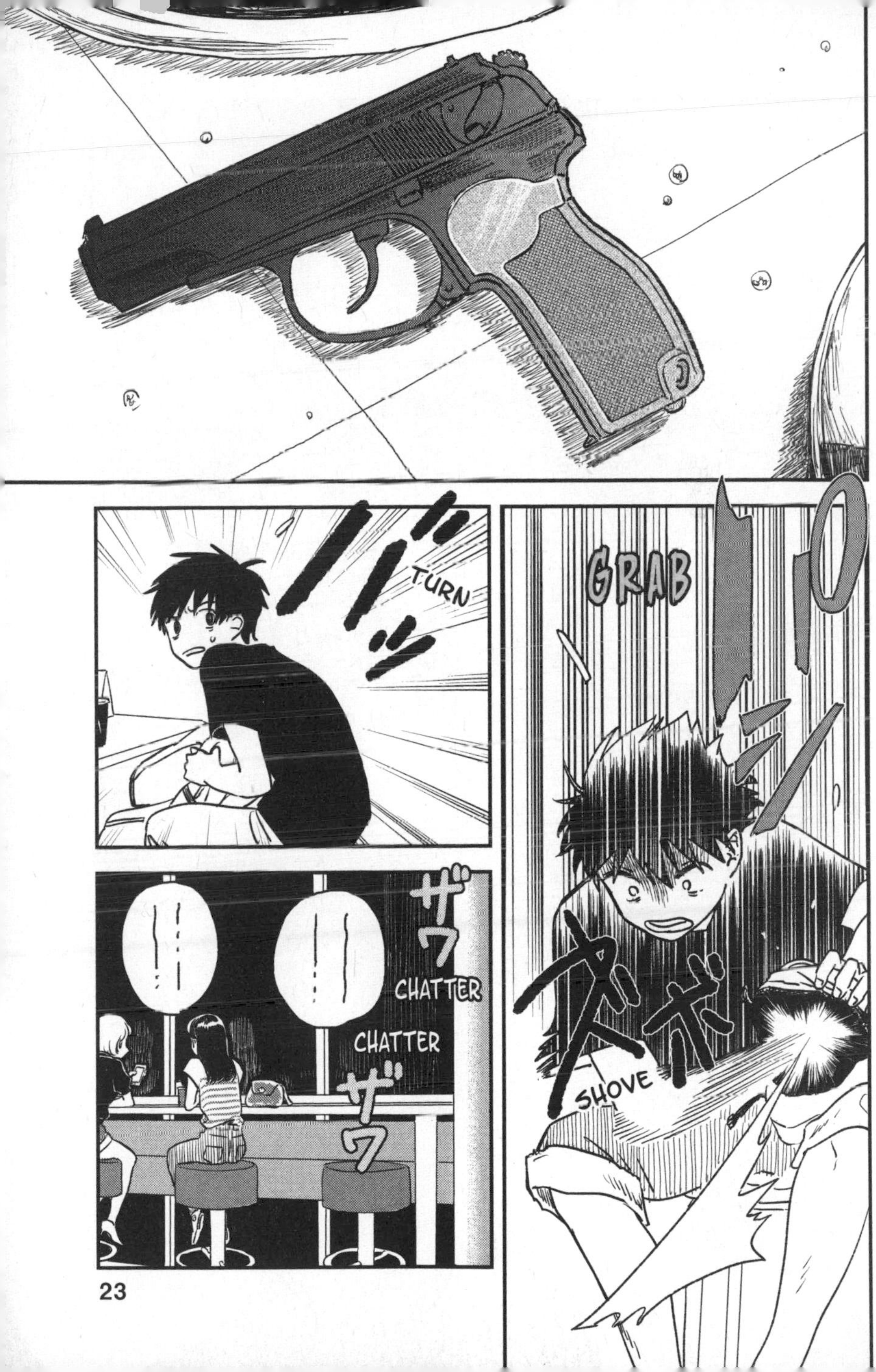
GRAB
SHOVE
TURN
ザワ
CHATTER
CHATTER
ザワ

...

CHATTER

CHATTER

It can't possibly be real...

THUNK

...

BDMP

BDMP

...

ZHAAA

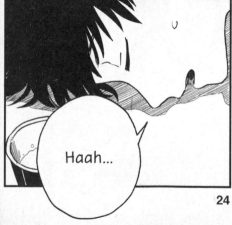

Haah...

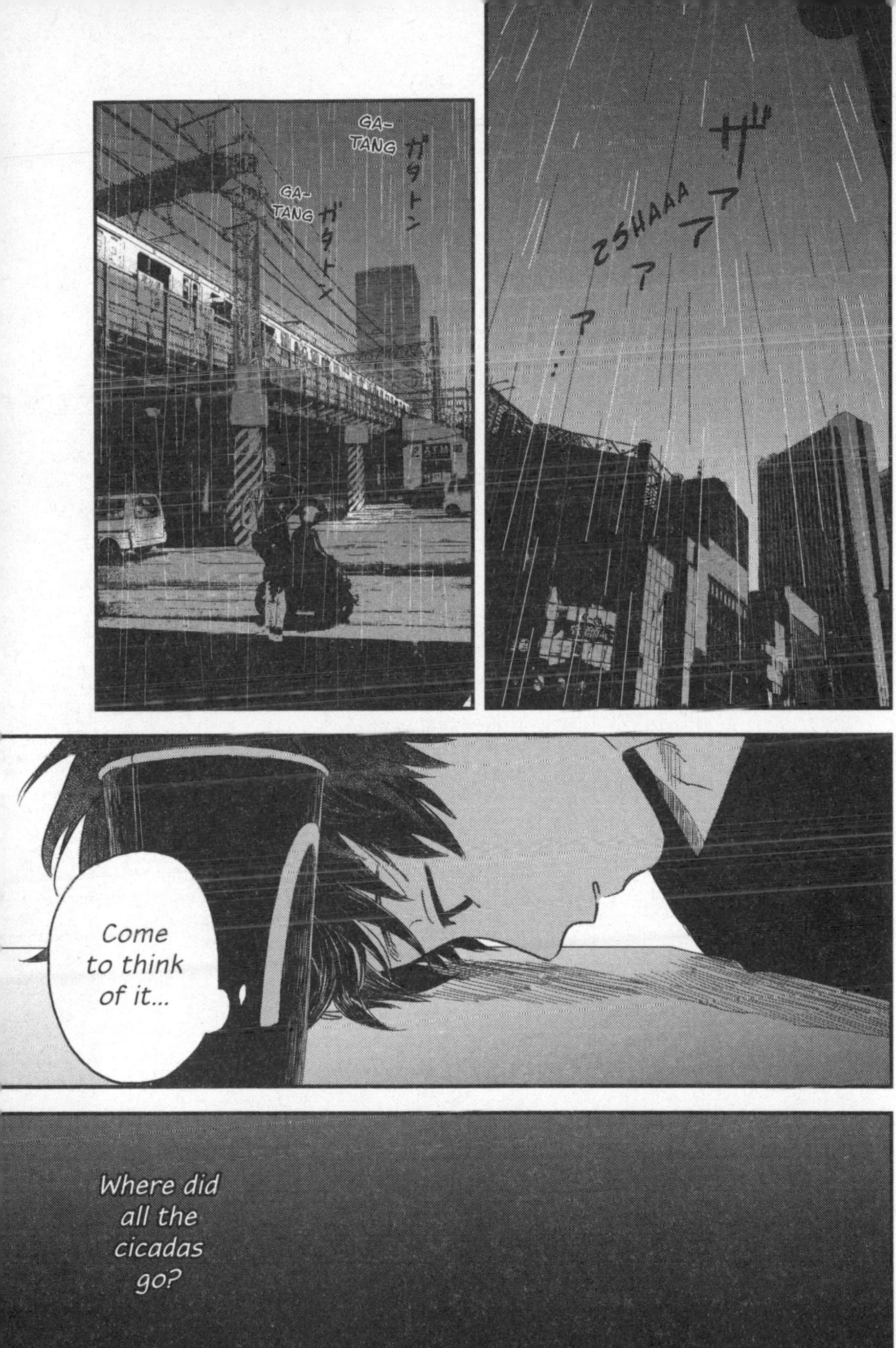
ザァァァ…
ZSHAAA
ガタトン
GA-TANG
ガタトン
GA-TANG
Come to think of it...
Where did all the cicadas go?

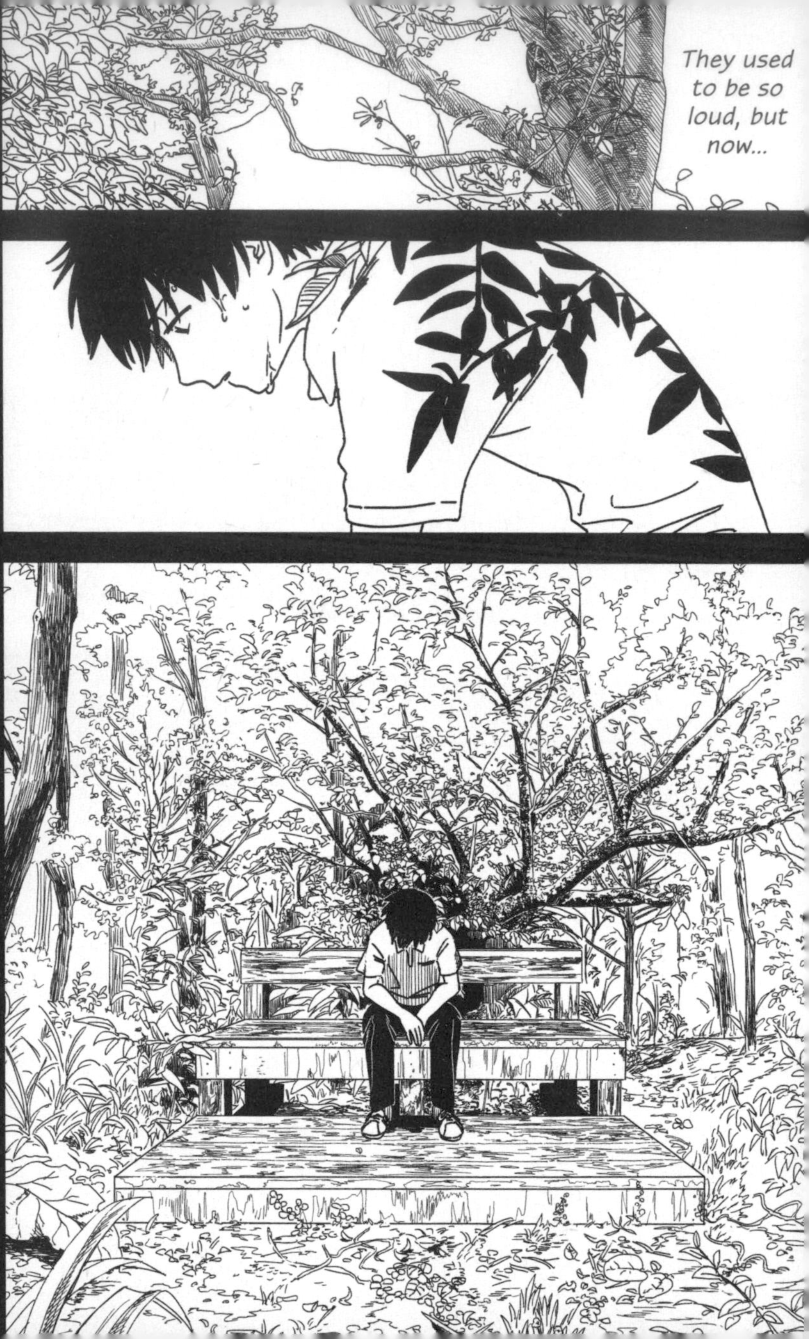
They used to be so loud, but now...

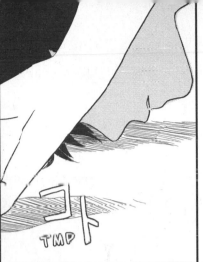

Did you

run away from home?

...

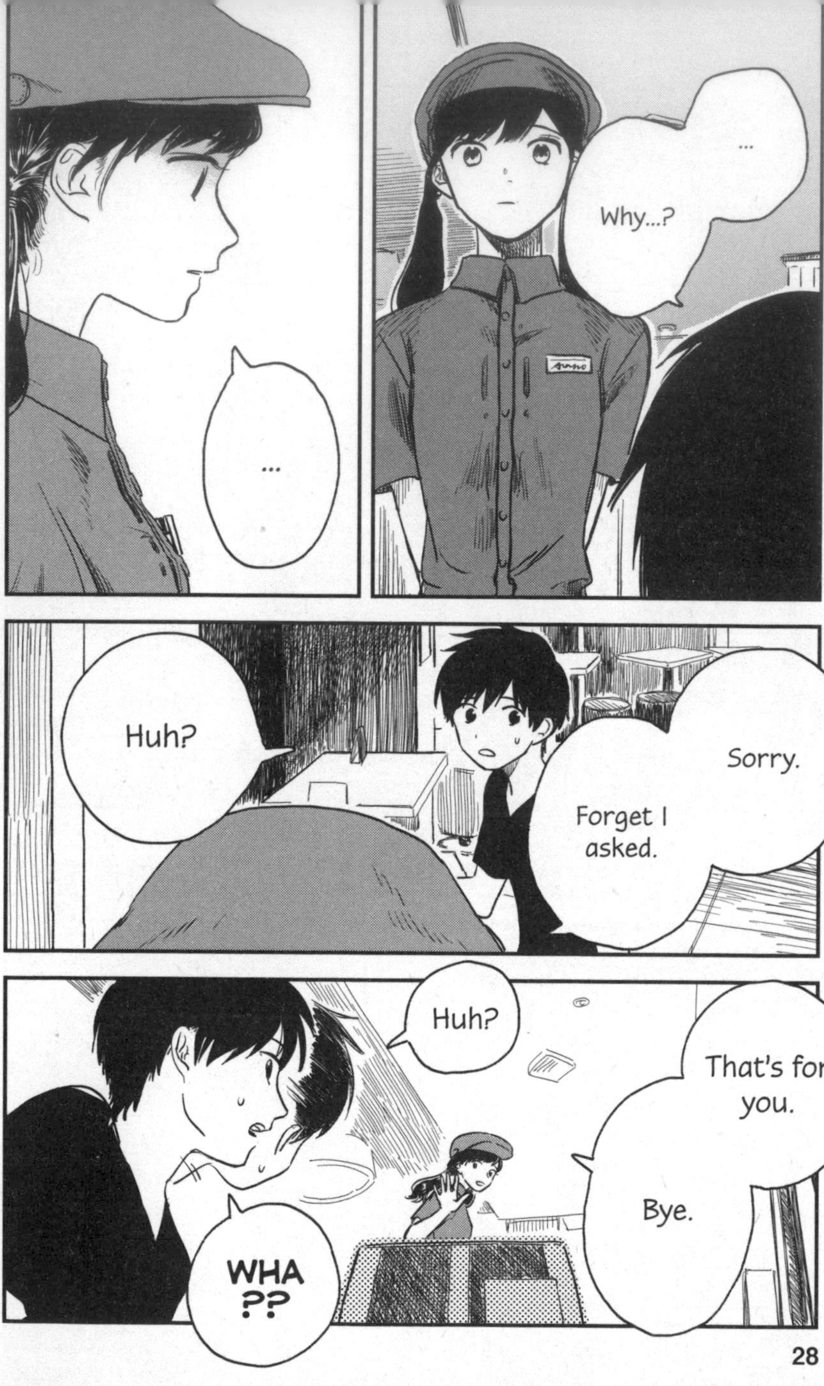
...
Why...?
...
Sorry.
Forget I asked.
Huh?
That's for you.
Bye.
Huh?
WHA ??

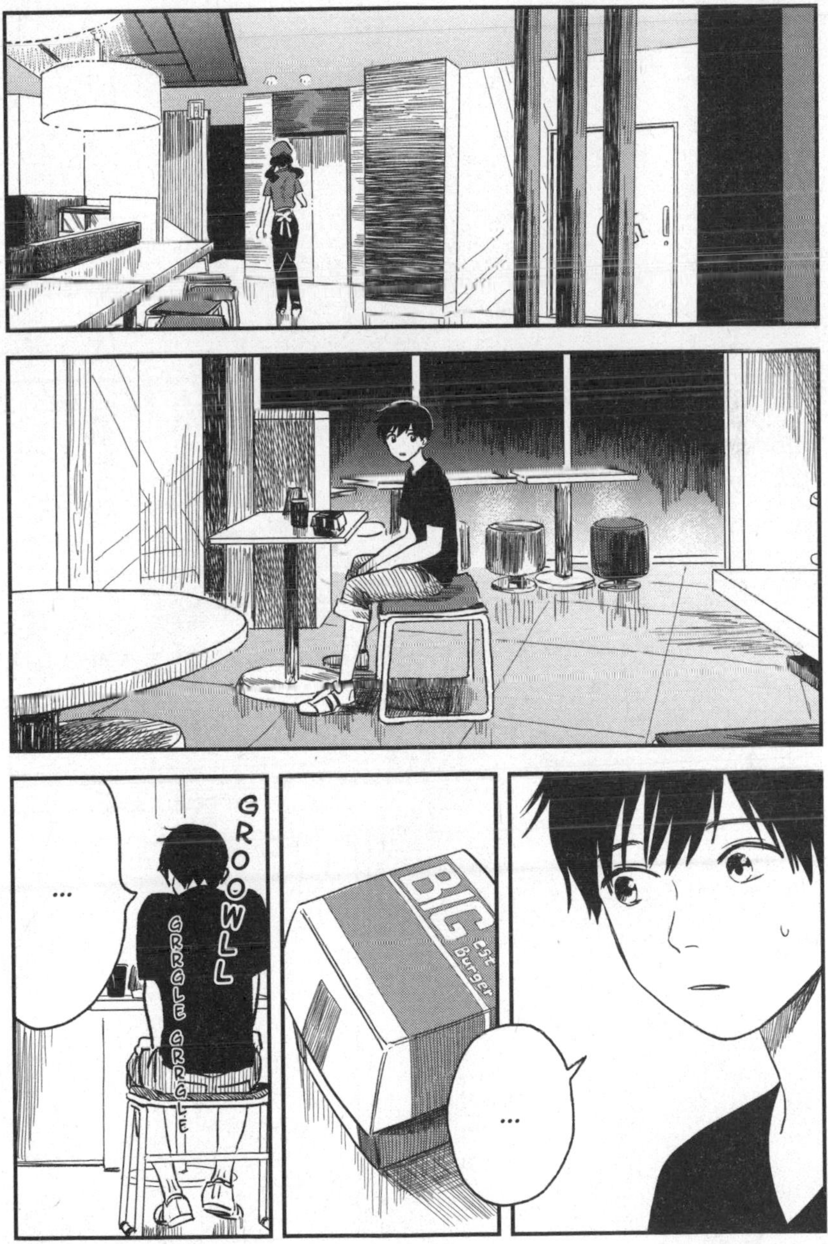
BIG est Burger
...
...
GROOOWLL
GRRGLE GRRGLE

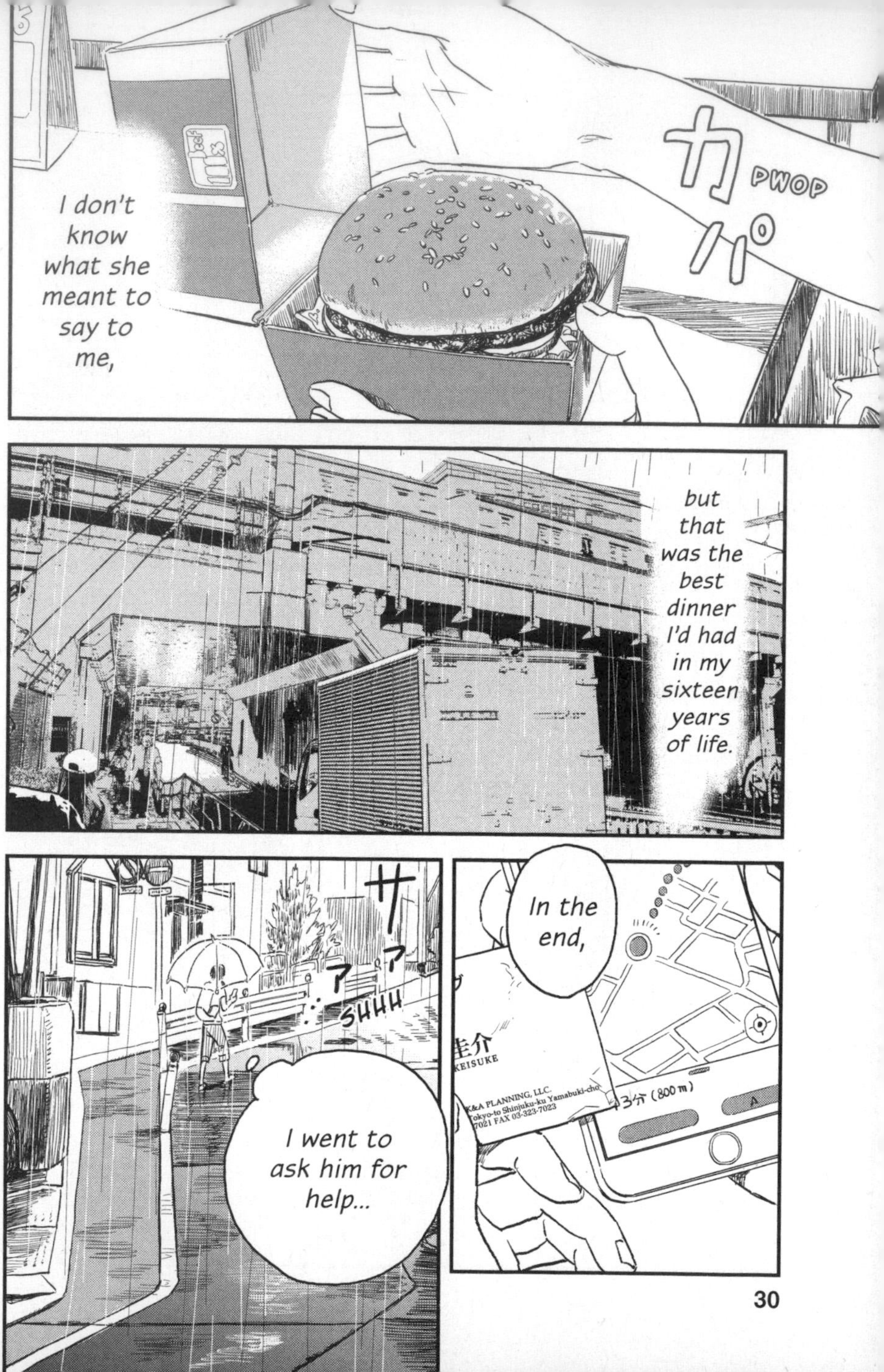

カパ
PWOP
I don't know what she meant to say to me,
but that was the best dinner I'd had in my sixteen years of life.
In the end,
圭介
KEISUKE
K&A PLANNING, LLC.
Tokyo-to Shinjuku-ku Yamabuki-cho
7021 FAX 03-323-7023
3分 (800m)
サァ
SHHH
I went to ask him for help...

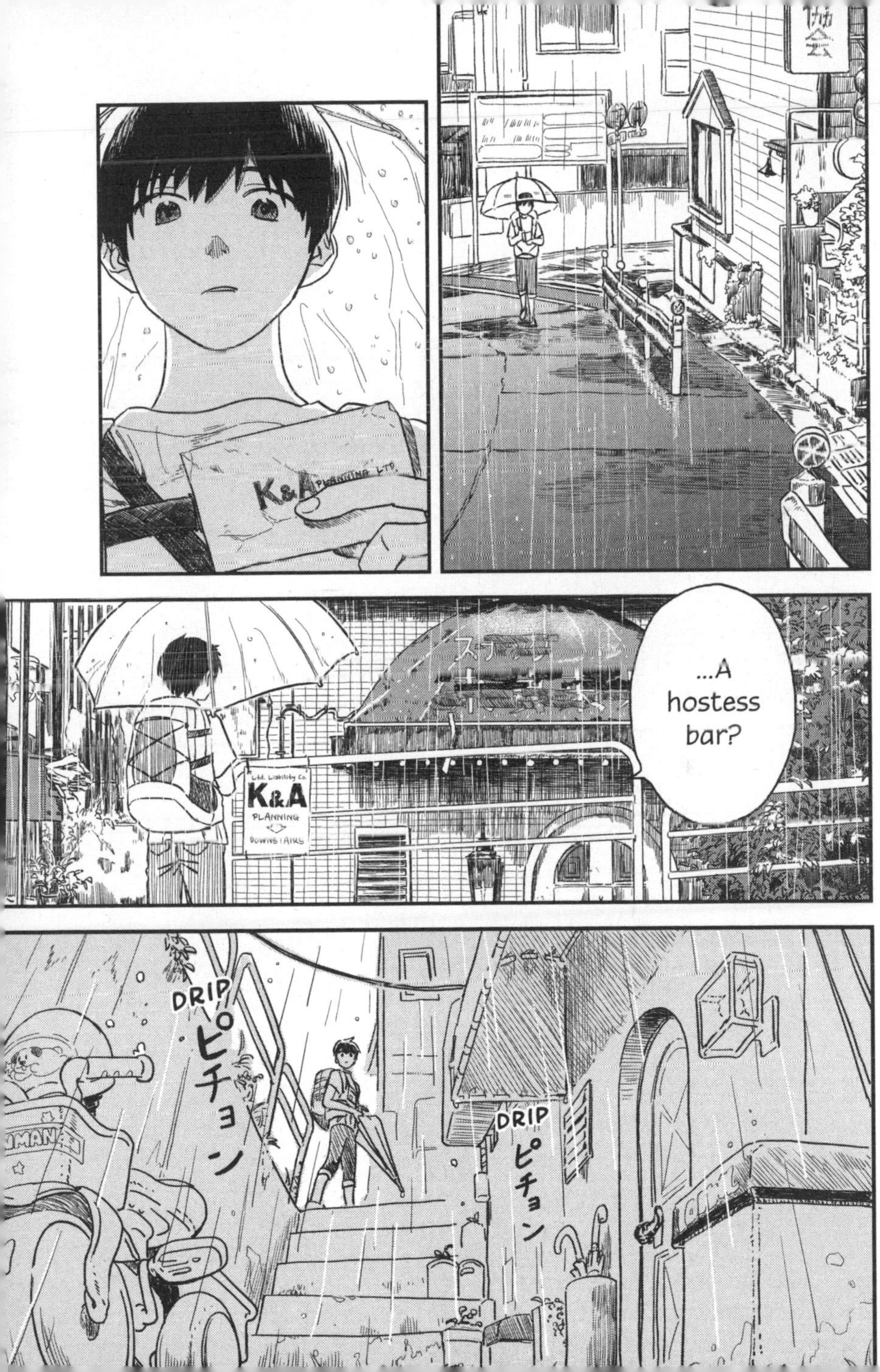
K&A PLANNING LTD.
Ltd. Liability Co.
K&A
PLANNING
DOWNSTAIRS
...A hostess bar?
DRIP
ピチョン
DRIP
ピチョン

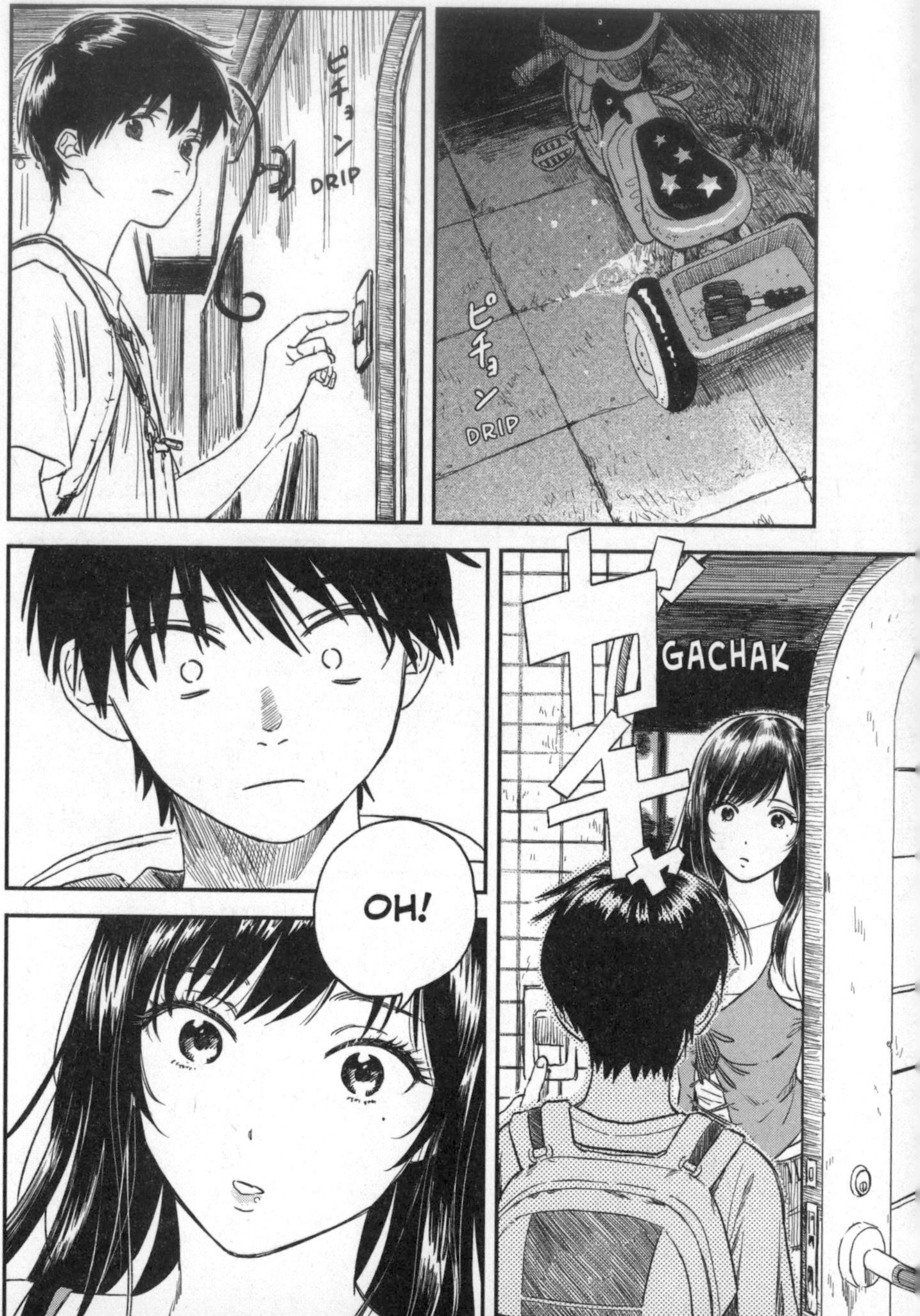
ピチョン
DRIP
ピチョン
DRIP
ガチャ
GACHAK
OH!

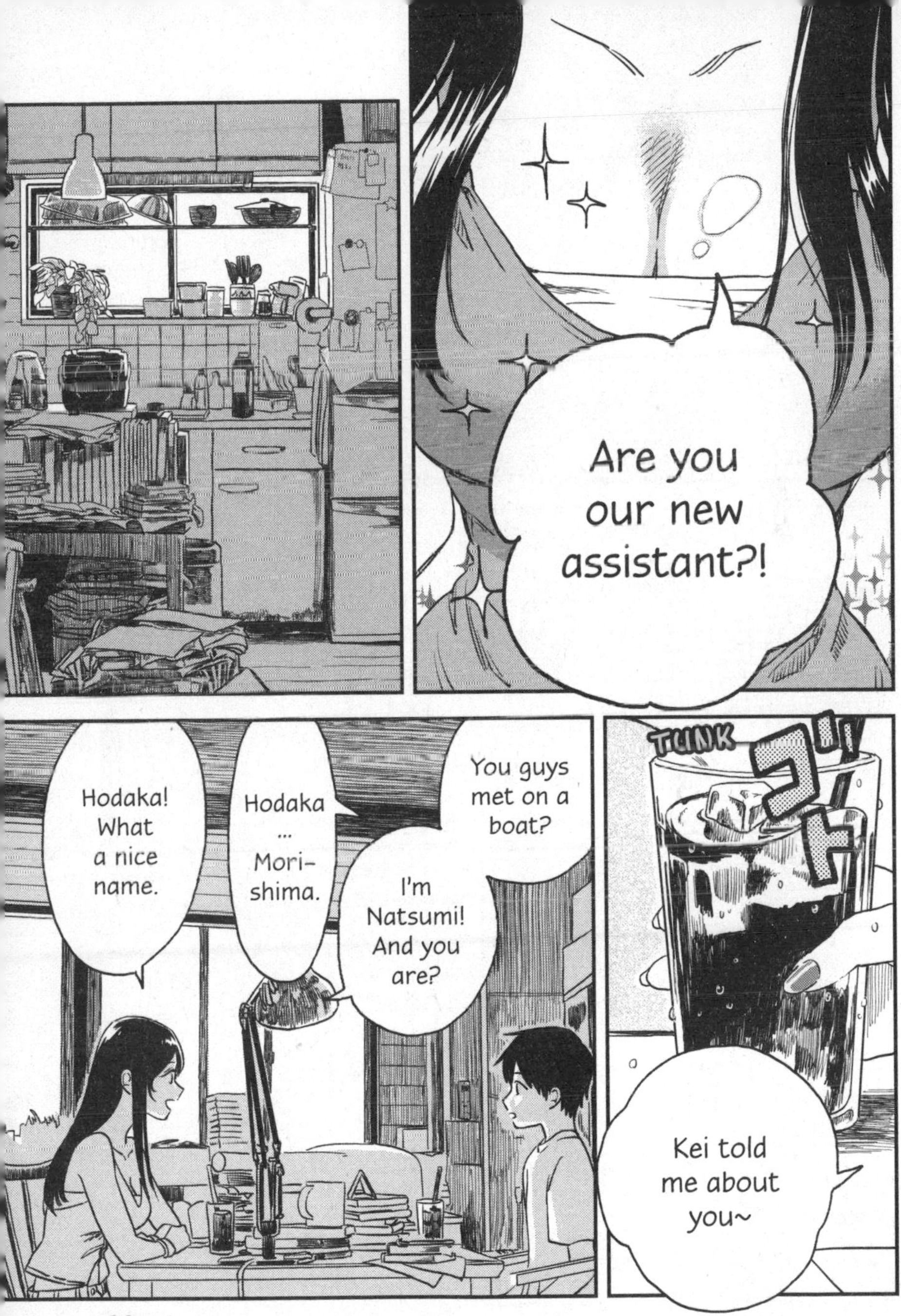
Are you our new assistant?!
TUNK
ゴト
Kei told me about you~
You guys met on a boat?
I'm Natsumi! And you are?
Hodaka ... Mori-shima.
Hodaka! What a nice name.

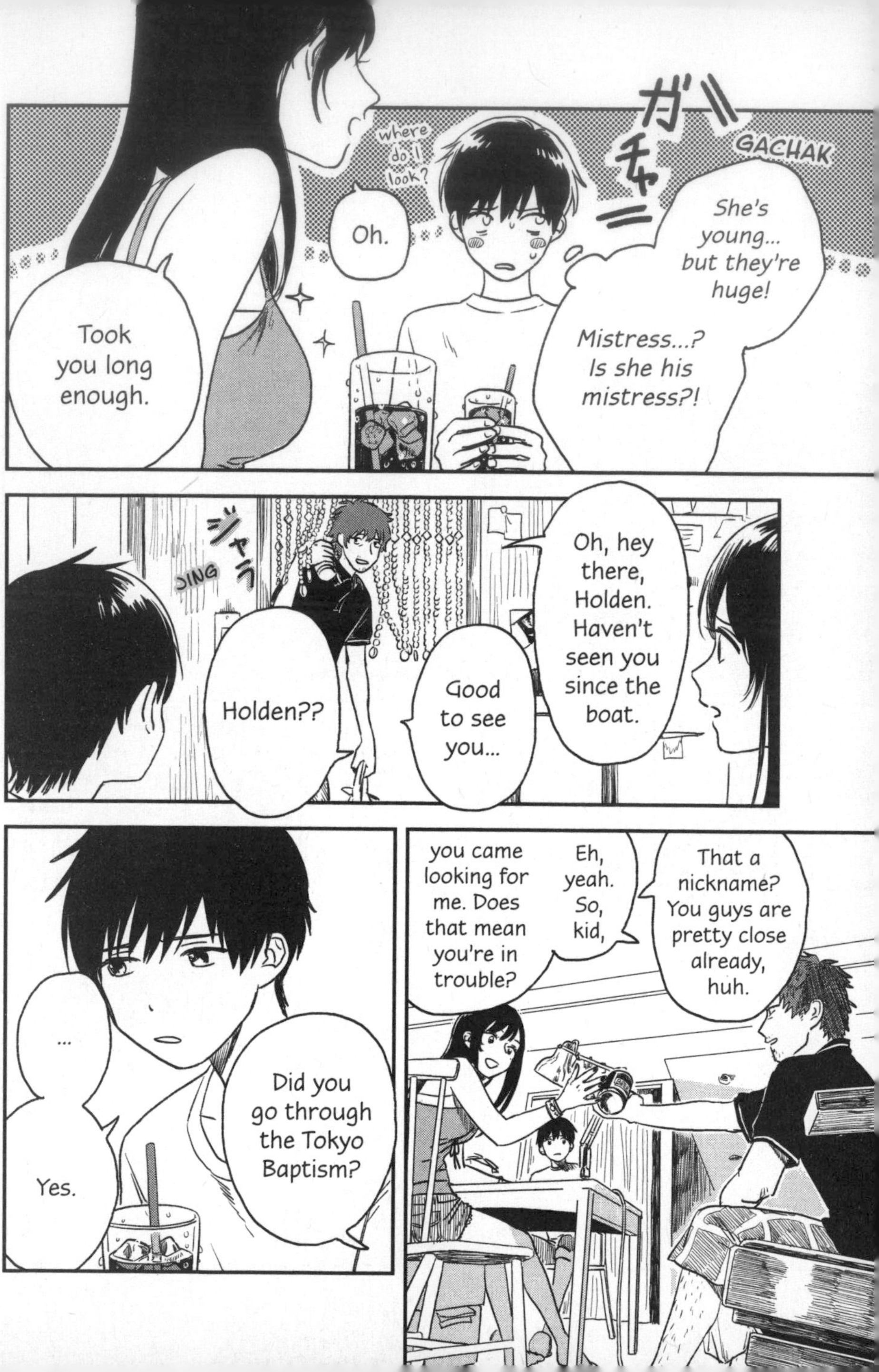

ガチャ
GACHAK
She's young... but they're huge!
Mistress...? Is she his mistress?!
where do I look?
Oh.
Took you long enough.
Oh, hey there, Holden. Haven't seen you since the boat.
Good to see you...
Holden??
ジャラ
JING
That a nickname? You guys are pretty close already, huh.
Eh, yeah. So, kid,
you came looking for me. Does that mean you're in trouble?
Did you go through the Tokyo Baptism?
...
Yes.

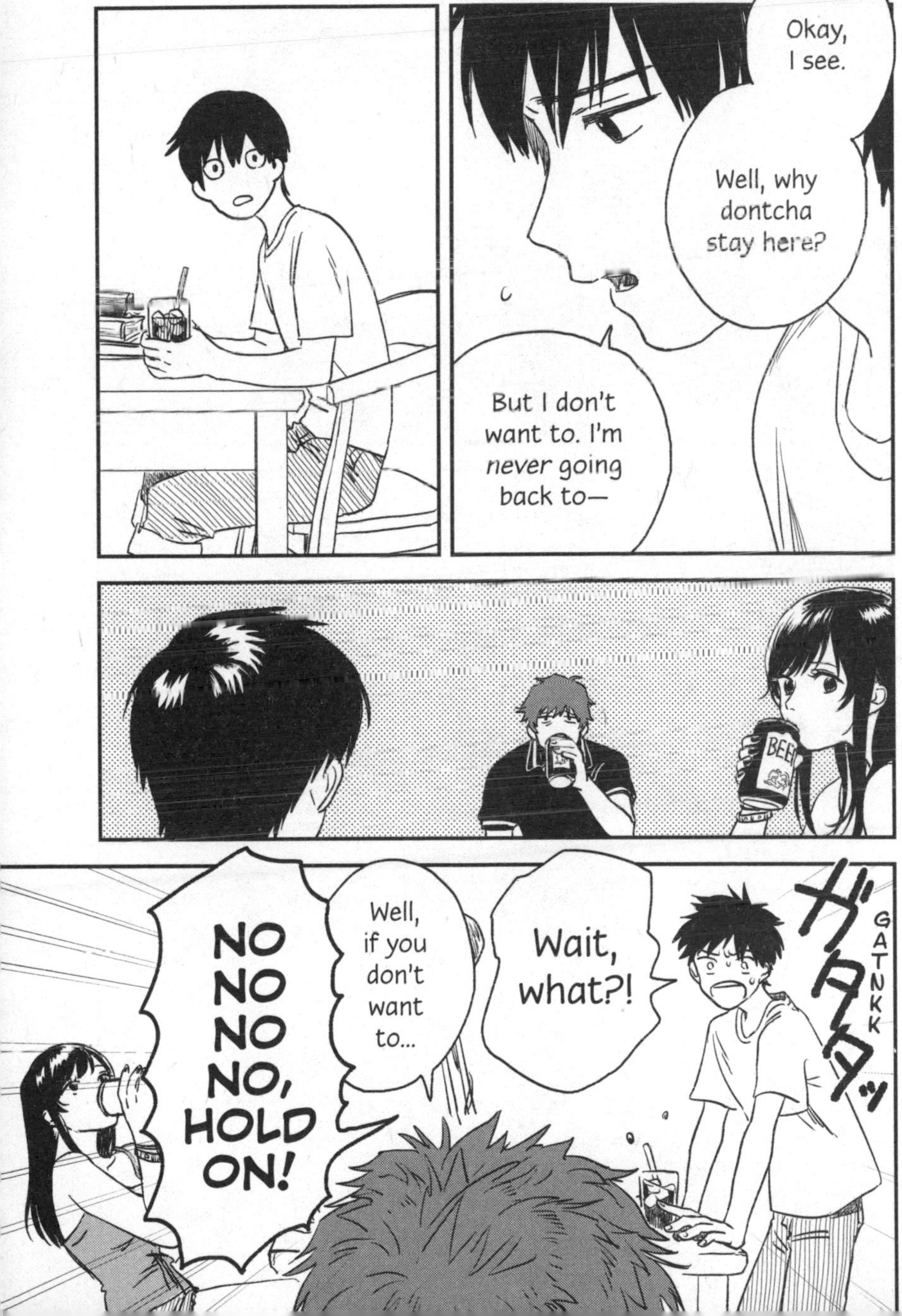
Okay, I see.
Well, why dontcha stay here?
But I don't want to. I'm *never* going back to—
BEER
ガタッ
GATNKK
Wait, what?!
Well, if you don't want to...
NO NO NO NO, HOLD ON!

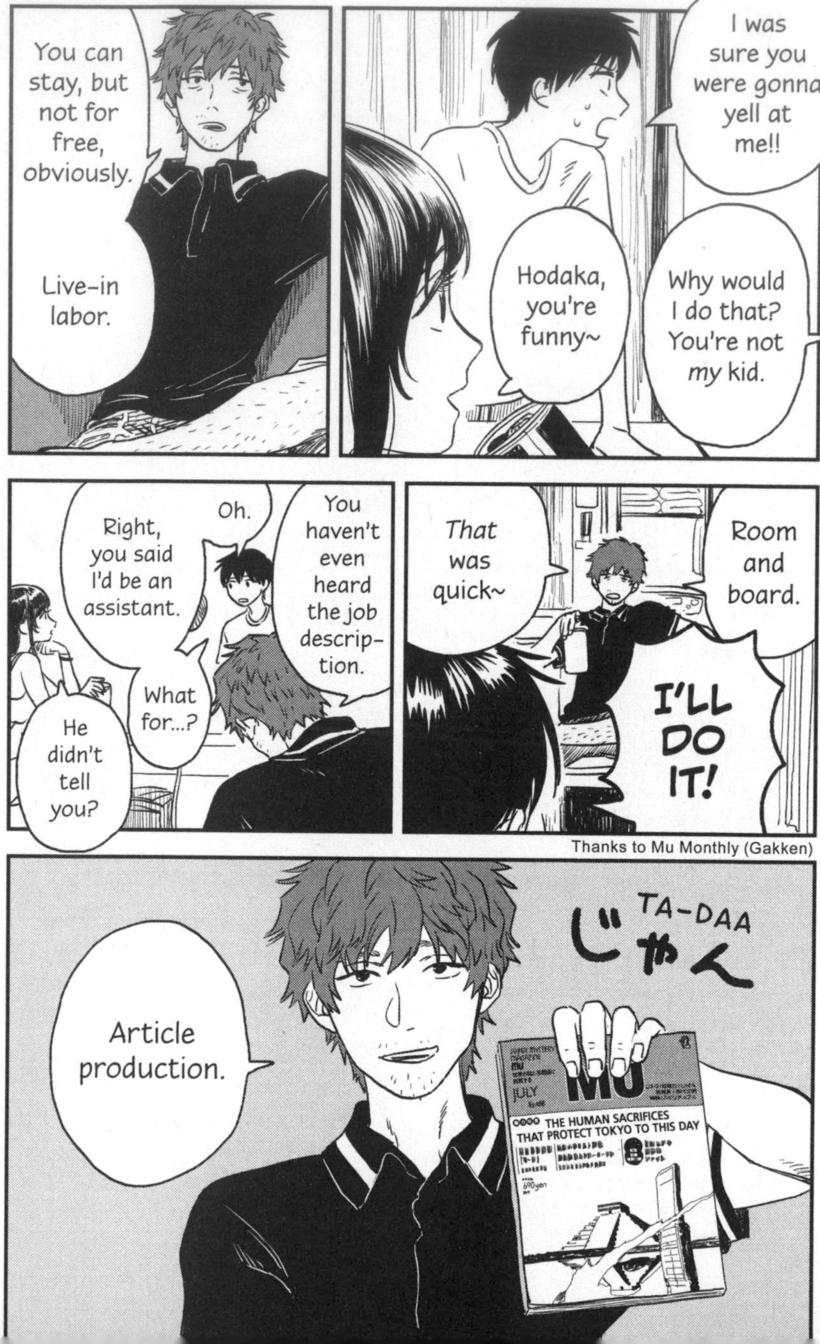
I was sure you were gonna yell at me!!
Why would I do that? You're not *my* kid.
Hodaka, you're funny~
You can stay, but not for free, obviously.
Live-in labor.
Room and board.
That was quick~
I'LL DO IT!
You haven't even heard the job description.
Oh.
Right, you said I'd be an assistant.
What for...?
He didn't tell you?
Thanks to Mu Monthly (Gakken)
じゃん TA-DAA
Article production.
MU
JULY
THE HUMAN SACRIFICES THAT PROTECT TOKYO TO THIS DAY
690yen

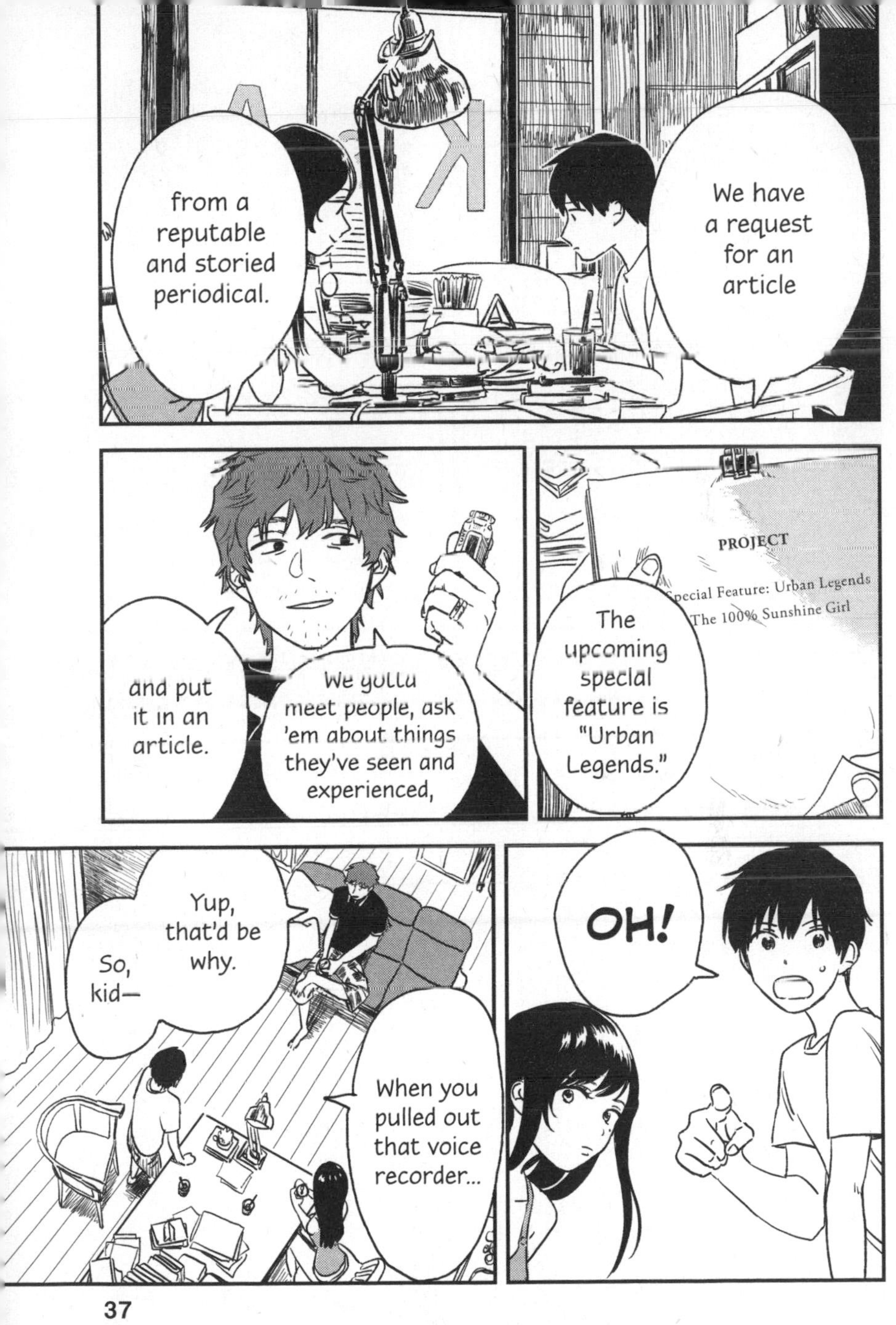
We have a request for an article
from a reputable and storied periodical.
PROJECT
Special Feature: Urban Legends
The 100% Sunshine Girl
The upcoming special feature is "Urban Legends."
We gotta meet people, ask 'em about things they've seen and experienced,
and put it in an article.
OH!
When you pulled out that voice recorder...
Yup, that'd be why.
So, kid—

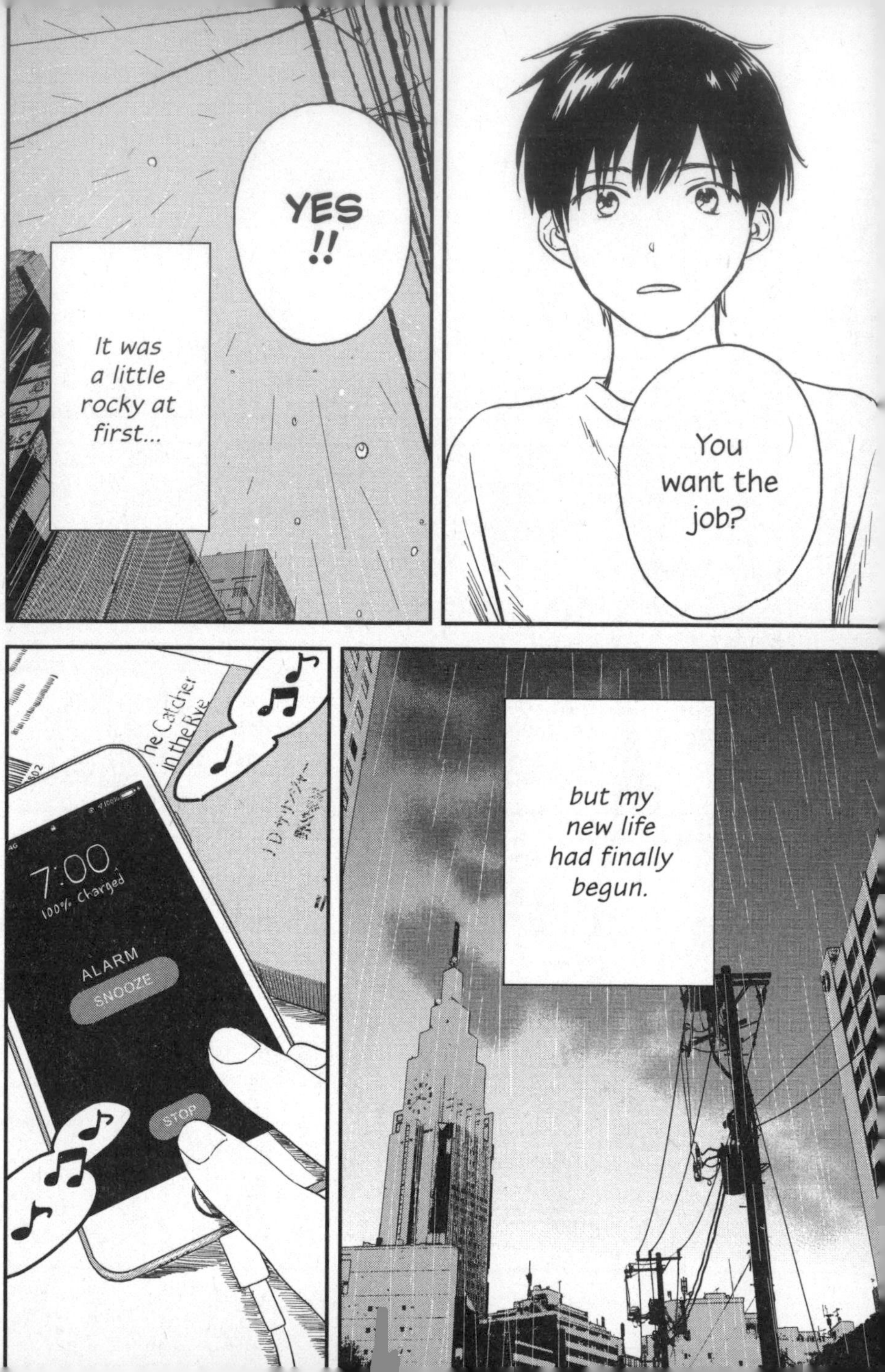
You want the job?
YES !!
It was a little rocky at first...
but my new life had finally begun.
he Catcher in the Rye
7:00
100% Charged
ALARM
SNOOZE
STOP

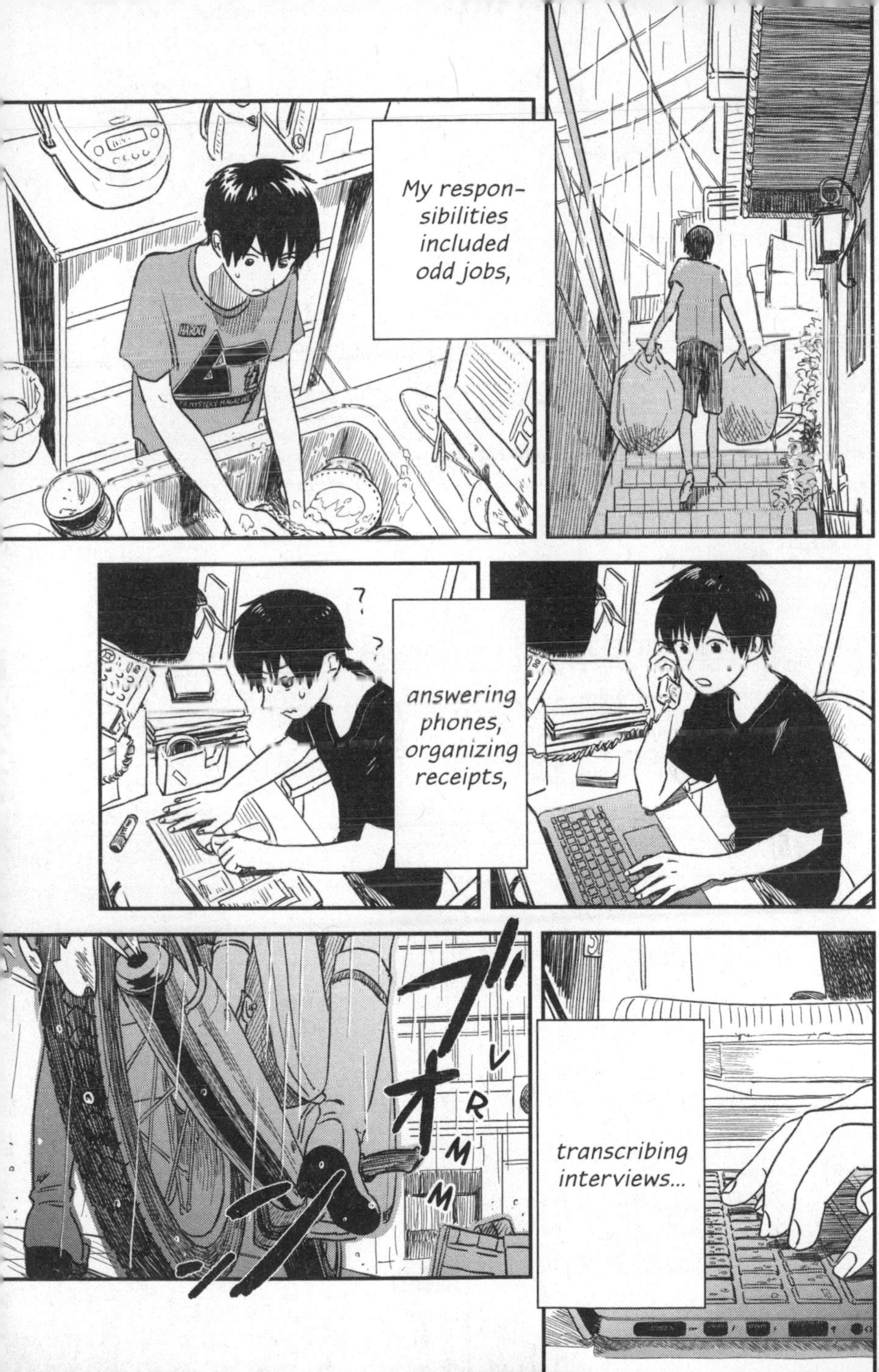
My responsibilities included odd jobs,
answering phones, organizing receipts,
?
?
transcribing interviews...
VRMM

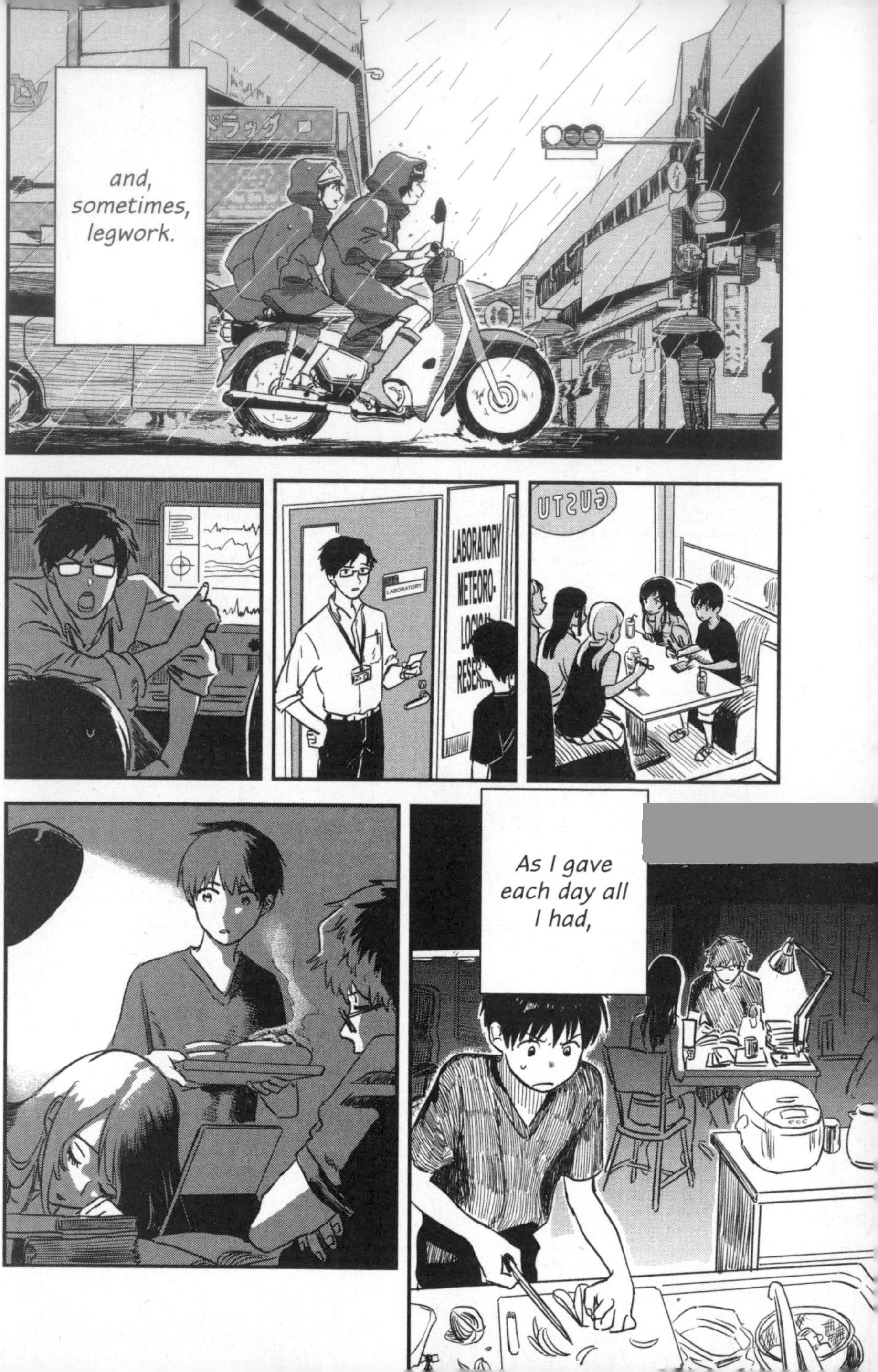

and, sometimes, legwork.
ドラッグ
LABORATORY
METEORO-
LABORATORY
As I gave each day all I had,

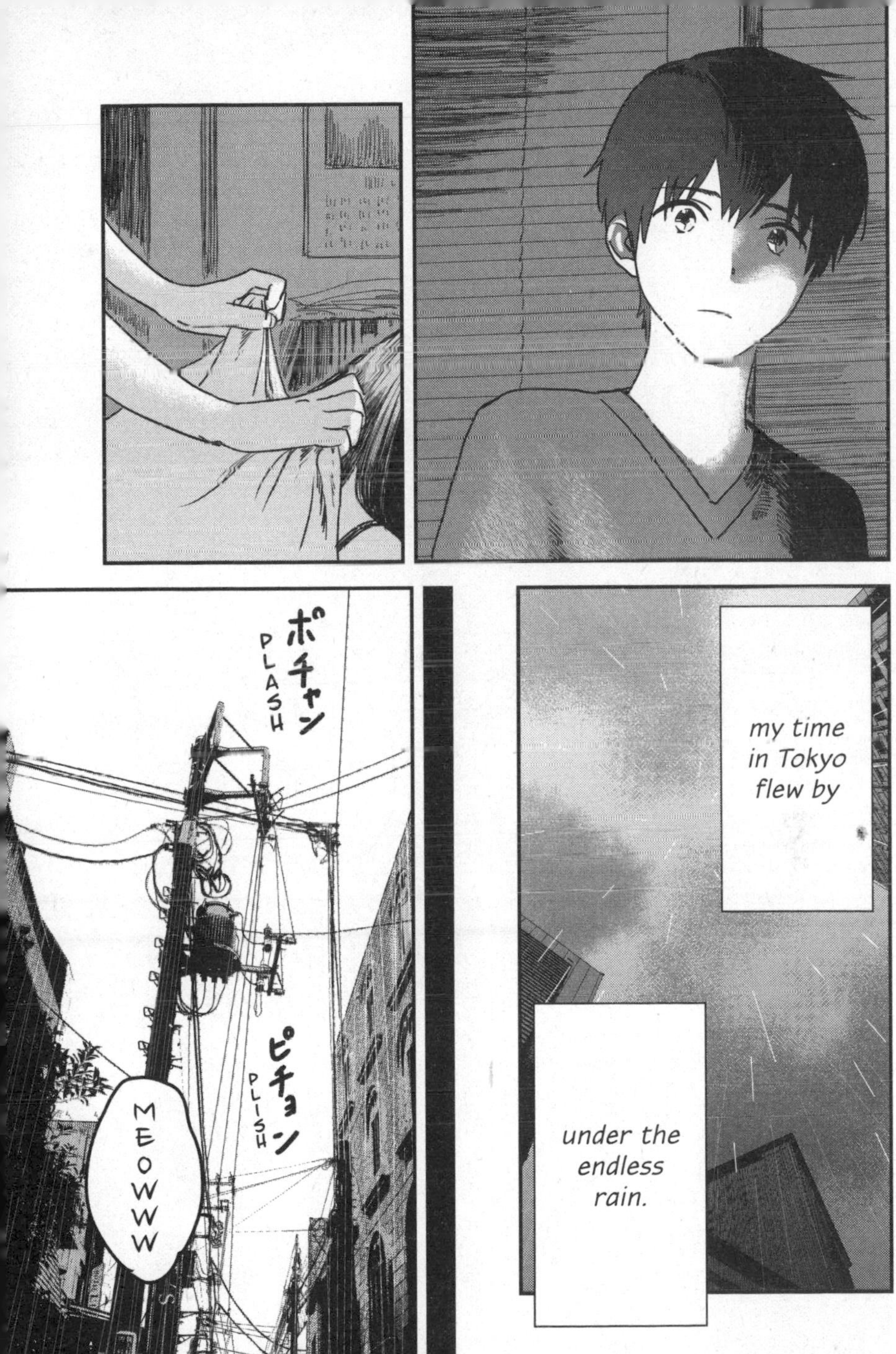
my time in Tokyo flew by
under the endless rain.
ポチャン
PLASH
ピチョン
PLISH
MEOWWW

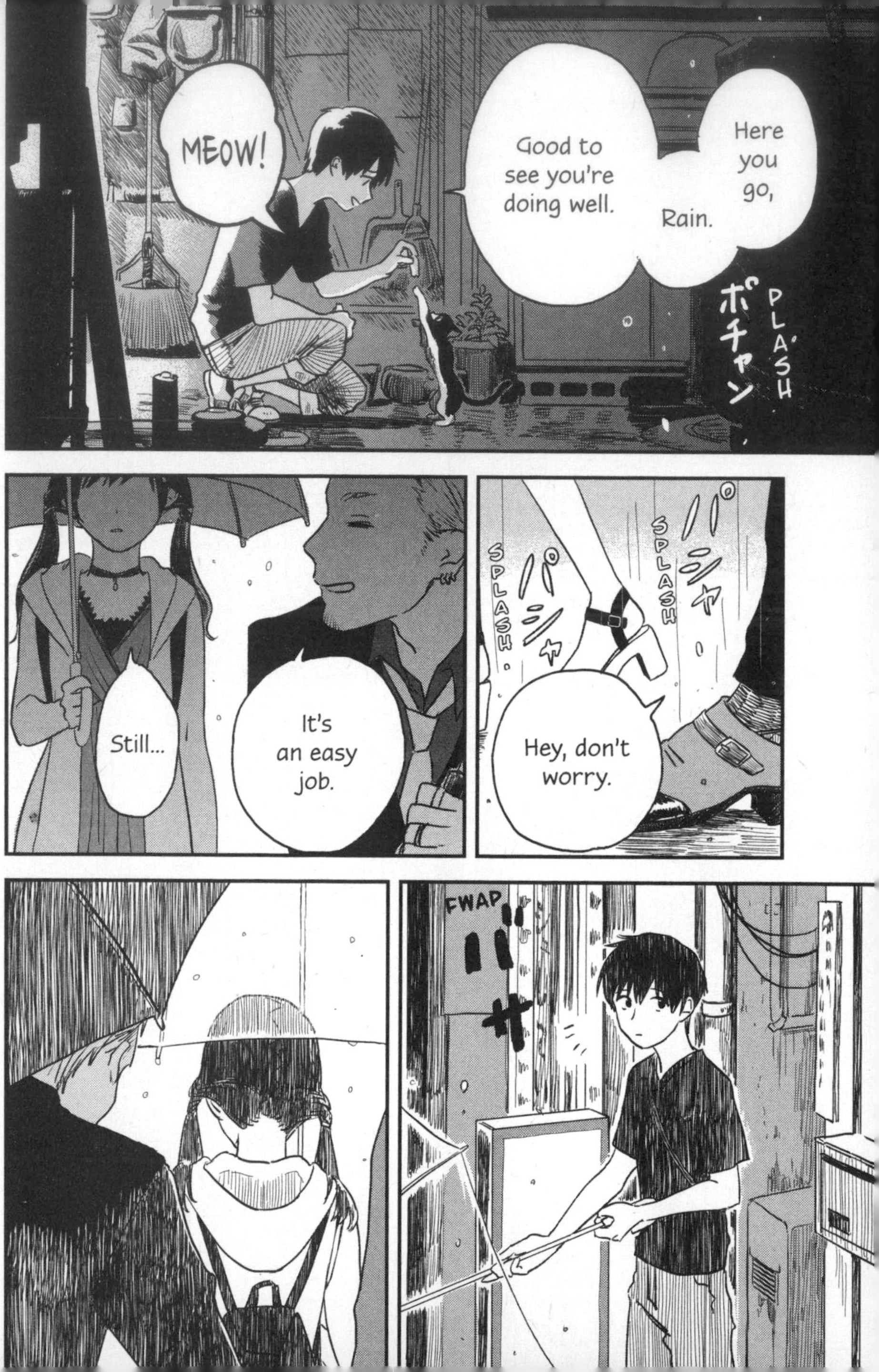
Here you go, Rain.
Good to see you're doing well.
MEOW!
ポチャン
PLASH
パシャ
SPLASH
パシャ
SPLASH
Hey, don't worry.
It's an easy job.
Still...
FWAP

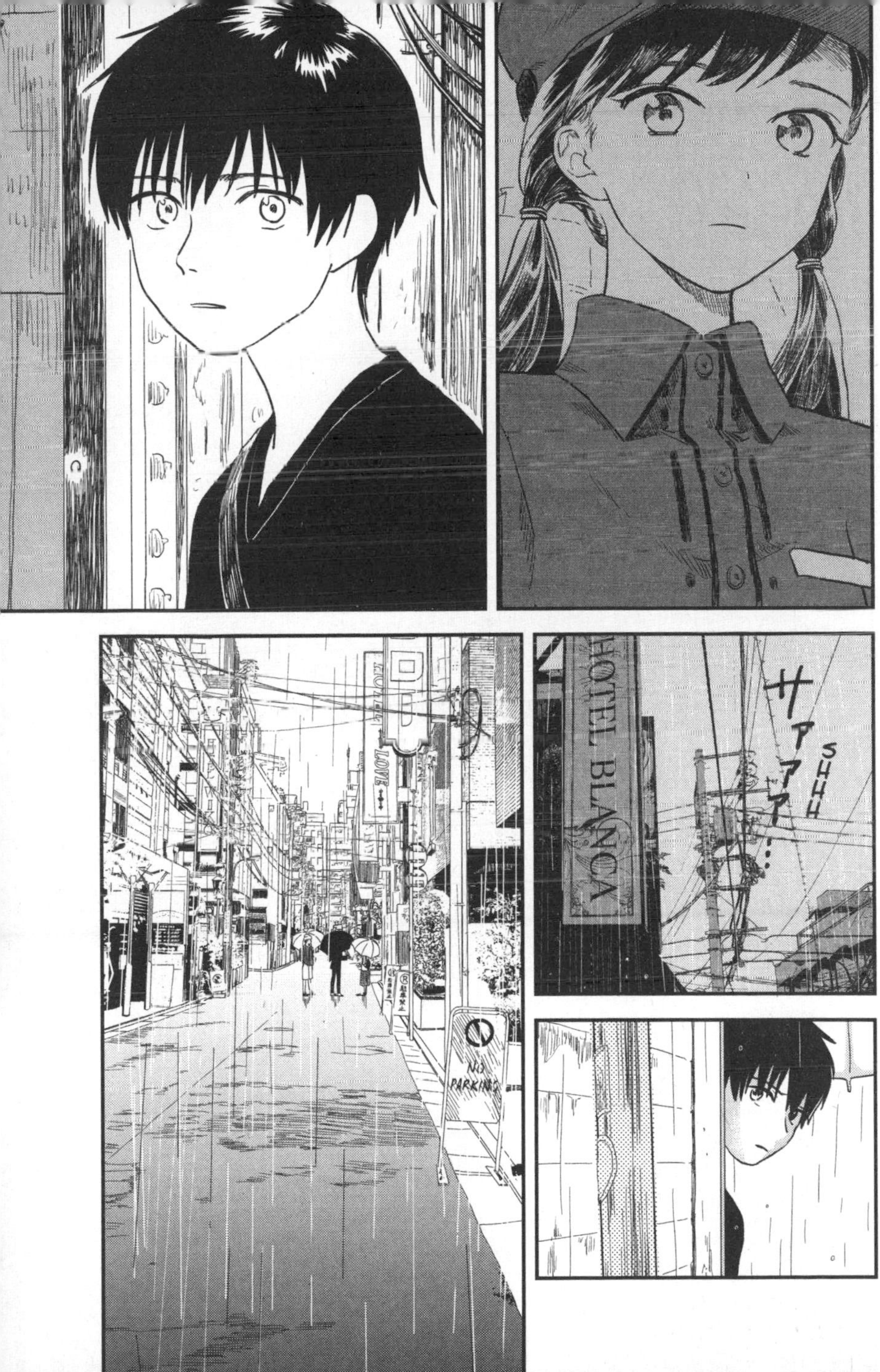
HOTEL BLANCA
サァァァ…
SHHH
LOVE
NO PARKING

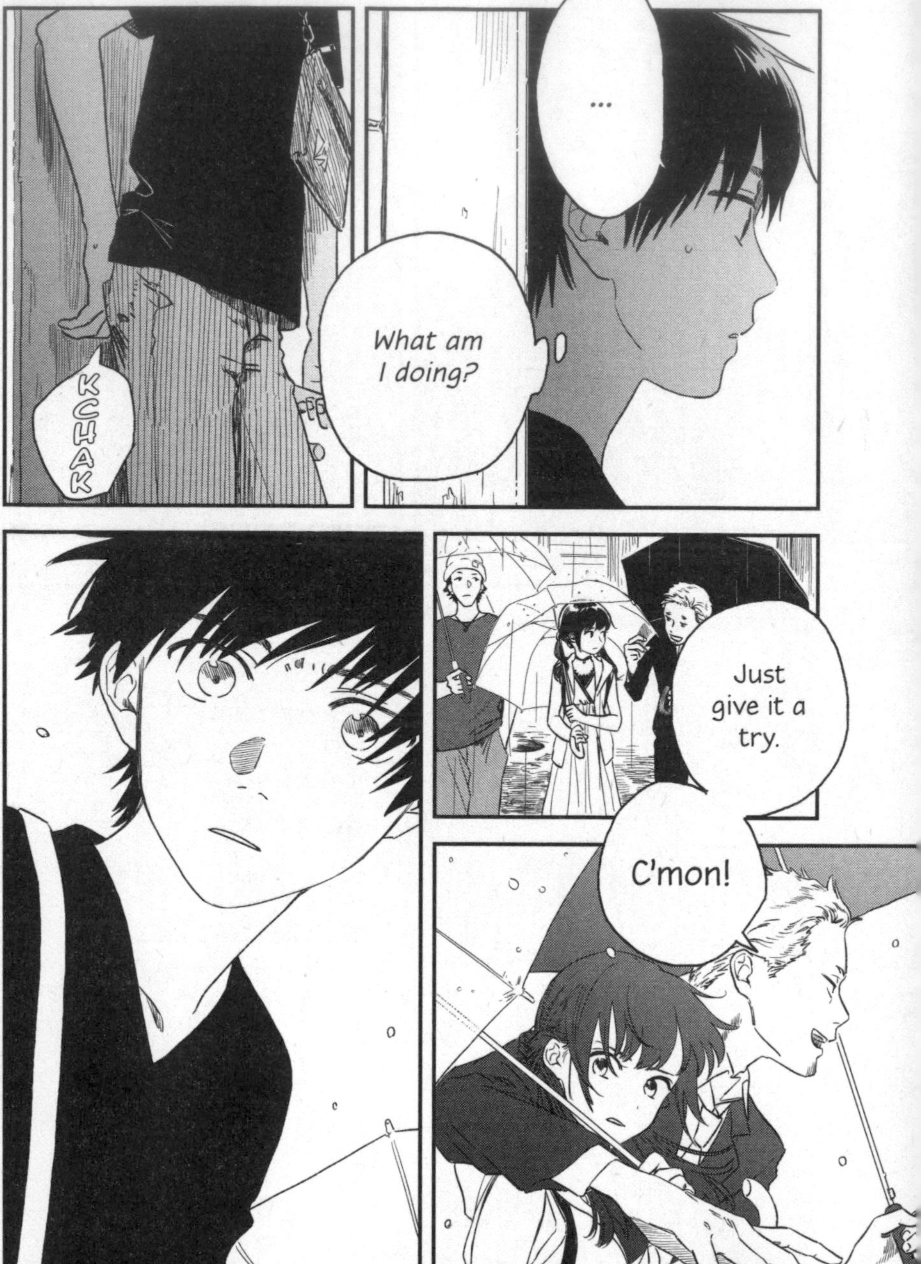
...
What am I doing?
KCHAK
Just give it a try.
C'mon!

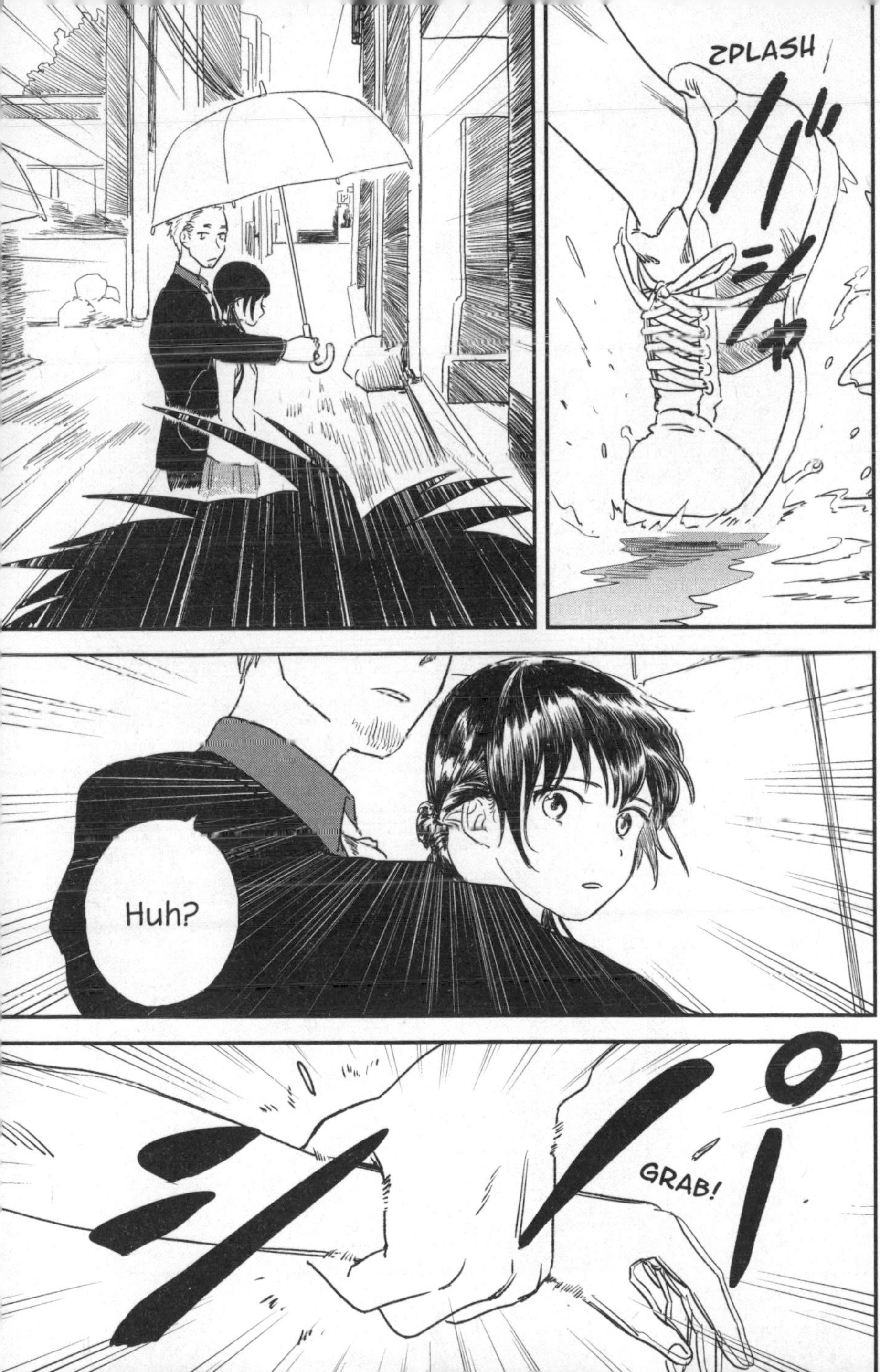
ZPLASH
Huh?
GRAB!

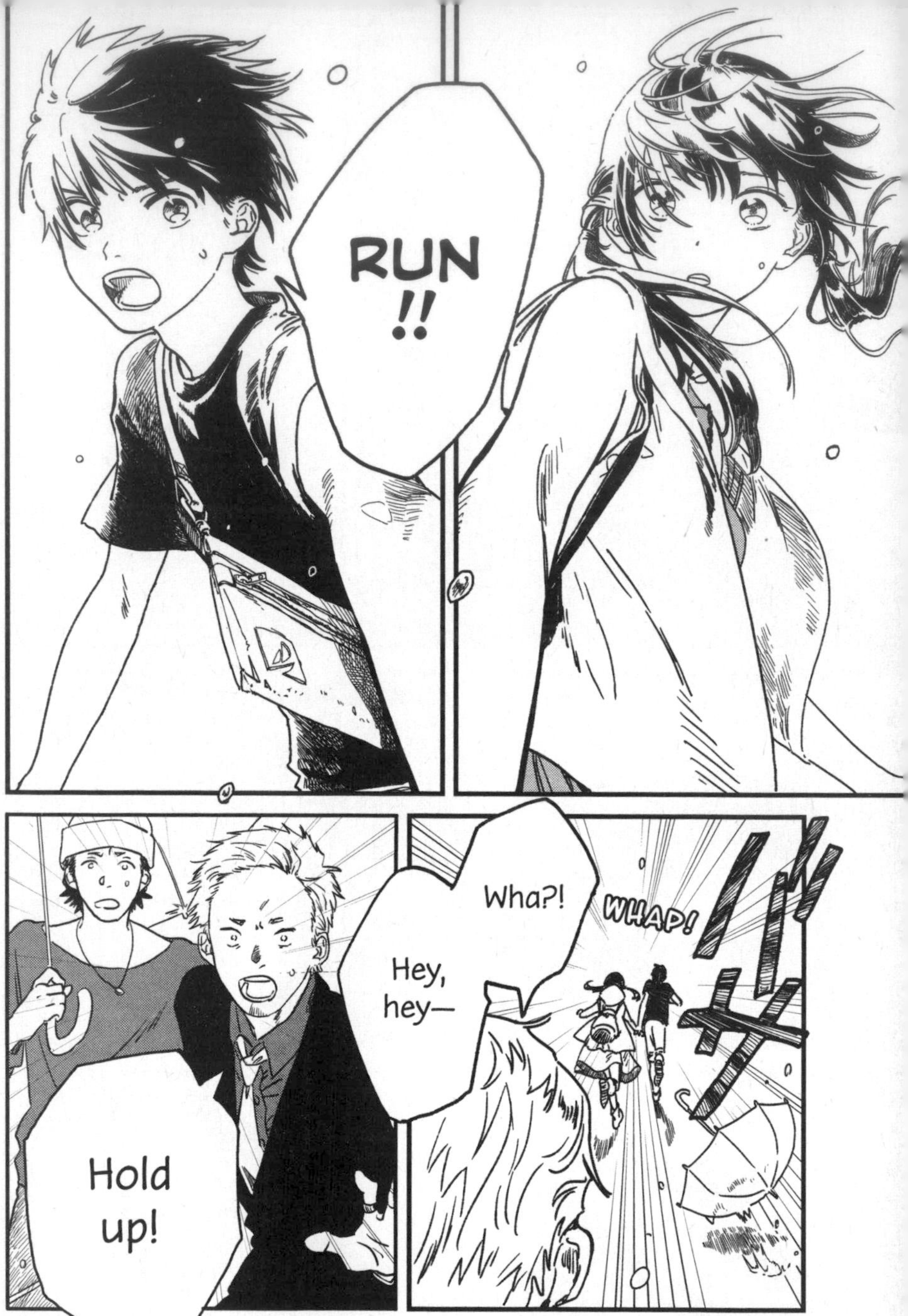
RUN !!
WHAP!
Wha?!
Hey, hey—
Hold up!

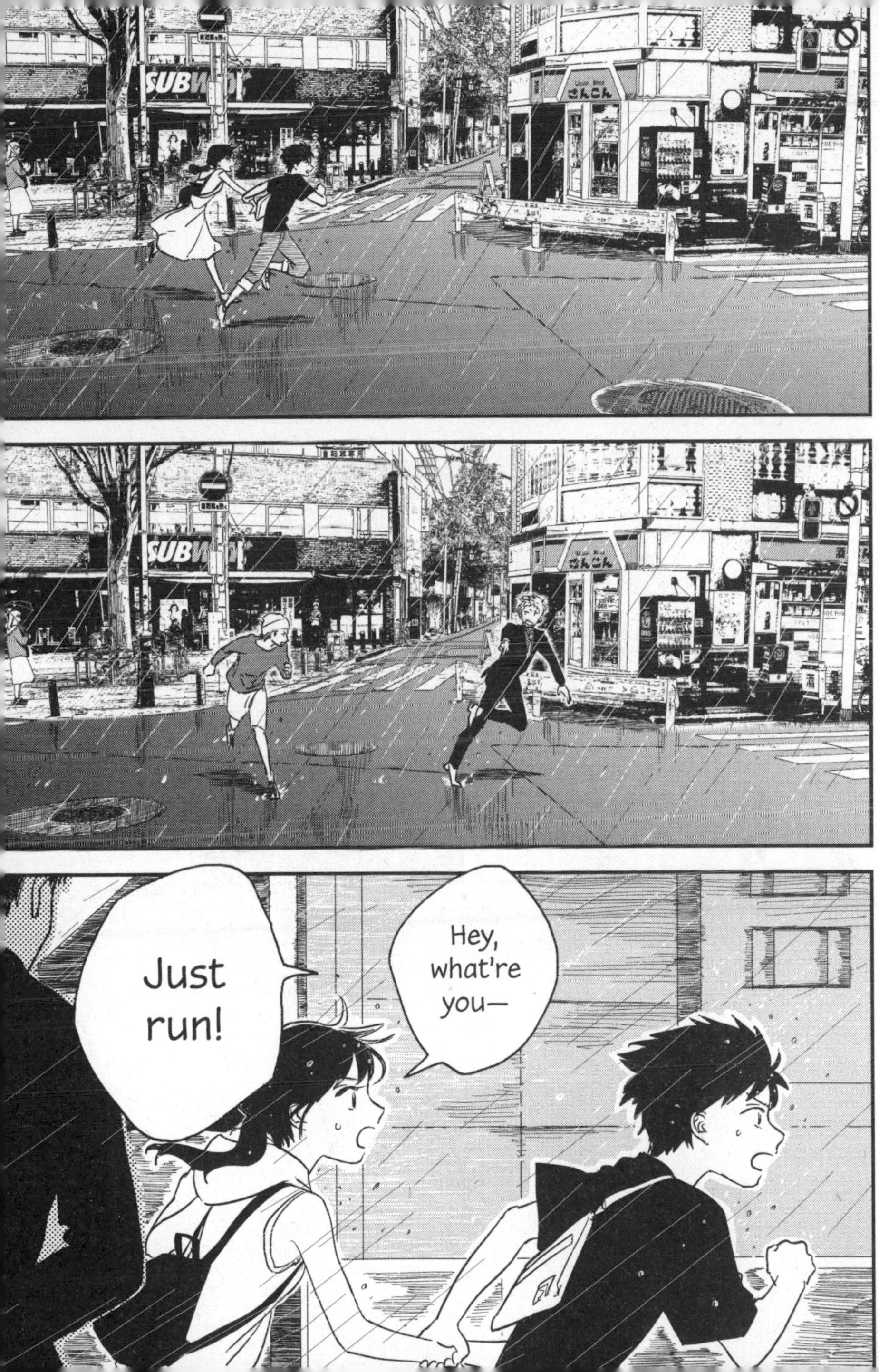
Hey, what're you—
Just run!

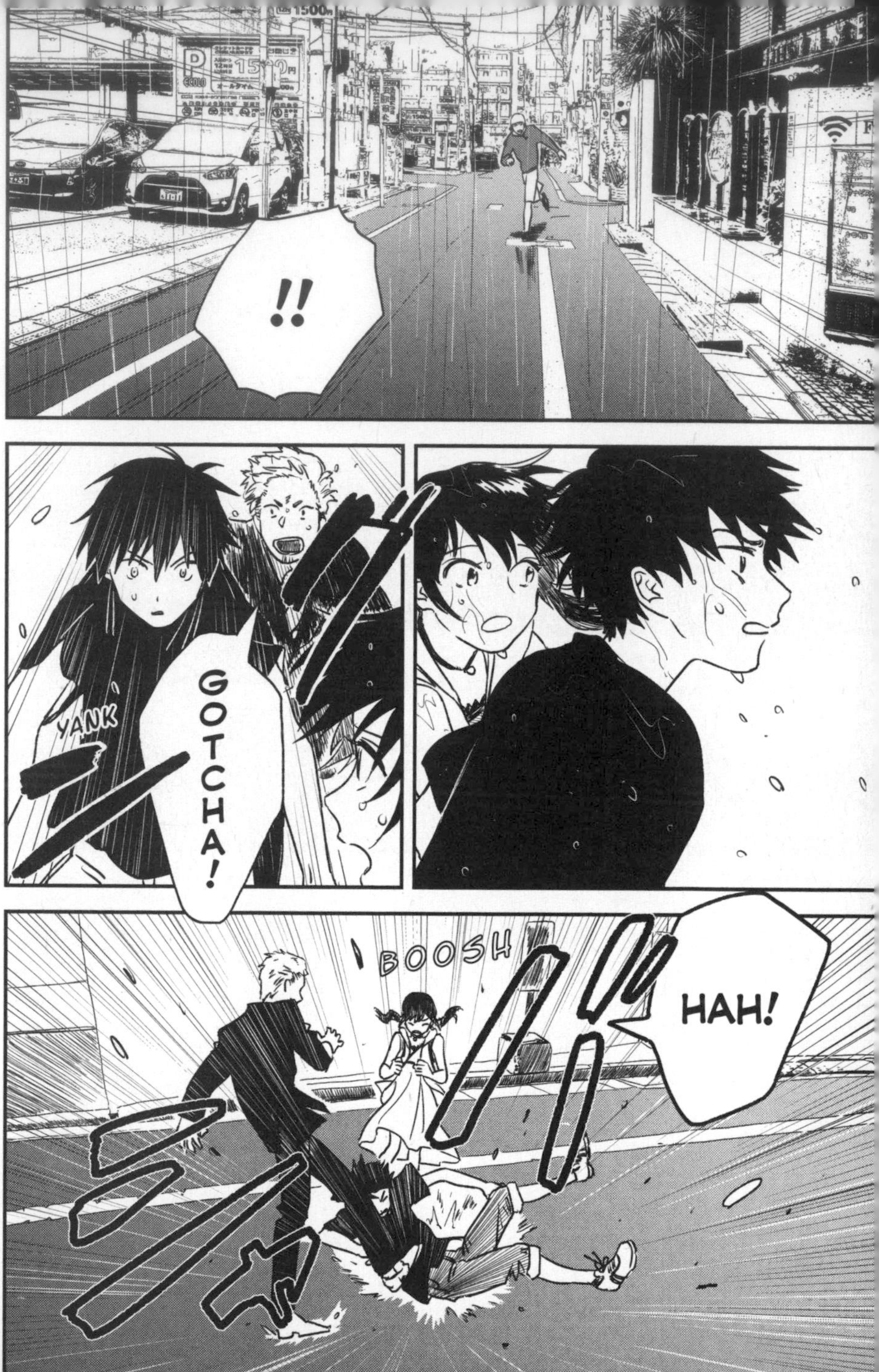
!!
GOTCHA!
YANK
HAH!
BOOSH

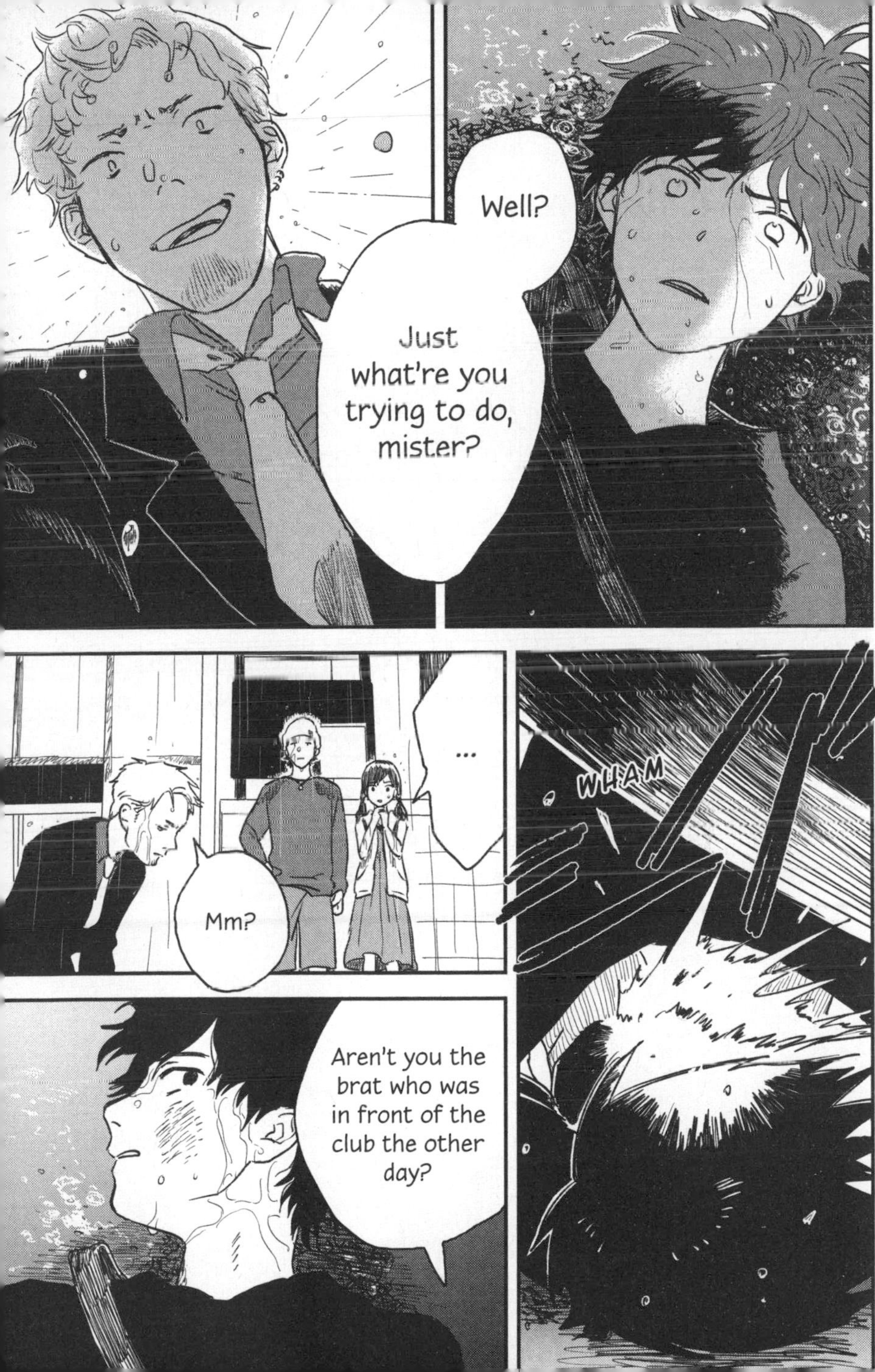
Well?
Just what're you trying to do, mister?
WHAM
...
Mm?
Aren't you the brat who was in front of the club the other day?

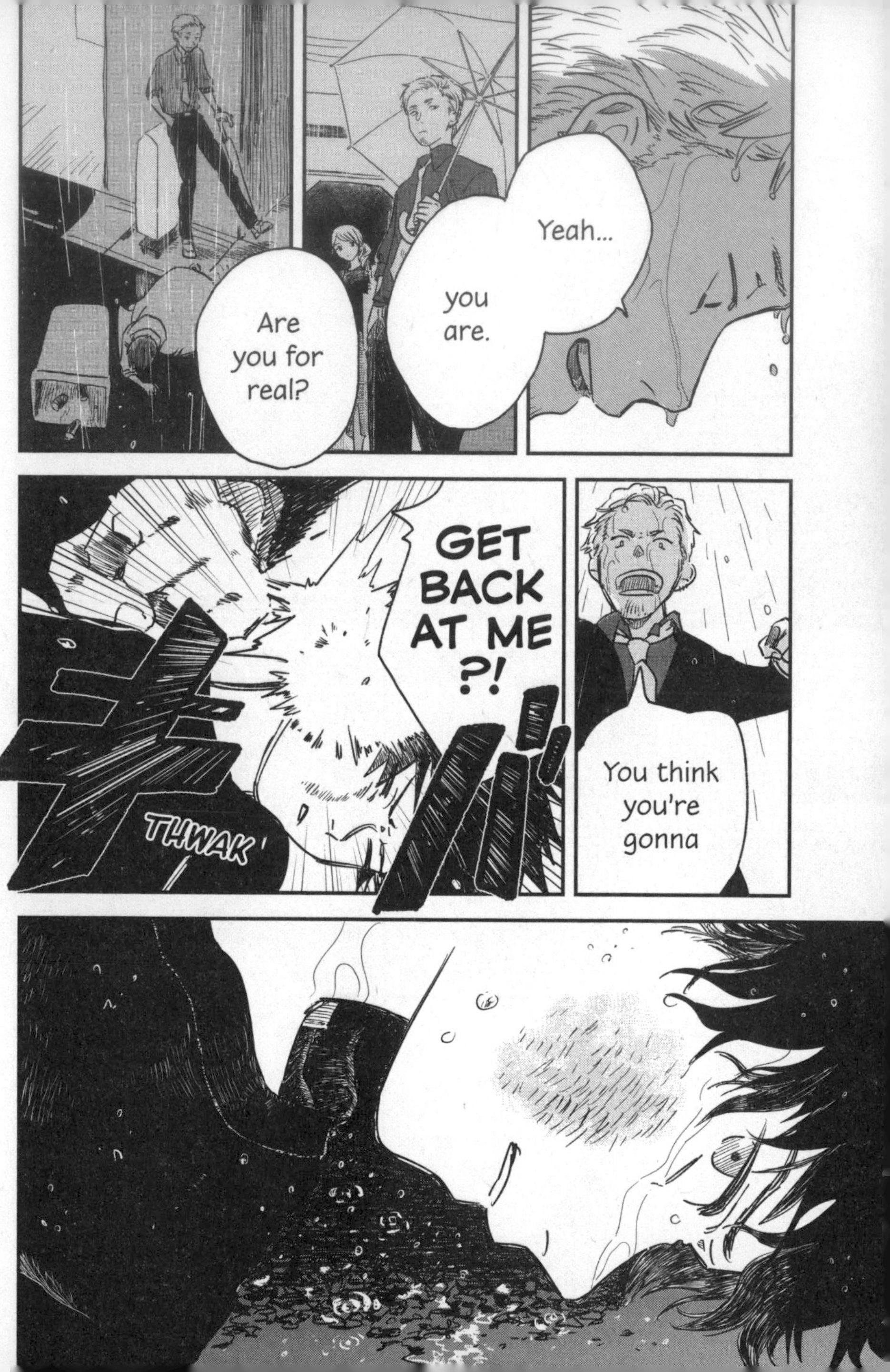
Yeah... you are.
Are you for real?
You think you're gonna
GET BACK AT ME ?!
THWAK

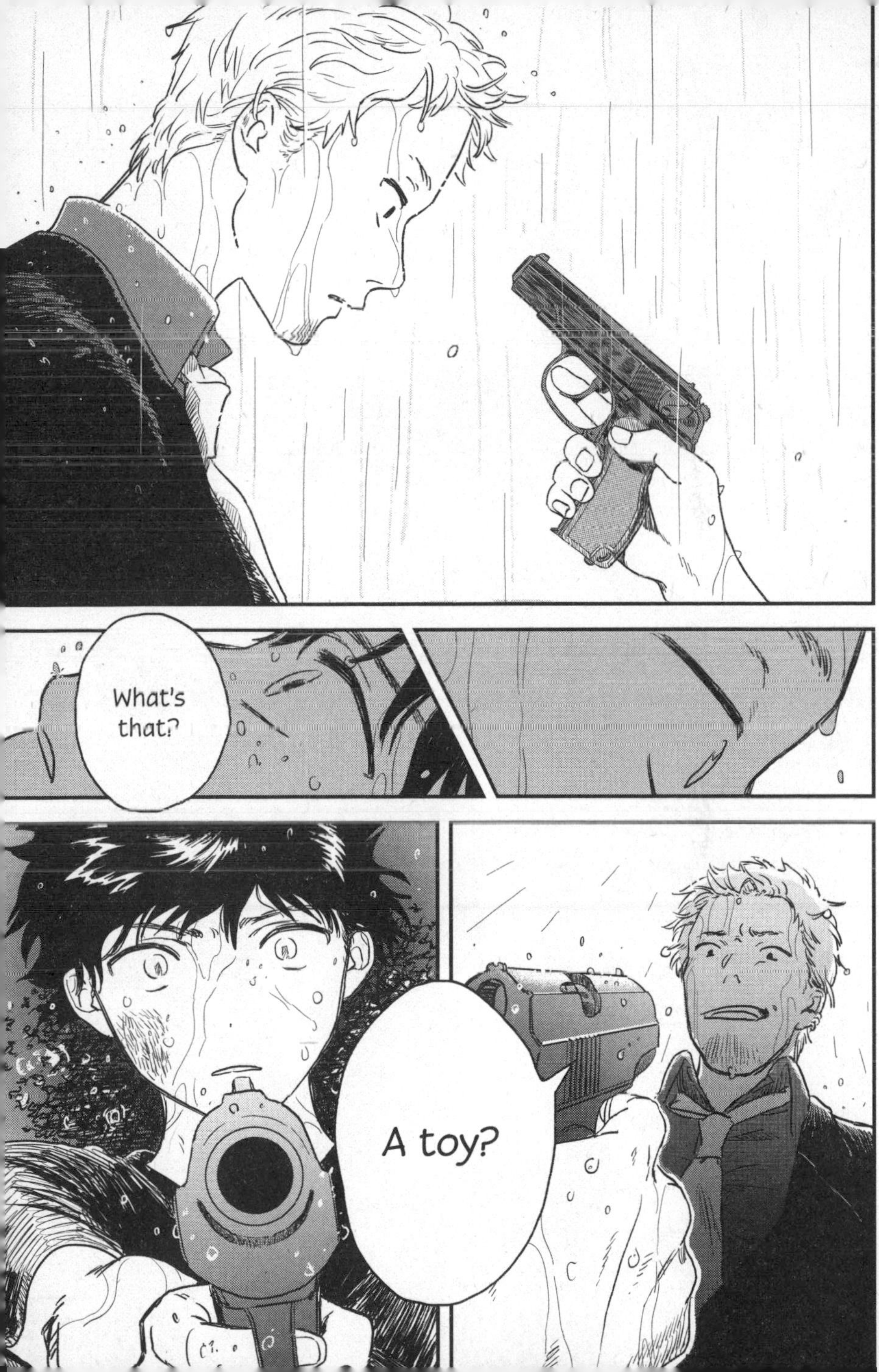
What's that?
A toy?

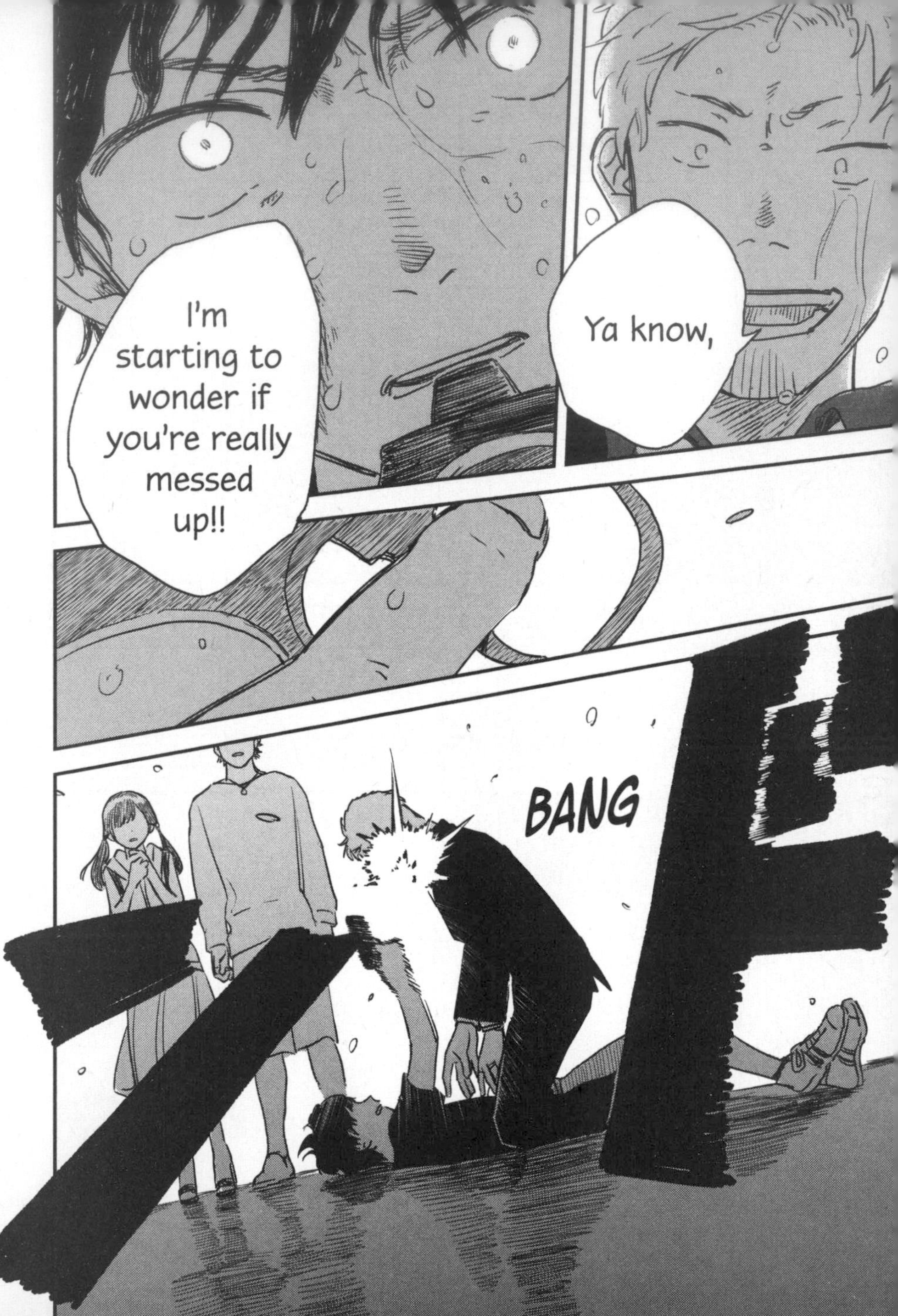
Ya know,
I'm starting to wonder if you're really messed up!!
BANG

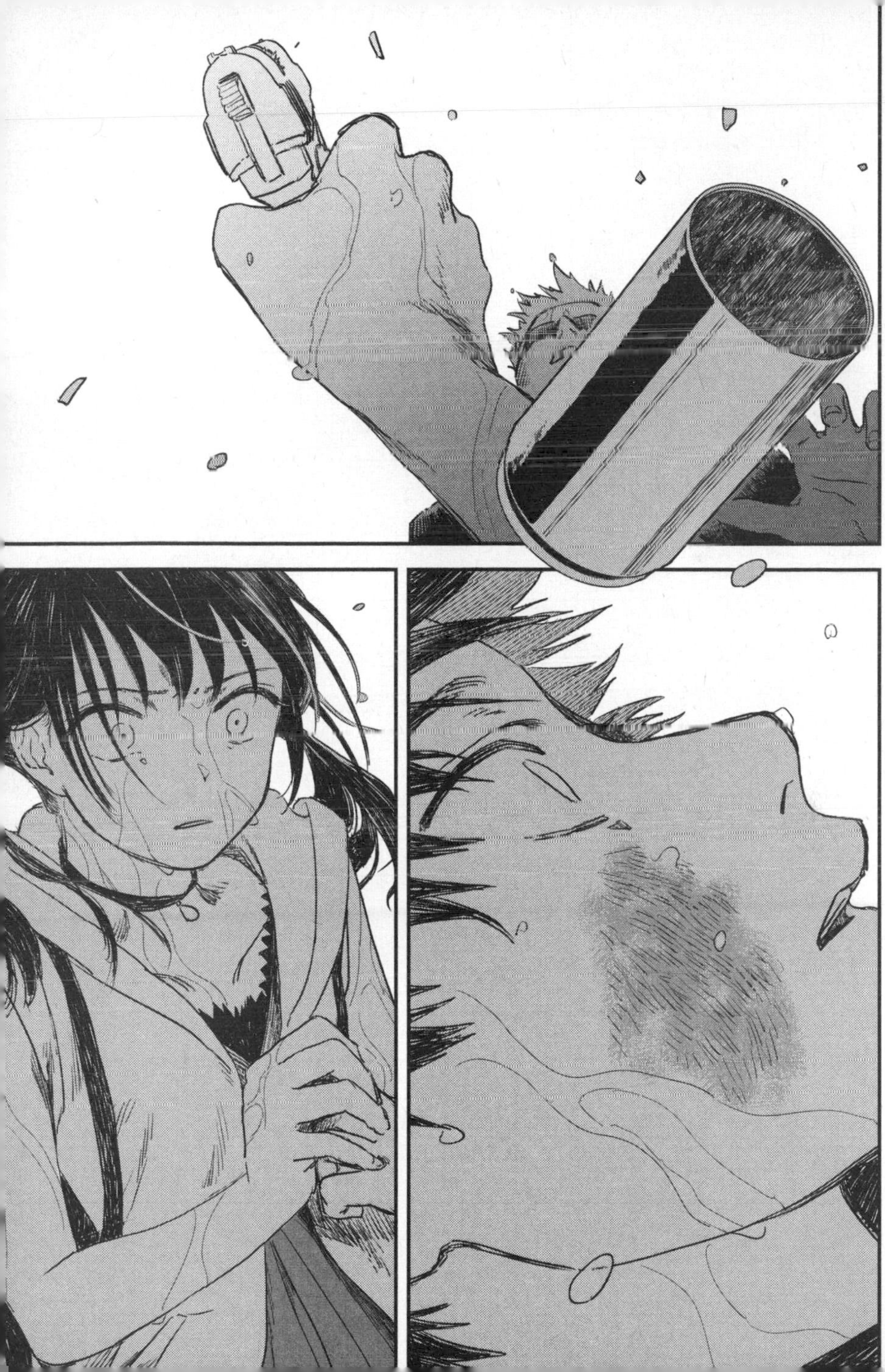

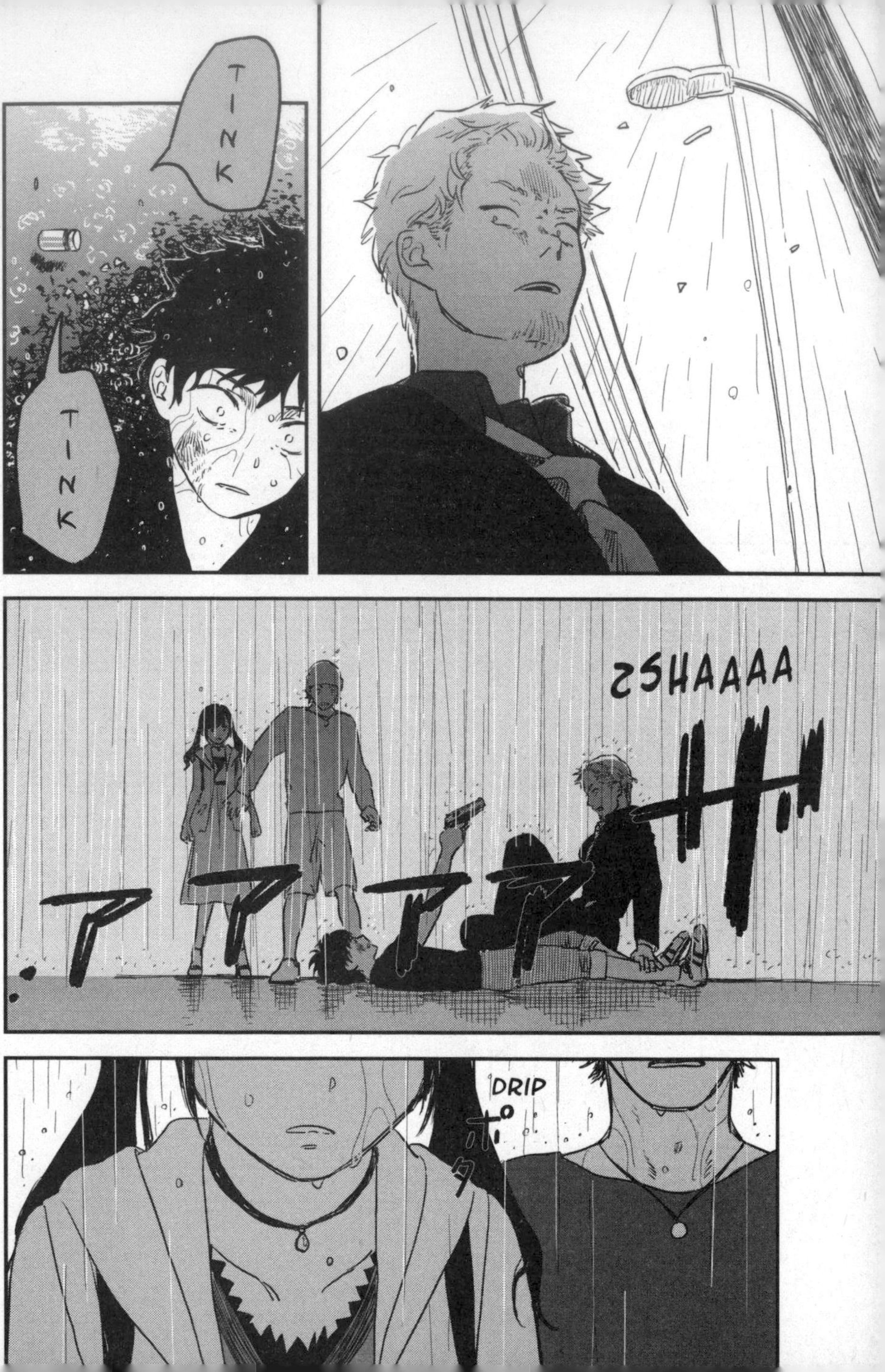
TINK
TINK
ZSHAAAA
DRIP
ポタ

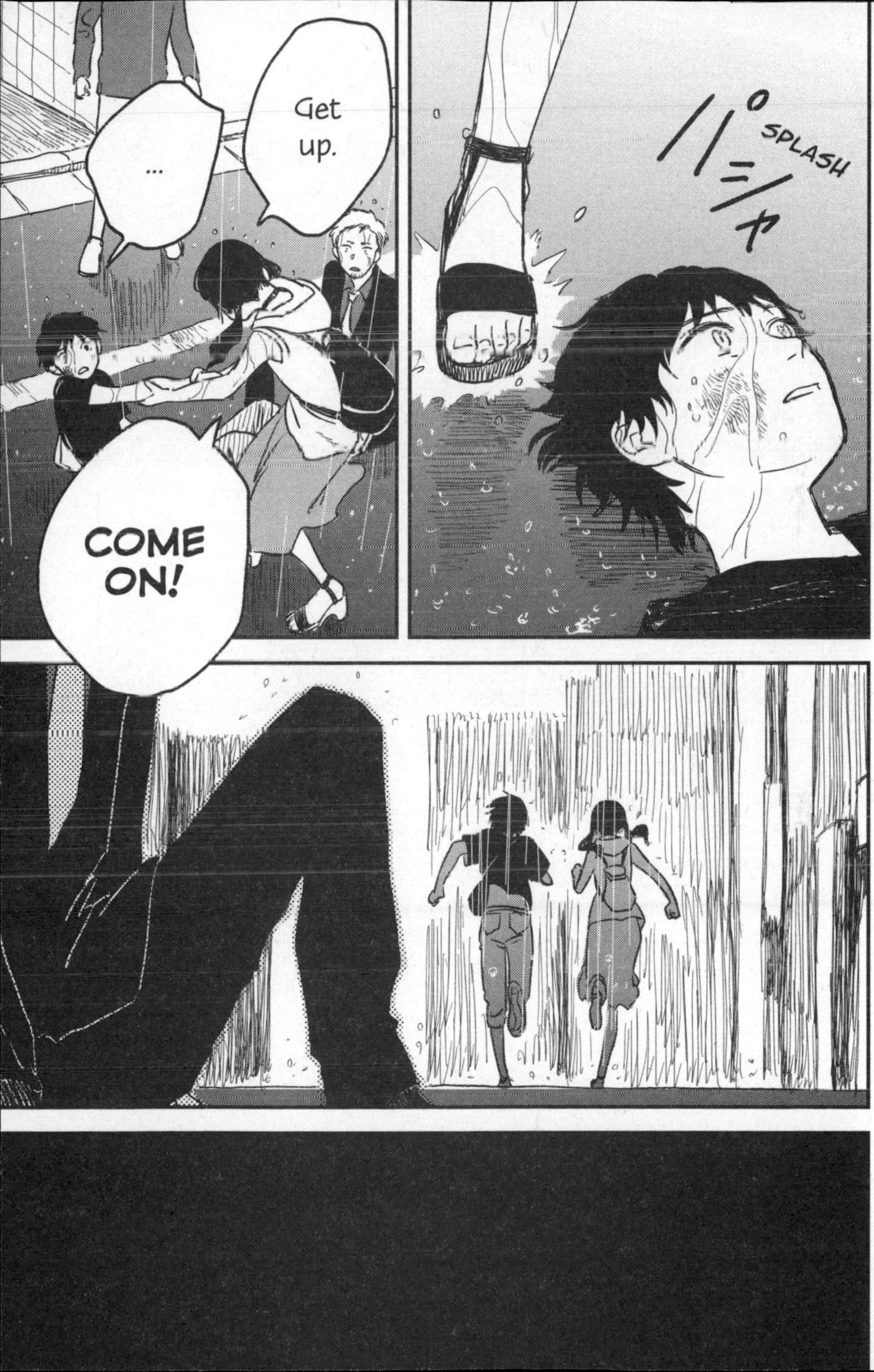
パシャ
SPLASH
Get up.
...
COME ON!

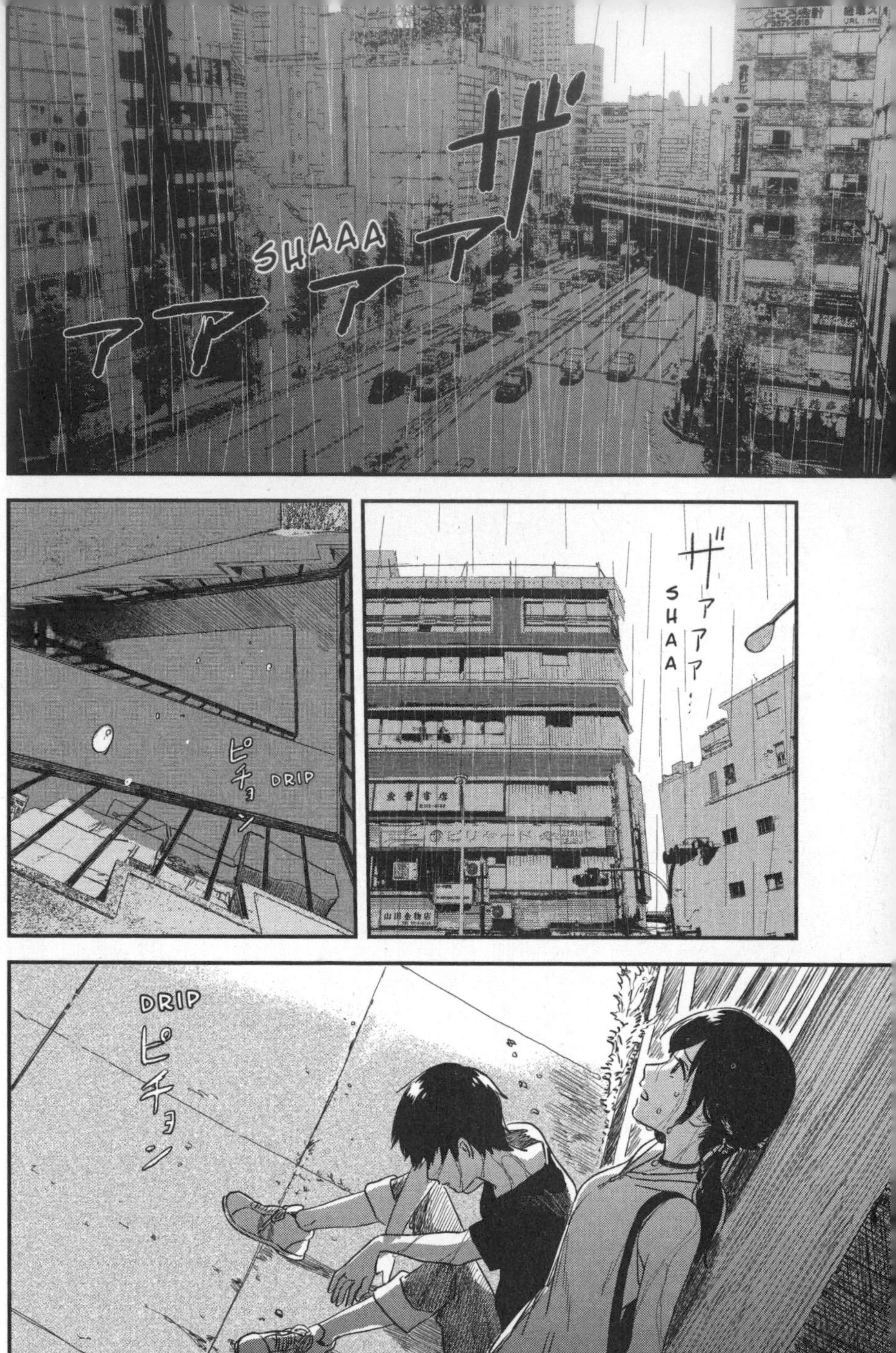
ザアアア
SHAAA
ザアアア…
SHAA
ピチョン
DRIP
DRIP
ピチョン

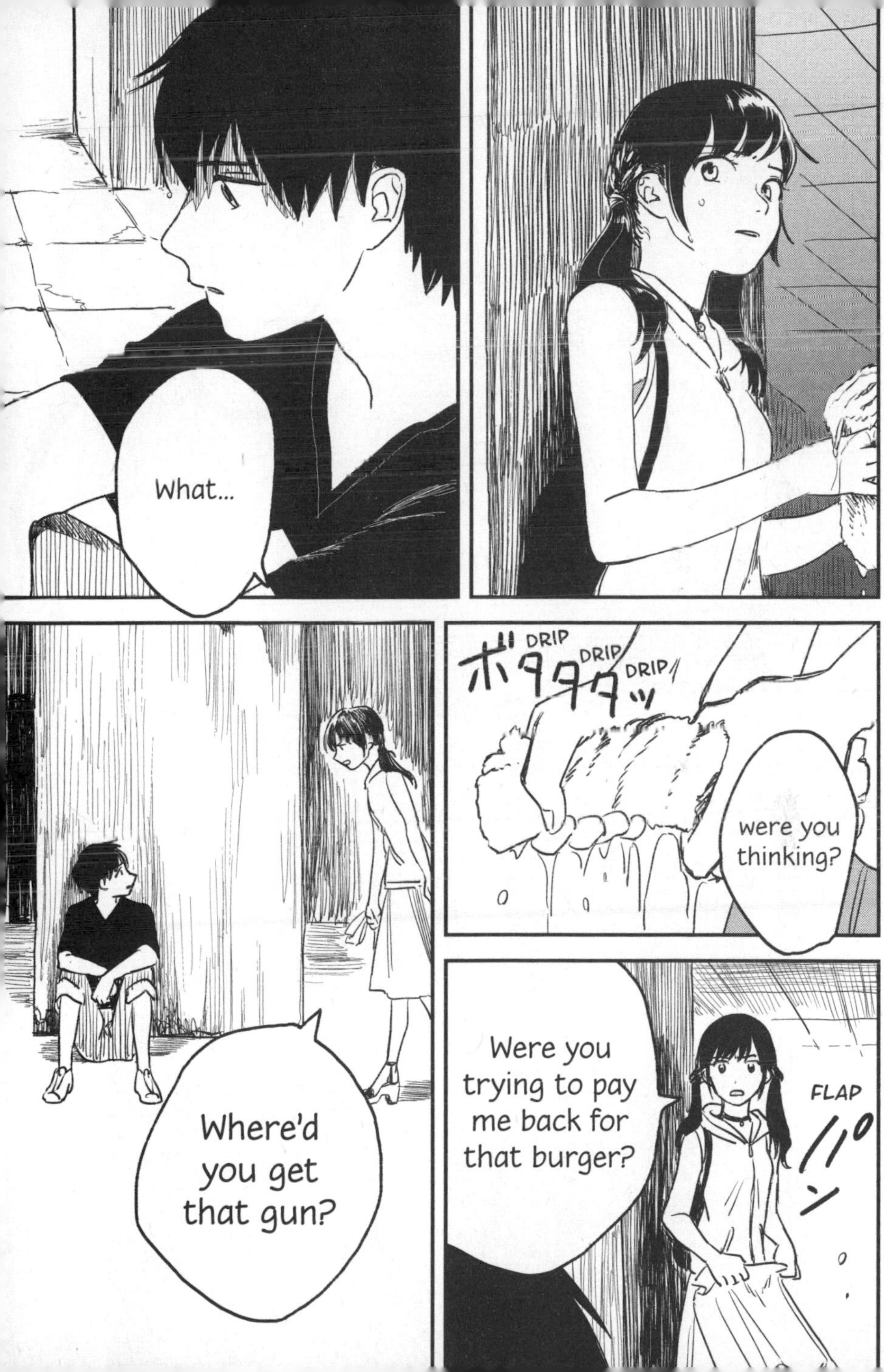
What...
ボタタタッ
DRIP DRIP DRIP
were you thinking?
Were you trying to pay me back for that burger?
パン
FLAP
Where'd you get that gun?

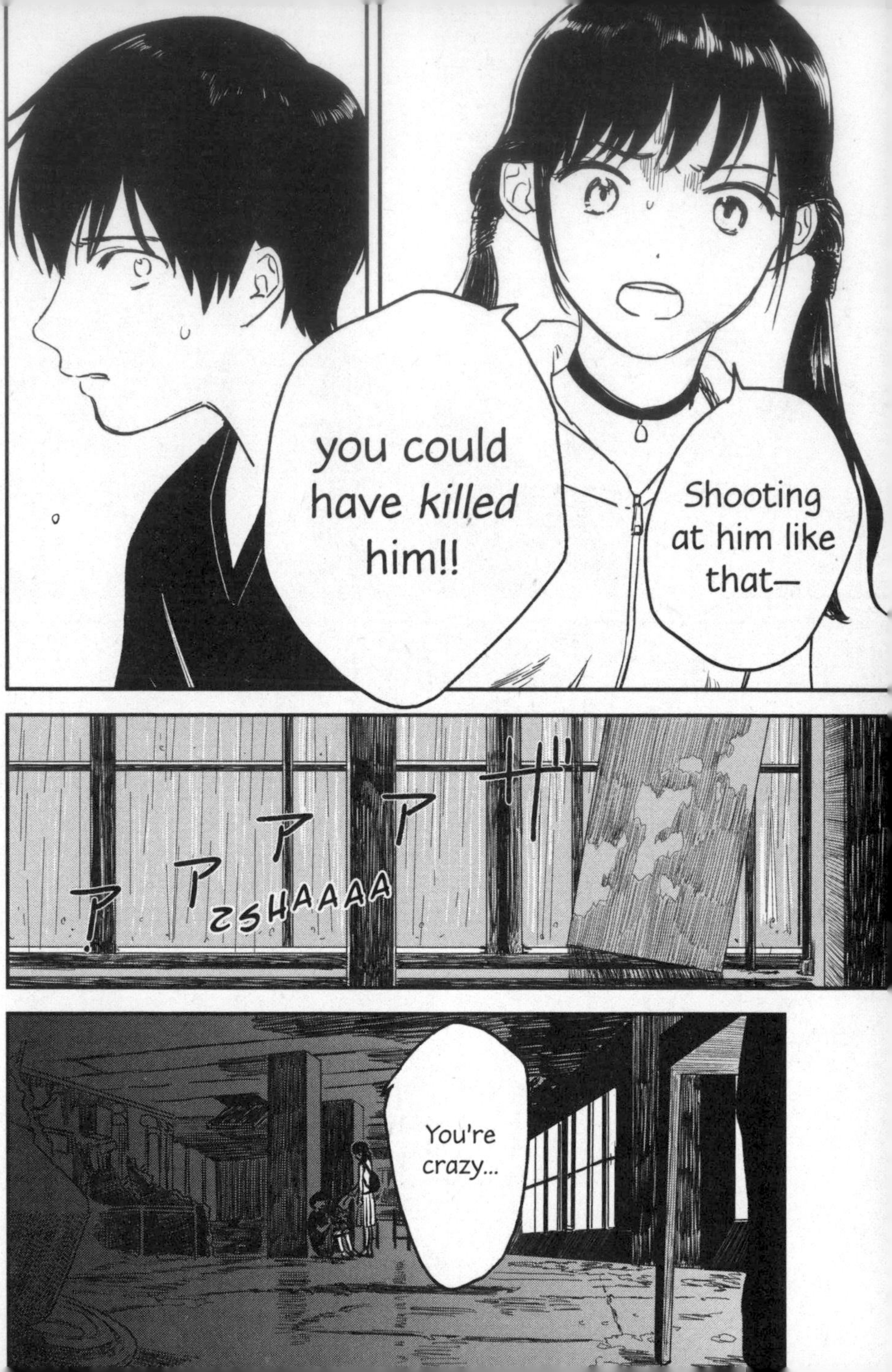
Shooting at him like that—
you could have *killed* him!!
ZSHAAAA
You're crazy...

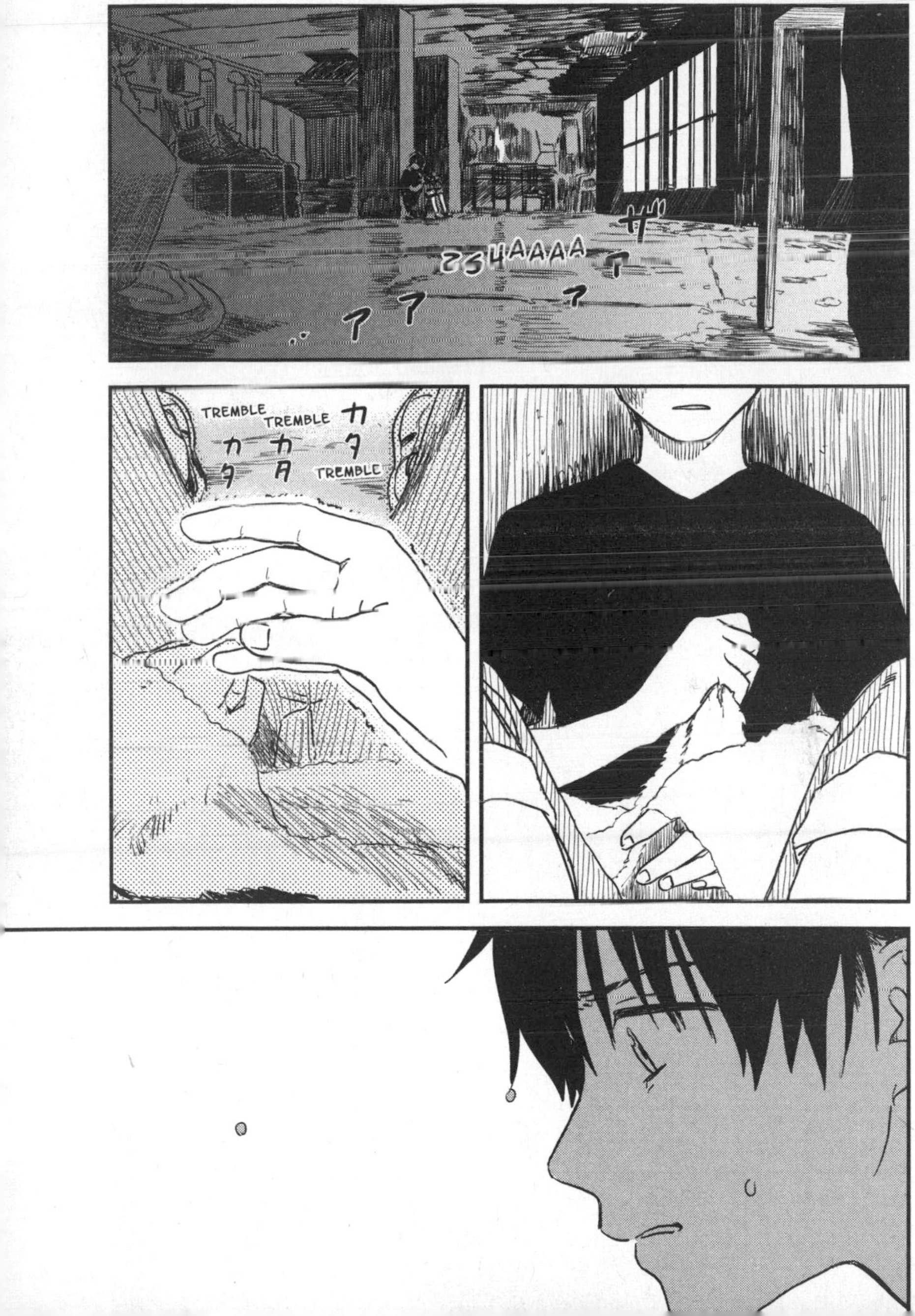

ZSHAAAA
TREMBLE
TREMBLE
TREMBLE

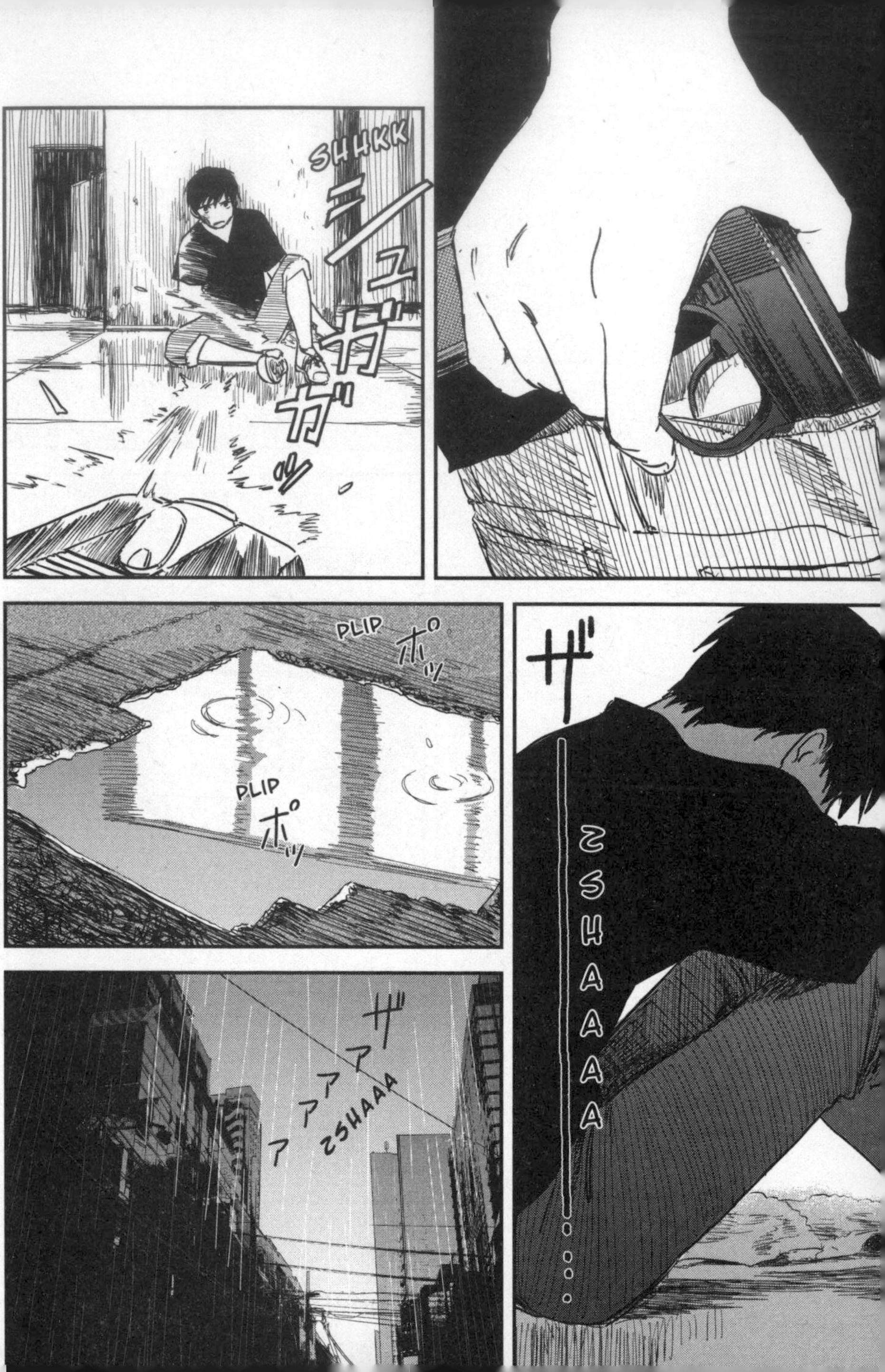
SHHKK
ニュ
ガガッ
ザ
ZSHAAAAA......
PLIP
ポッ
PLIP
ポッ
ザアアア
ZSHAAA

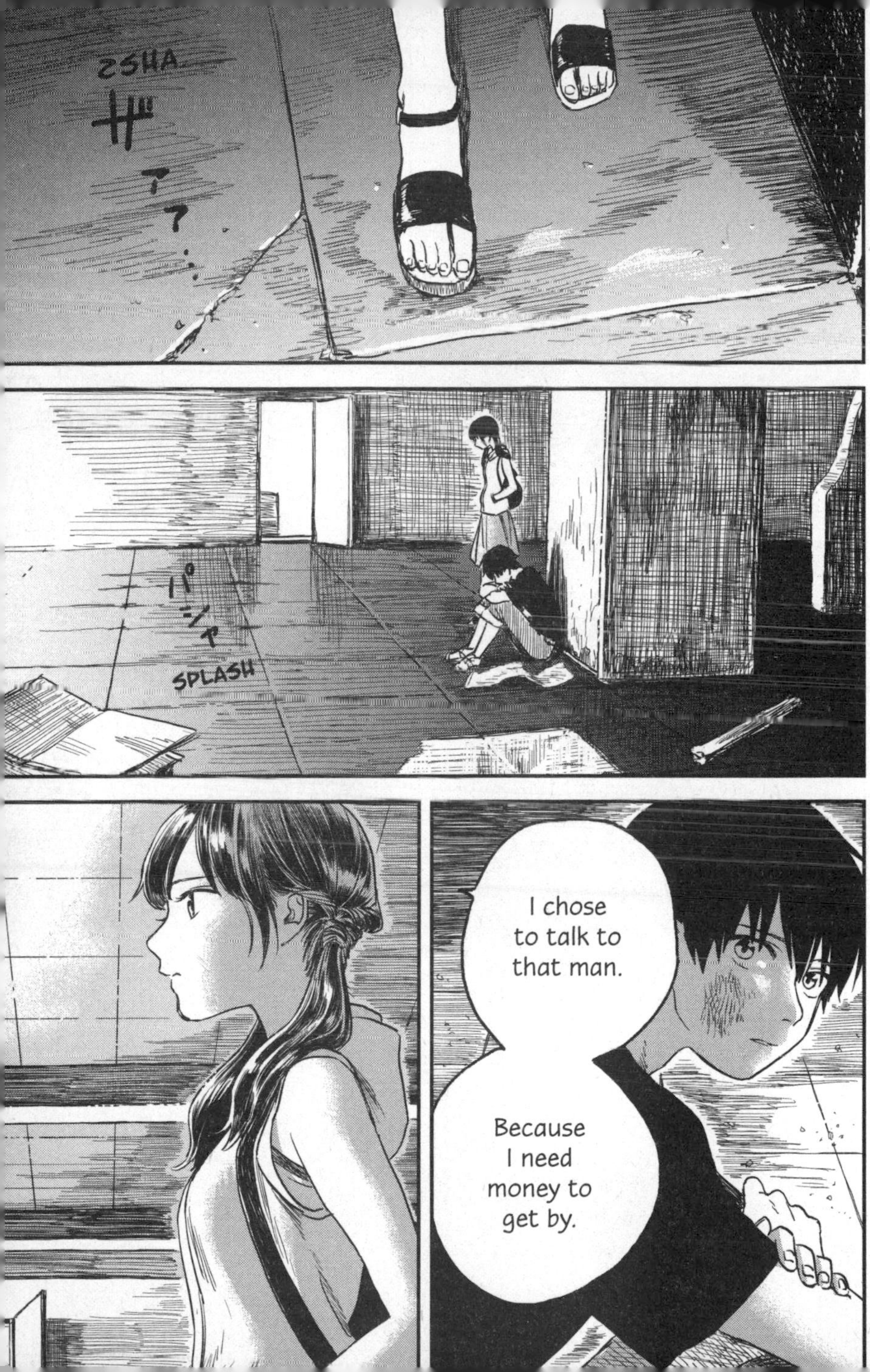
ZSHA
SPLASH
I chose to talk to that man.
Because I need money to get by.

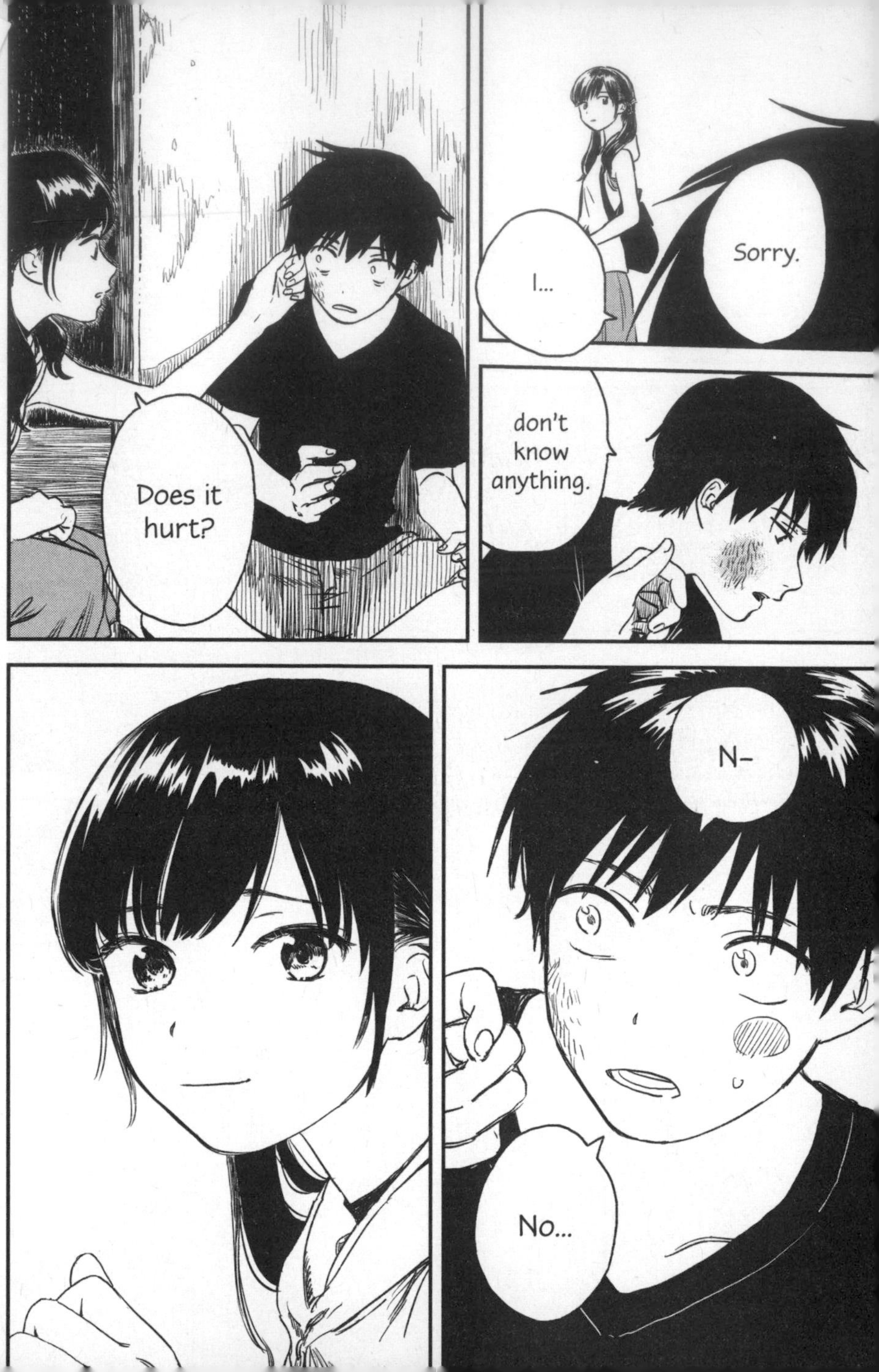
Sorry.
I...
don't know anything.
Does it hurt?
N-
No...

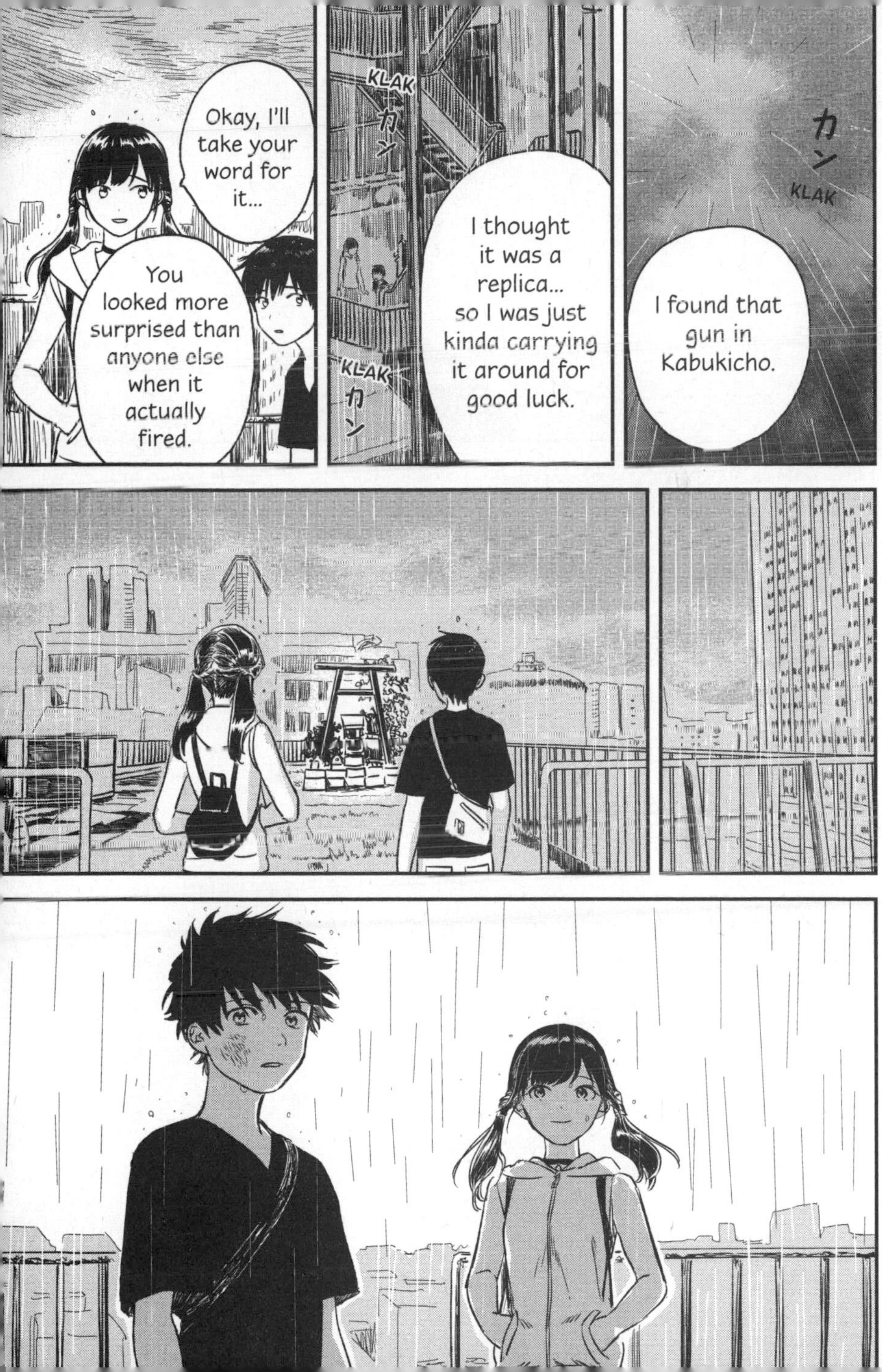
カン
KLAK
I found that gun in Kabukicho.
KLAK
カン
I thought it was a replica... so I was just kinda carrying it around for good luck.
KLAK
カン
Okay, I'll take your word for it...
You looked more surprised than anyone else when it actually fired.

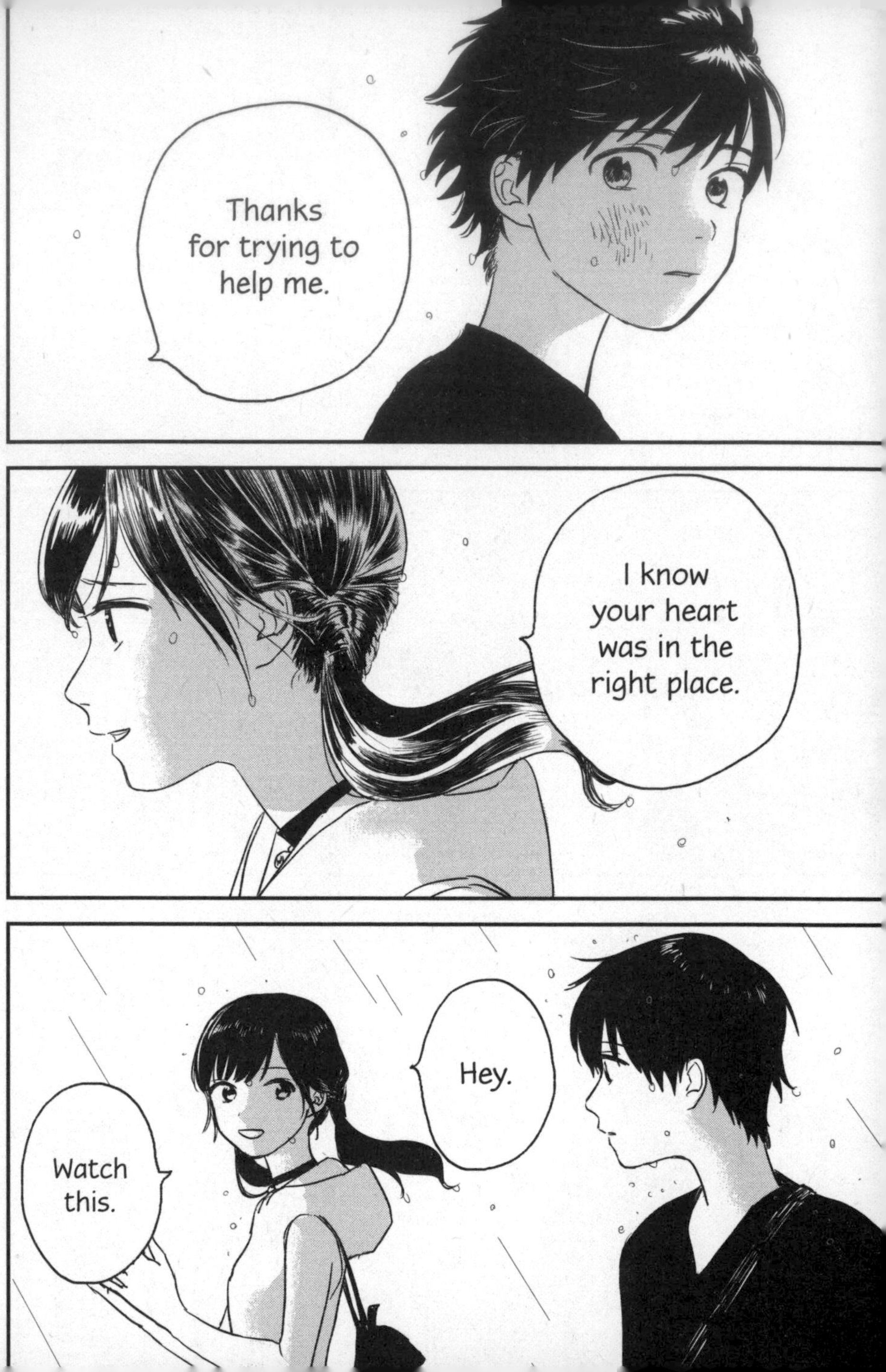
Thanks for trying to help me.
I know your heart was in the right place.
Hey.
Watch this.

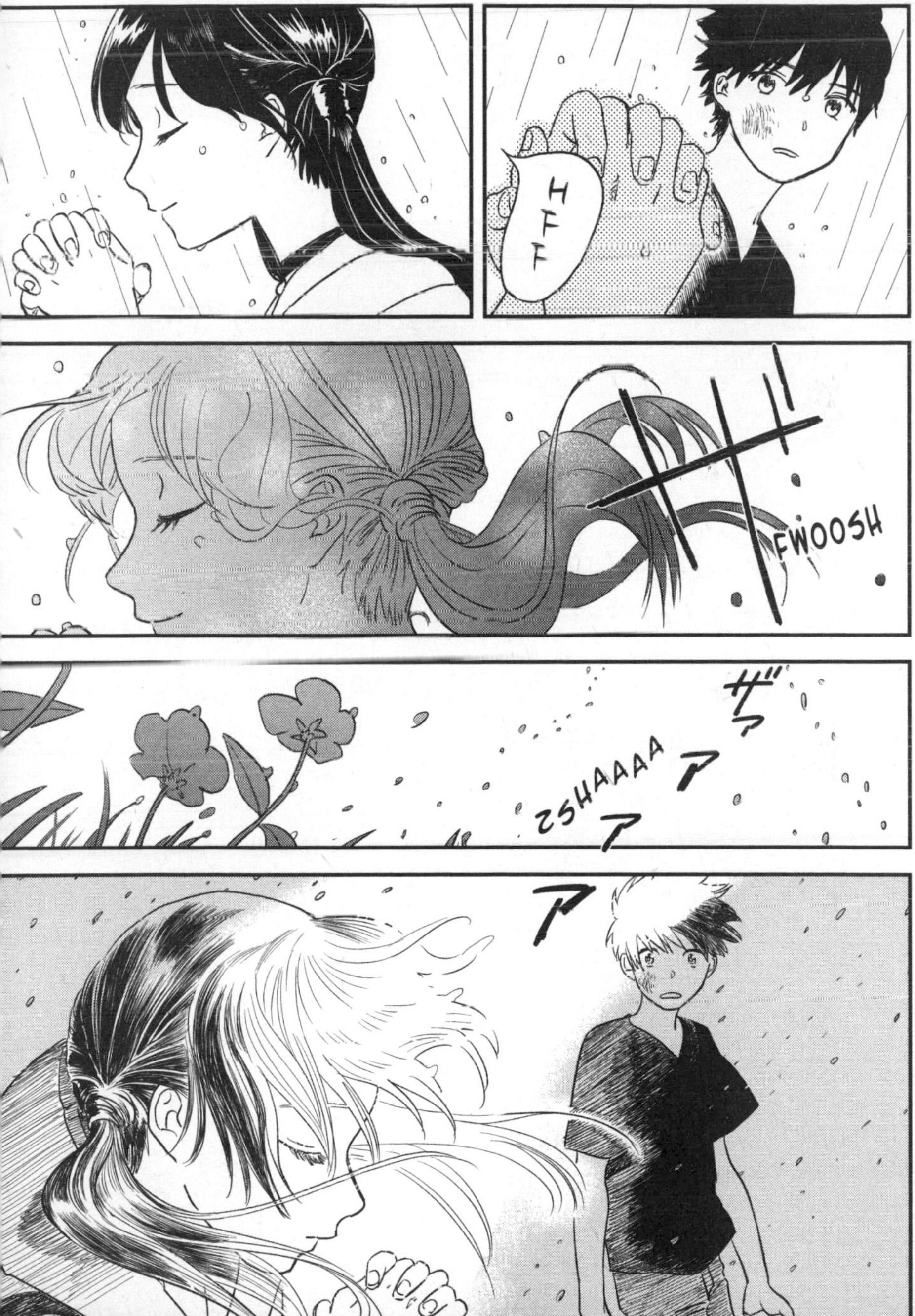
HFFF
FWOOSH
ザァアアア
ZSHAAAA

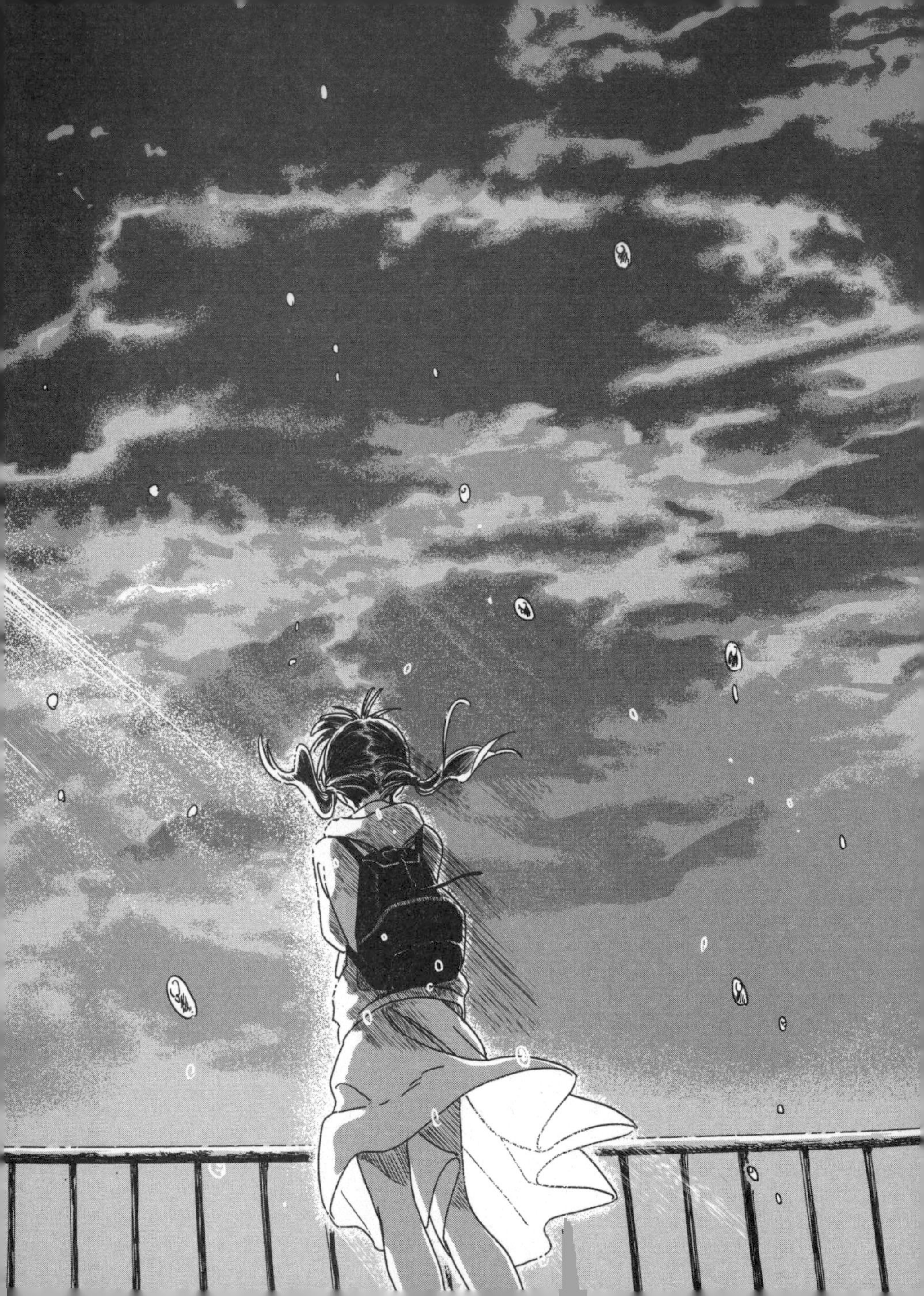

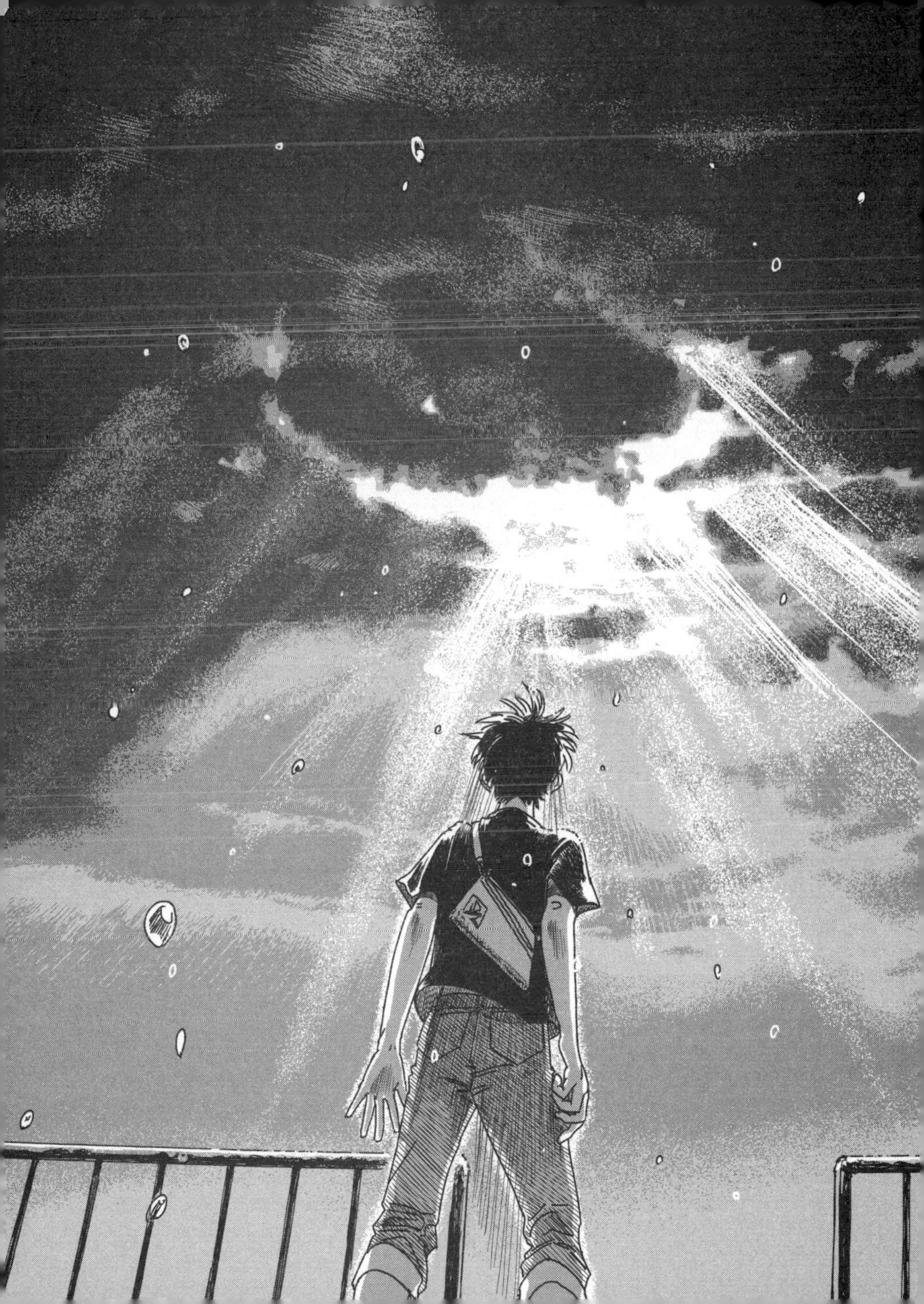

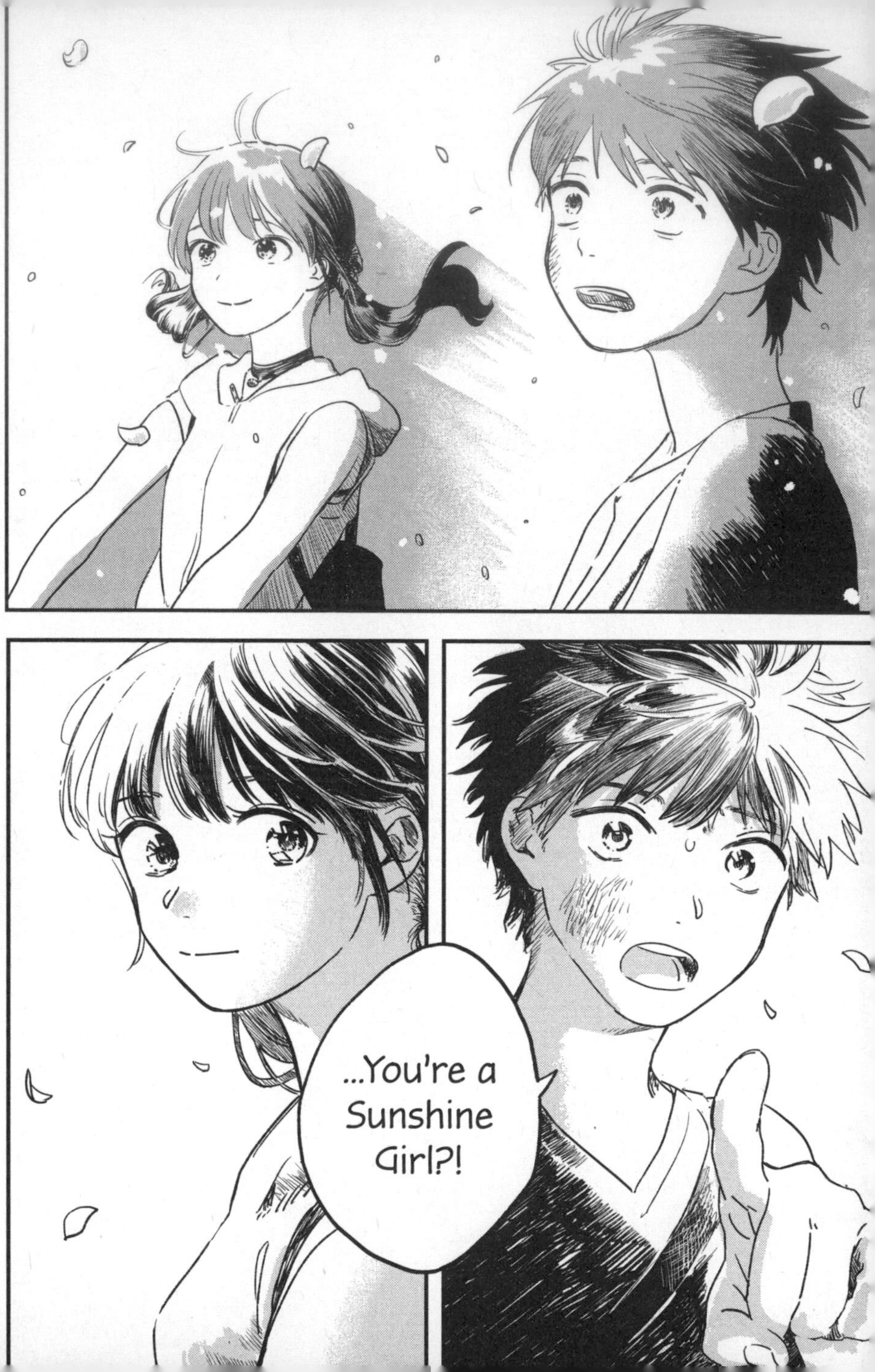
...You're a Sunshine Girl?!

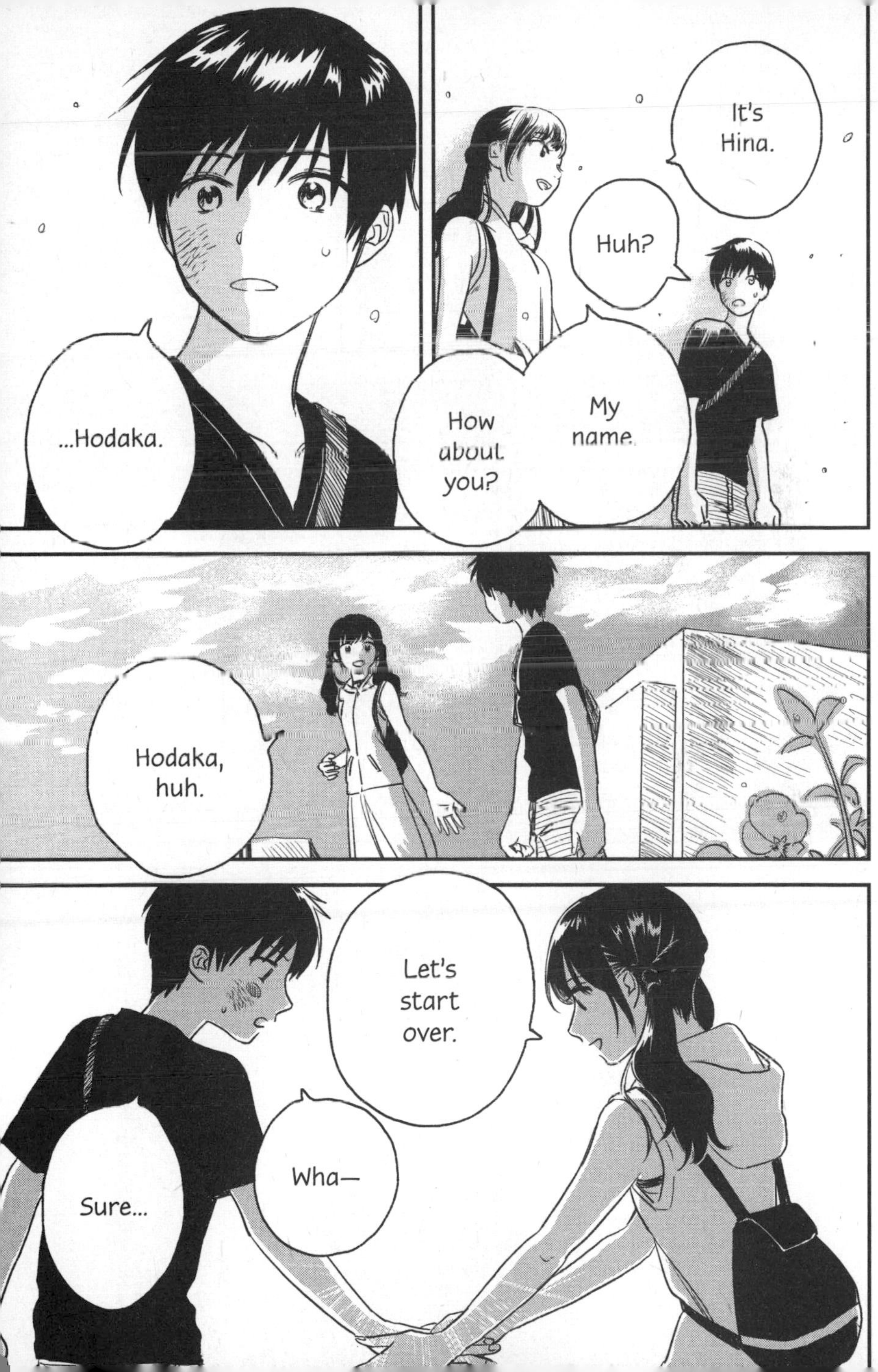
It's Hina.
Huh?
My name.
How about you?
...Hodaka.
Hodaka, huh.
Let's start over.
Wha—
Sure...

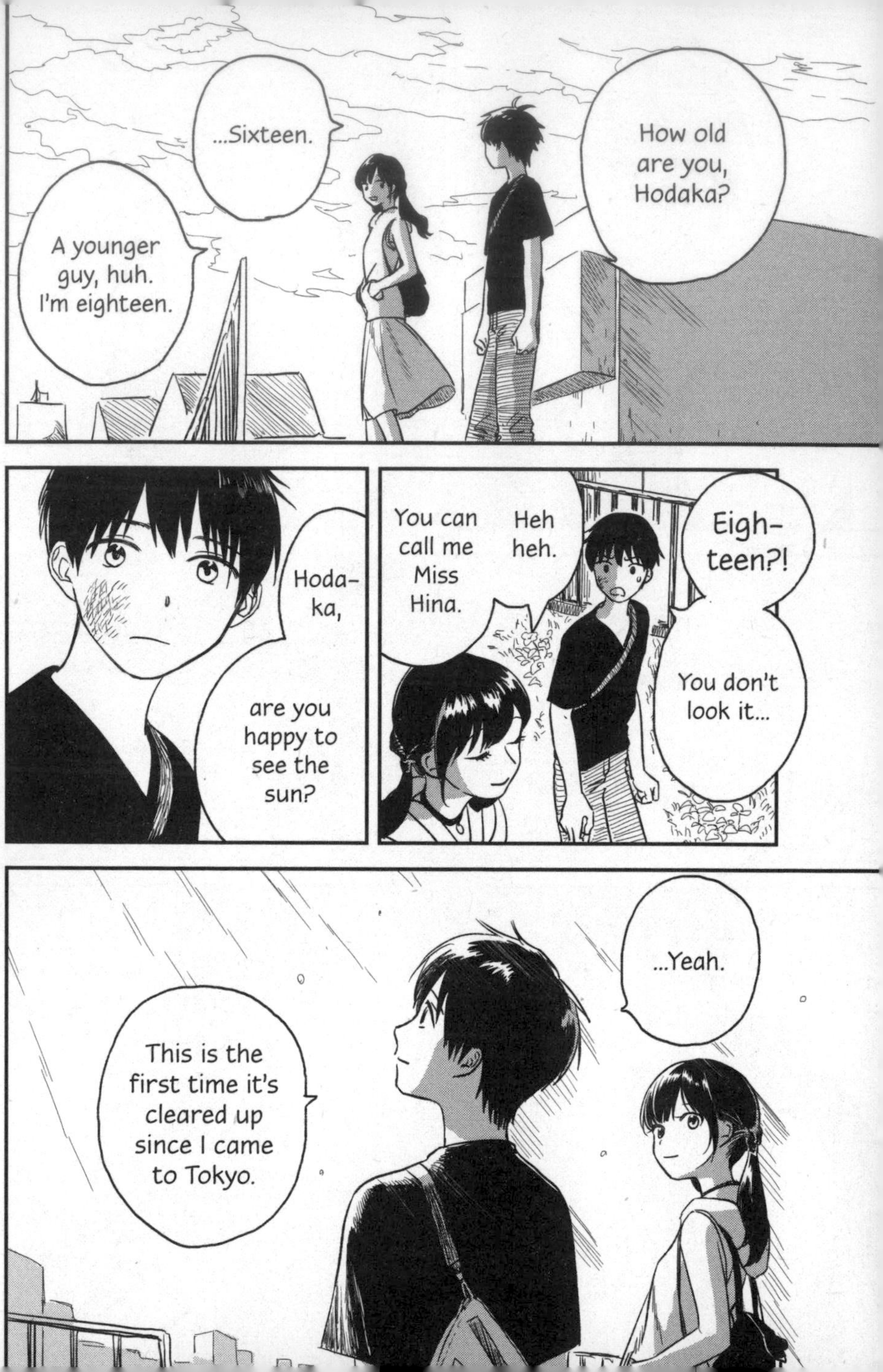
How old are you, Hodaka?
...Sixteen.
A younger guy, huh. I'm eighteen.
Eigh-teen?!
You don't look it...
Heh heh.
You can call me Miss Hina.
Hoda-ka,
are you happy to see the sun?
...Yeah.
This is the first time it's cleared up since I came to Tokyo.

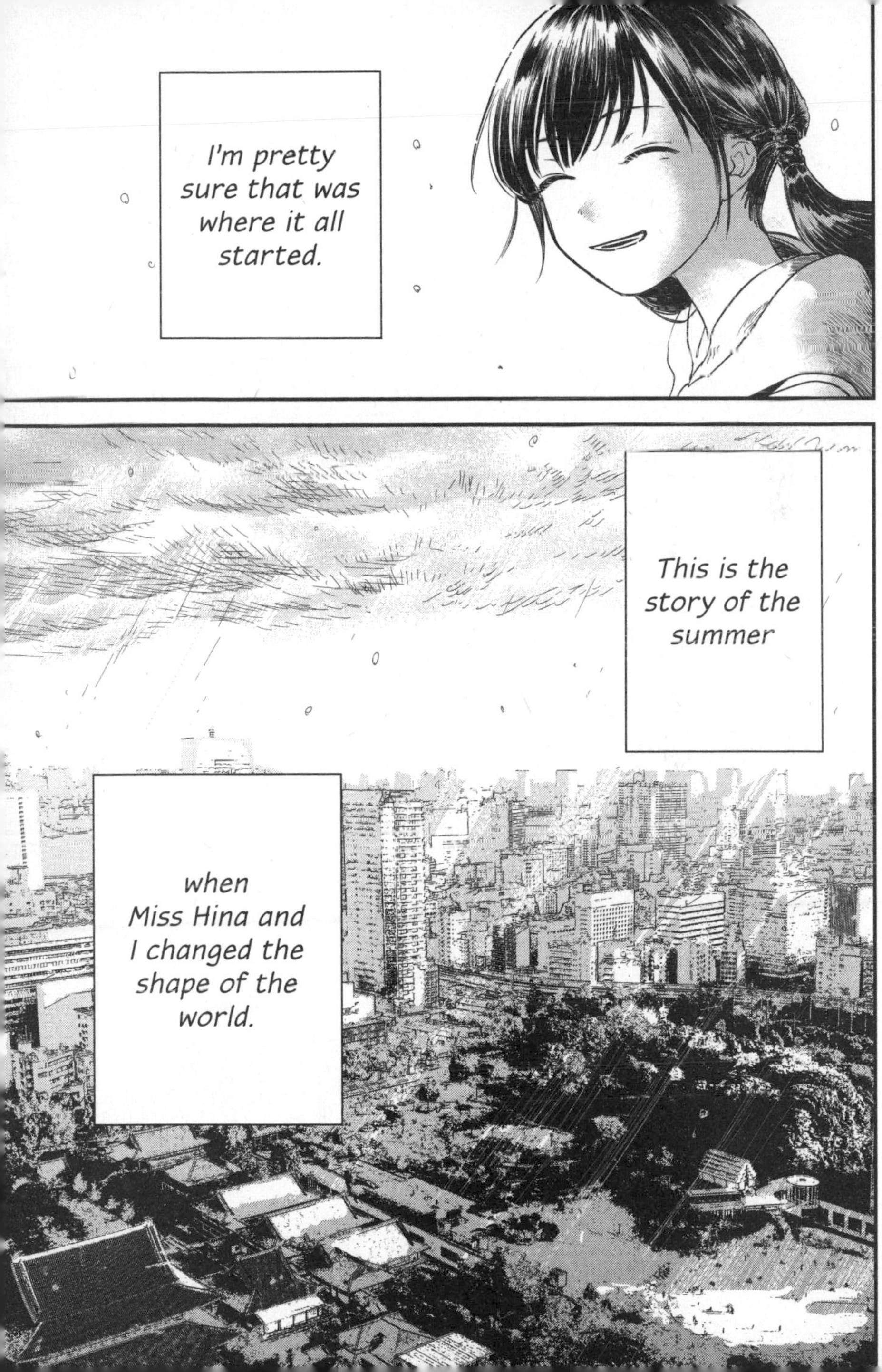
I'm pretty sure that was where it all started.
This is the story of the summer
when Miss Hina and I changed the shape of the world.

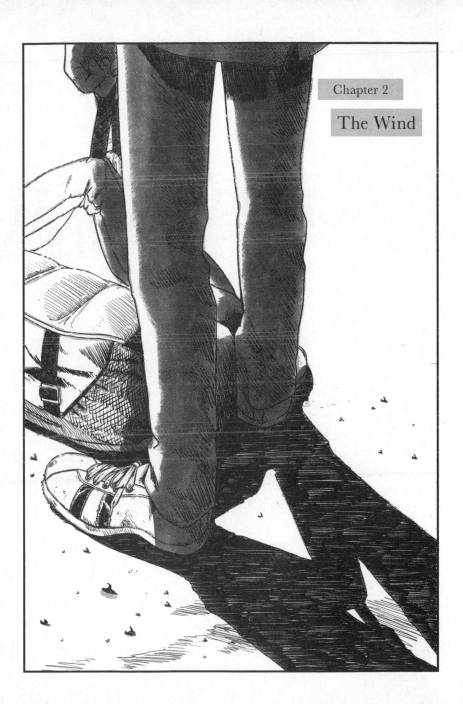

Chapter 2

The Wind

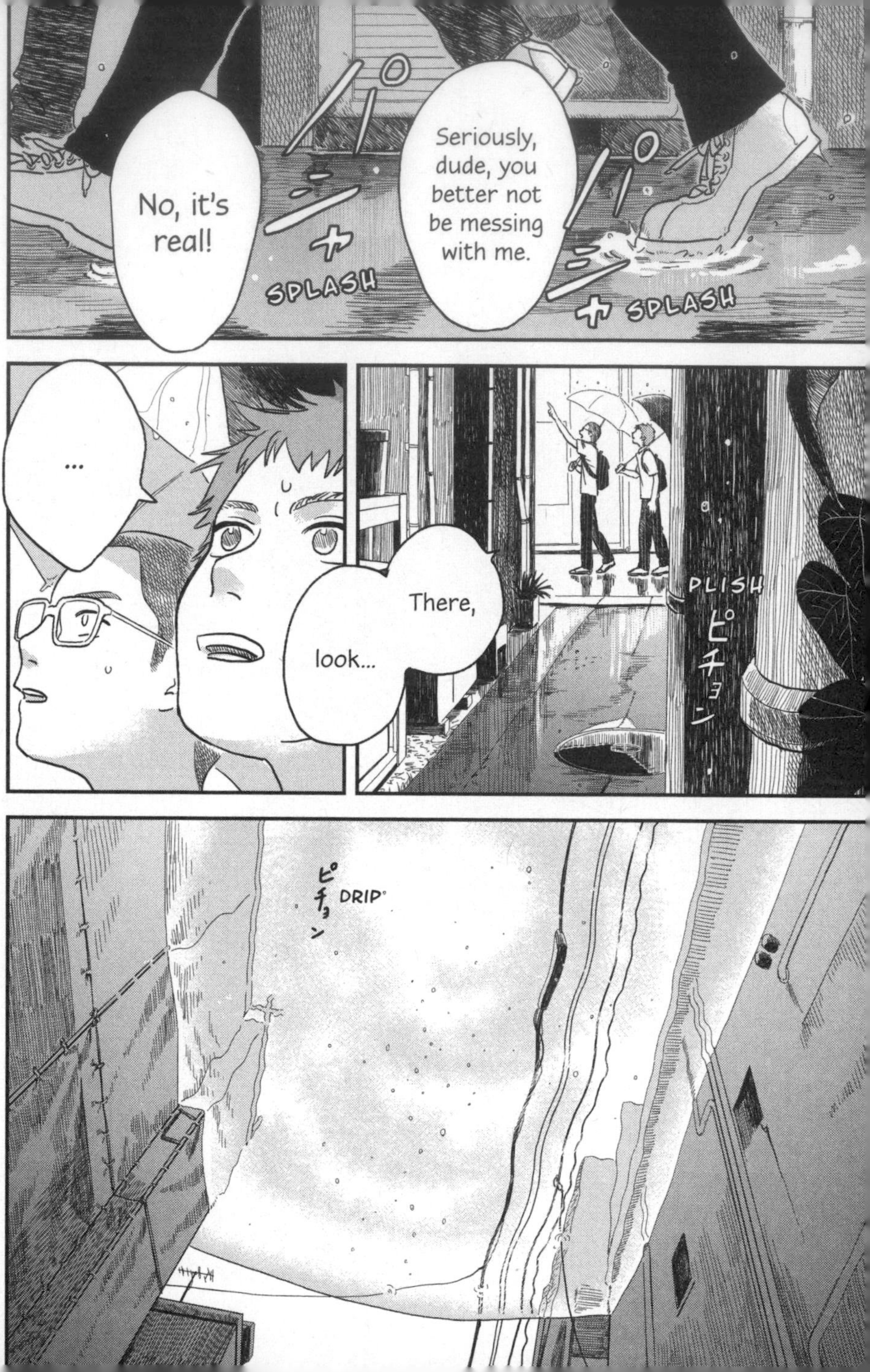
SPLASH
Seriously, dude, you better not be messing with me.
SPLASH
No, it's real!
PLISH
ピチョン
There, look...
...
ピチョン
DRIP

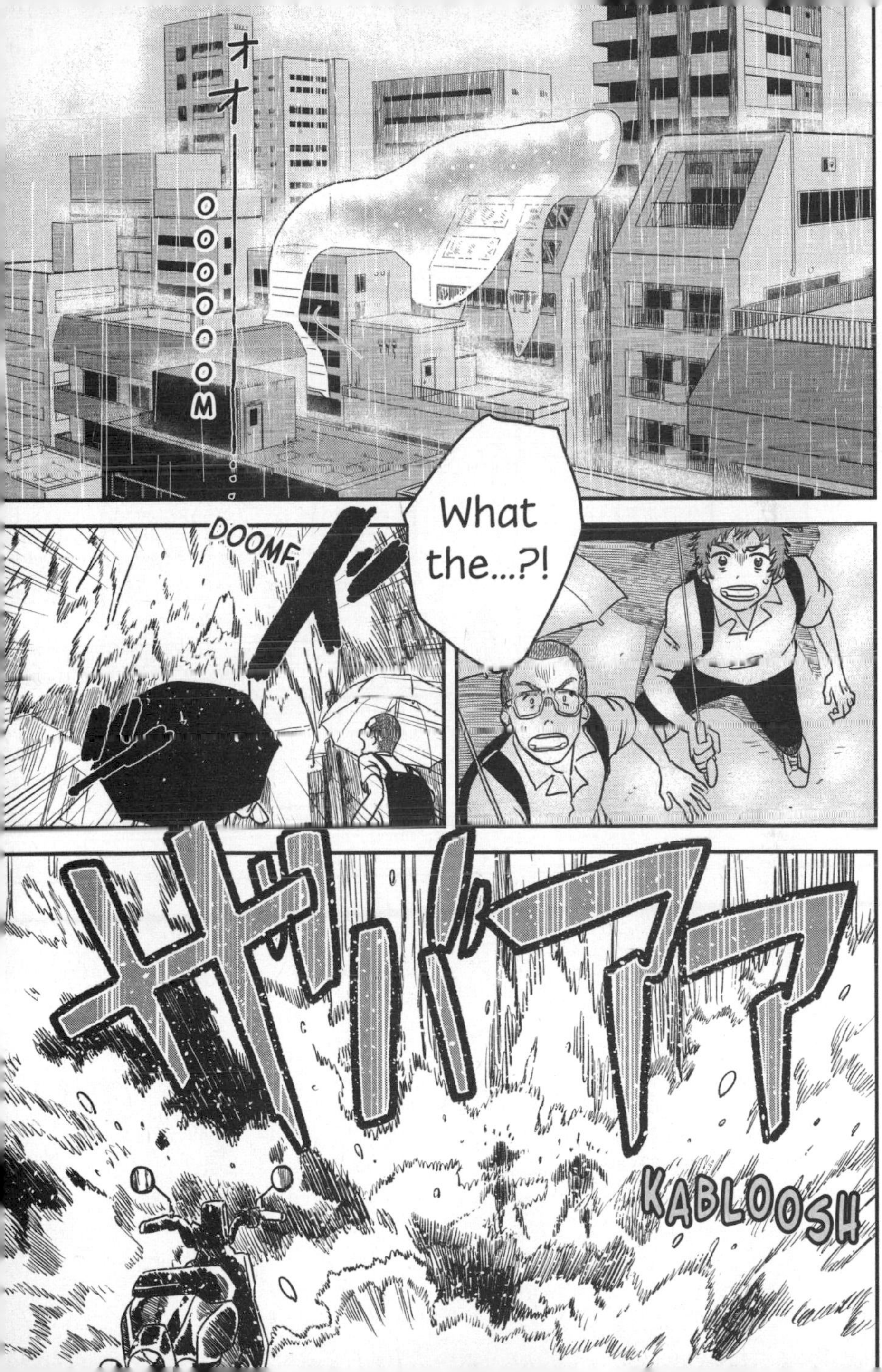
オオー
OOOOOOOM
What the...?!
DOOMF
ド
KABLOOSH

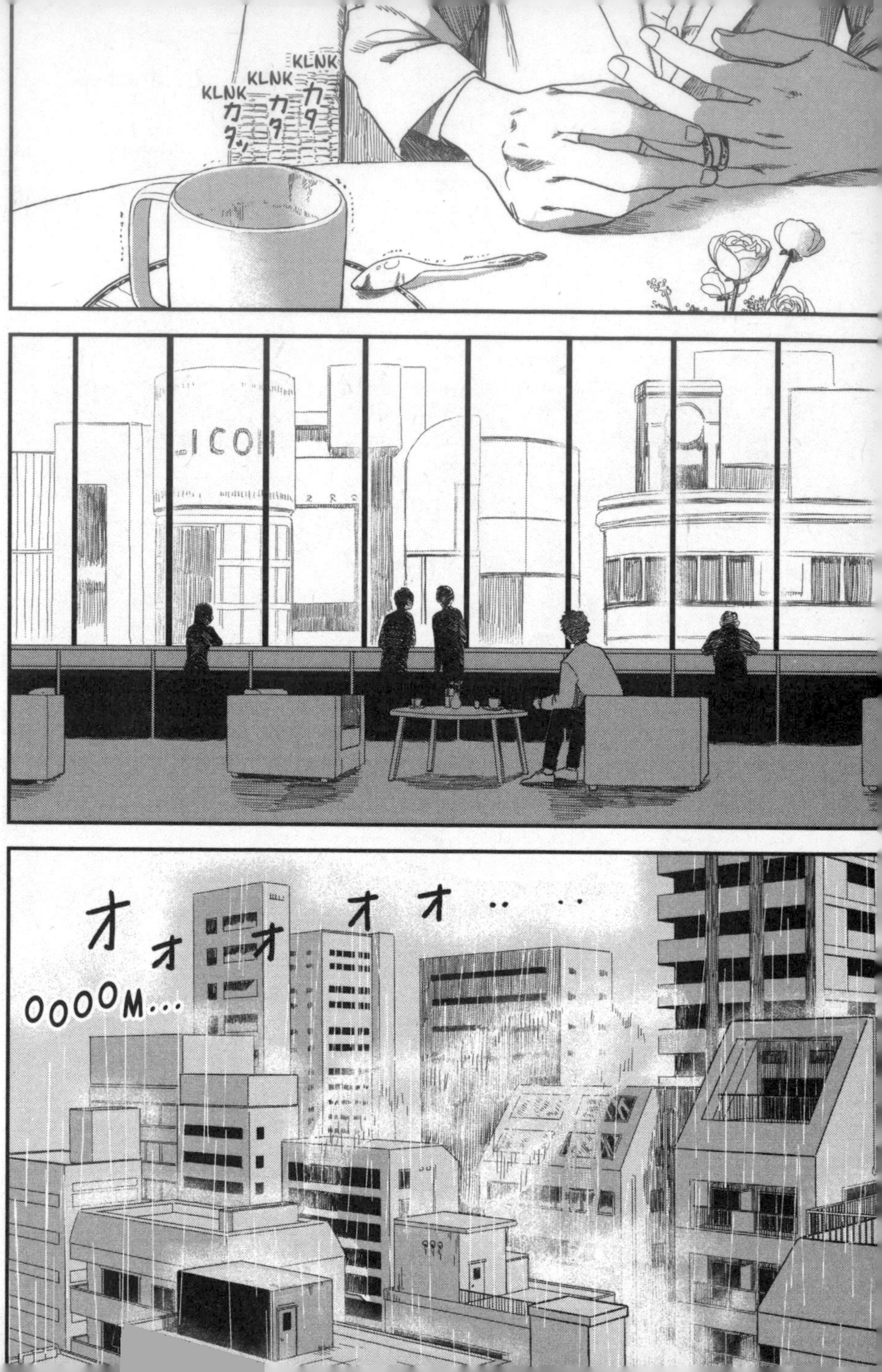
KLNK
カタ
KLNK
カタ
KLNK
カタッ
ICOH
オォォオオ‥‥
OOOOM...

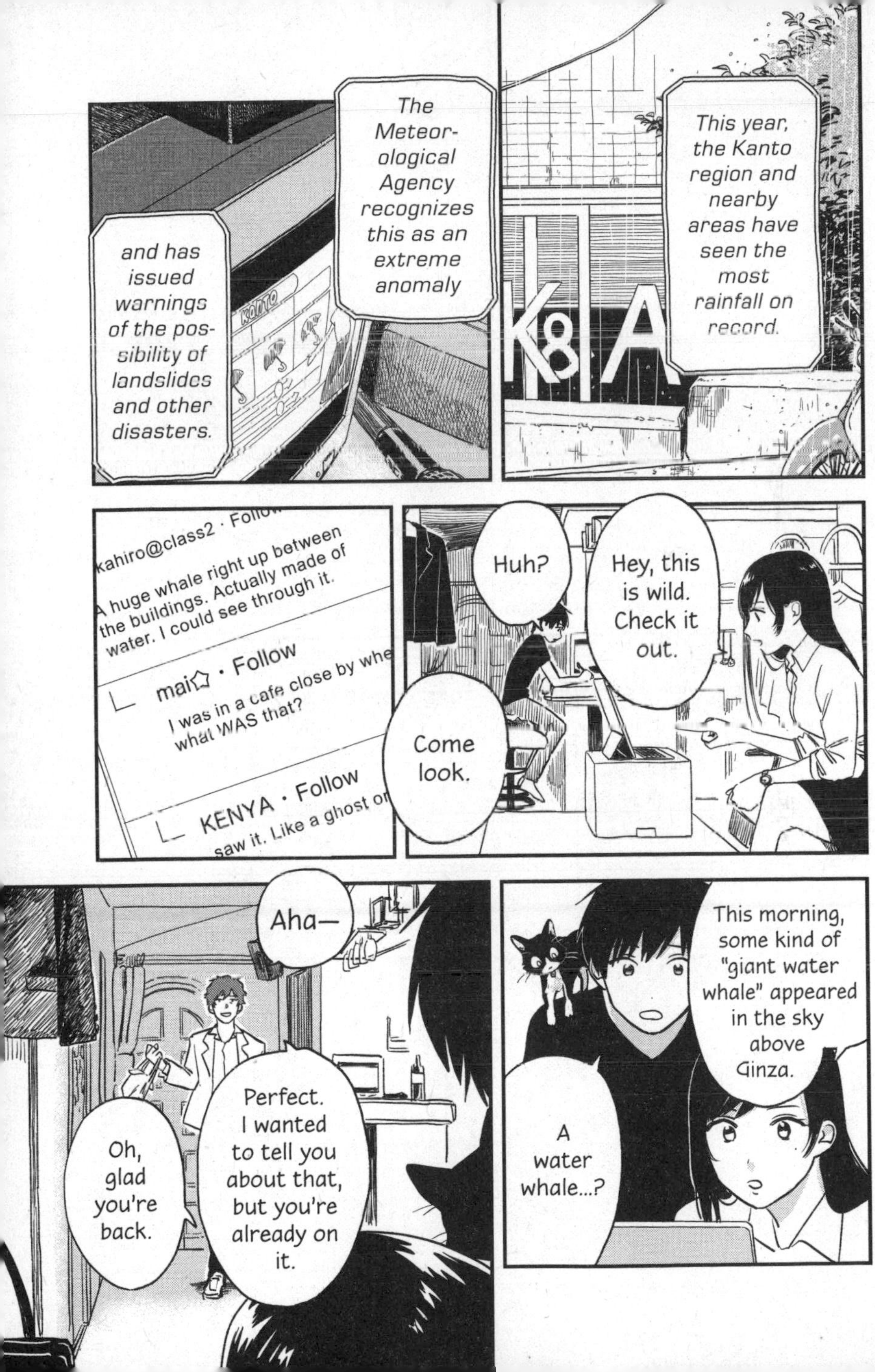
This year, the Kanto region and nearby areas have seen the most rainfall on record.
The Meteorological Agency recognizes this as an extreme anomaly
and has issued warnings of the possibility of landslides and other disasters.
Hey, this is wild. Check it out.
Huh?
Come look.
kahiro@class2 · Follo
A huge whale right up between the buildings. Actually made of water. I could see through it.
mai✩ · Follow
I was in a cafe close by whe
what WAS that?
KENYA · Follow
saw it. Like a ghost or
This morning, some kind of "giant water whale" appeared in the sky above Ginza.
A water whale...?
Aha—
Perfect. I wanted to tell you about that, but you're already on it.
Oh, glad you're back.

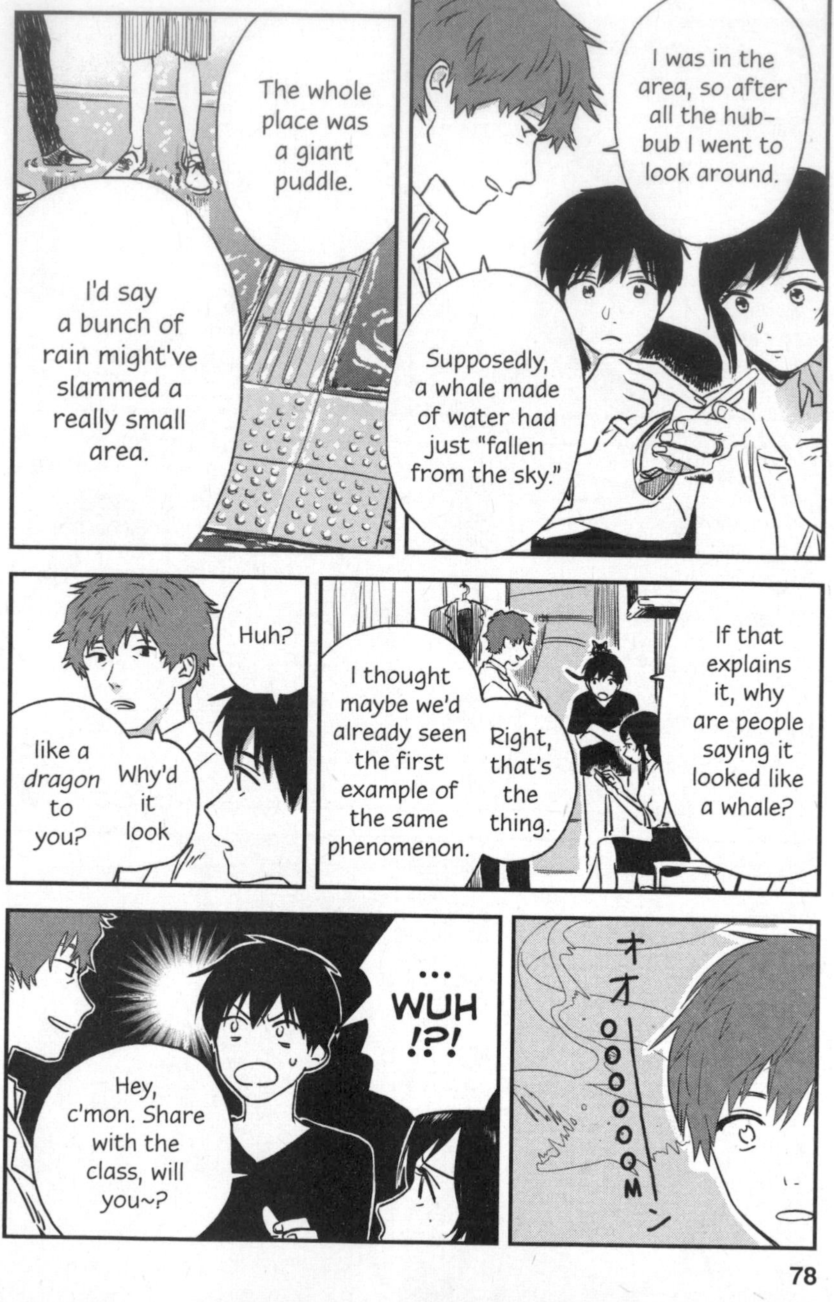
I was in the area, so after all the hub-bub I went to look around.
Supposedly, a whale made of water had just "fallen from the sky."
The whole place was a giant puddle.
I'd say a bunch of rain might've slammed a really small area.
If that explains it, why are people saying it looked like a whale?
Right, that's the thing.
I thought maybe we'd already seen the first example of the same phenomenon.
Huh?
Why'd it look
like a dragon to you?
オオ
OOOOOOM
ン
... WUH !?!
Hey, c'mon. Share with the class, will you~?

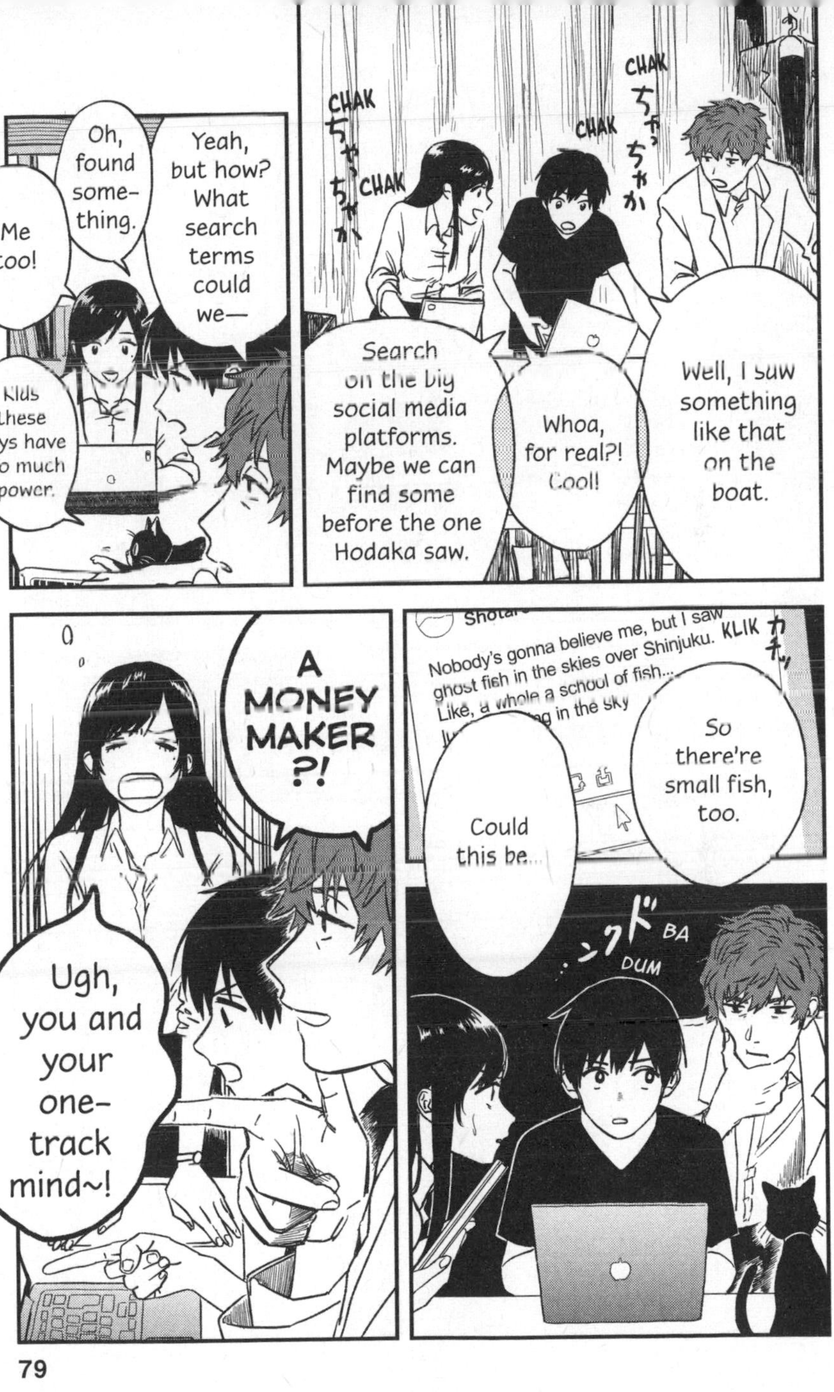
CHAK
CHAK
CHAK
CHAK
Well, I saw something like that on the boat.
Whoa, for real?! Cool!
Search on the big social media platforms. Maybe we can find some before the one Hodaka saw.
Yeah, but how? What search terms could we—
Oh, found something.
Me too!
Kids these days have too much power.
Nobody's gonna believe me, but I saw ghost fish in the skies over Shinjuku.
Like, a whole a school of fish...
KLIK
So there're small fish, too.
Could this be...
BA DUM
A MONEY MAKER?!
Ugh, you and your one-track mind~!

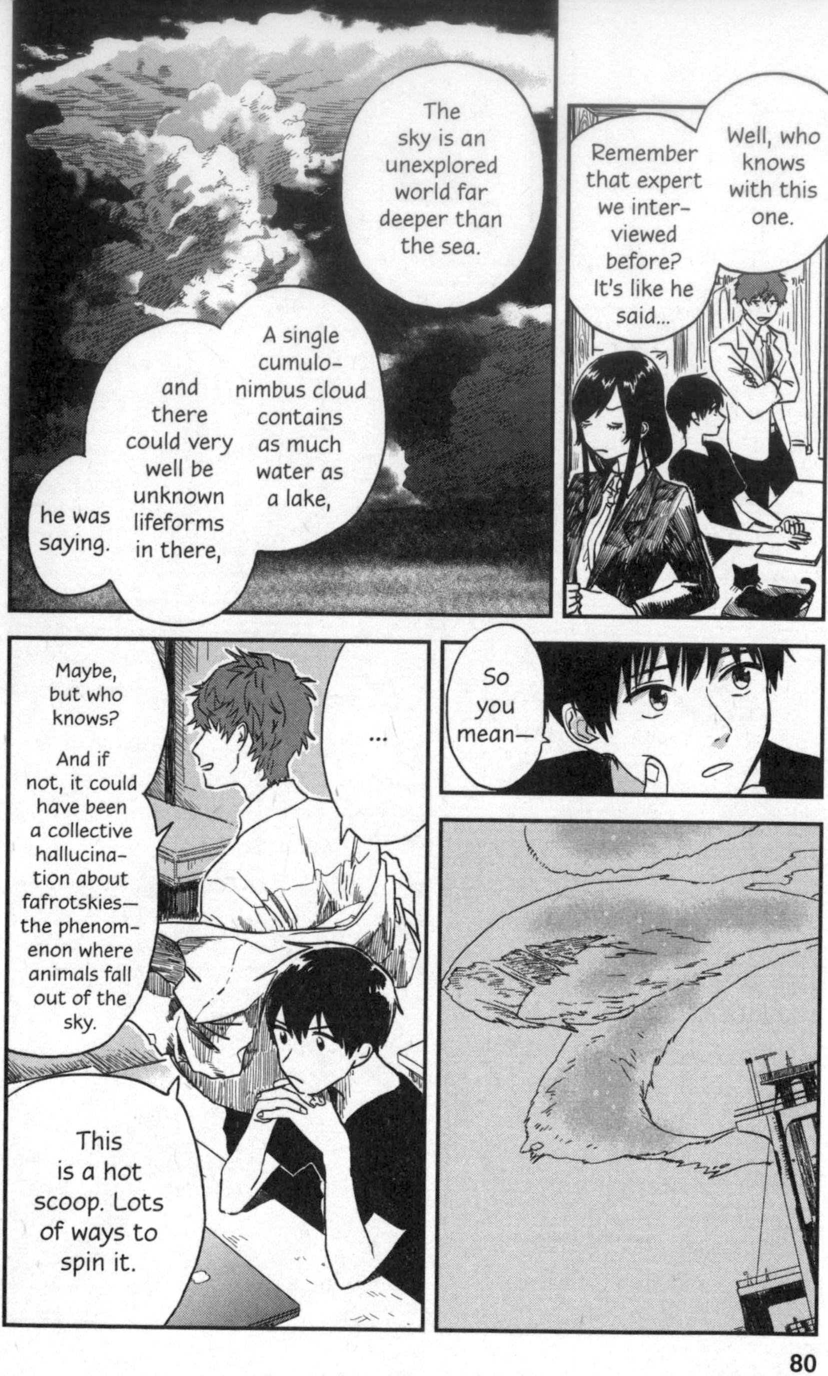

Well, who knows with this one.
Remember that expert we interviewed before? It's like he said...
The sky is an unexplored world far deeper than the sea.
A single cumulonimbus cloud contains as much water as a lake,
and there could very well be unknown lifeforms in there,
he was saying.
So you mean—
...
Maybe, but who knows?
And if not, it could have been a collective hallucination about fafrotskies—the phenomenon where animals fall out of the sky.
This is a hot scoop. Lots of ways to spin it.

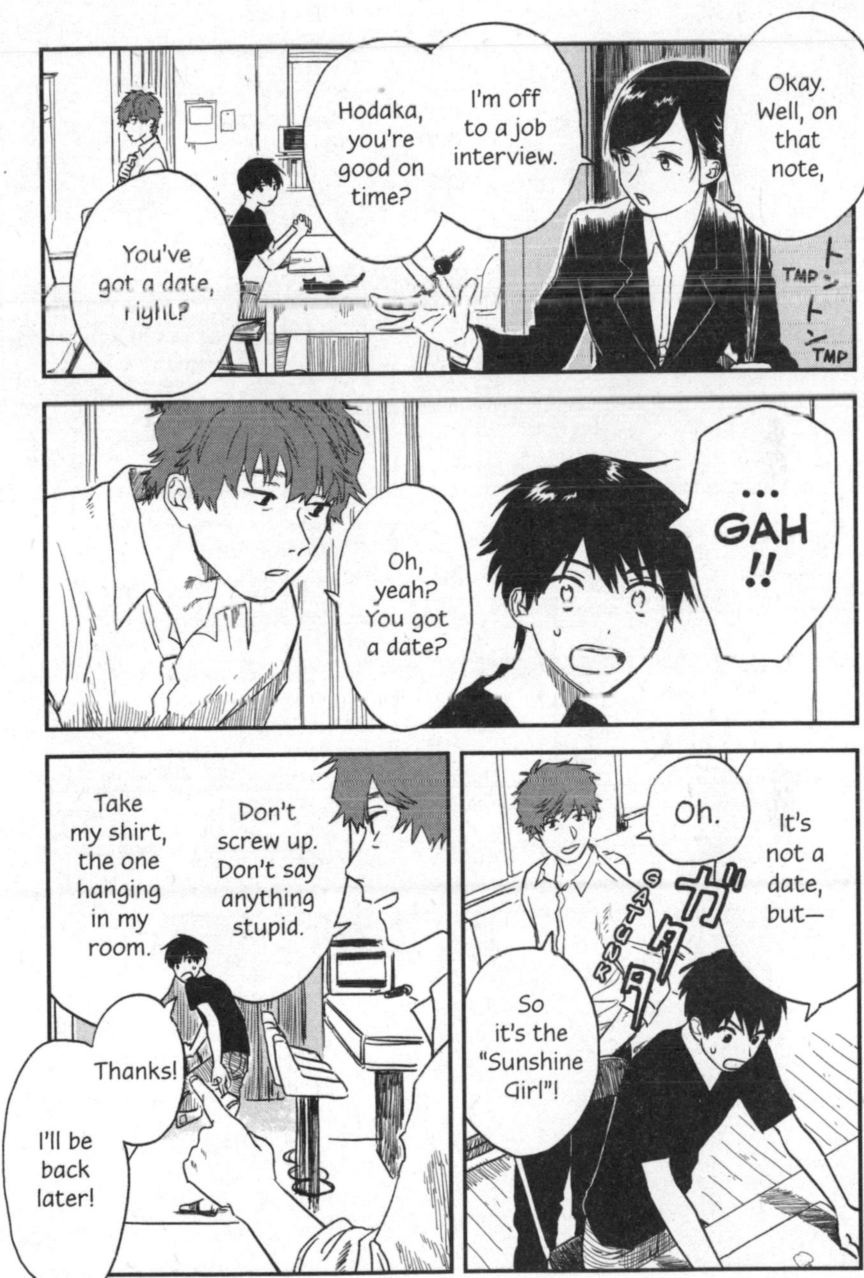
Okay. Well, on that note,
I'm off to a job interview.
Hodaka, you're good on time?
You've got a date, right?
TMP トン
TMP トン
... GAH !!
Oh, yeah? You got a date?
It's not a date, but—
Oh.
GATUNK ガタタ
So it's the "Sunshine Girl"!
Don't screw up. Don't say anything stupid.
Take my shirt, the one hanging in my room.
Thanks!
I'll be back later!

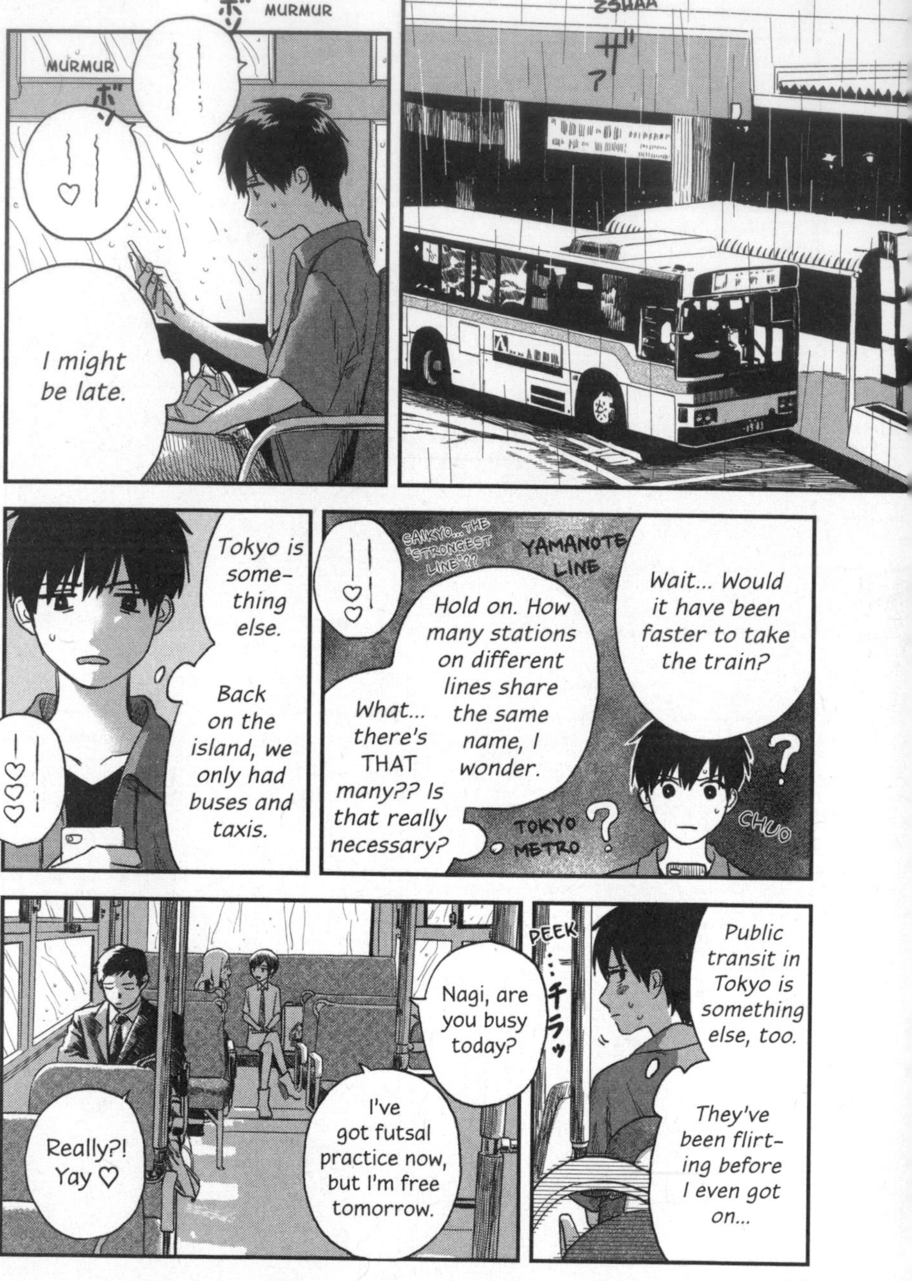
ZSHAA
ザァ
MURMUR
ボソ
MURMUR
ボソ
I might be late.
Wait... Would it have been faster to take the train?
SAIKYO... THE "STRONGEST LINE"??
YAMANOTE LINE
CHUO
TOKYO METRO
Hold on. How many stations on different lines share the same name, I wonder.
What... there's THAT many?? Is that really necessary?
Tokyo is something else.
Back on the island, we only had buses and taxis.
PEEK
チラッ
Public transit in Tokyo is something else, too.
They've been flirting before I even got on...
Nagi, are you busy today?
I've got futsal practice now, but I'm free tomorrow.
Really?! Yay ♡

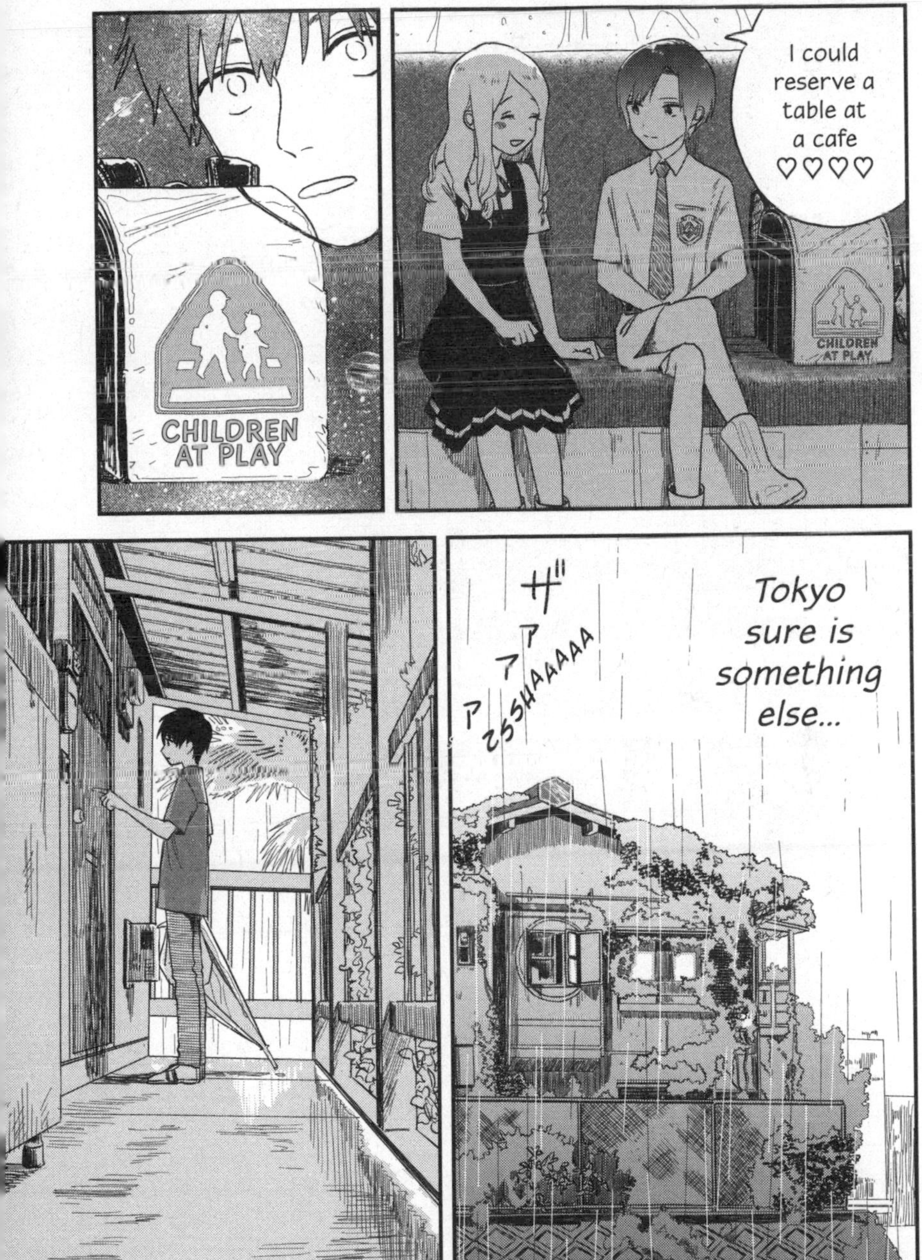
I could reserve a table at a cafe ♡♡♡♡
CHILDREN AT PLAY
CHILDREN AT PLAY
ザ
アアア
ZSSHAAAAA
Tokyo sure is something else...

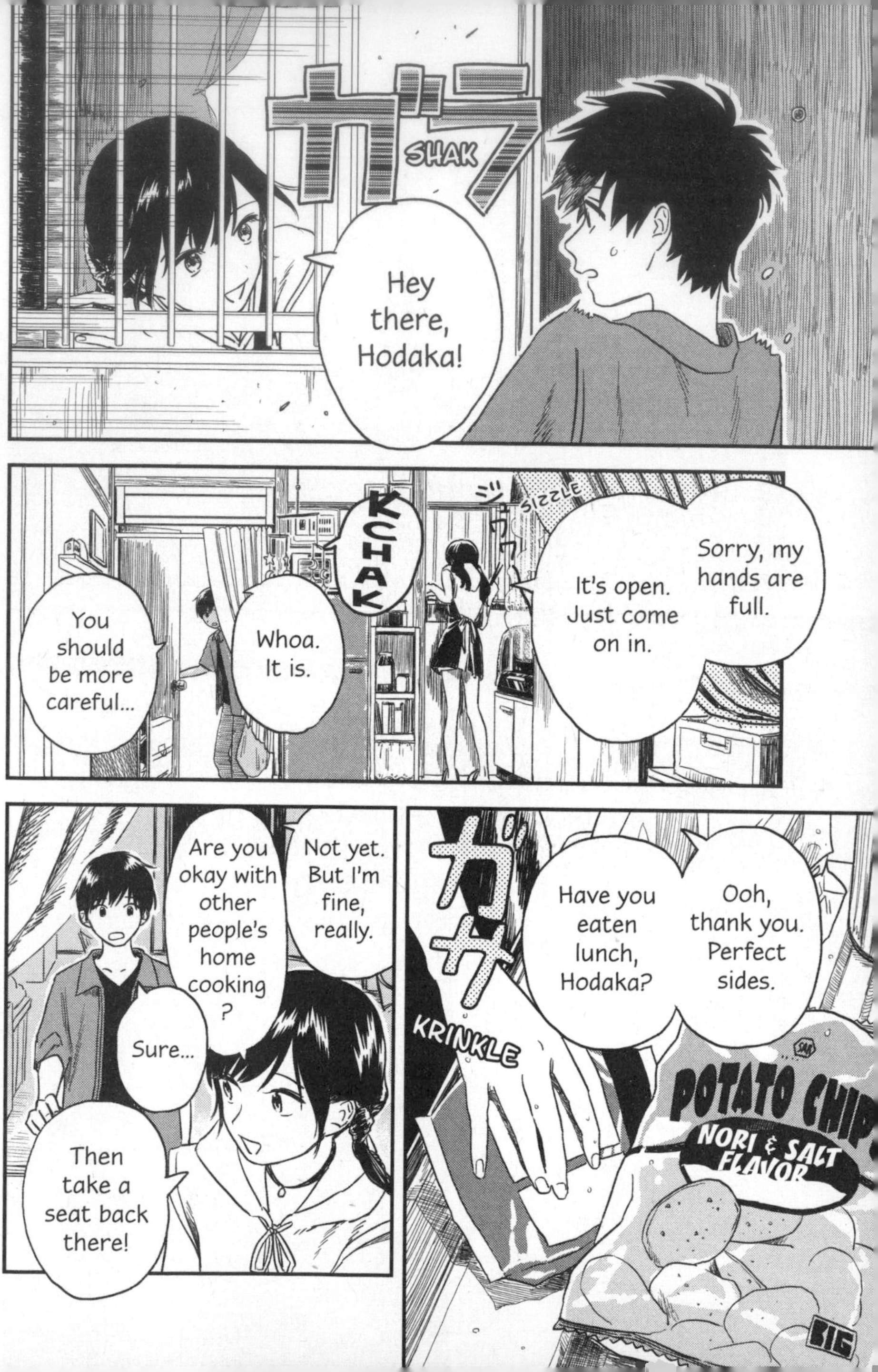
ガラ
SHAK
Hey there, Hodaka!
SIZZLE
Sorry, my hands are full.
It's open. Just come on in.
KCHAK
Whoa. It is.
You should be more careful...
ガサ
KRINKLE
Ooh, thank you. Perfect sides.
Have you eaten lunch, Hodaka?
POTATO CHIP
NORI & SALT FLAVOR
BIG
Not yet. But I'm fine, really.
Are you okay with other people's home cooking?
Sure...
Then take a seat back there!

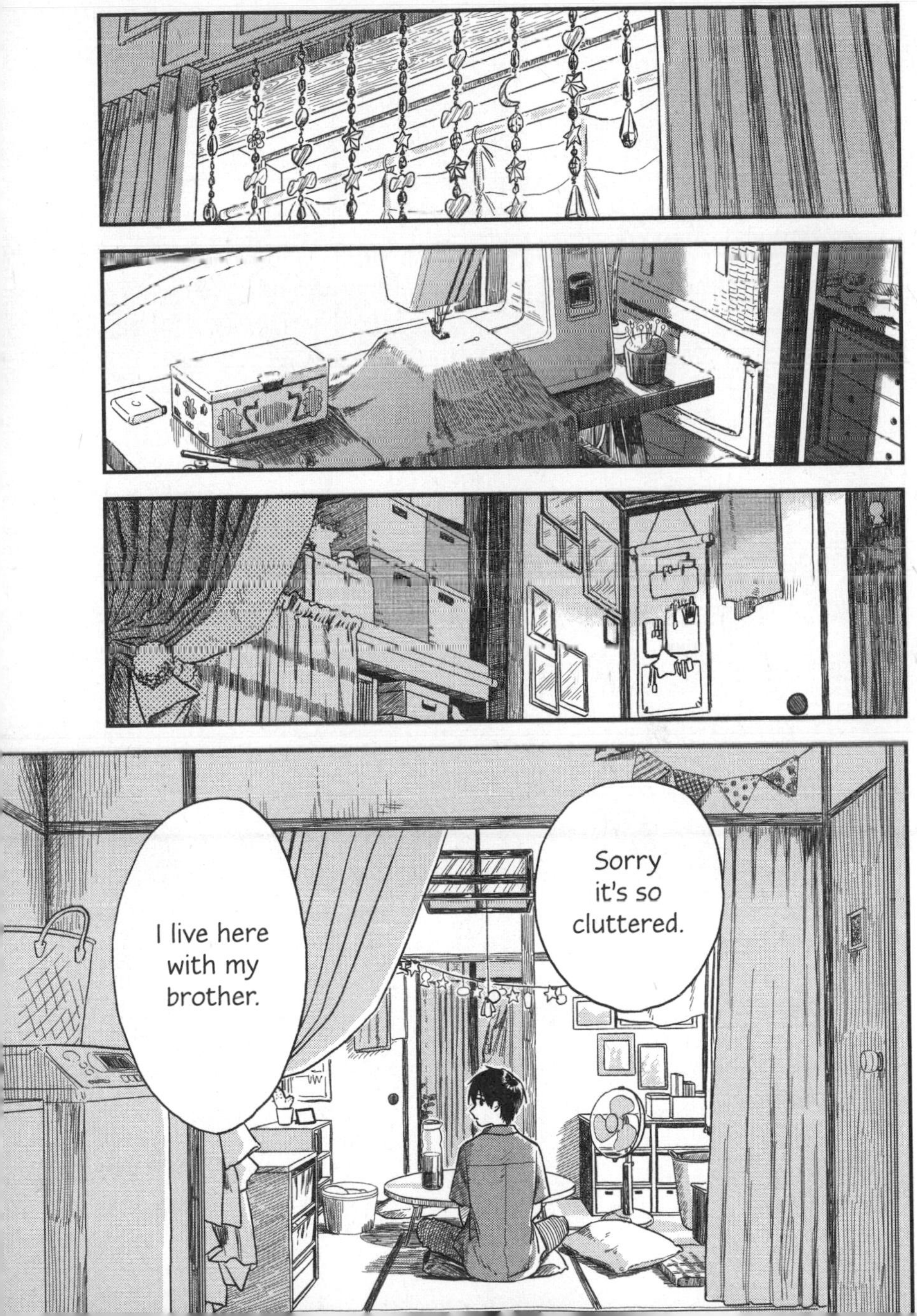
Sorry it's so cluttered.
I live here with my brother.

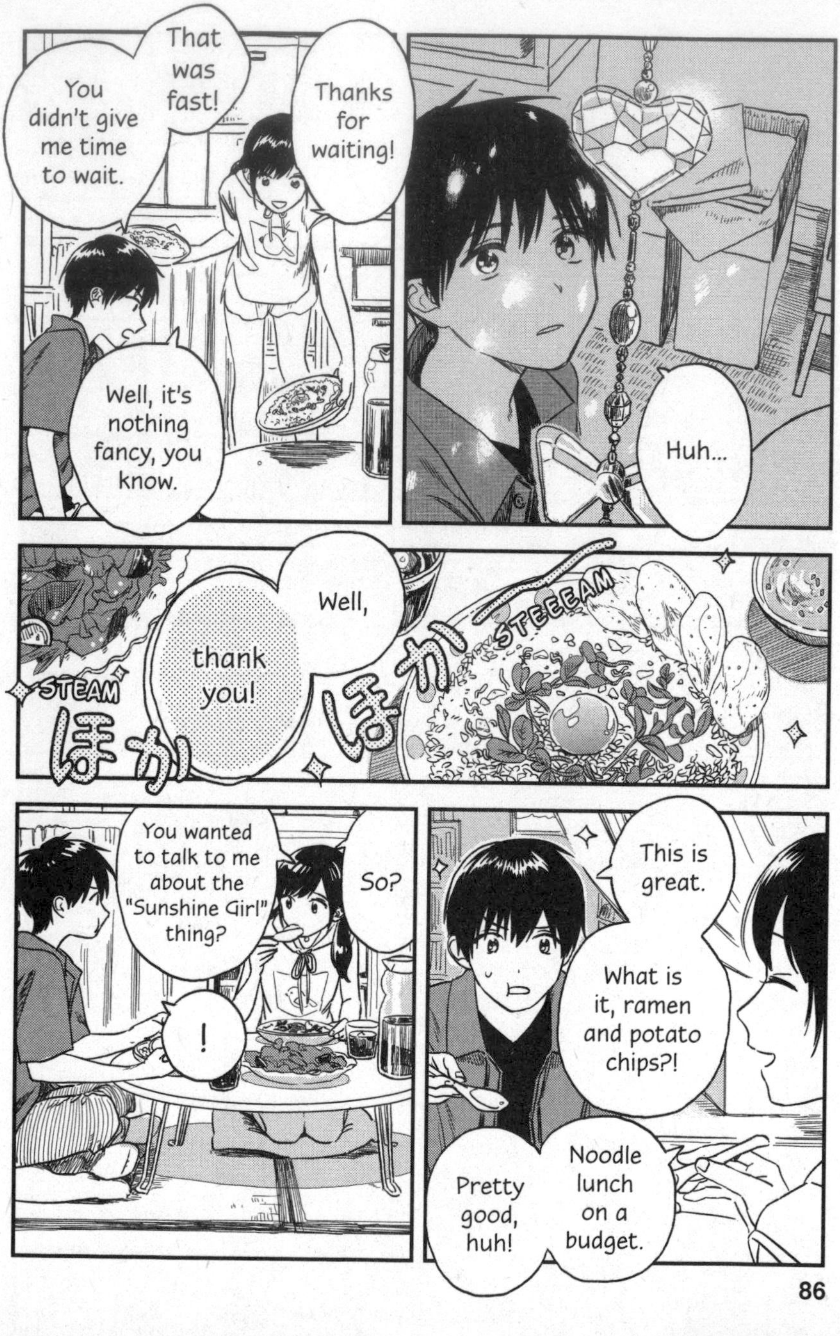
Huh...
Thanks for waiting!
That was fast!
You didn't give me time to wait.
Well, it's nothing fancy, you know.
STEEEAM
ほか
Well,
thank you!
STEAM
ほか
This is great.
What is it, ramen and potato chips?!
Noodle lunch on a budget.
Pretty good, huh!
So?
You wanted to talk to me about the "Sunshine Girl" thing?
!

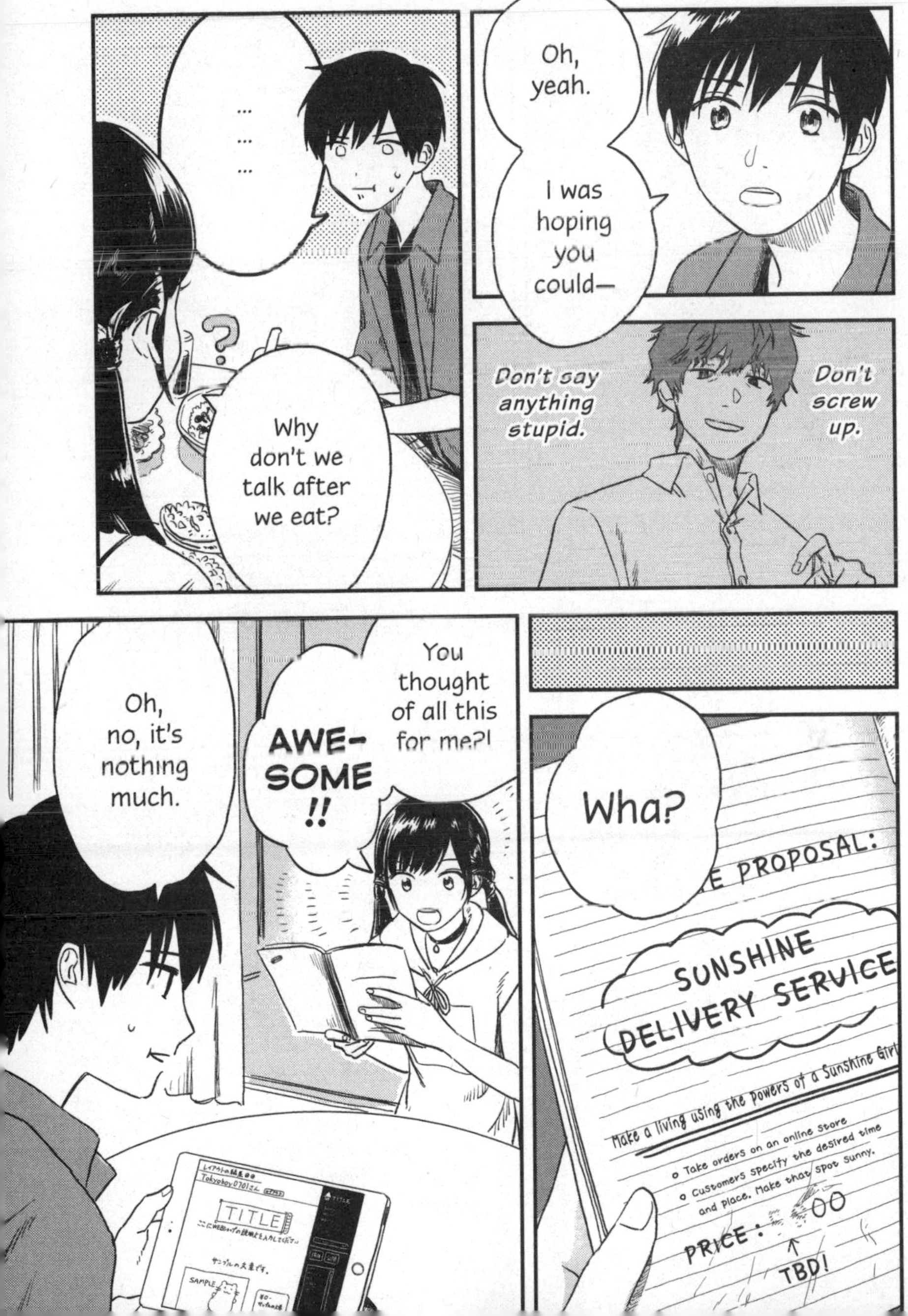
Oh, yeah.
I was hoping you could—
Don't say anything stupid.
Don't screw up.
...
...
...
Why don't we talk after we eat?
Wha?
E PROPOSAL:
SUNSHINE DELIVERY SERVICE
Make a living using the powers of a Sunshine Girl
Take orders on an online store
Customers specify the desired time and place. Make that spot sunny.
PRICE:
00
TBD!
You thought of all this for me?!
AWE-SOME!!
Oh, no, it's nothing much.
TITLE
SAMPLE

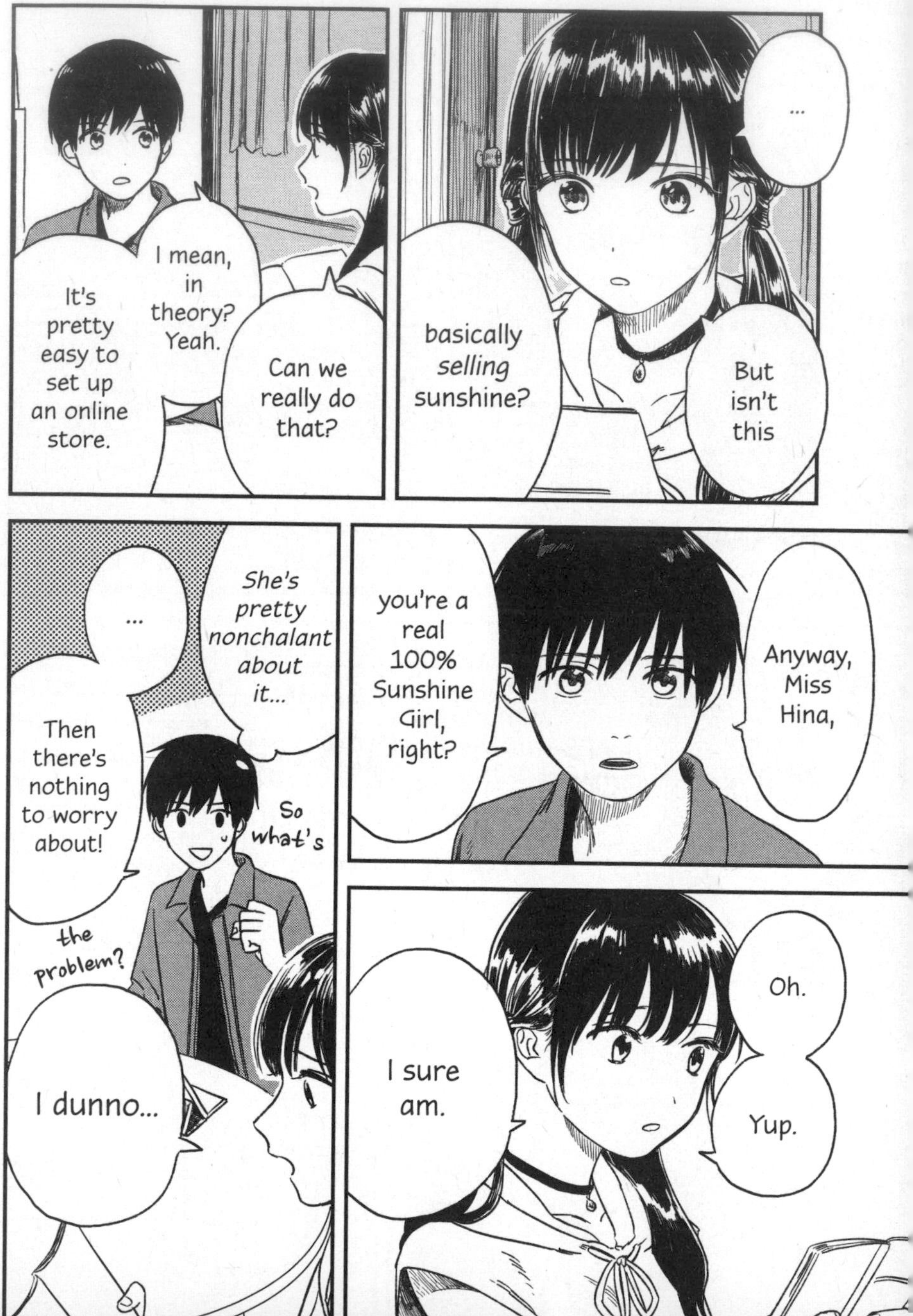
...
But isn't this
basically *selling* sunshine?
Can we really do that?
I mean, in theory? Yeah.
It's pretty easy to set up an online store.
Anyway, Miss Hina,
you're a real 100% Sunshine Girl, right?
Oh.
Yup.
I sure am.
She's pretty nonchalant about it...
...
Then there's nothing to worry about!
So what's the problem?
I dunno...

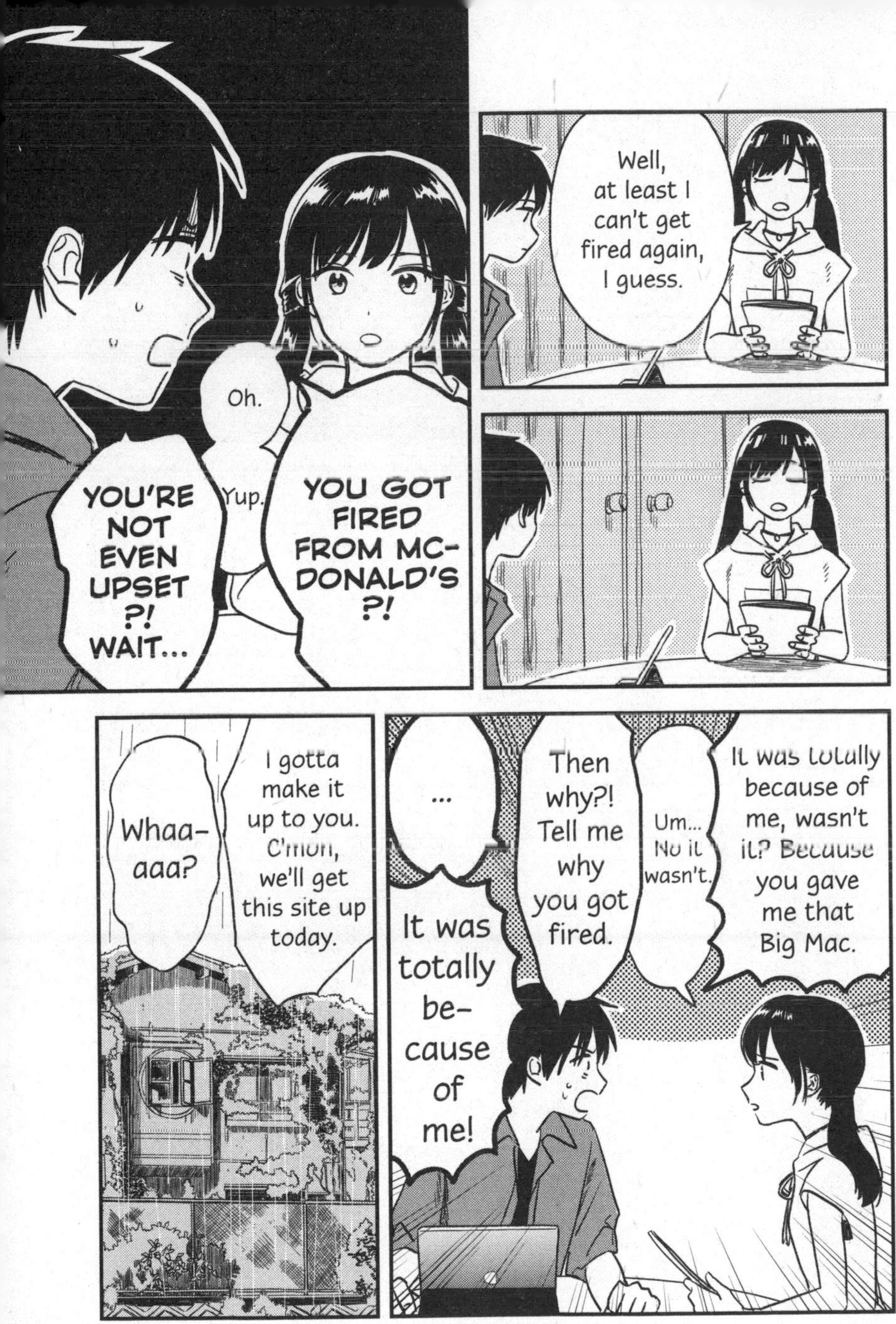
Well, at least I can't get fired again, I guess.
YOU GOT FIRED FROM MC-DONALD'S?!
Oh.
Yup.
YOU'RE NOT EVEN UPSET?! WAIT...
It was totally because of me, wasn't it? Because you gave me that Big Mac.
Um... No it wasn't.
Then why?! Tell me why you got fired.
...
It was totally be-cause of me!
I gotta make it up to you. C'mon, we'll get this site up today.
Whaa-aaa?

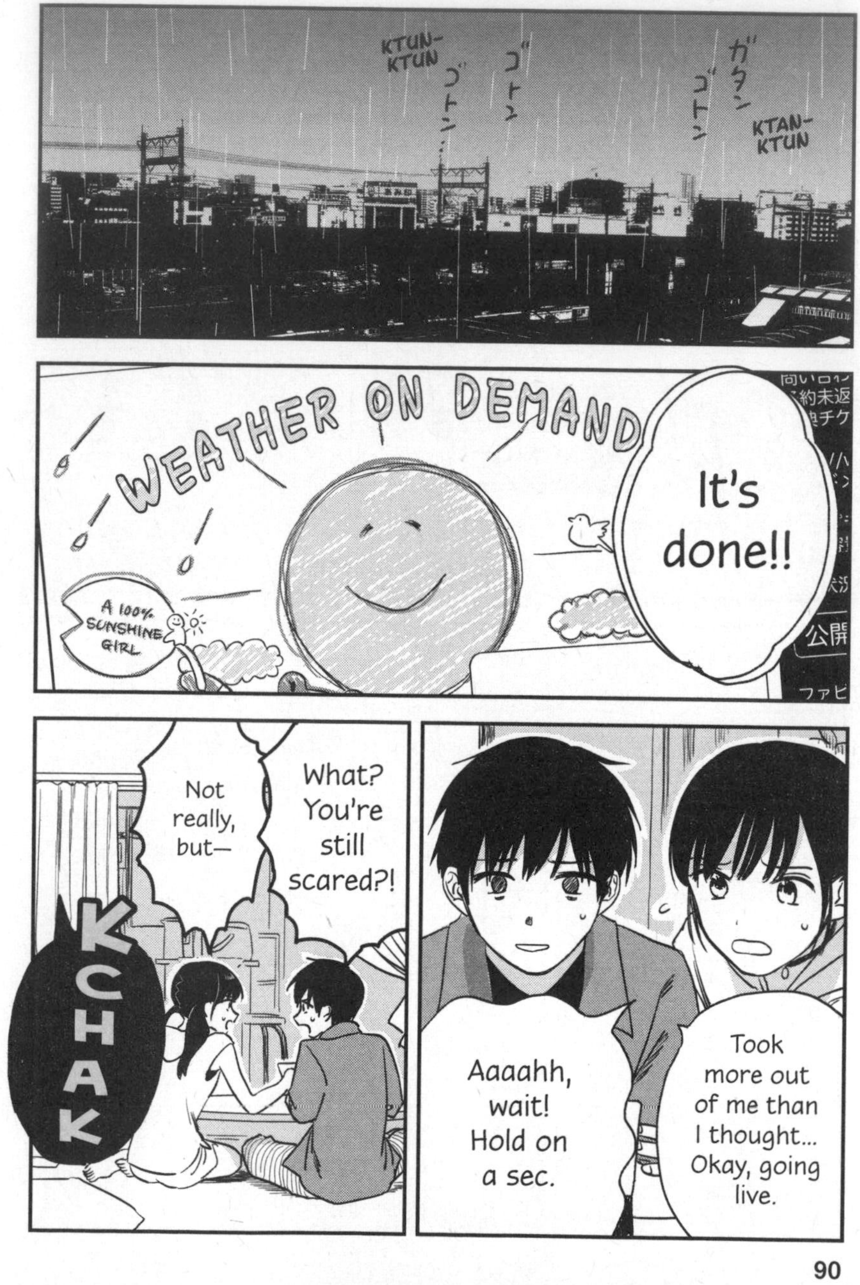
KTAN-KTUN
ガタン ゴトン
ゴトン ゴトン…
KTUN-KTUN
It's done!!
WEATHER ON DEMAND
A 100% SUNSHINE GIRL
公開
Took more out of me than I thought... Okay, going live.
Aaaahh, wait! Hold on a sec.
What? You're still scared?!
Not really, but—
KCHAK

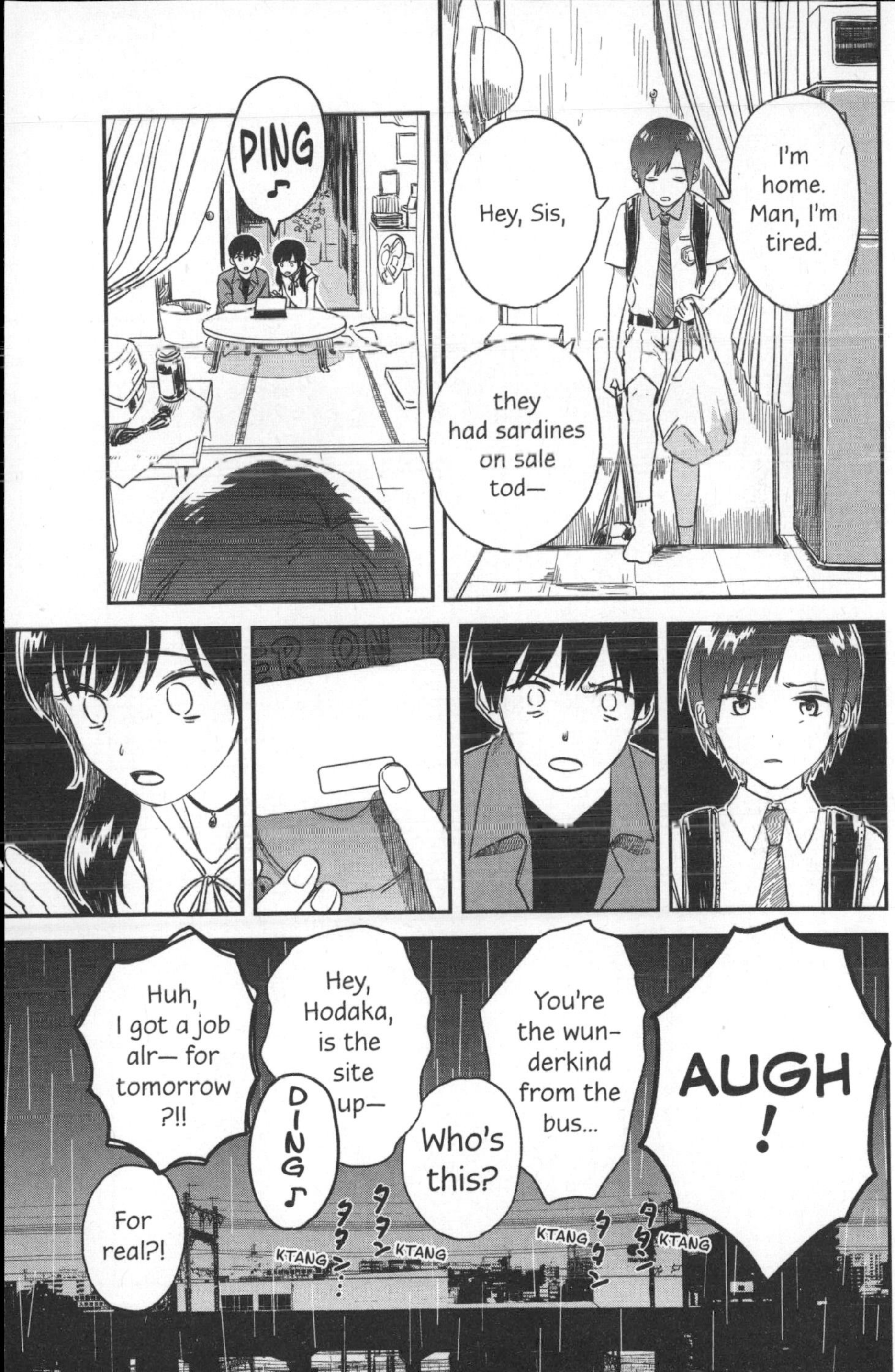
I'm home. Man, I'm tired.
Hey, Sis,
they had sardines on sale tod—
PING ♪
AUGH!
You're the wunderkind from the bus...
Who's this?
Hey, Hodaka, is the site up—
DING ♪
Huh, I got a job alr— for tomorrow?!!
For real?!
タタン
KTANG
タタン
KTANG
タタン
KTANG
タタン…
KTANG

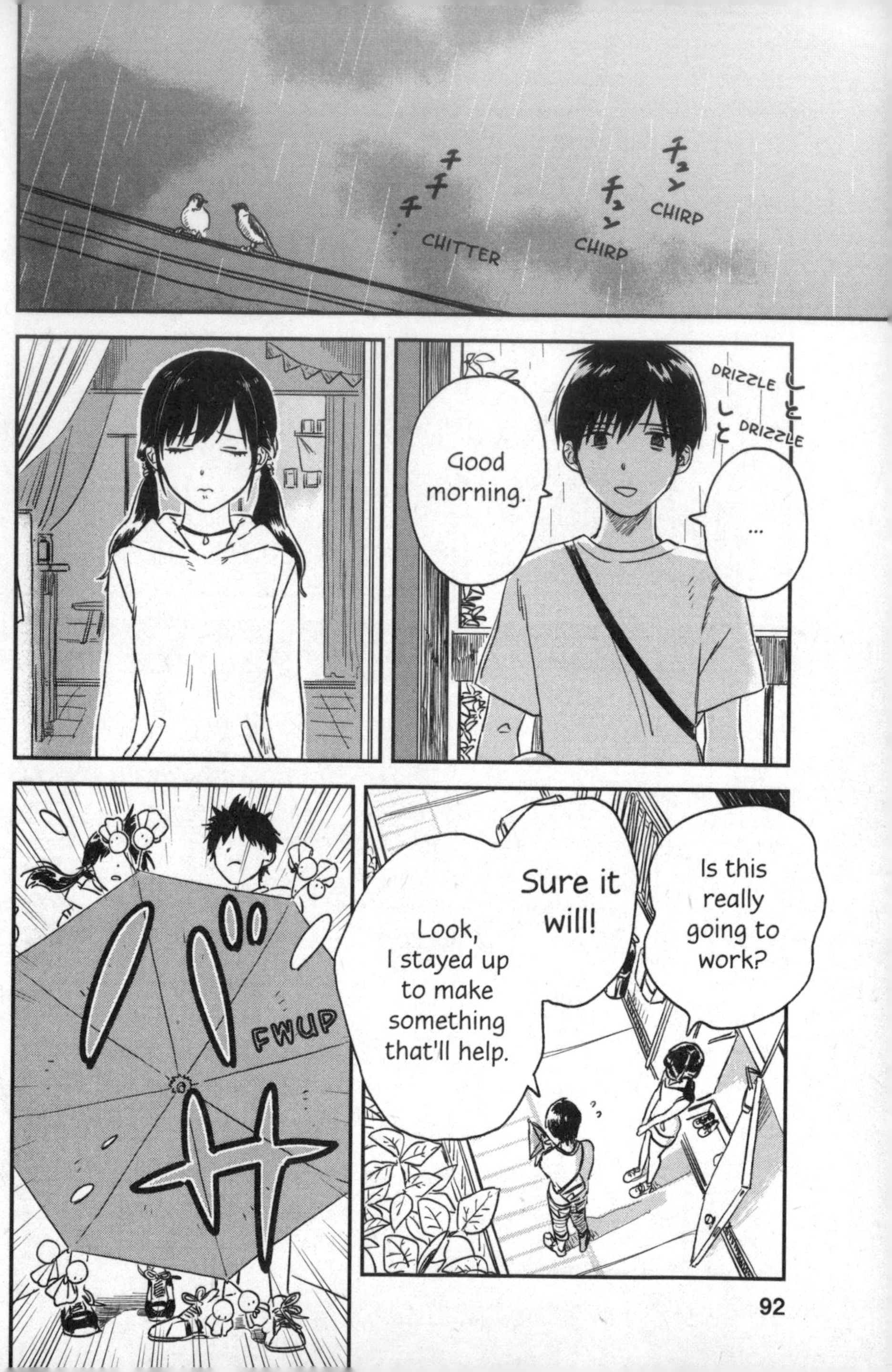
チュン
CHIRP
チュン
CHIRP
チチチ
CHITTER
DRIZZLE
しとしと
DRIZZLE
Good morning.
...
Is this really going to work?
Sure it will!
Look, I stayed up to make something that'll help.
FWUP

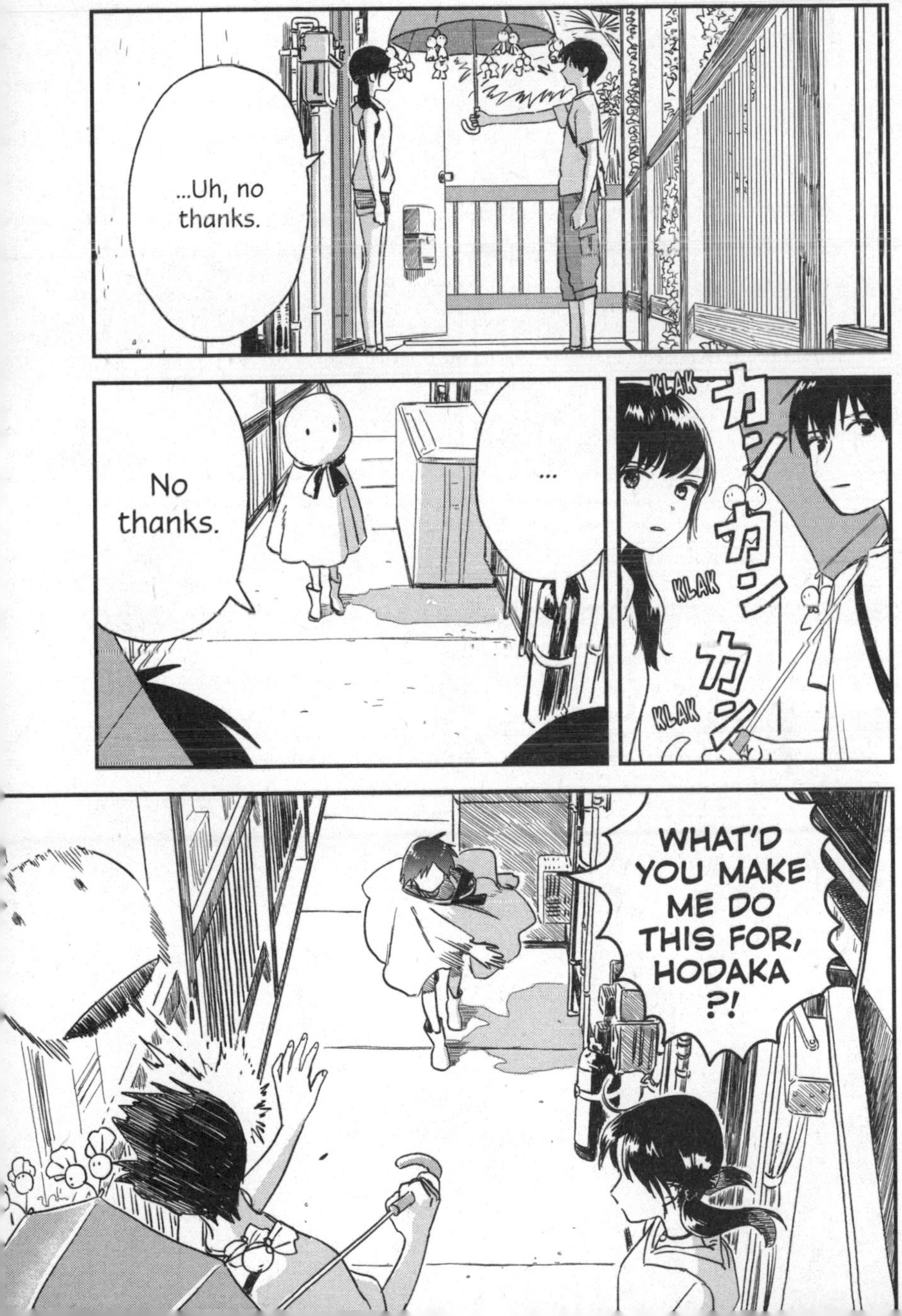
...Uh, no thanks.
KLAK...
カン
KLAK
カン
KLAK
カン
...
No thanks.
WHAT'D YOU MAKE ME DO THIS FOR, HODAKA?!

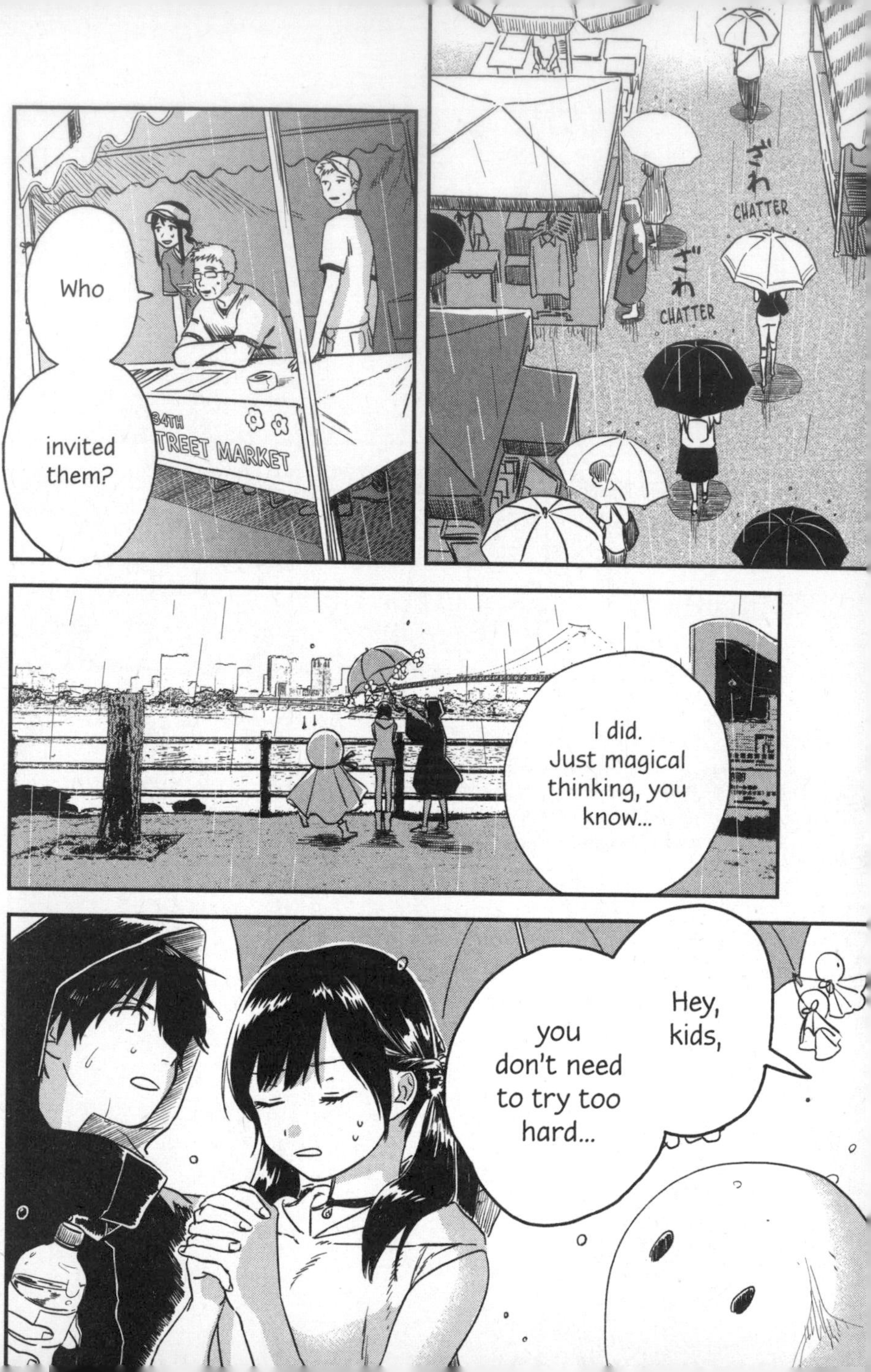
ざわ
CHATTER
ざわ
CHATTER
Who invited them?
34TH
TREET MARKET
I did. Just magical thinking, you know...
Hey, kids, you don't need to try too hard...

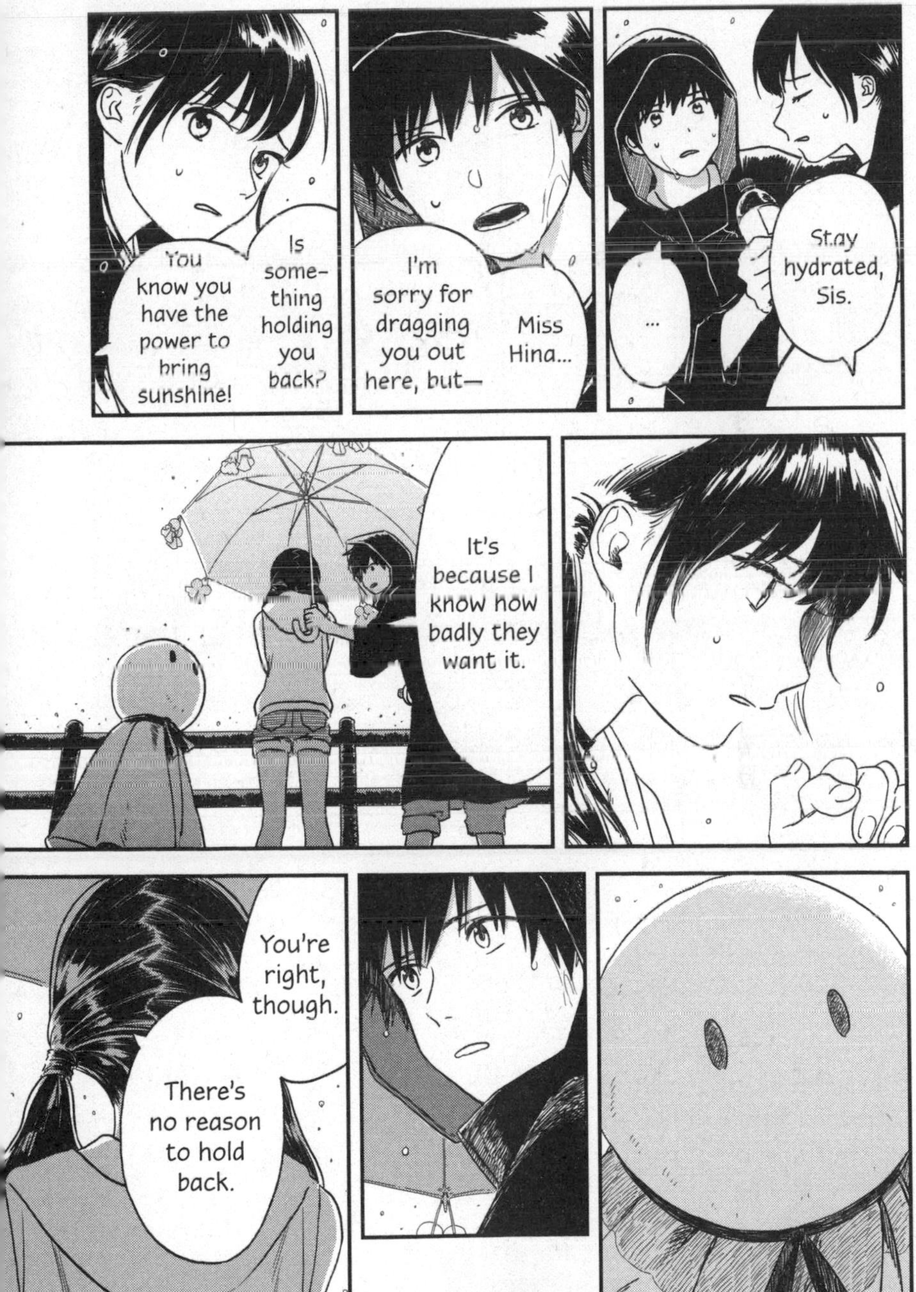
Stay hydrated, Sis.
...
Miss Hina...
I'm sorry for dragging you out here, but—
Is something holding you back?
You know you have the power to bring sunshine!
It's because I know how badly they want it.
You're right, though.
There's no reason to hold back.

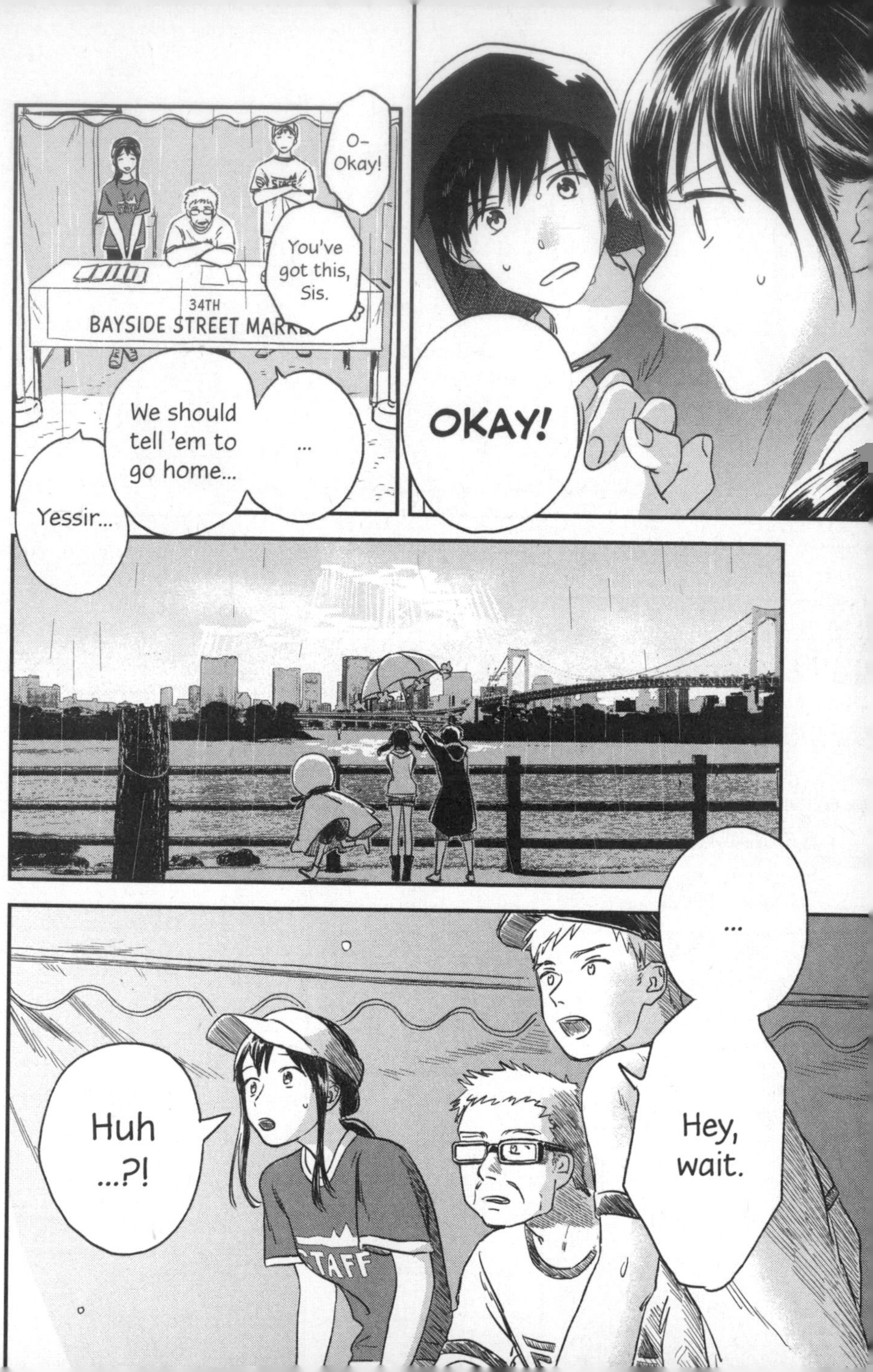
OKAY!
O-Okay!
You've got this, Sis.
34TH
BAYSIDE STREET
...
We should tell 'em to go home...
Yessir...
...
Hey, wait.
Huh ...?!

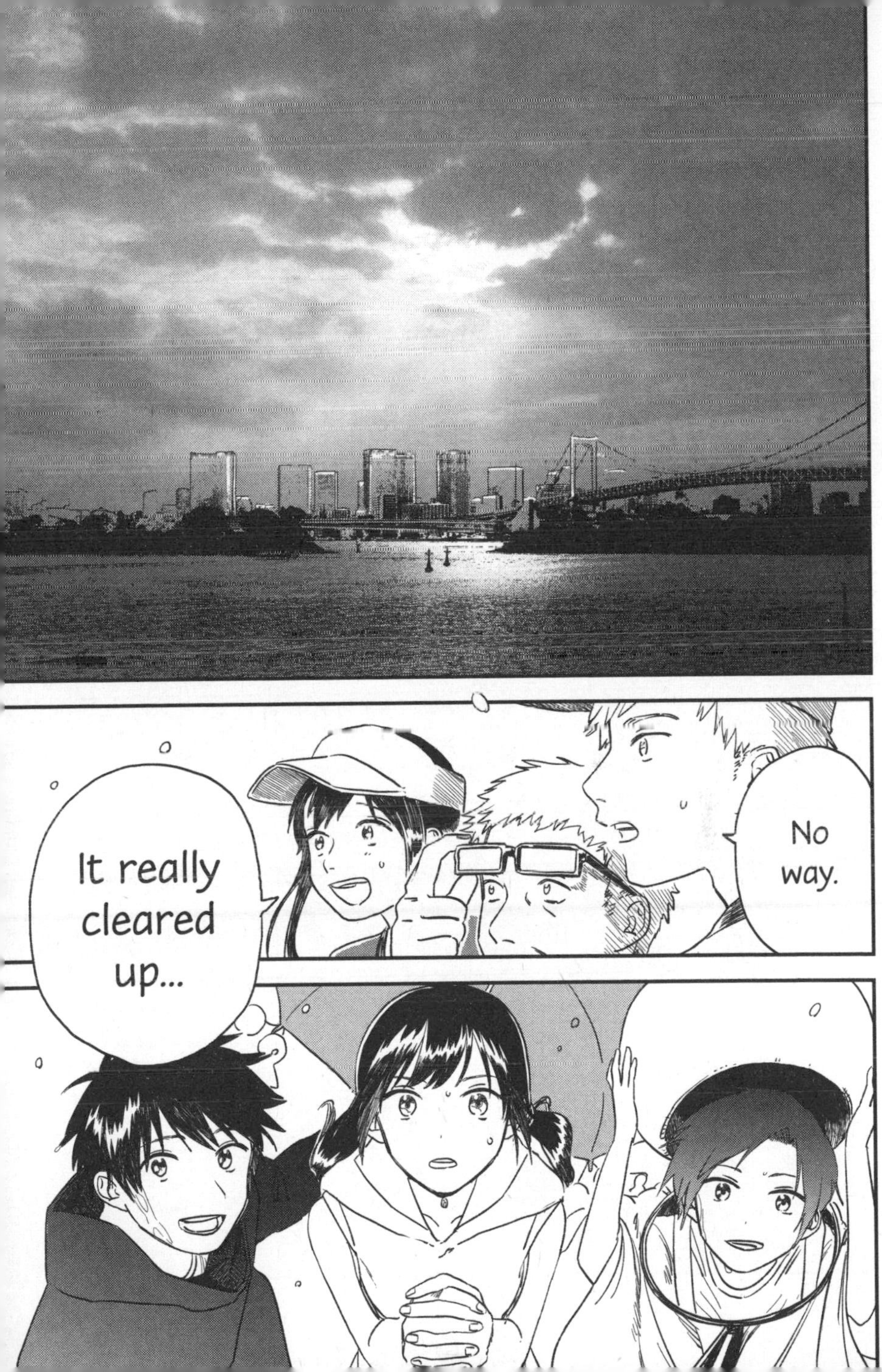
No way.
It really cleared up...

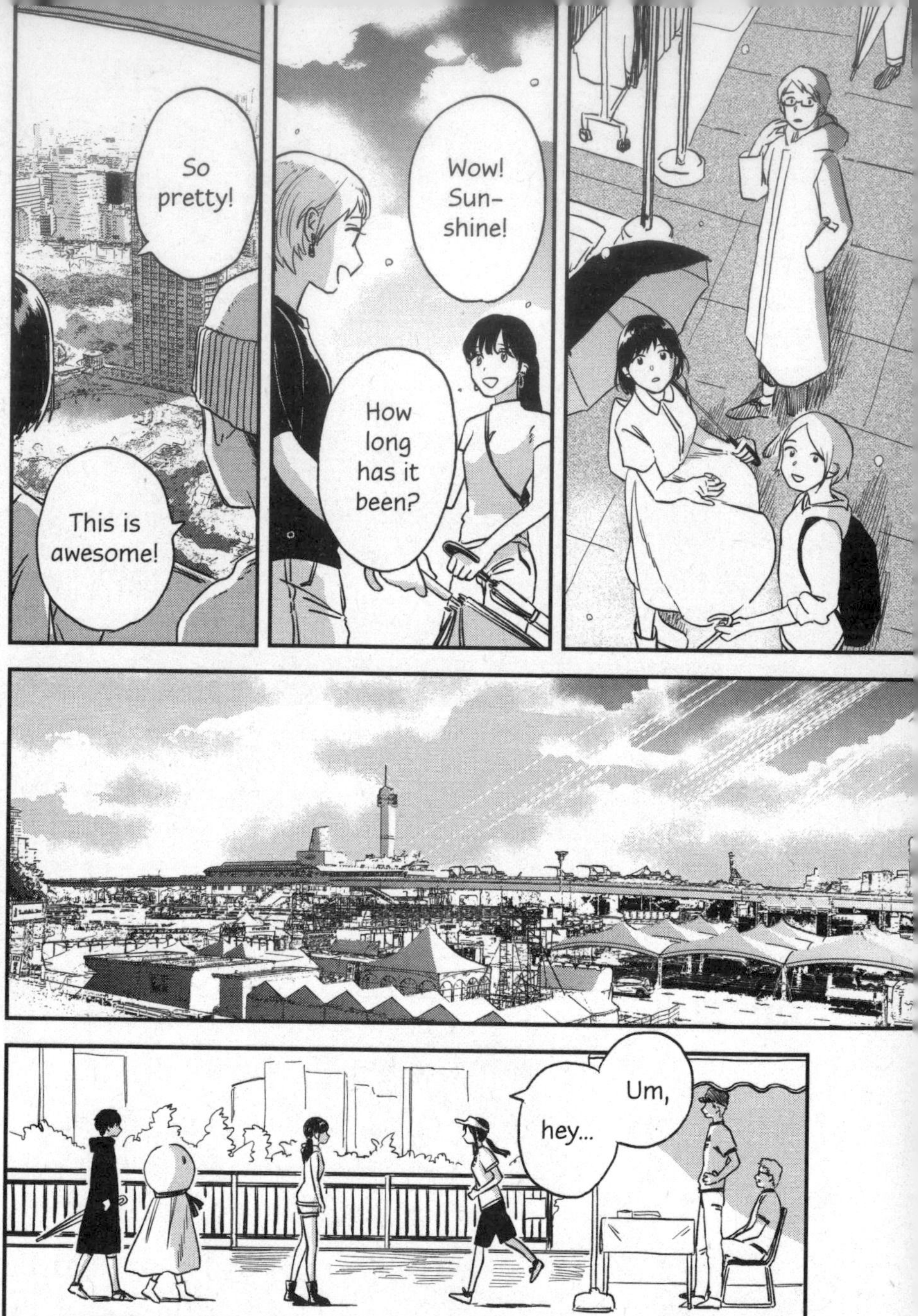
Wow! Sun-shine!
How long has it been?
So pretty!
This is awesome!
Um, hey...

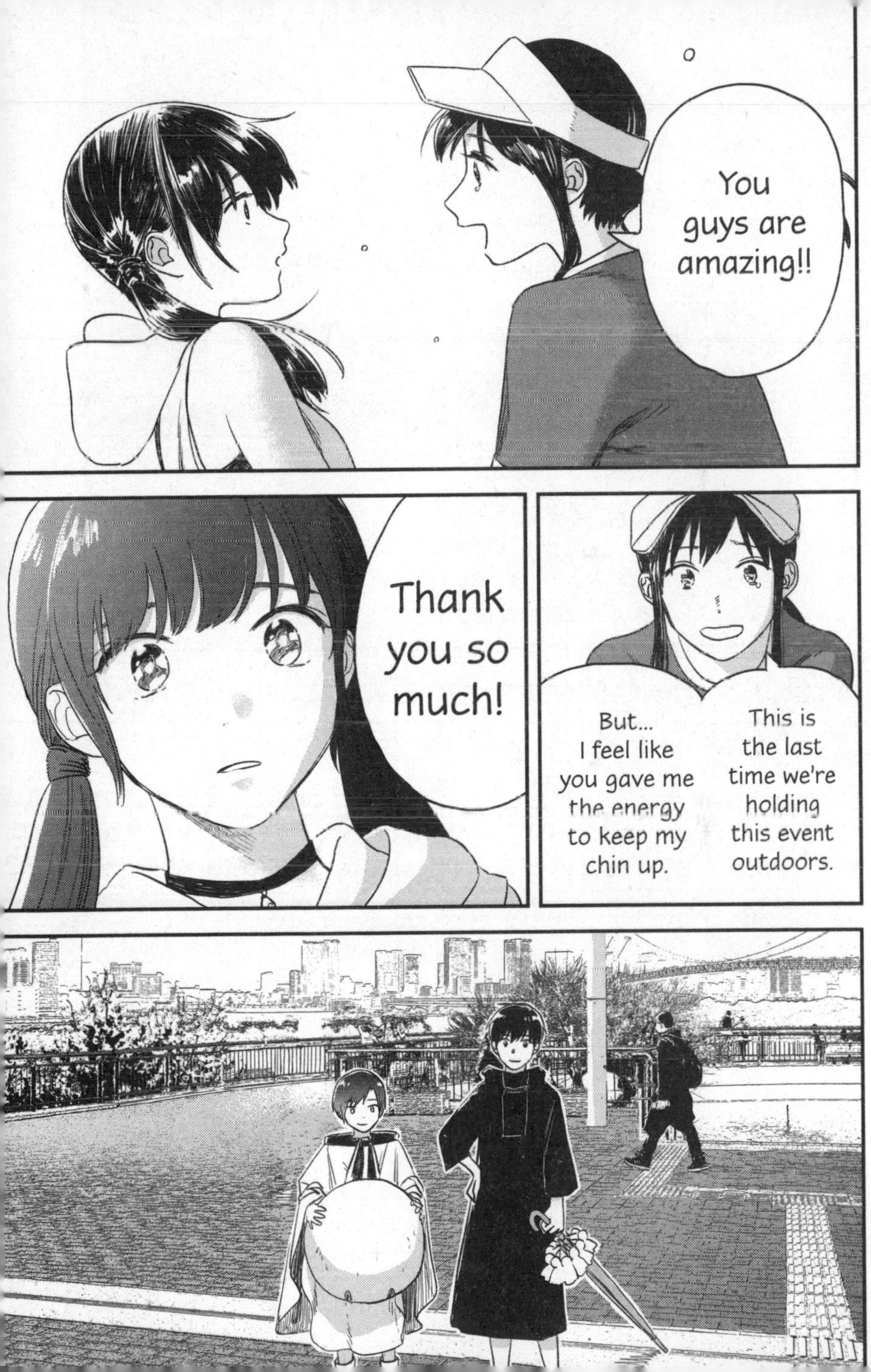
You guys are amazing!!
This is the last time we're holding this event outdoors.
But... I feel like you gave me the energy to keep my chin up.
Thank you so much!

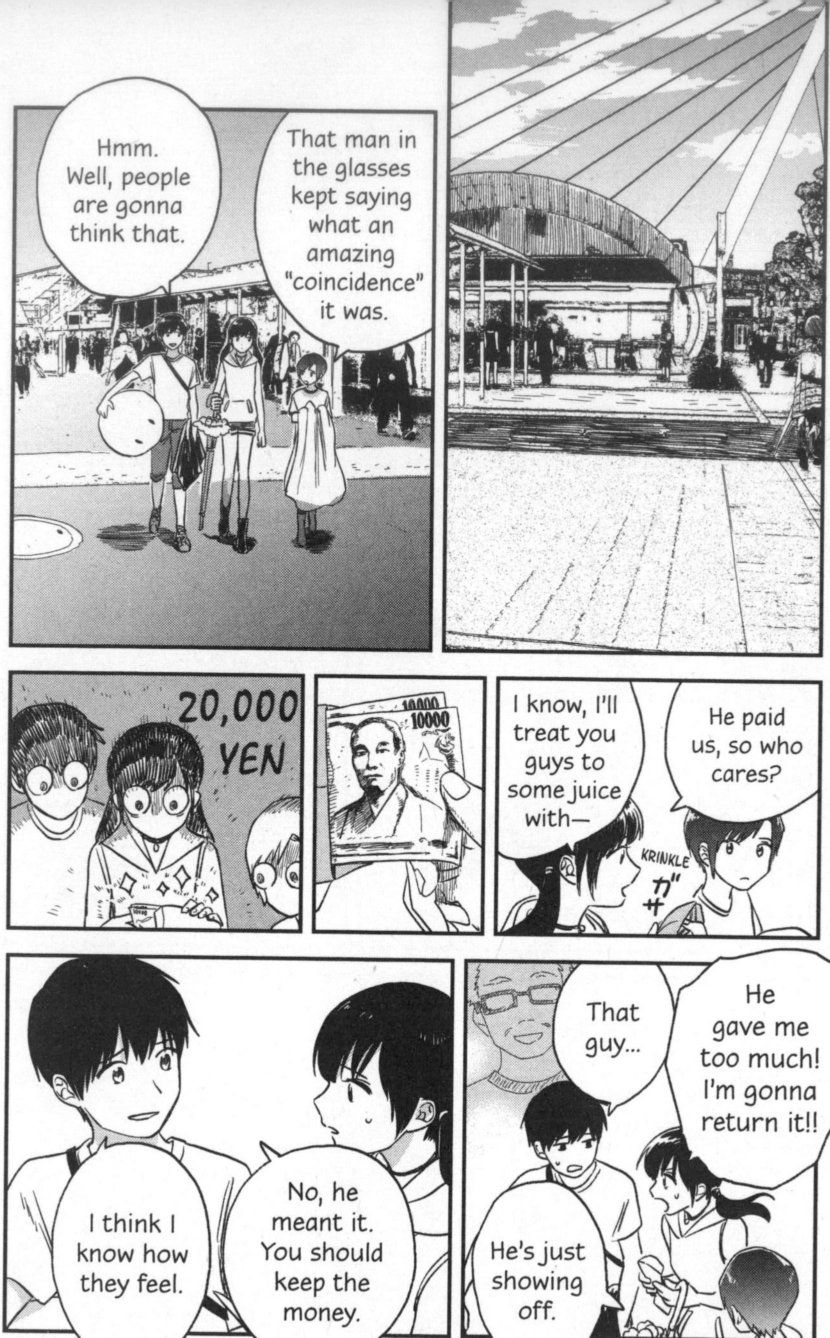
That man in the glasses kept saying what an amazing "coincidence" it was.
Hmm. Well, people are gonna think that.
He paid us, so who cares?
I know, I'll treat you guys to some juice with—
KRINKLE
ガサ
10000
20,000 YEN
He gave me too much! I'm gonna return it!!
That guy...
He's just showing off.
No, he meant it. You should keep the money.
I think I know how they feel.

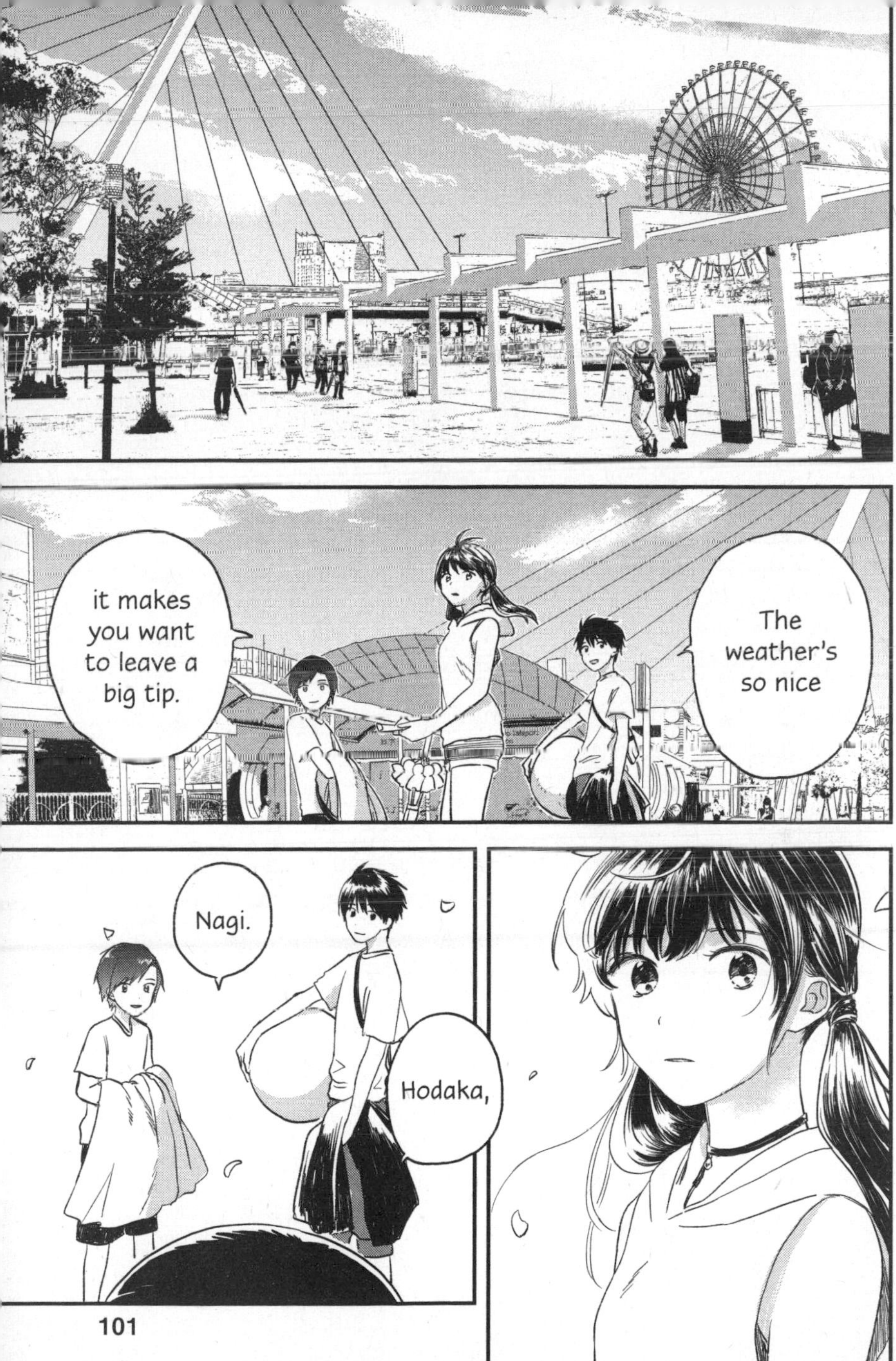
The weather's so nice
it makes you want to leave a big tip.
Hodaka,
Nagi.

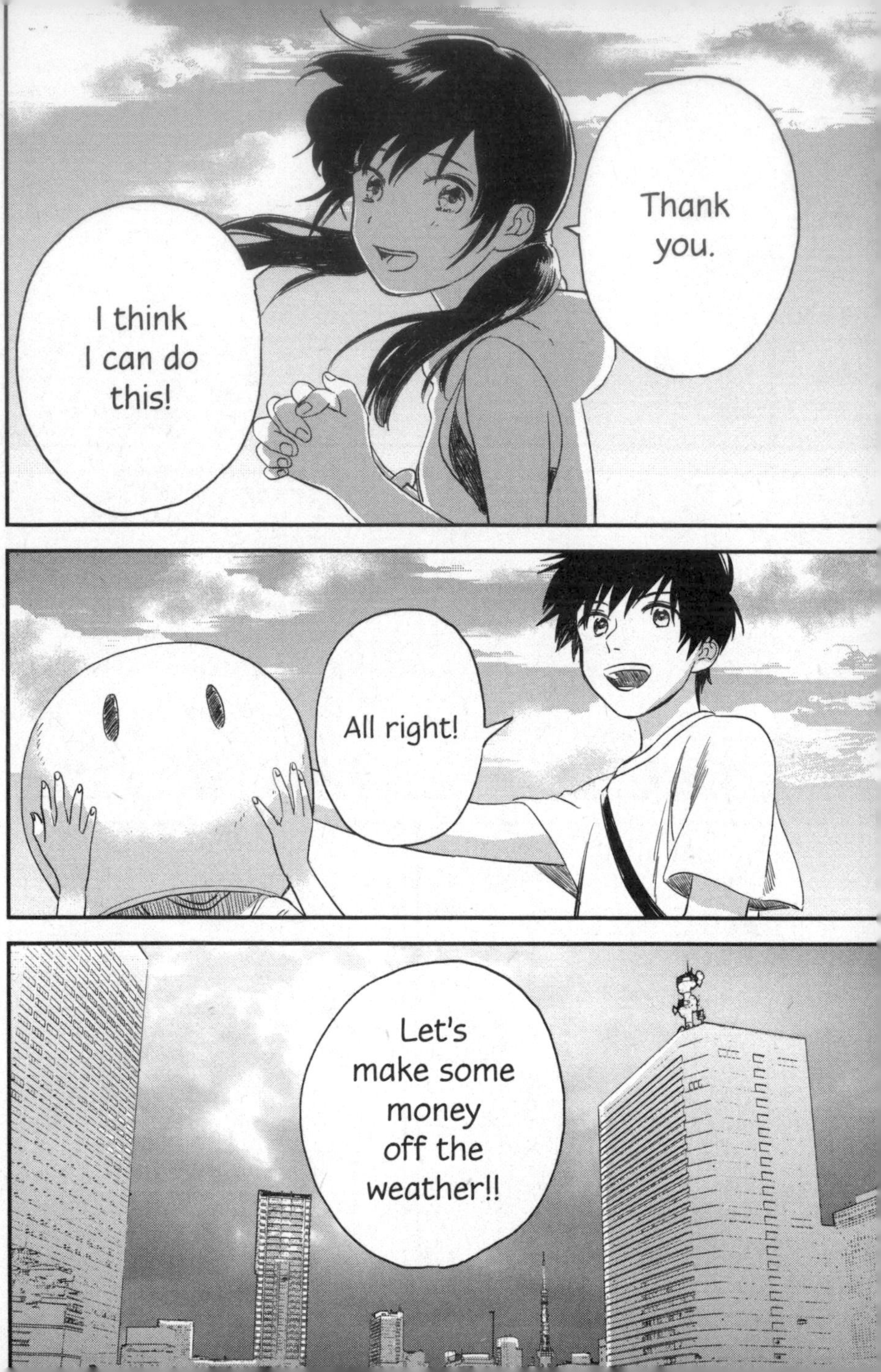
Thank you.
I think I can do this!
All right!
Let's make some money off the weather!!

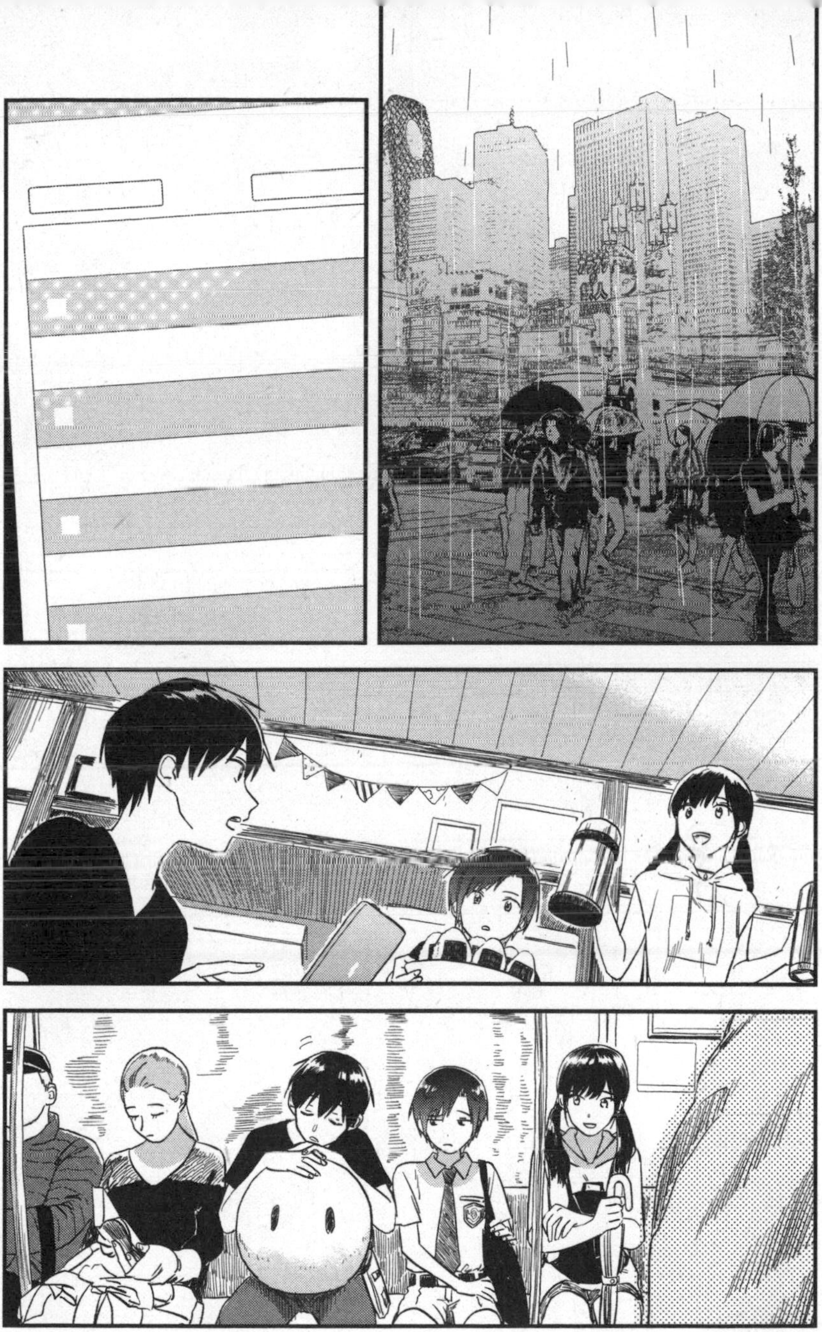

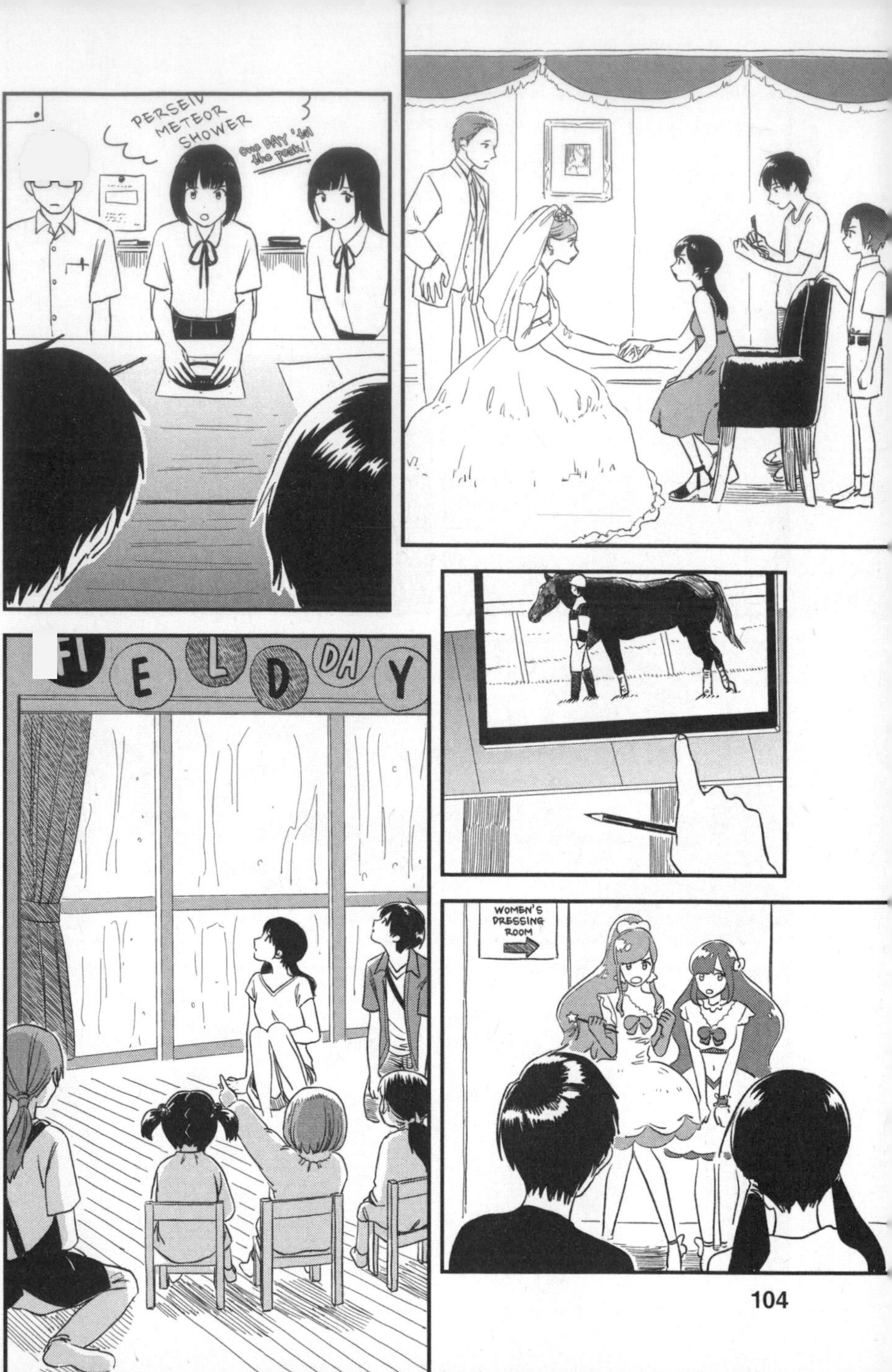
PERSEID METEOR SHOWER
one DAY 'til the peak!!
WOMEN'S DRESSING ROOM
FI E L D DA Y

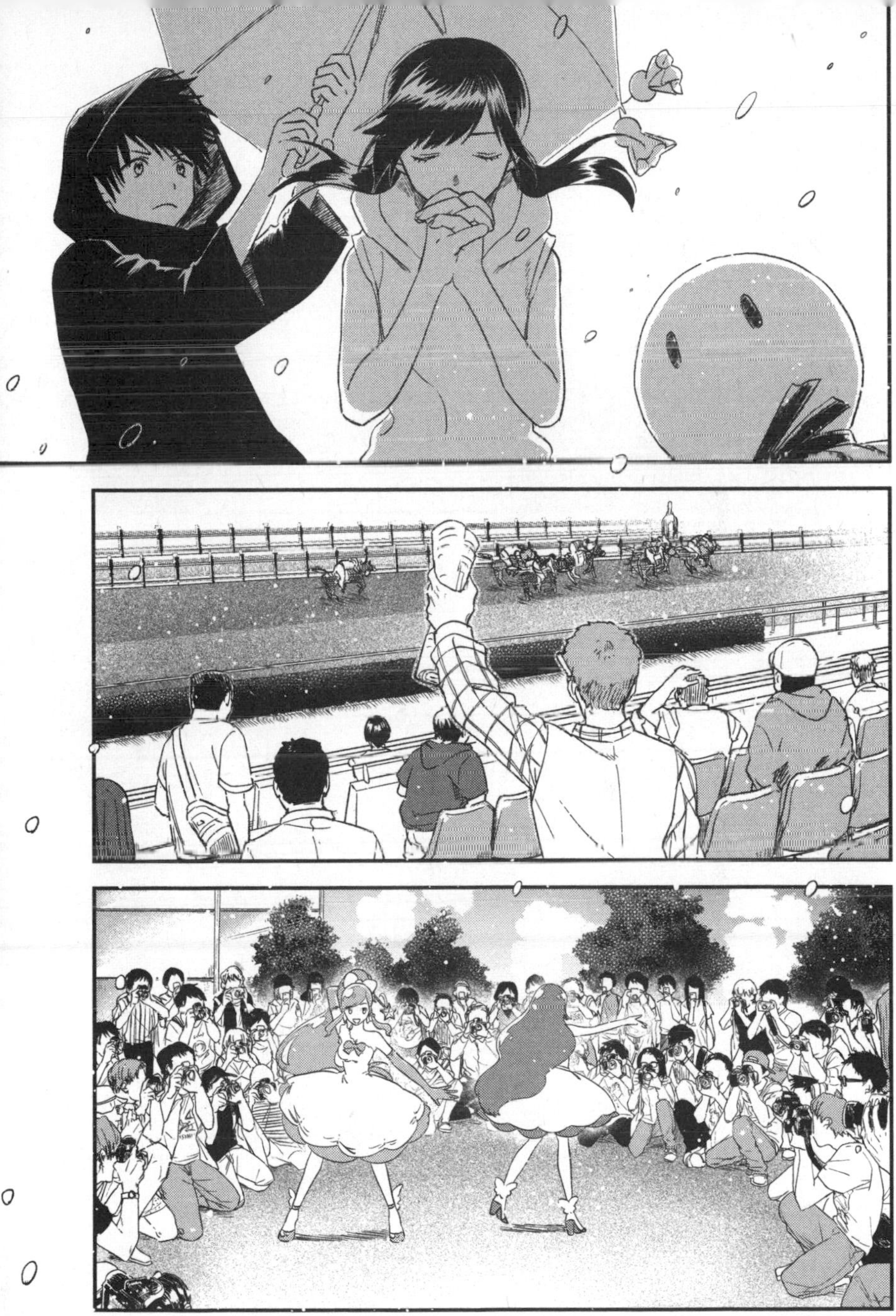

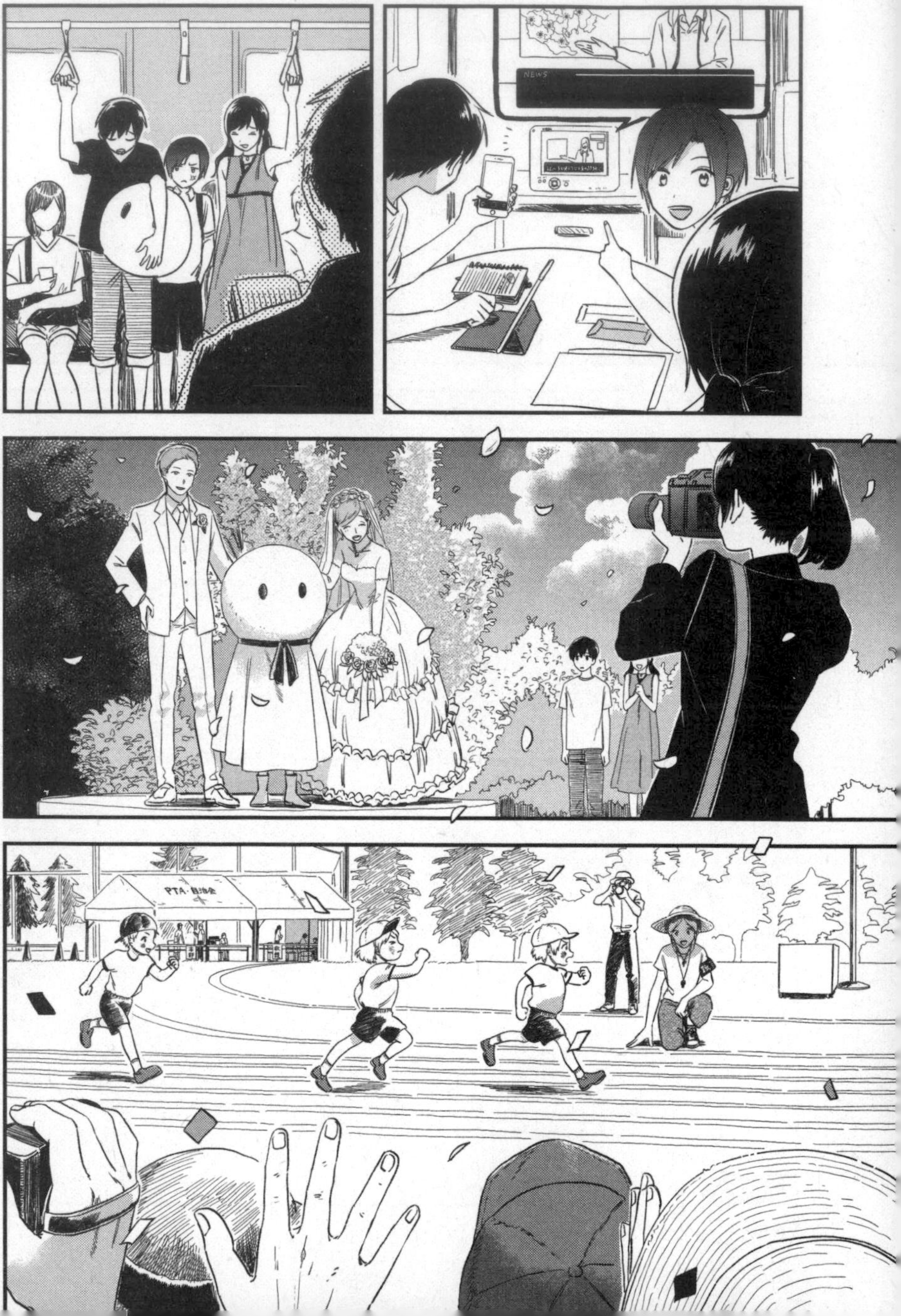
NEWS
PTA・自治会

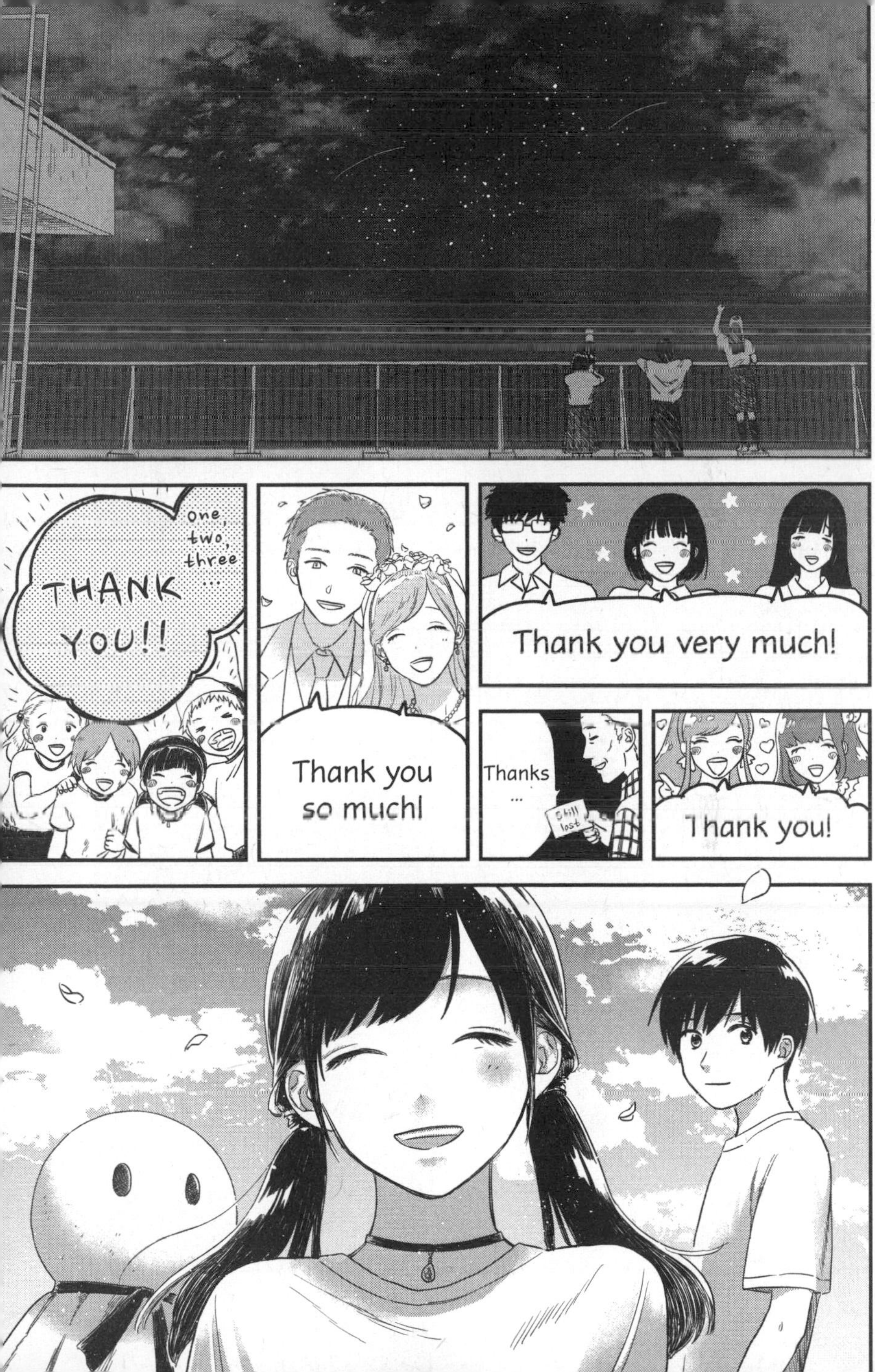
Thank you very much!
Thank you!
Thanks ...
Still lost
Thank you so much!
one, two, three ...
THANK YOU!!

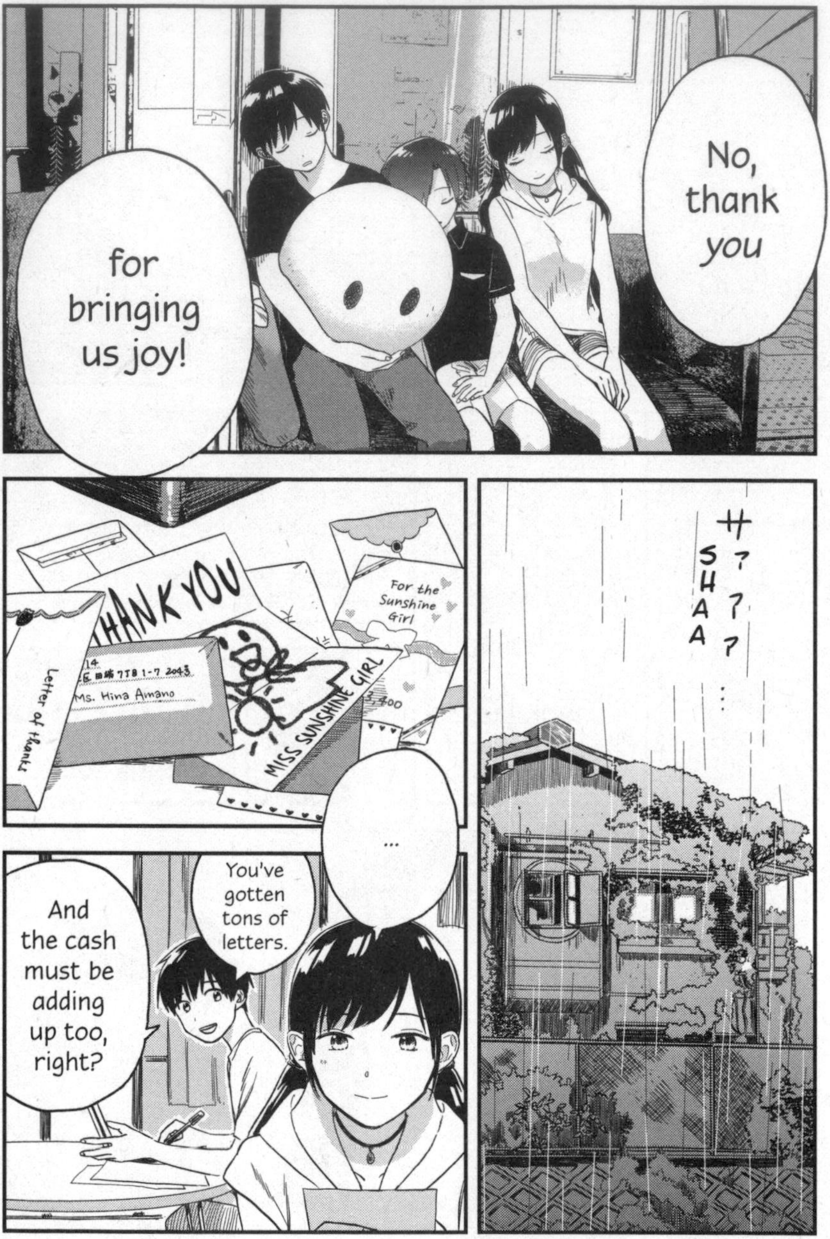
No, thank you
for bringing us joy!
SHAA...
THANK YOU
For the Sunshine Girl
Ms. Hina Amano
Letter of thanks
MISS SUNSHINE GIRL
...
You've gotten tons of letters.
And the cash must be adding up too, right?

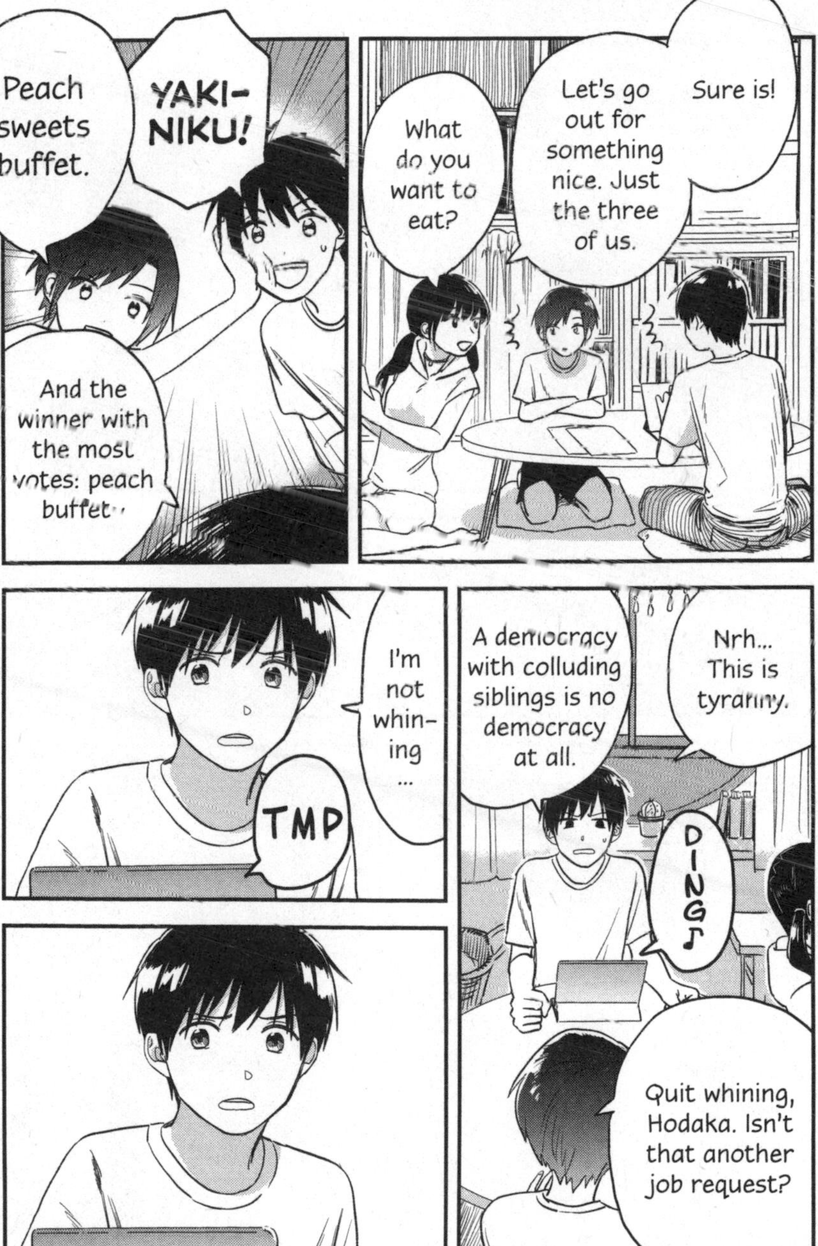
Sure is!
Let's go out for something nice. Just the three of us.
What do you want to eat?
YAKI-NIKU!
Peach sweets buffet.
And the winner with the most votes: peach buffet..
Nrh... This is tyranny.
A democracy with colluding siblings is no democracy at all.
DING♪
Quit whining, Hodaka. Isn't that another job request?
I'm not whin-ing...
TMP

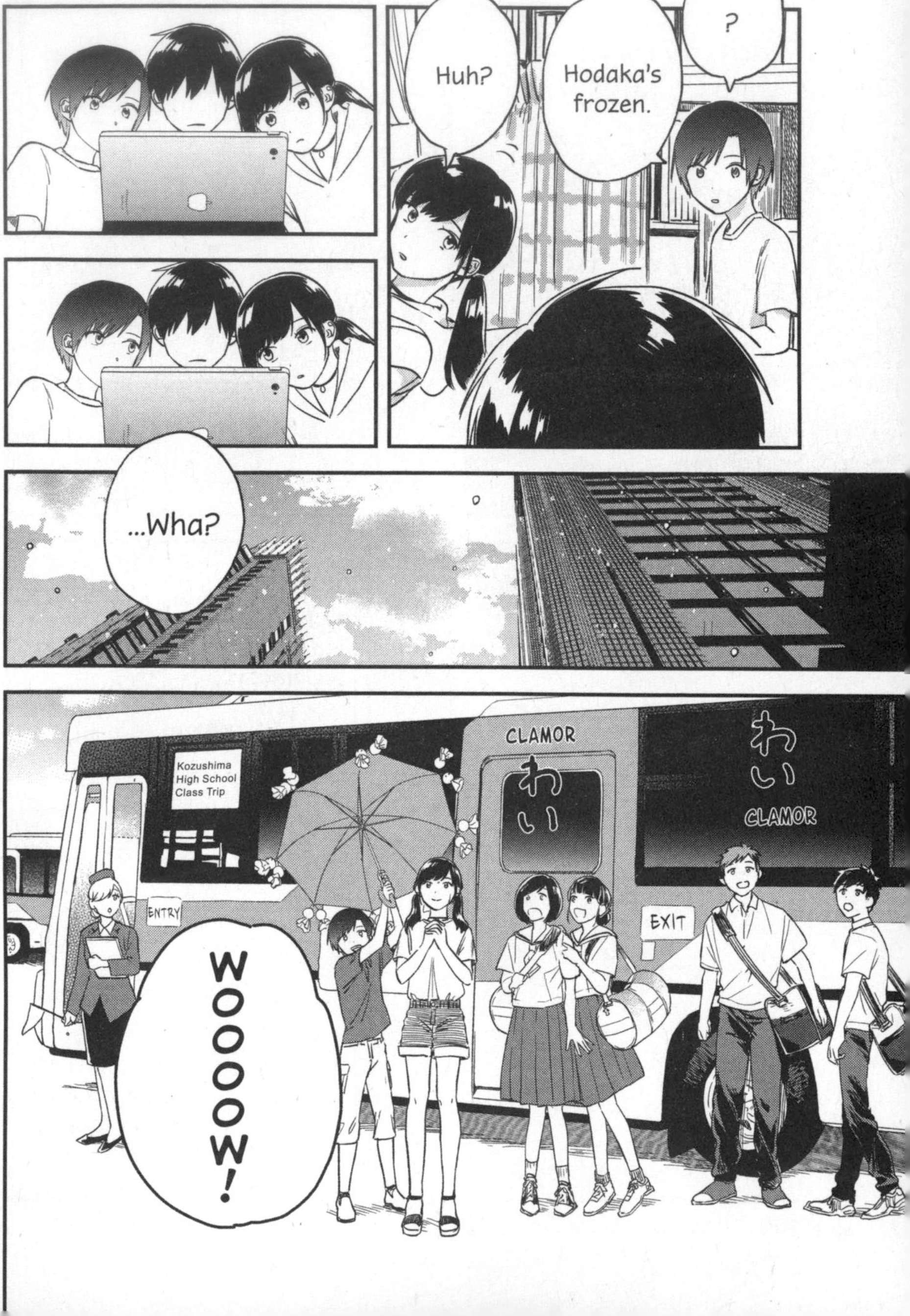
?
Hodaka's frozen.
Huh?
...Wha?
わい
CLAMOR
CLAMOR
わい
Kozushima High School Class Trip
EXIT
ENTRY
WOOOOOW!

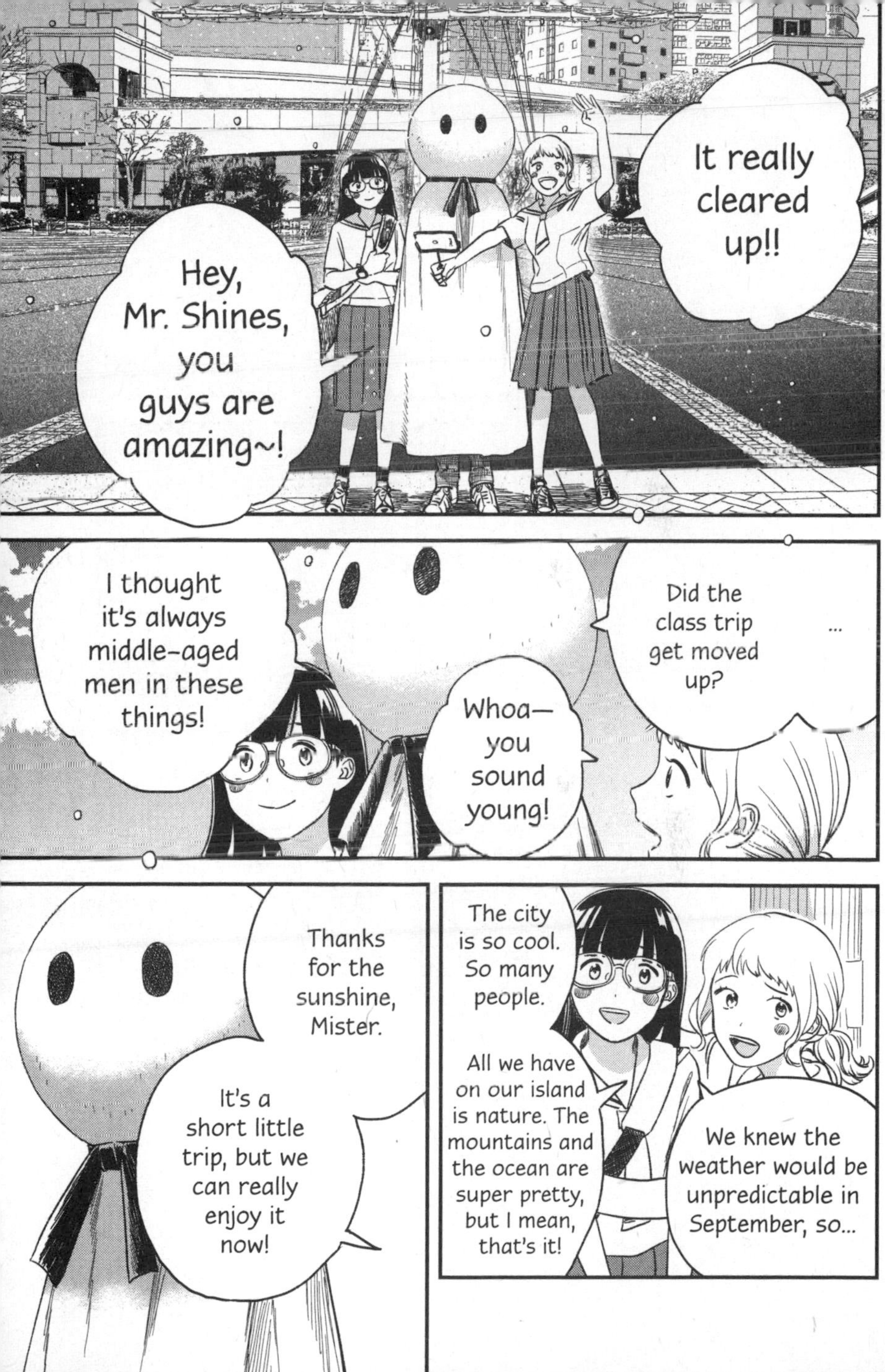
It really cleared up!!
Hey, Mr. Shines, you guys are amazing~!
...
Did the class trip get moved up?
Whoa— you sound young!
I thought it's always middle-aged men in these things!
The city is so cool. So many people.
All we have on our island is nature. The mountains and the ocean are super pretty, but I mean, that's it!
We knew the weather would be unpredictable in September, so...
Thanks for the sunshine, Mister.
It's a short little trip, but we can really enjoy it now!

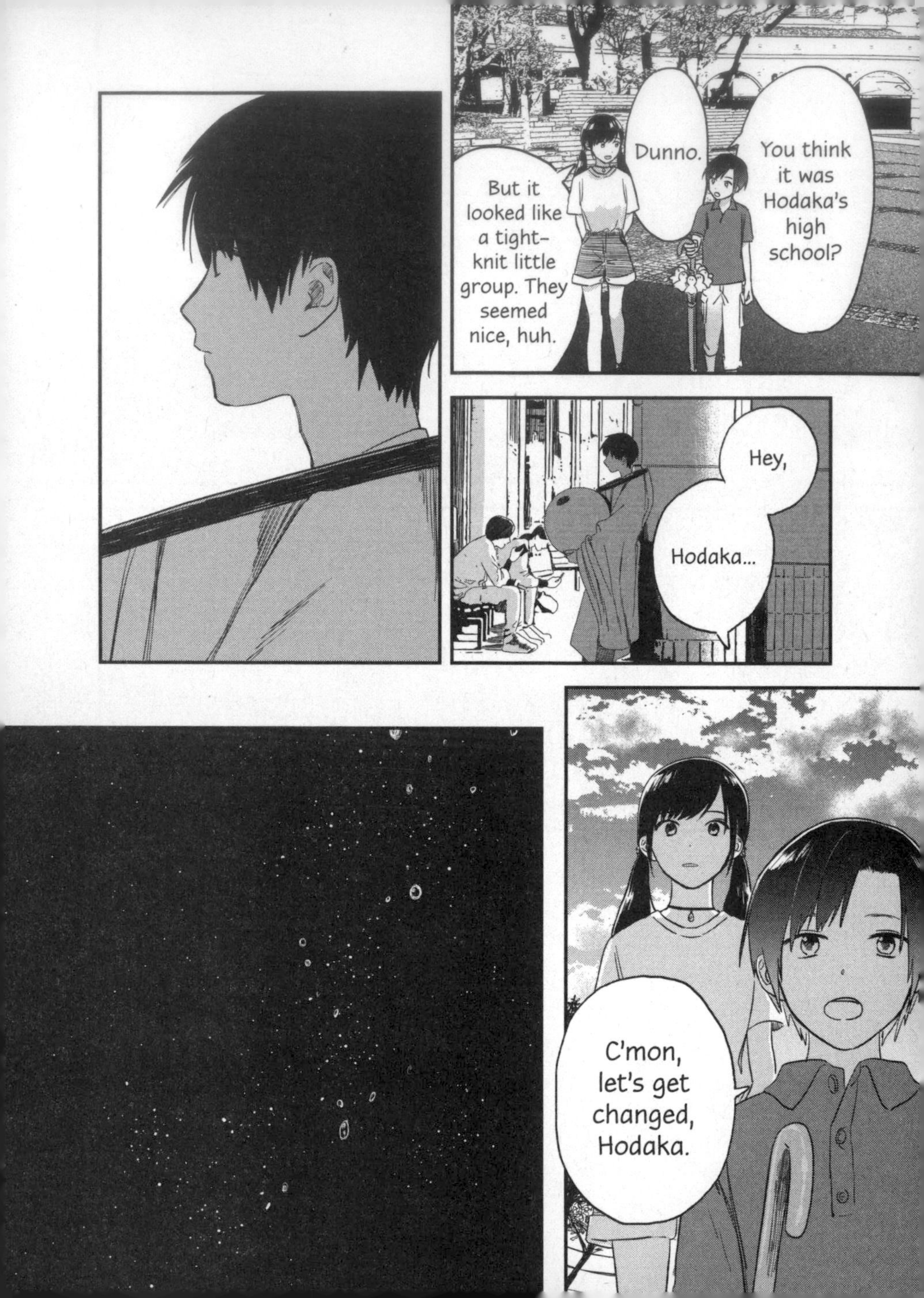
You think it was Hodaka's high school?
Dunno.
But it looked like a tight-knit little group. They seemed nice, huh.
Hey,
Hodaka...
C'mon, let's get changed, Hodaka.

GLUBBUB
ゴポポッ
GLUB
ゴポ

TWITCH
ビク

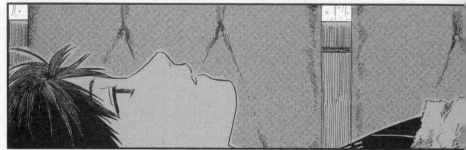

JING
ジャラ

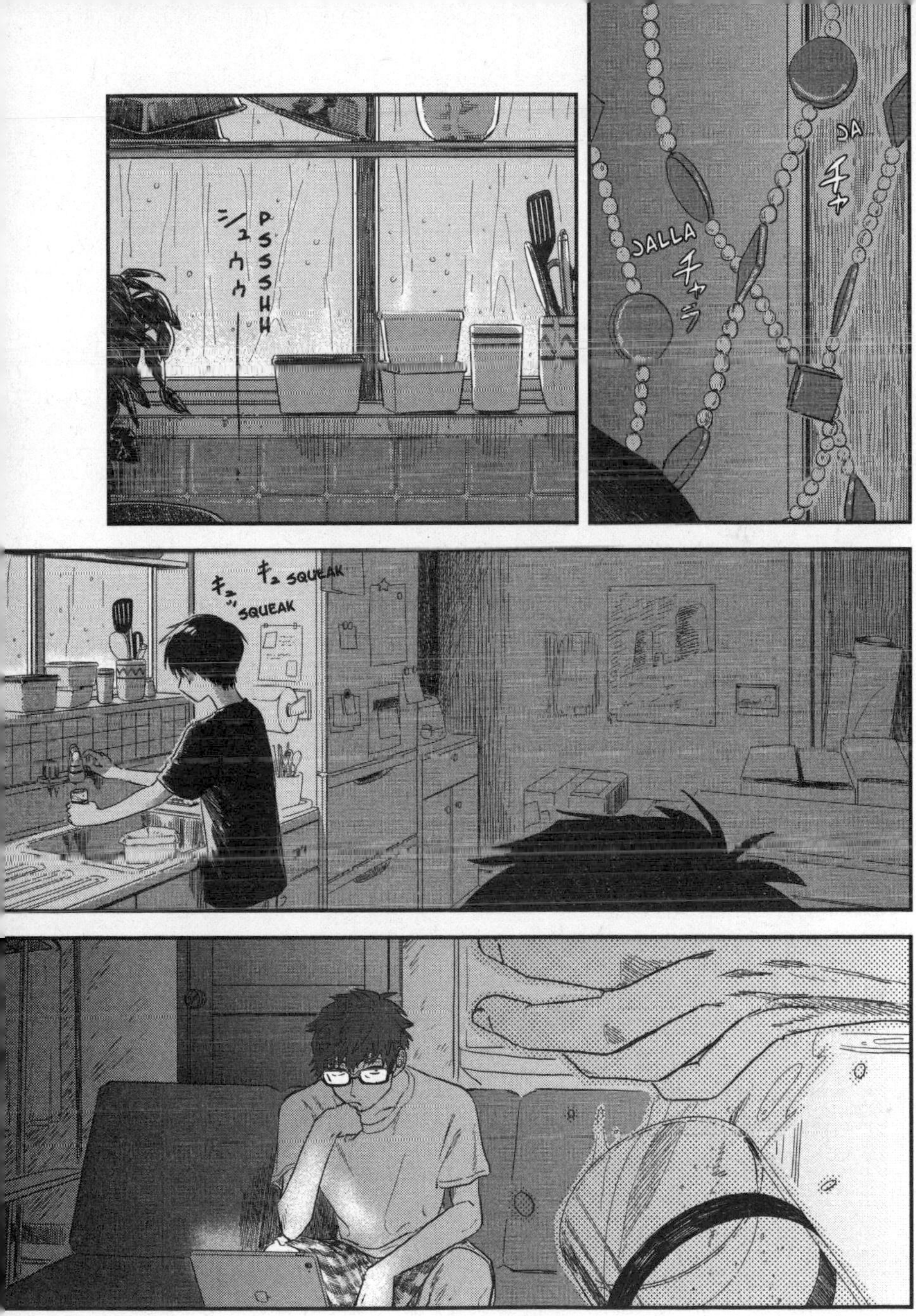
DA
チャ
JALLA
チャラ
シュウウ
PSSSHH
キュ
SQUEAK
キュ
SQUEAK

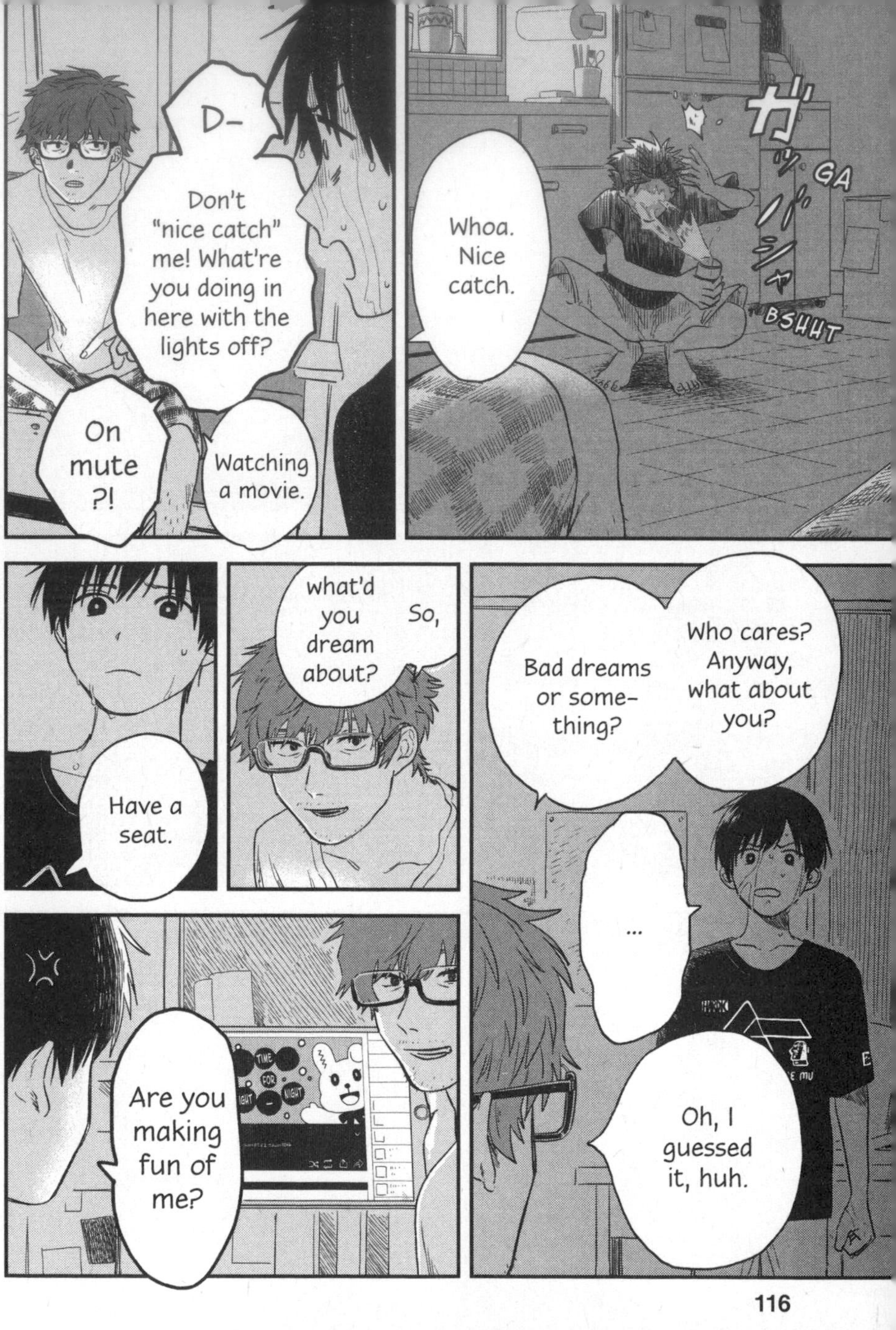
ガッ GA
シャ BSHHT
Whoa. Nice catch.
D–
Don't "nice catch" me! What're you doing in here with the lights off?
Watching a movie.
On mute ?!
Bad dreams or some-thing?
Who cares? Anyway, what about you?
...
Oh, I guessed it, huh.
So, what'd you dream about?
Have a seat.
Are you making fun of me?

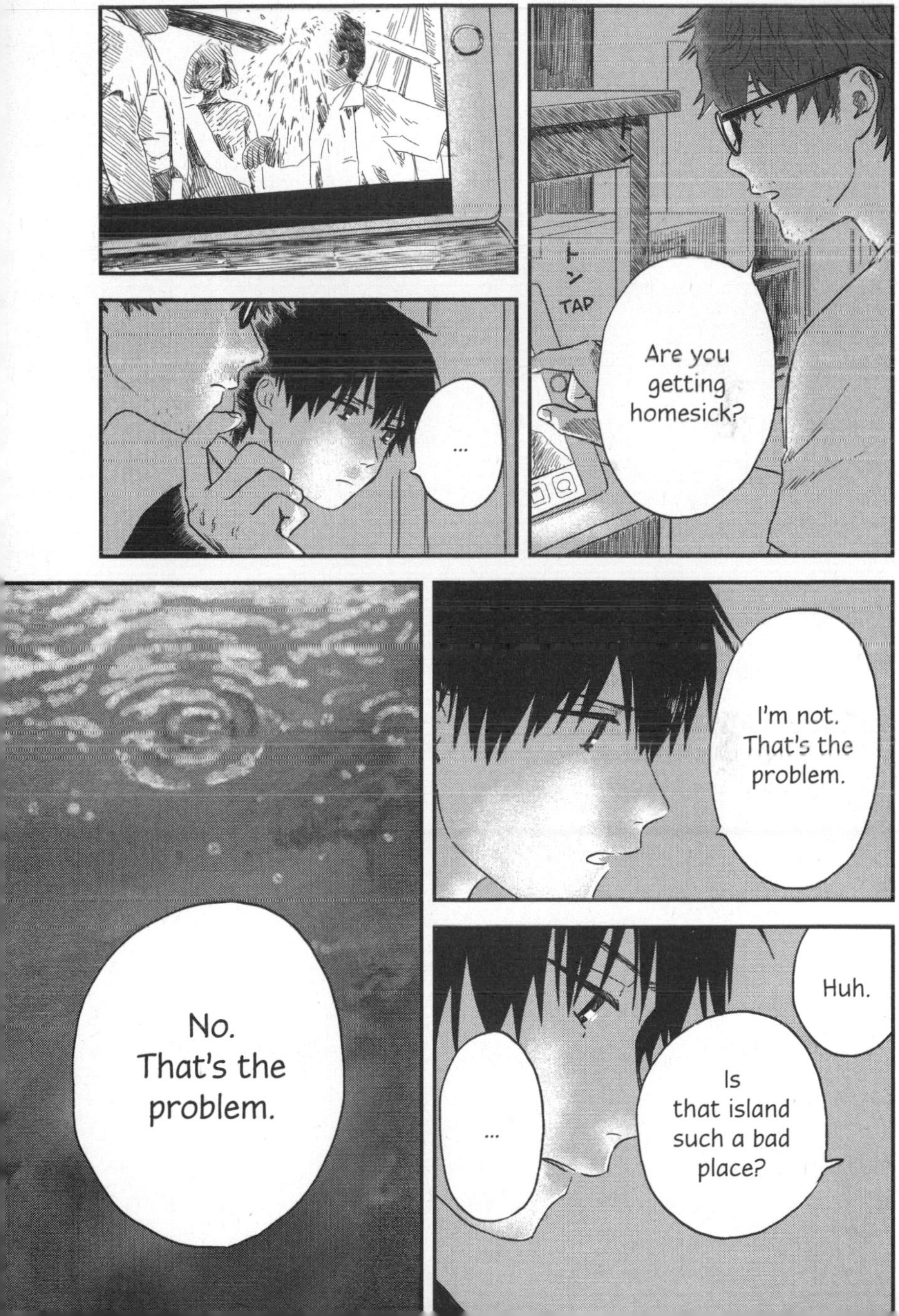

TAP
Are you getting homesick?
...
I'm not. That's the problem.
Huh.
Is that island such a bad place?
...
No. That's the problem.

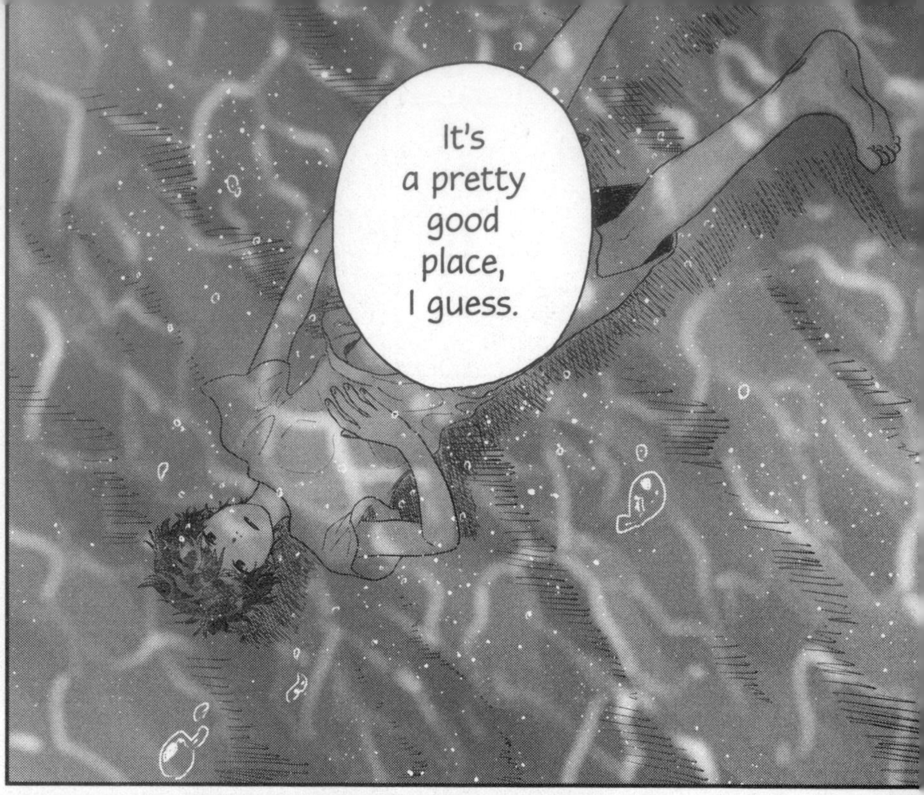
It's a pretty good place, I guess.
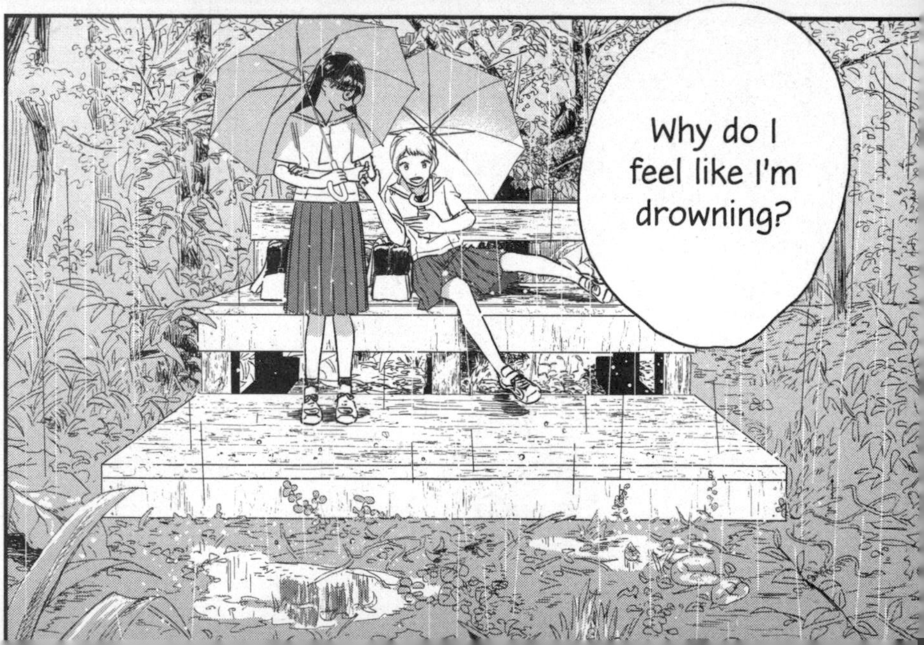
Why do I feel like I'm drowning?

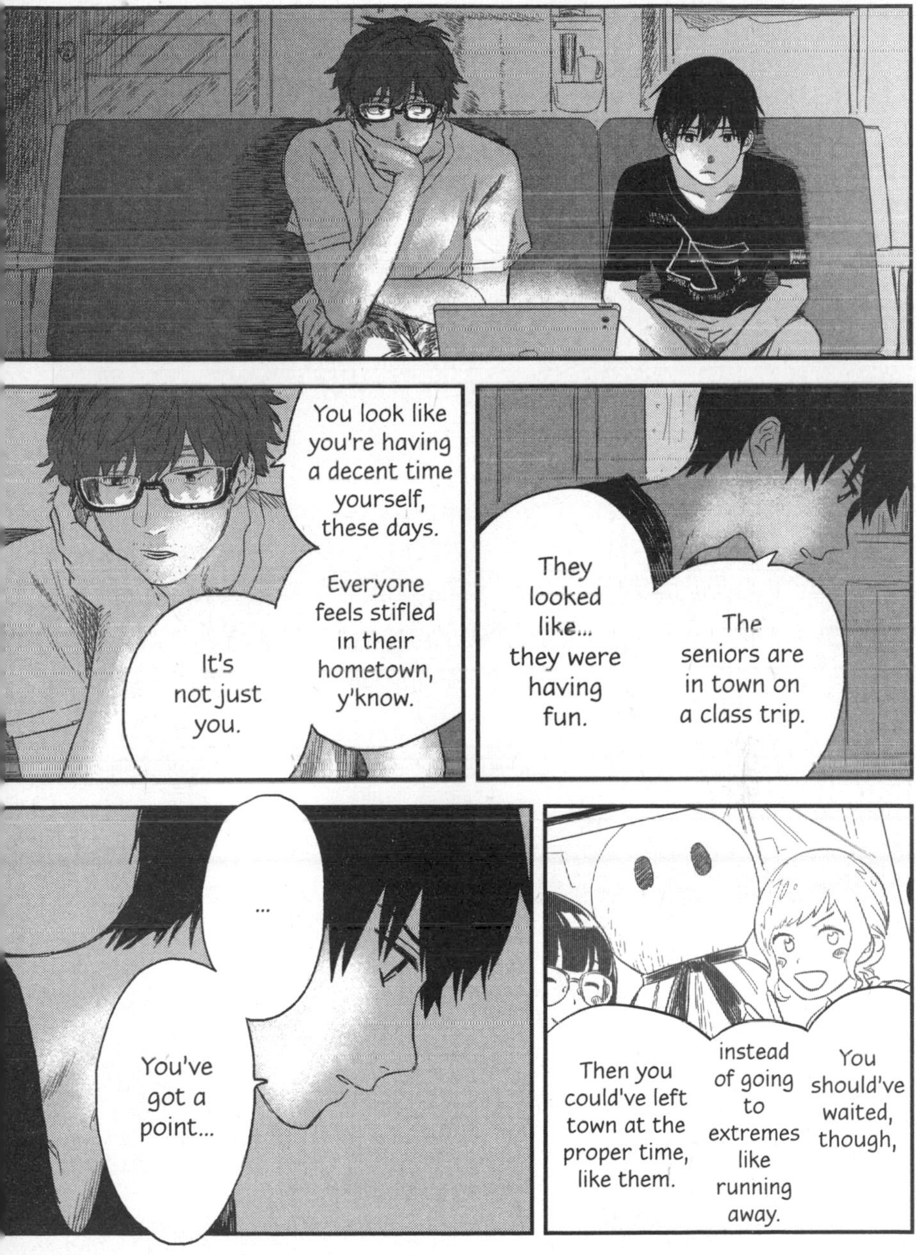
The seniors are in town on a class trip.
They looked like... they were having fun.
You look like you're having a decent time yourself, these days.
Everyone feels stifled in their hometown, y'know.
It's not just you.
You should've waited, though,
instead of going to extremes like running away.
Then you could've left town at the proper time, like them.
...
You've got a point...

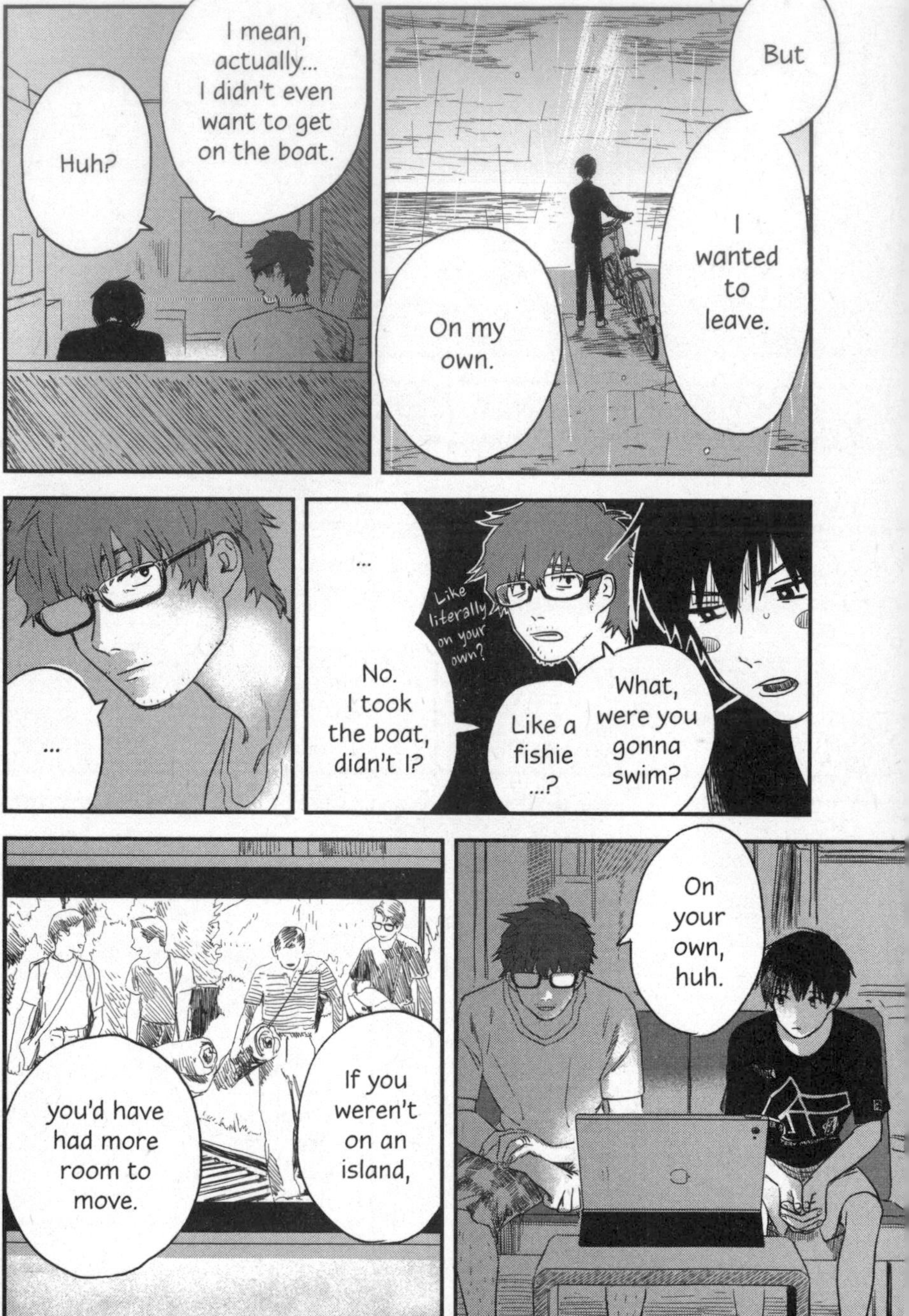
But
I wanted to leave.
On my own.
I mean, actually... I didn't even want to get on the boat.
Huh?
...
Like literally on your own?
What, were you gonna swim?
Like a fishie ...?
No. I took the boat, didn't I?
...
On your own, huh.
If you weren't on an island,
you'd have had more room to move.

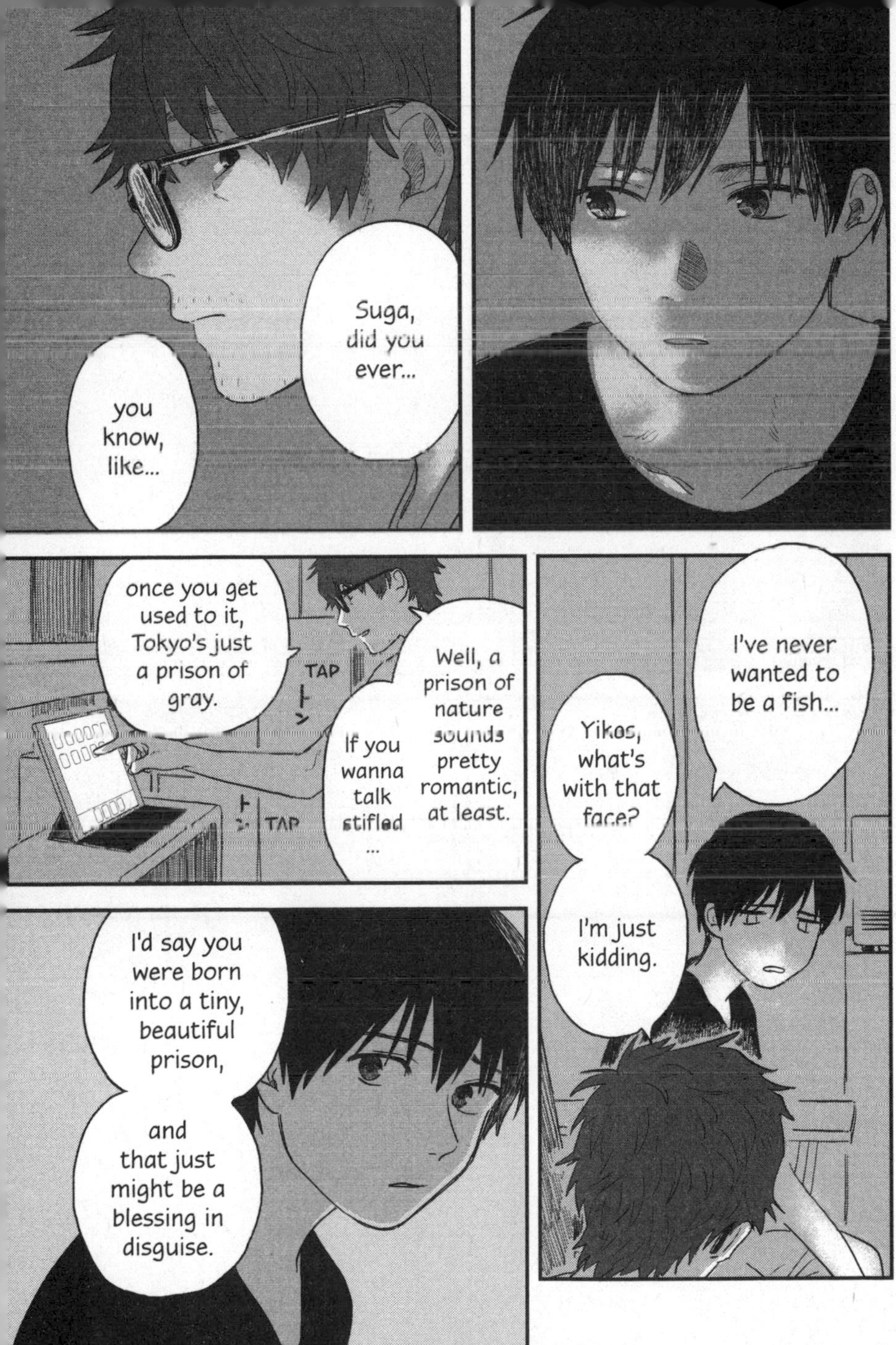
Suga, did you ever...
you know, like...
I've never wanted to be a fish...
Yikos, what's with that face?
I'm just kidding.
once you get used to it, Tokyo's just a prison of gray.
TAP
TAP
Well, a prison of nature sounds pretty romantic, at least.
If you wanna talk stifled ...
I'd say you were born into a tiny, beautiful prison,
and that just might be a blessing in disguise.

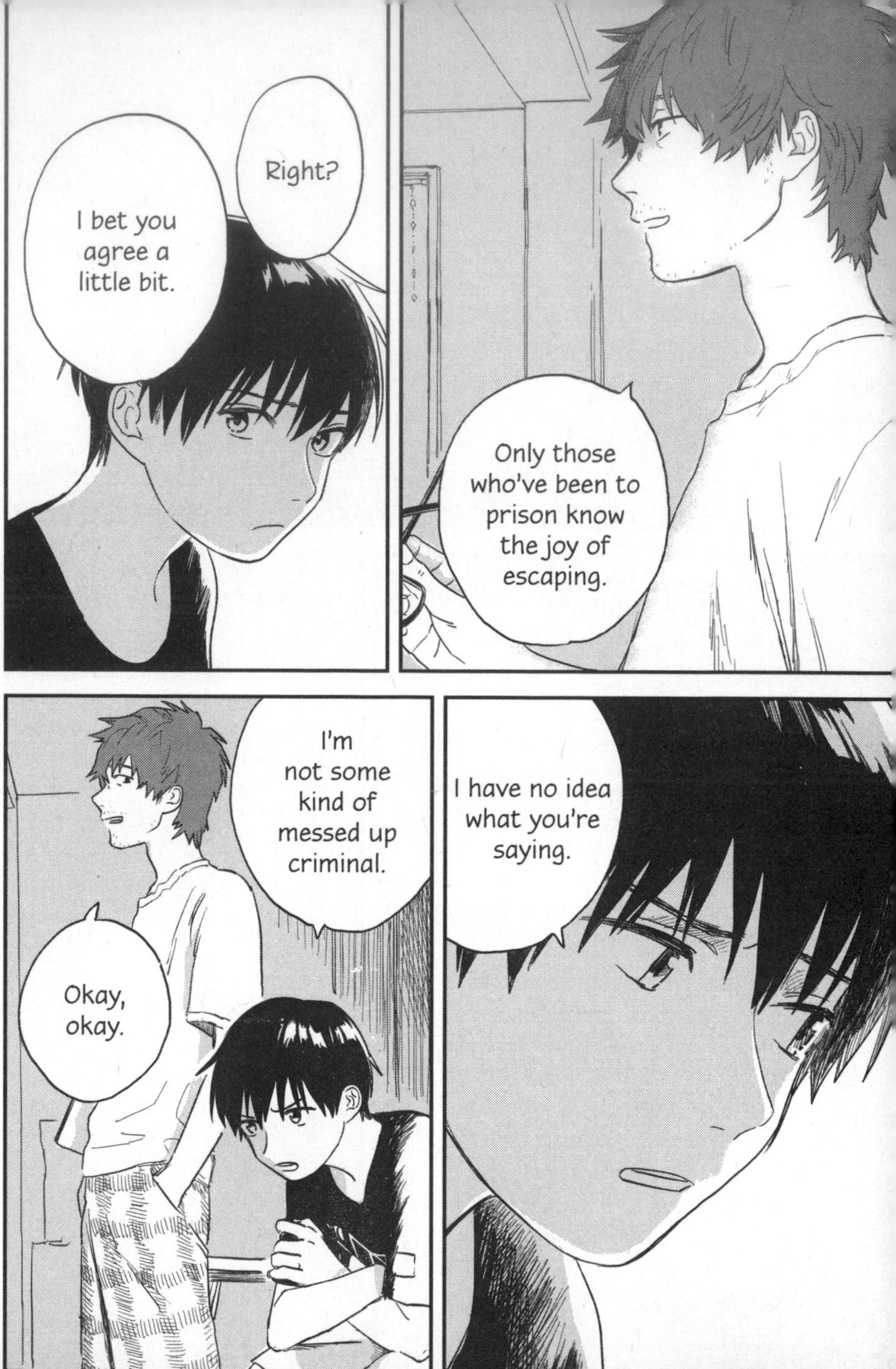
Only those who've been to prison know the joy of escaping.
Right?
I bet you agree a little bit.
I have no idea what you're saying.
I'm not some kind of messed up criminal.
Okay, okay.

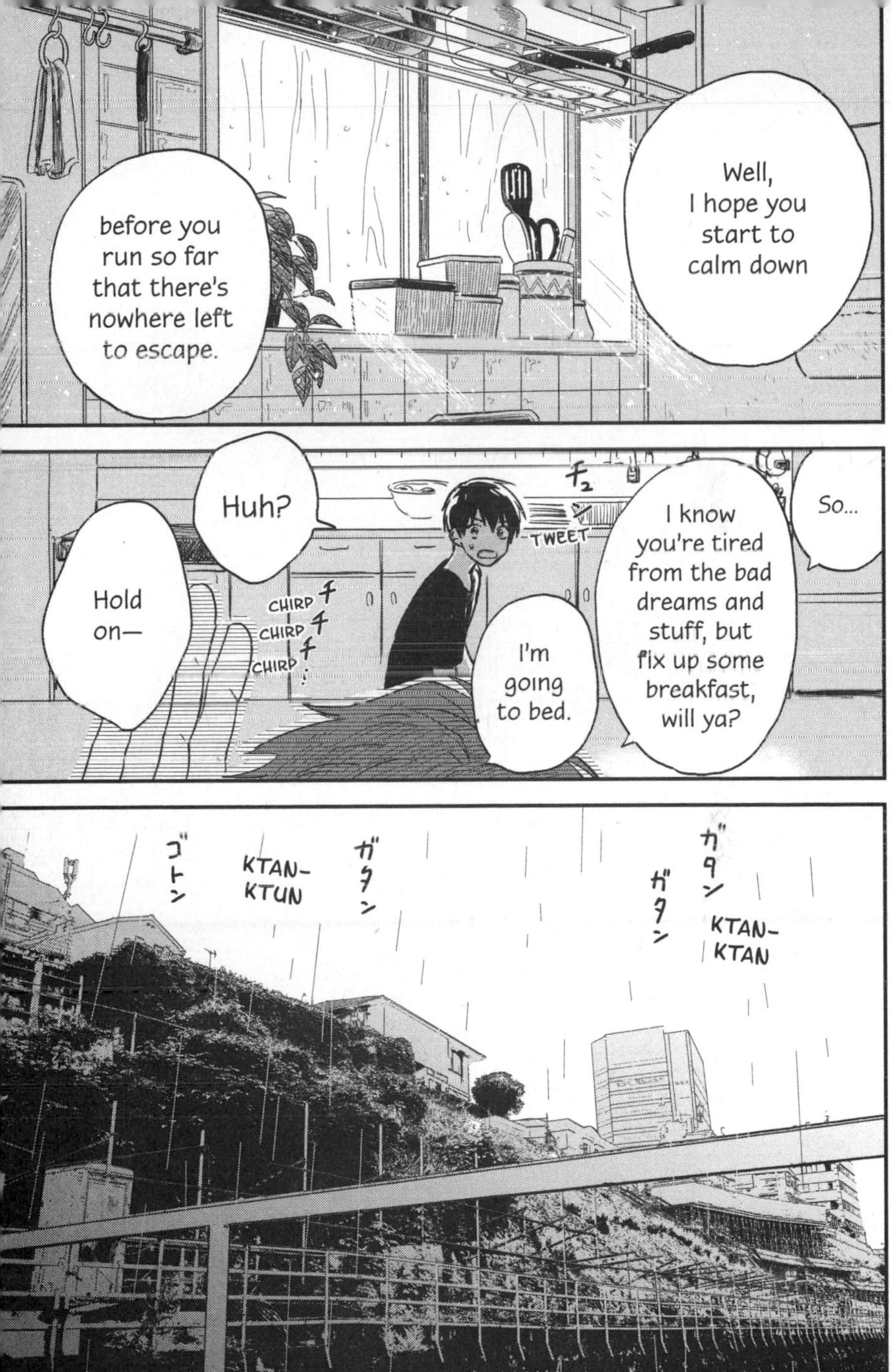
Well, I hope you start to calm down
before you run so far that there's nowhere left to escape.
So...
I know you're tired from the bad dreams and stuff, but fix up some breakfast, will ya?
チュン
TWEET
I'm going to bed.
Huh?
チチチ…
CHIRP CHIRP CHIRP
Hold on—
ガタン ガタン
KTAN-KTAN
ガタン
ゴトン
KTAN-KTUN

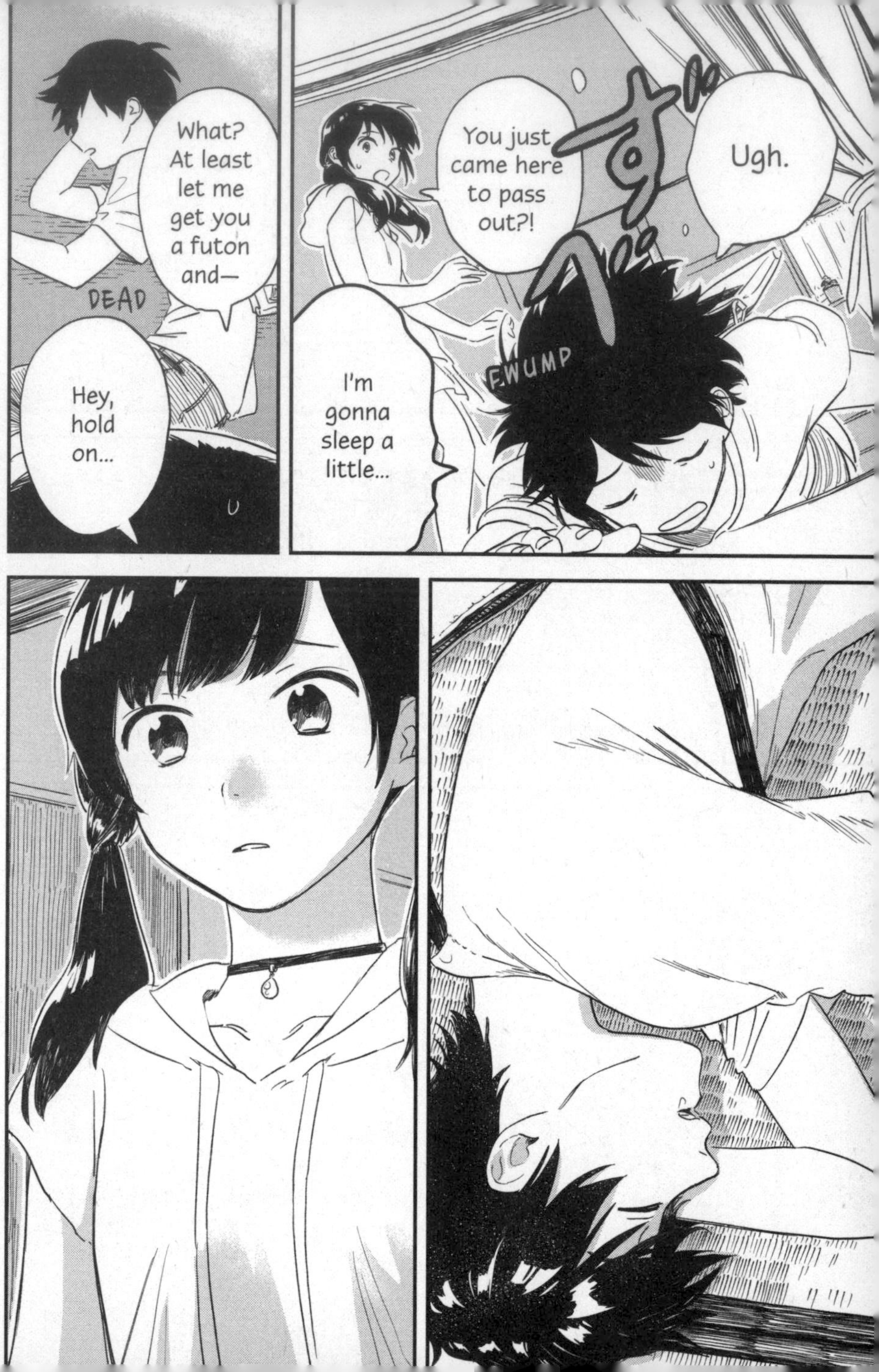
Ugh.
You just came here to pass out?!
FWUMP
I'm gonna sleep a little...
What? At least let me get you a futon and—
DEAD
Hey, hold on...

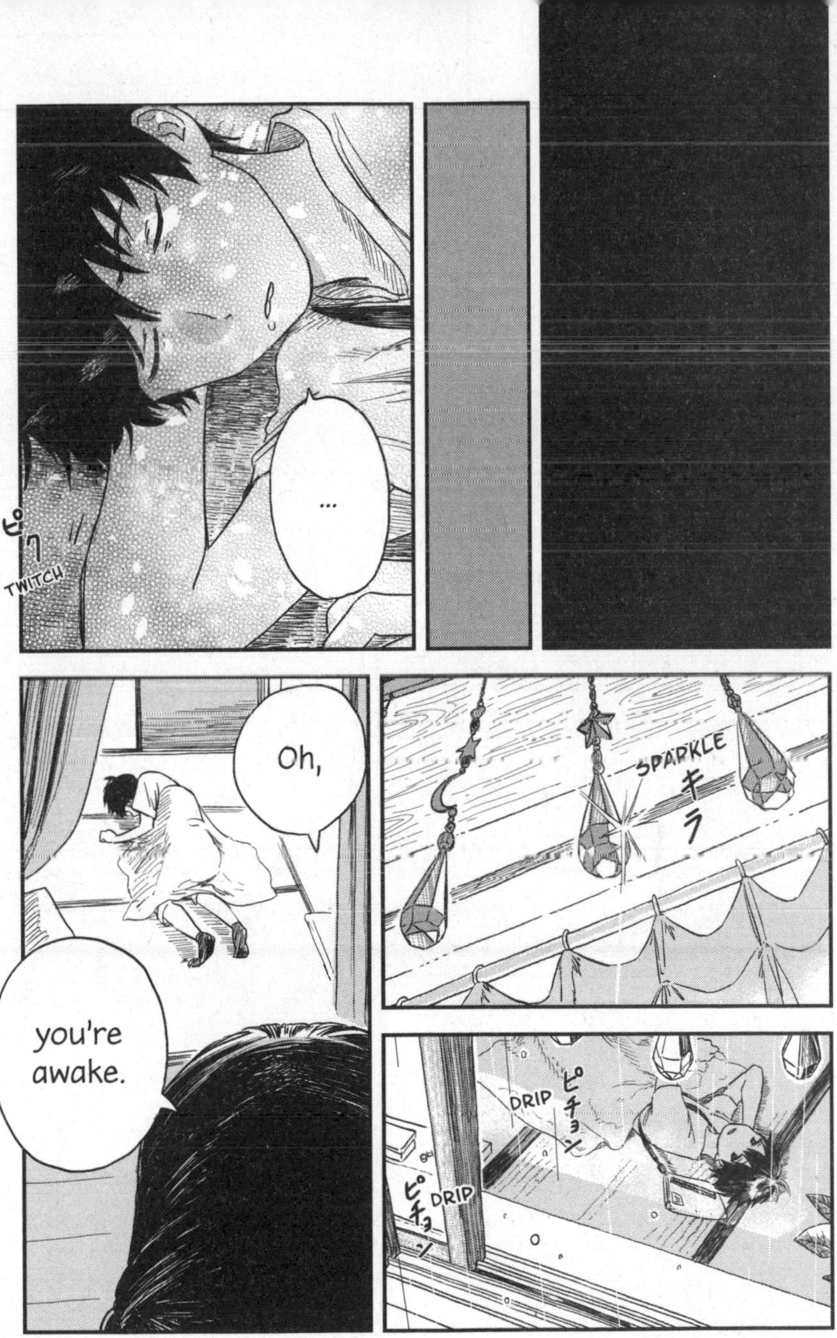
...
ピク
TWITCH
SPARKLE
キラ
DRIP
ピチョン
DRIP
ピチョン
Oh,
you're awake.

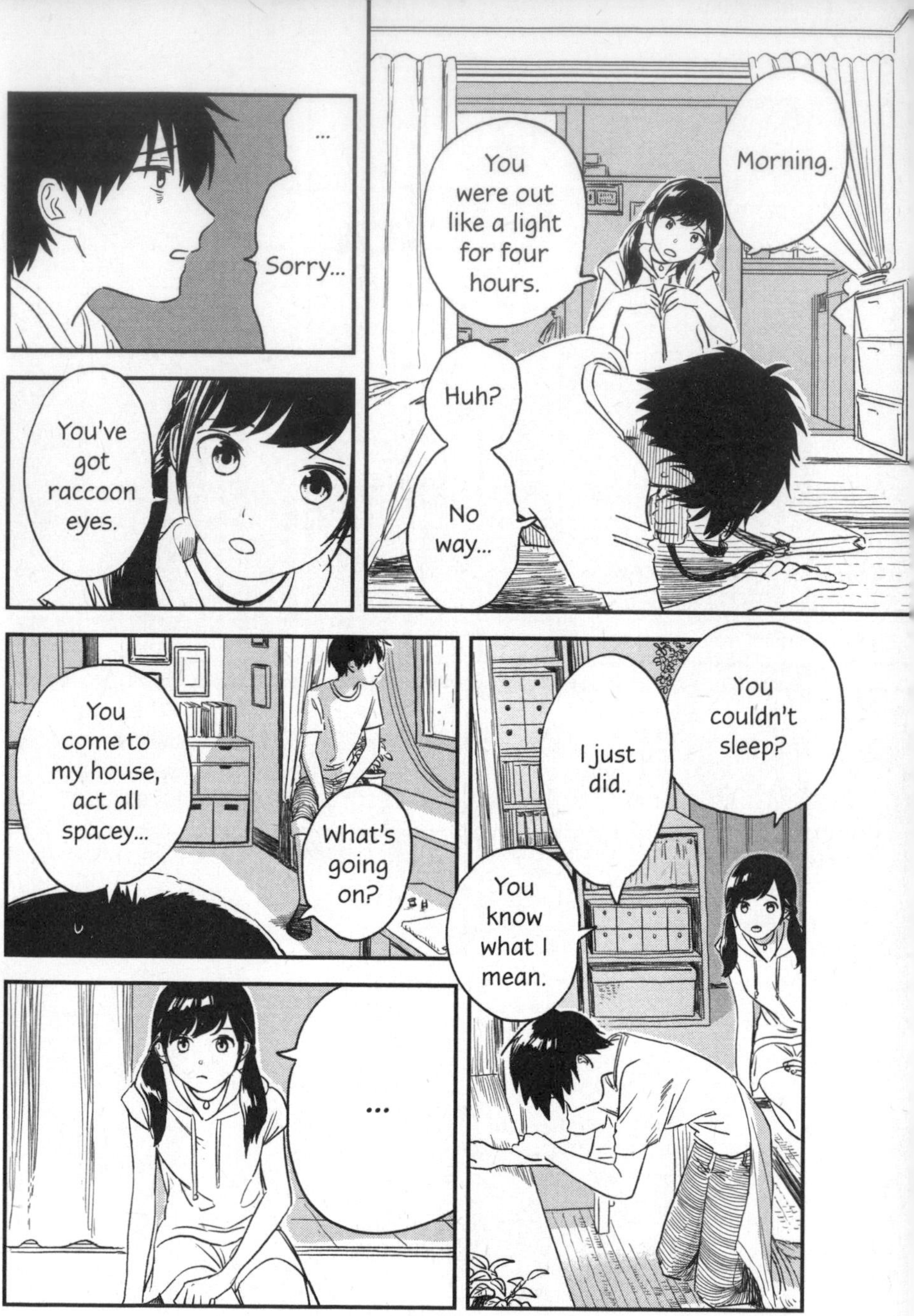

Morning.
You were out like a light for four hours.
Huh?
No way...
...
Sorry...
You've got raccoon eyes.
You couldn't sleep?
I just did.
You know what I mean.
You come to my house, act all spacey...
What's going on?
...

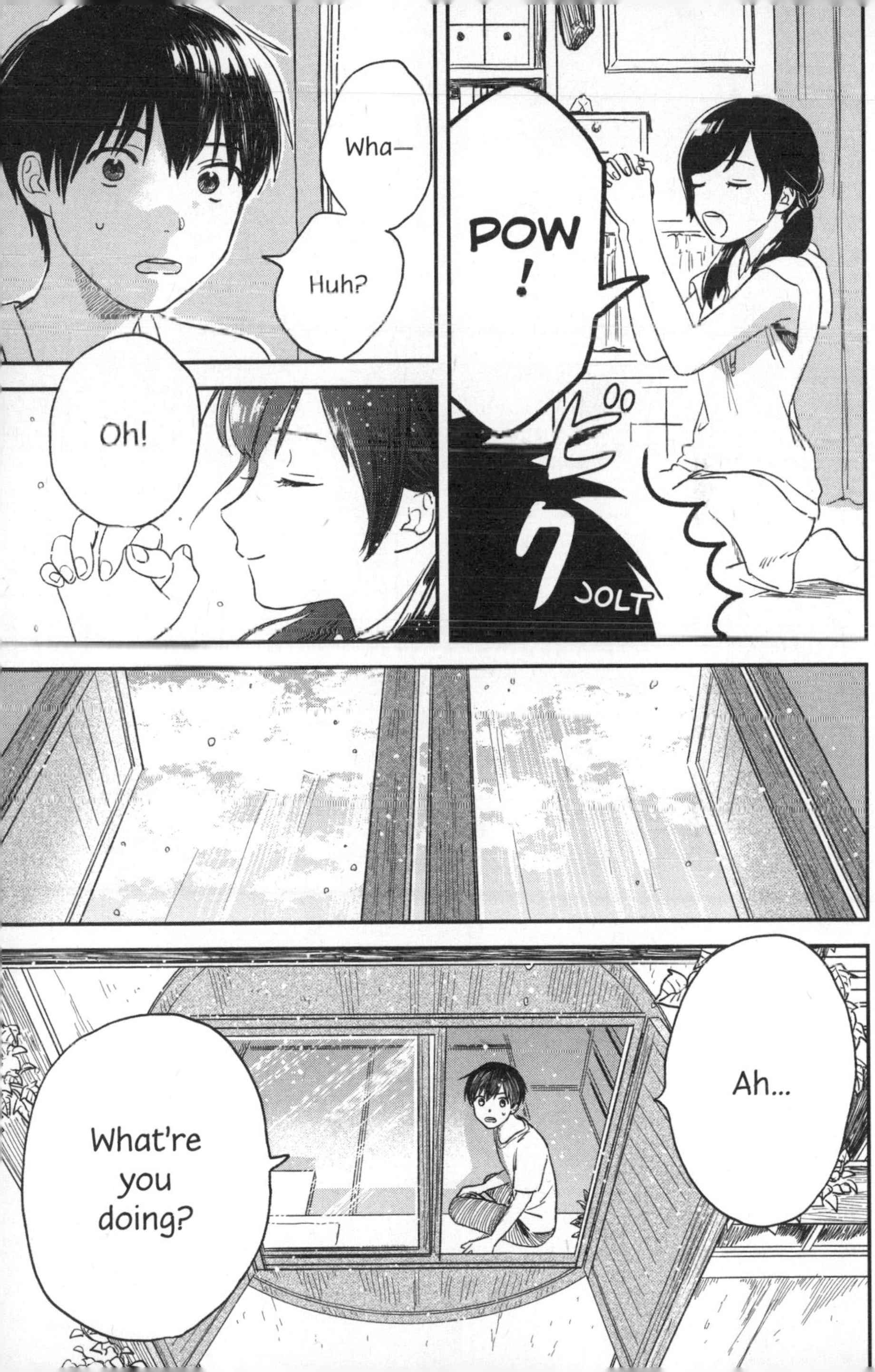
POW!
ビク
JOLT
Wha—
Huh?
Oh!
Ah...
What're you doing?

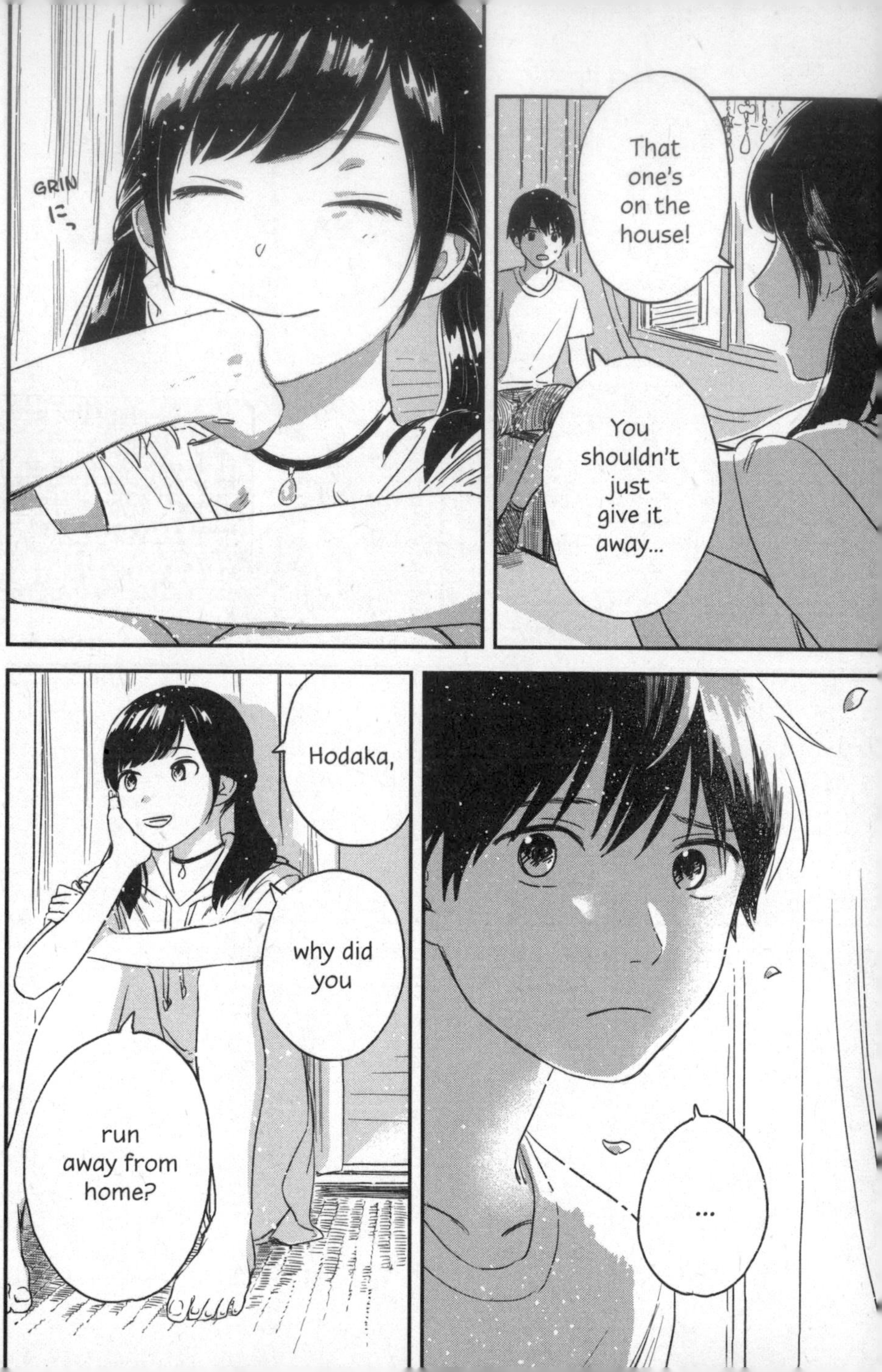
That one's on the house!
You shouldn't just give it away...
GRIN
に、
Hodaka,
why did you
run away from home?
...

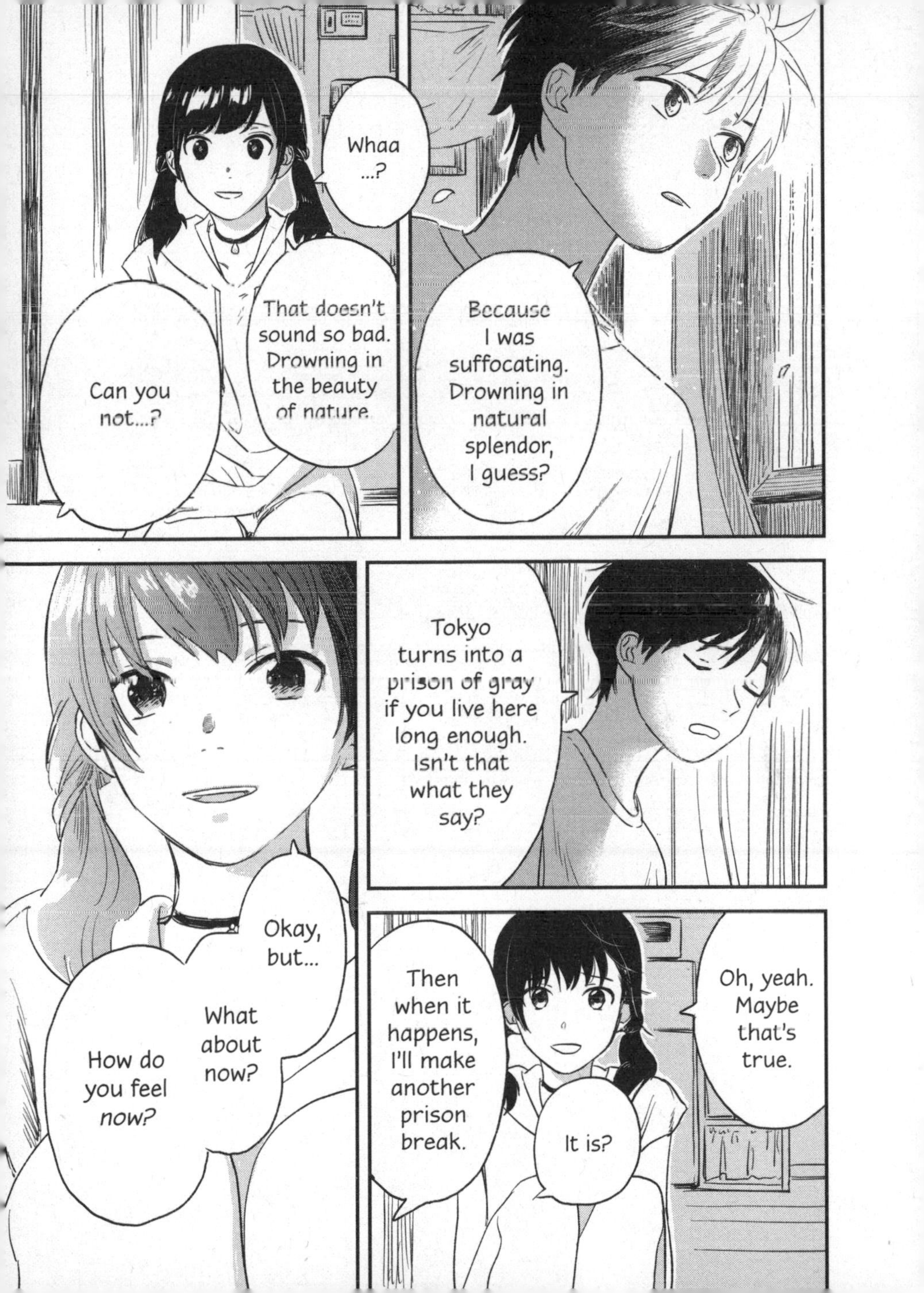
Because I was suffocating. Drowning in natural splendor, I guess?
Whaa ...?
That doesn't sound so bad. Drowning in the beauty of nature.
Can you not...?
Tokyo turns into a prison of gray if you live here long enough. Isn't that what they say?
Oh, yeah. Maybe that's true.
It is?
Then when it happens, I'll make another prison break.
Okay, but...
What about now?
How do you feel *now?*

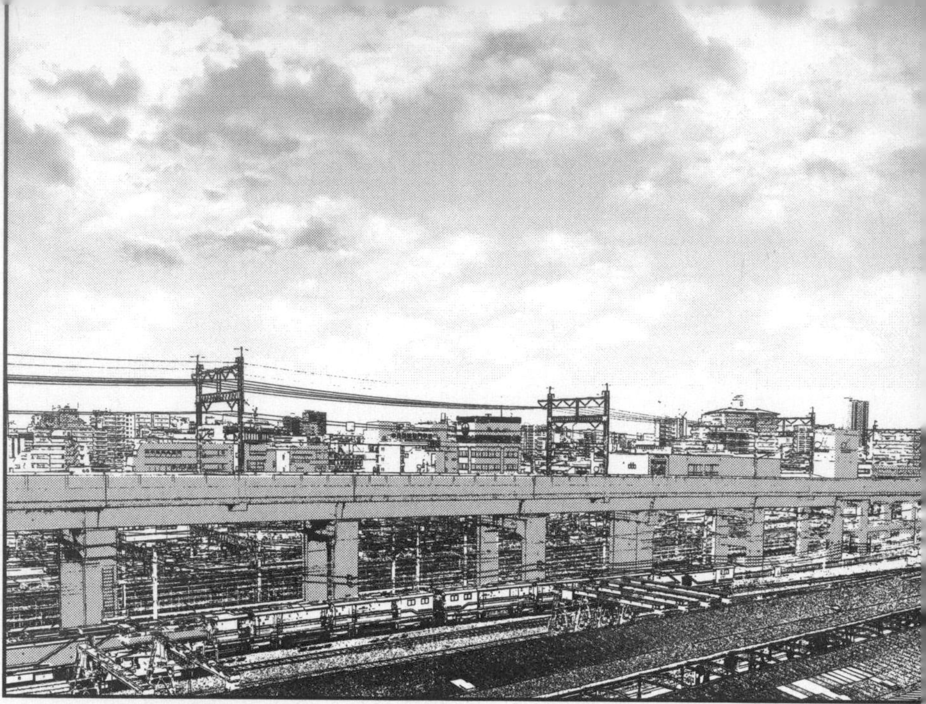
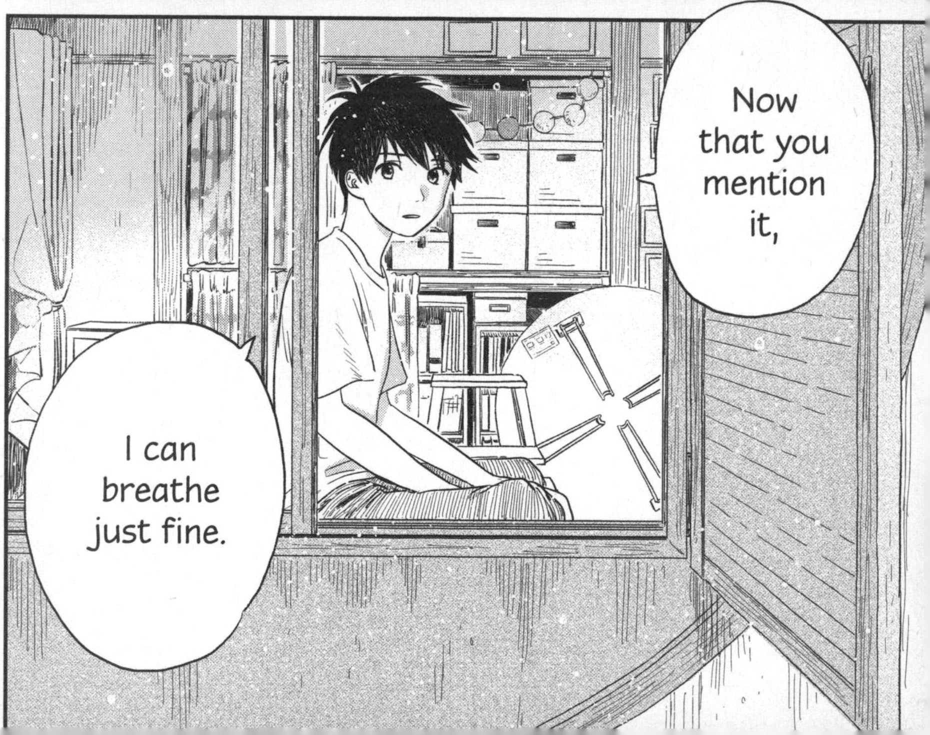
Now that you mention it,
I can breathe just fine.

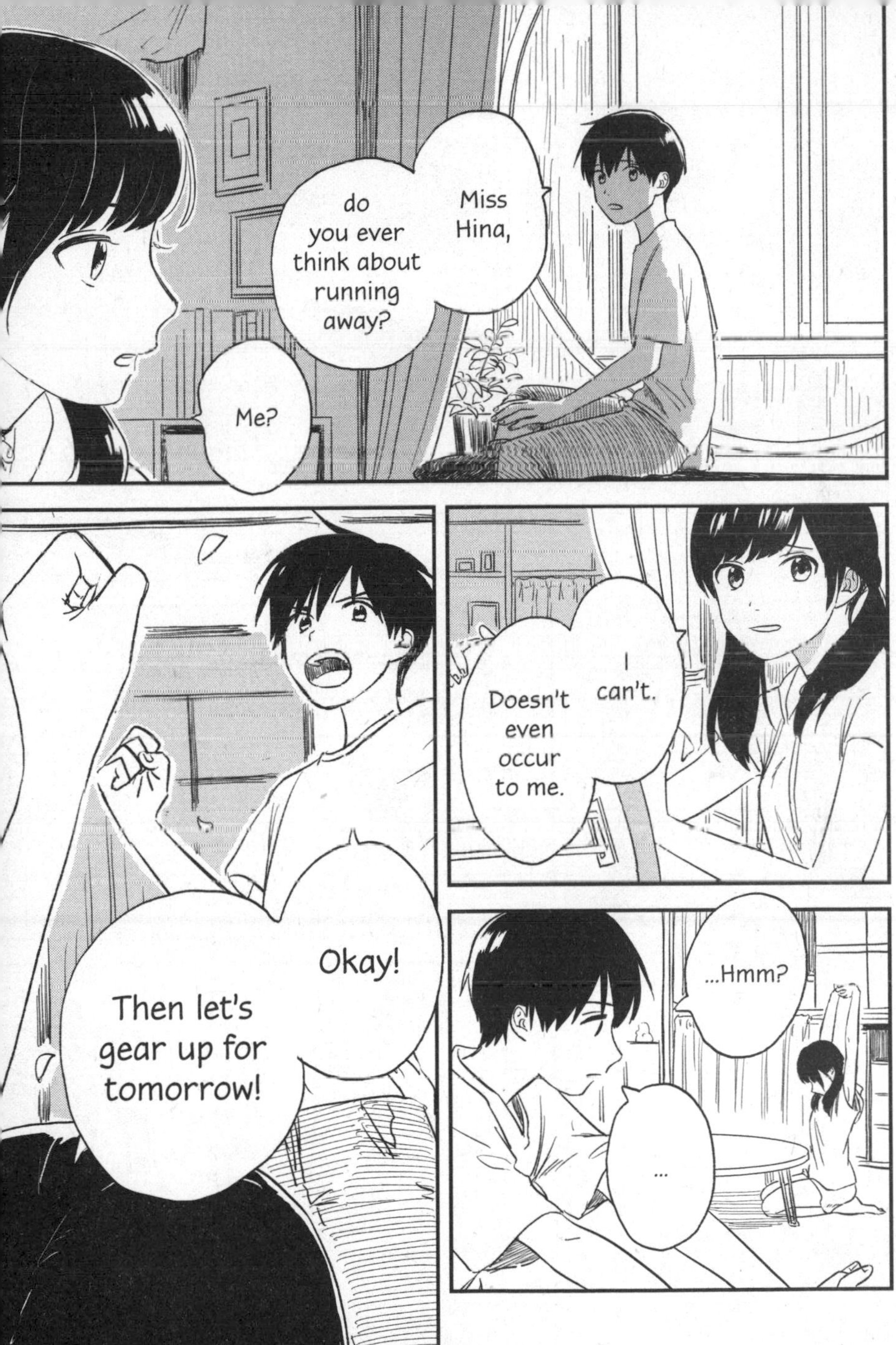
Miss Hina,
do you ever think about running away?
Me?
I can't.
Doesn't even occur to me.
...Hmm?
...
Okay!
Then let's gear up for tomorrow!

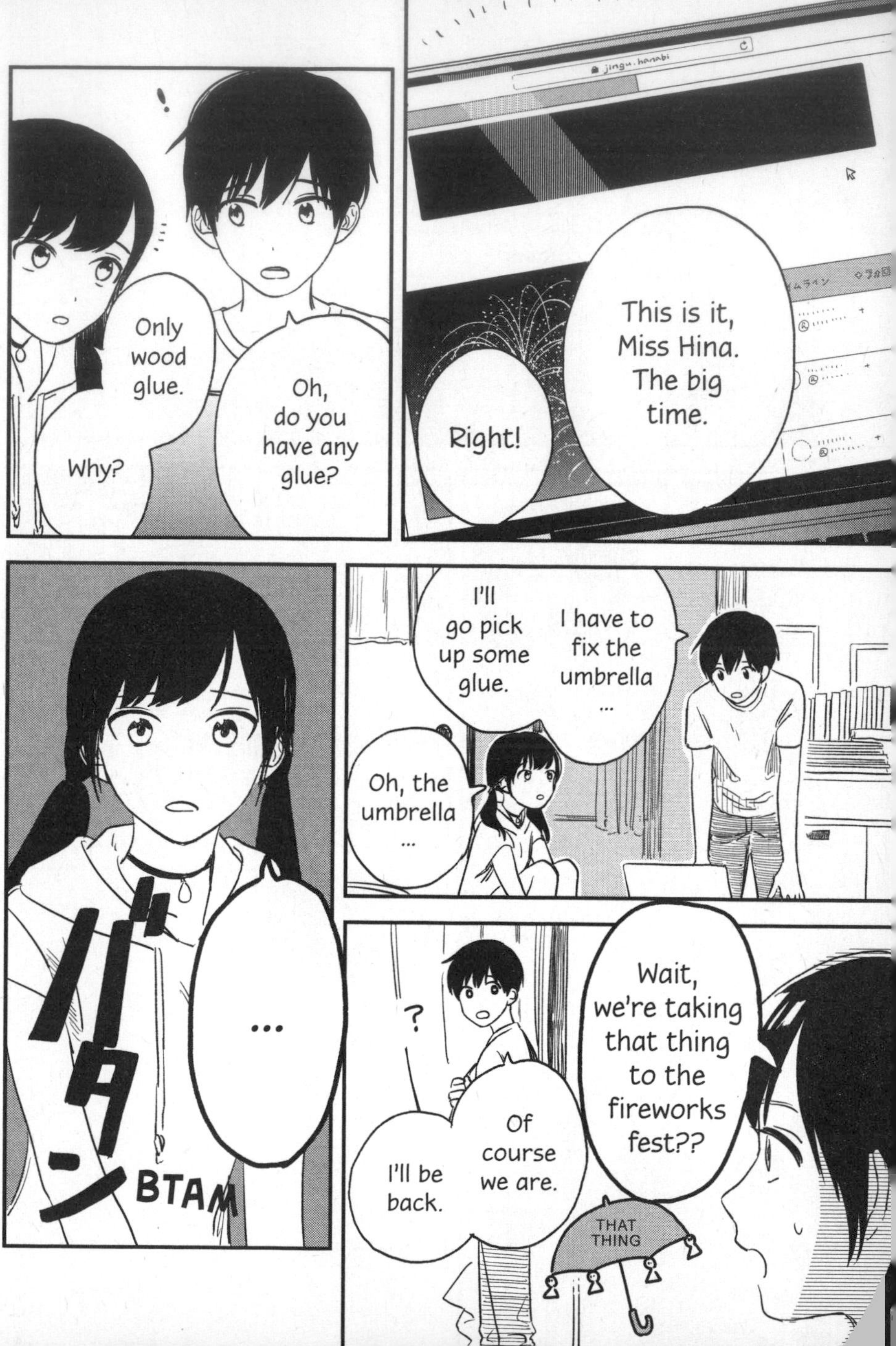

jingu.hanabi
This is it, Miss Hina. The big time.
Right!
!
Oh, do you have any glue?
Only wood glue.
Why?
I have to fix the umbrella ...
I'll go pick up some glue.
Oh, the umbrella ...
Wait, we're taking that thing to the fireworks fest??
?
Of course we are.
I'll be back.
THAT THING
...
バタン
BTAM

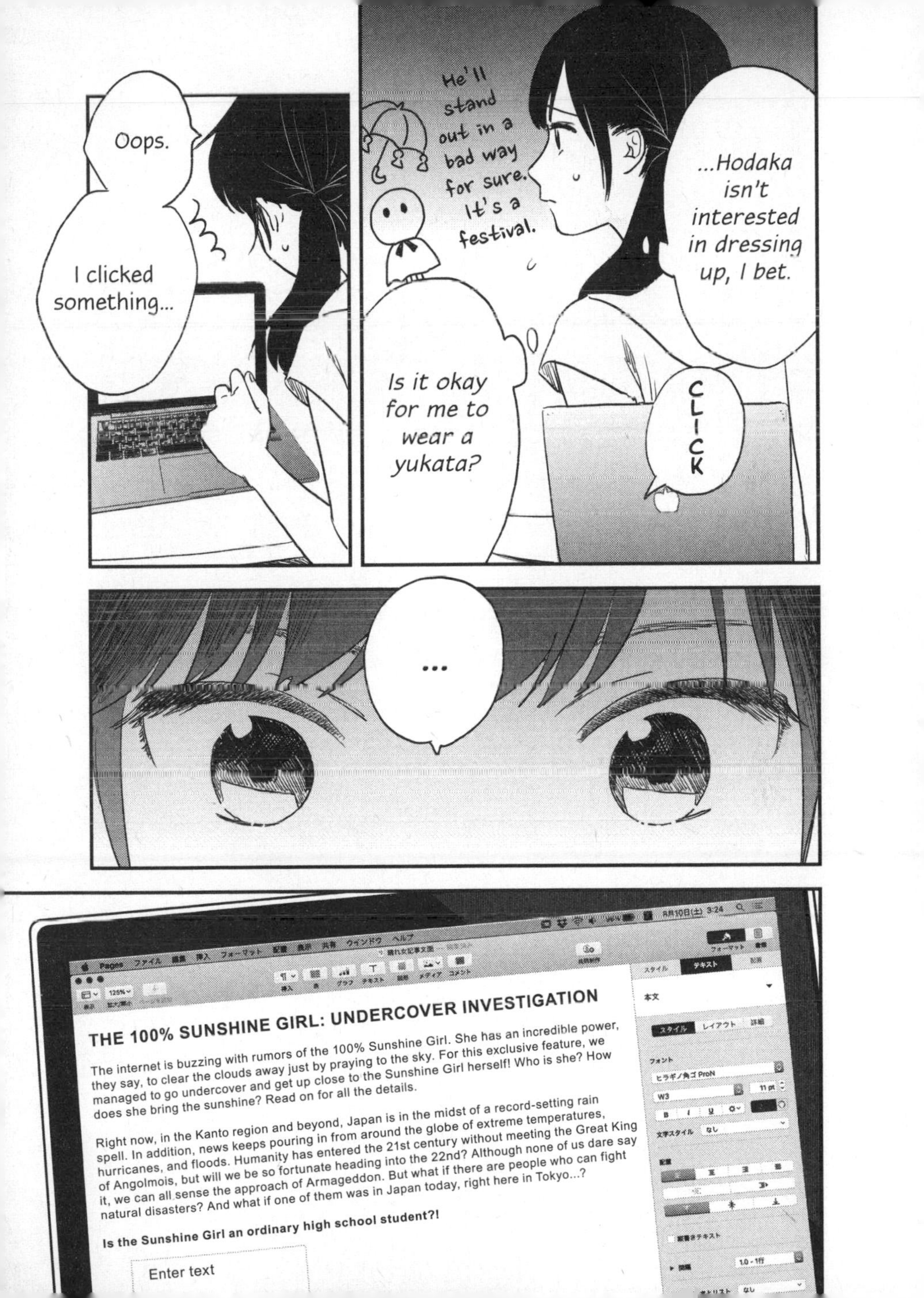
...Hodaka isn't interested in dressing up, I bet.
He'll stand out in a bad way for sure. It's a festival.
CLICK
Is it okay for me to wear a yukata?
Oops.
I clicked something...
...
THE 100% SUNSHINE GIRL: UNDERCOVER INVESTIGATION
The internet is buzzing with rumors of the 100% Sunshine Girl. She has an incredible power, they say, to clear the clouds away just by praying to the sky. For this exclusive feature, we managed to go undercover and get up close to the Sunshine Girl herself! Who is she? How does she bring the sunshine? Read on for all the details.
Right now, in the Kanto region and beyond, Japan is in the midst of a record-setting rain spell. In addition, news keeps pouring in from around the globe of extreme temperatures, hurricanes, and floods. Humanity has entered the 21st century without meeting the Great King of Angolmois, but will we be so fortunate heading into the 22nd? Although none of us dare say it, we can all sense the approach of Armageddon. But what if there are people who can fight natural disasters? And what if one of them was in Japan today, right here in Tokyo...?
Is the Sunshine Girl an ordinary high school student?!
Enter text

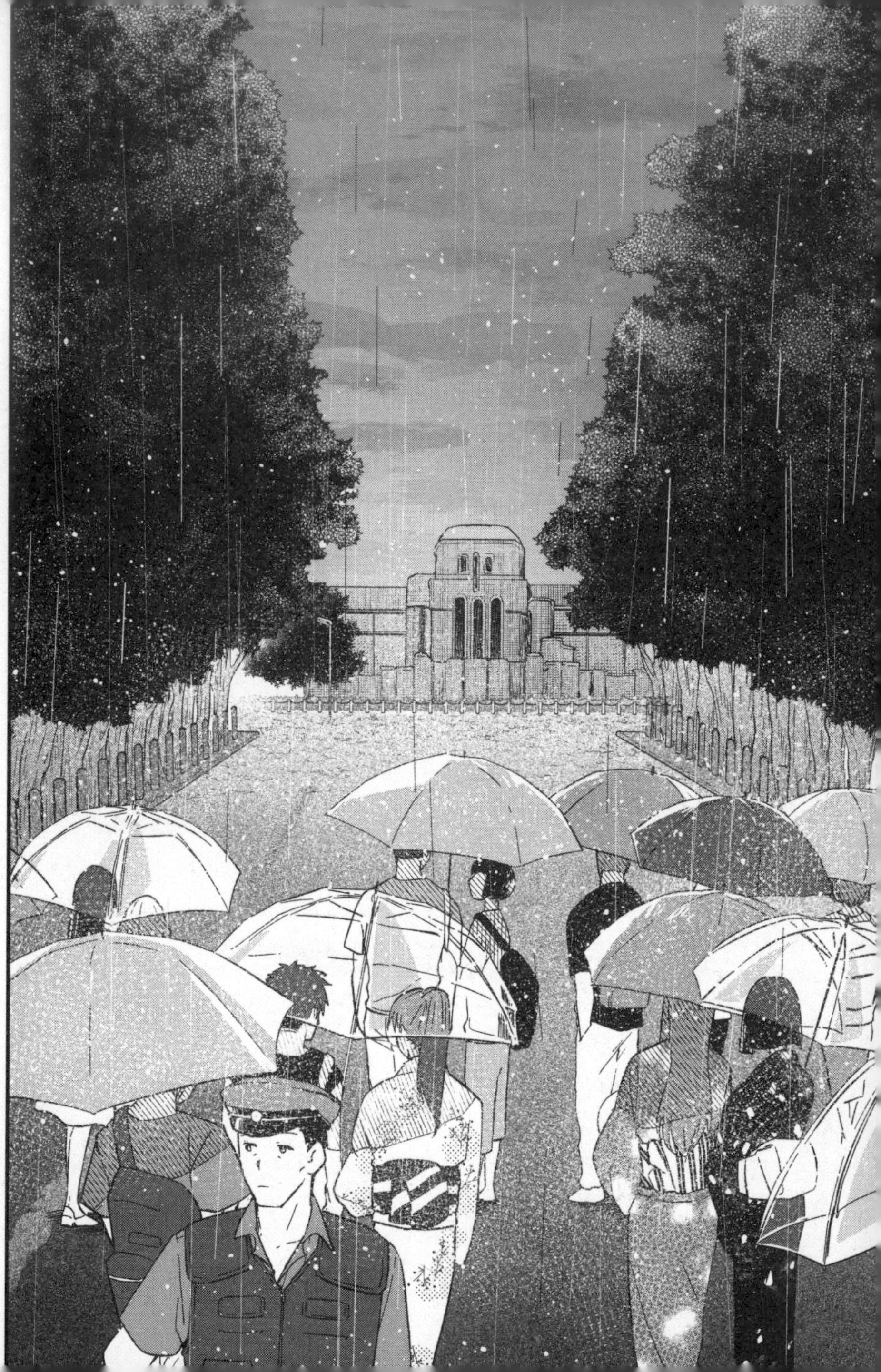

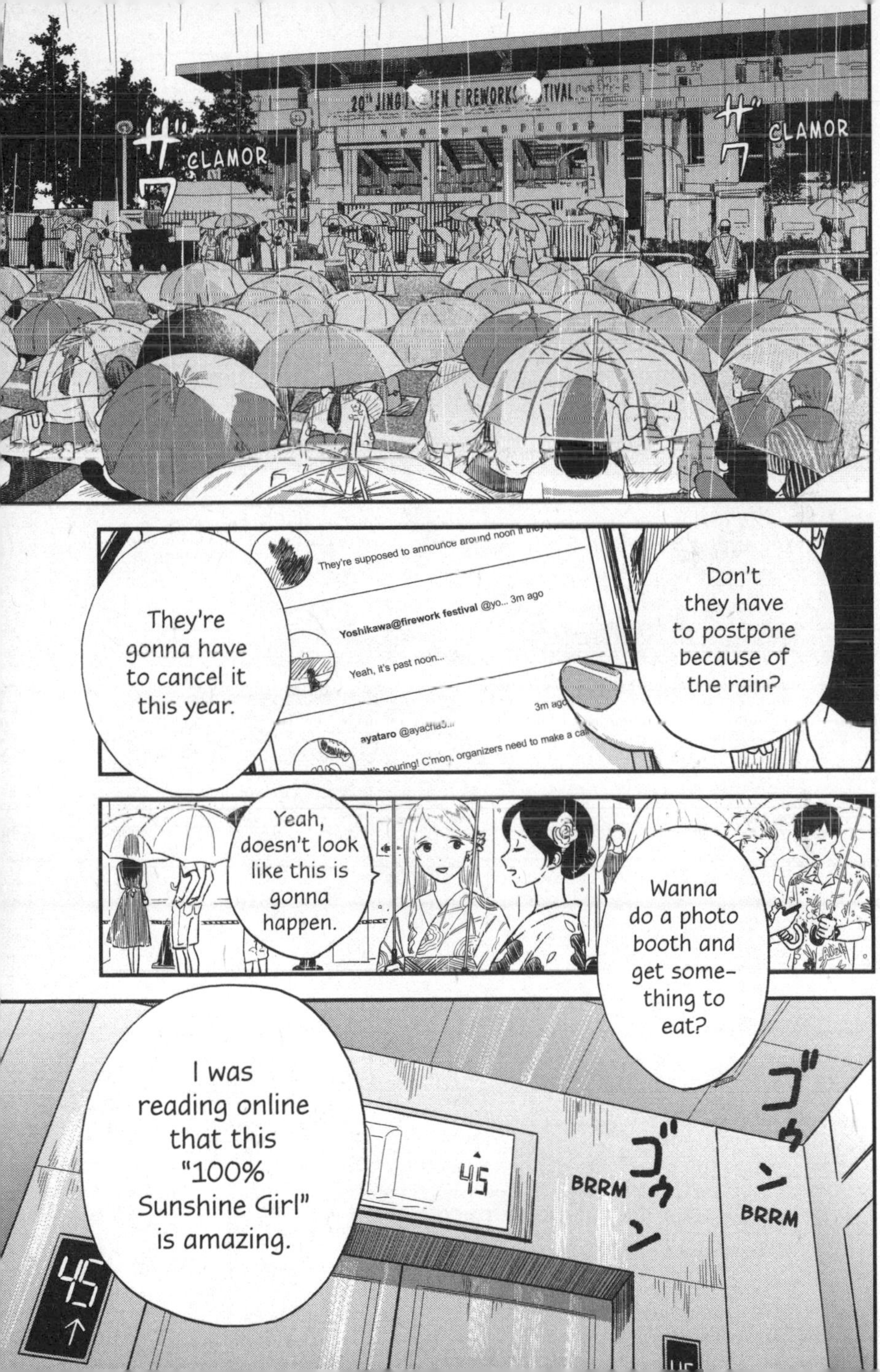
ザワ
CLAMOR
ザワ
CLAMOR
Don't they have to postpone because of the rain?
They're supposed to announce around noon if they
Yoshikawa@firework festival @yo... 3m ago
Yeah, it's past noon...
3m ago
They're gonna have to cancel it this year.
Wanna do a photo booth and get some-thing to eat?
Yeah, doesn't look like this is gonna happen.
ゴウン
BRRM
ゴウン
BRRM
45
I was reading online that this "100% Sunshine Girl" is amazing.
45

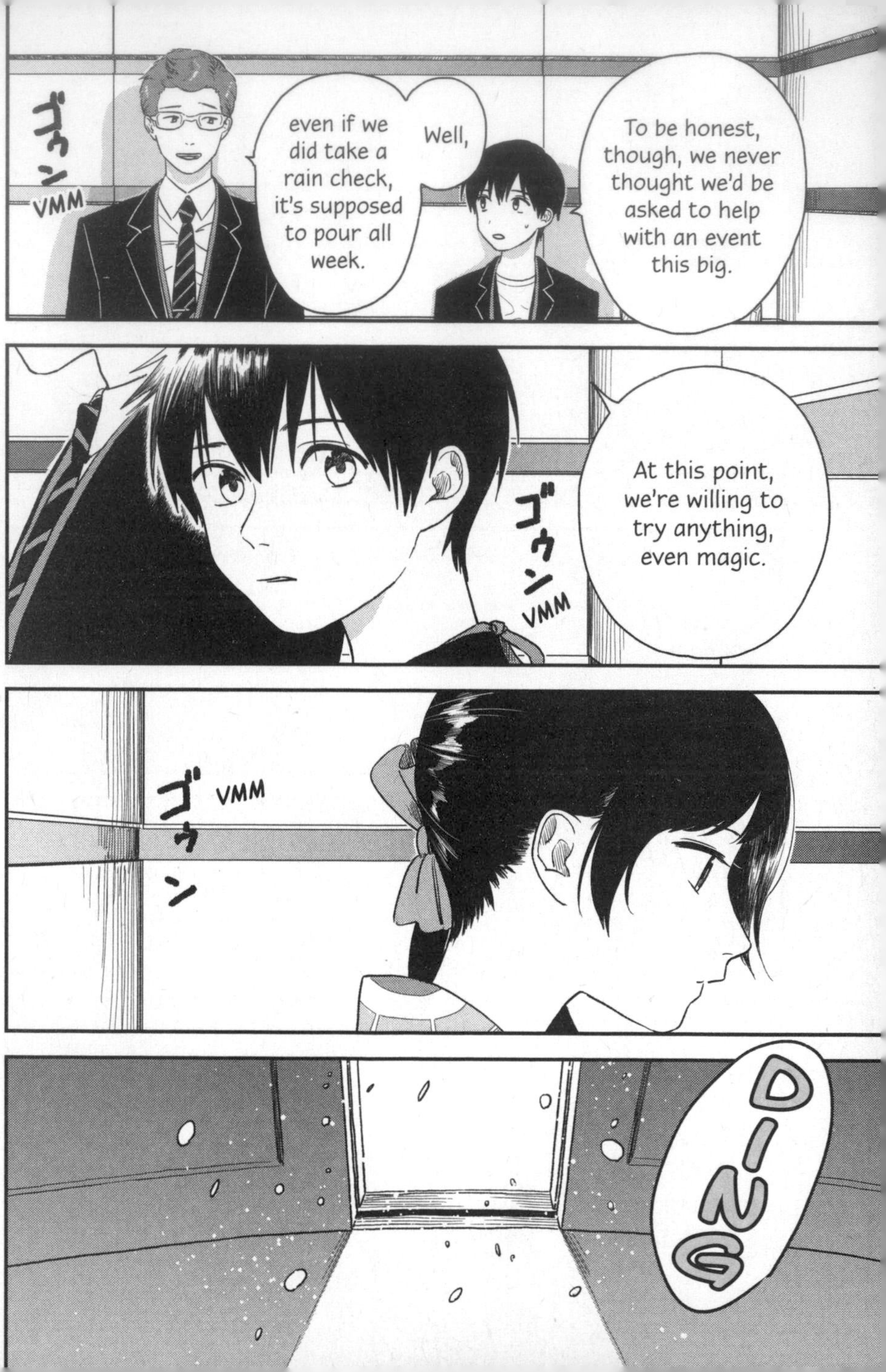
To be honest, though, we never thought we'd be asked to help with an event this big.
Well,
even if we did take a rain check, it's supposed to pour all week.
ゴウン
VMM
At this point, we're willing to try anything, even magic.
ゴウン
VMM
ゴウン
VMM
DING

Chapter 3
Rainclouds

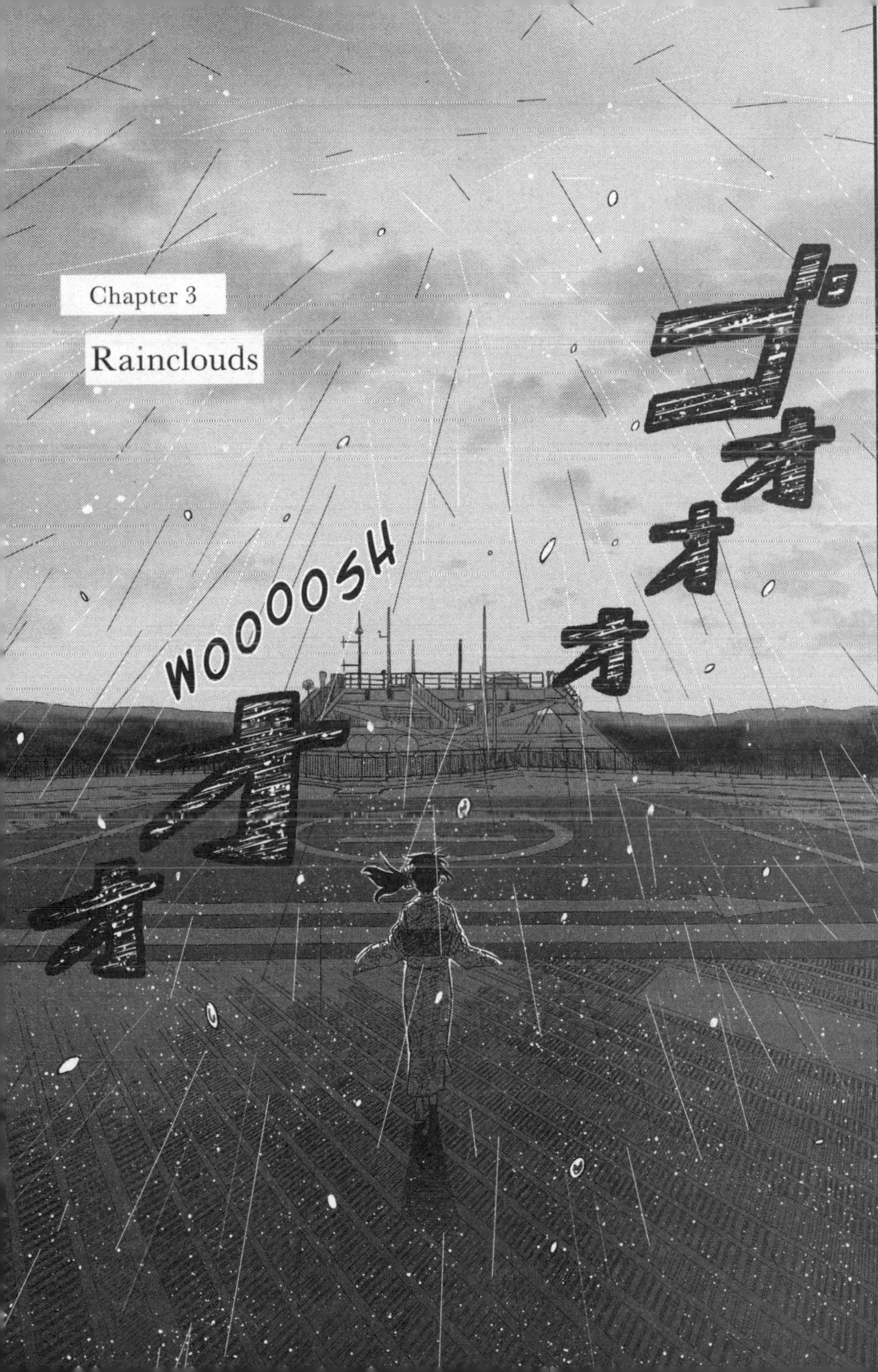
ゴオオオオオ
WOOOOSH

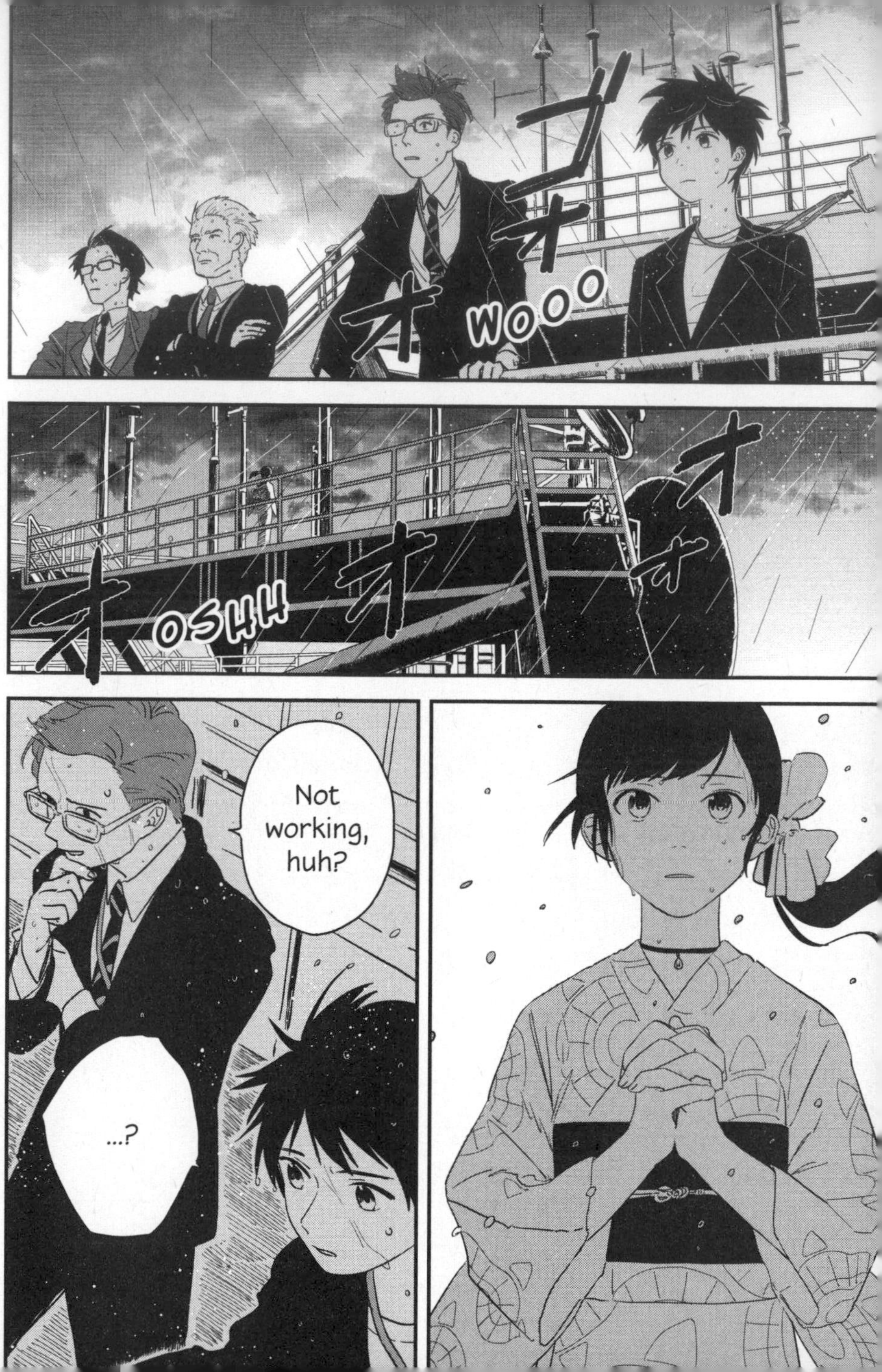
WOOO
OSHH
Not working, huh?
...?

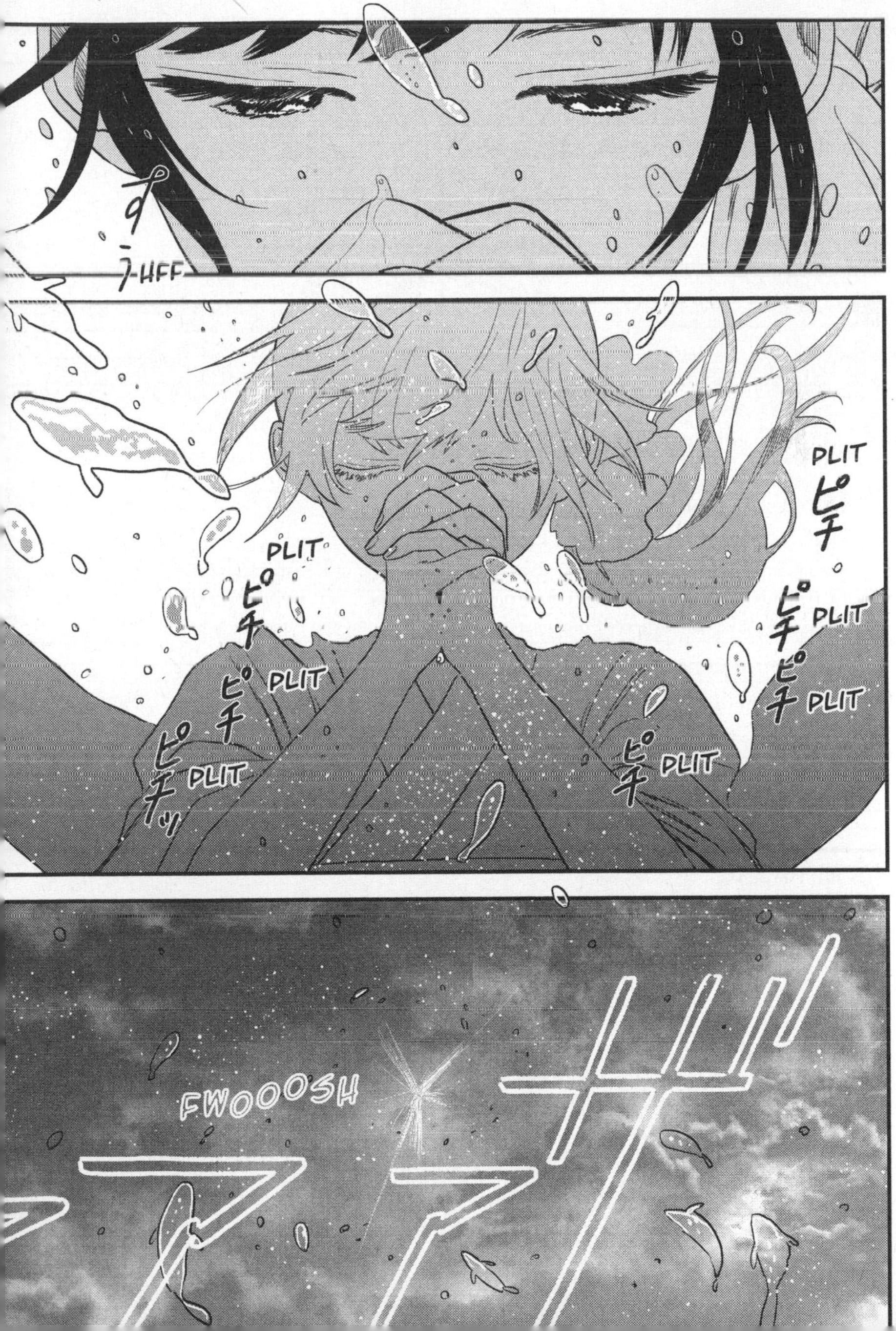
HFF
PLIT
ピチ
PLIT
ピチ
PLIT
ピチ
PLIT
ピチ
PLIT
ピチ
PLIT
ピチ
PLIT
ピチッ
FWOOOSH
ザァァ

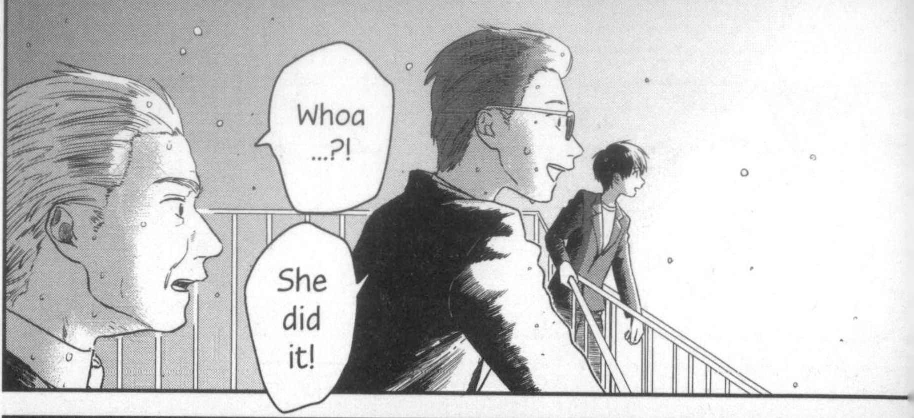
Whoa ...?!
She did it!
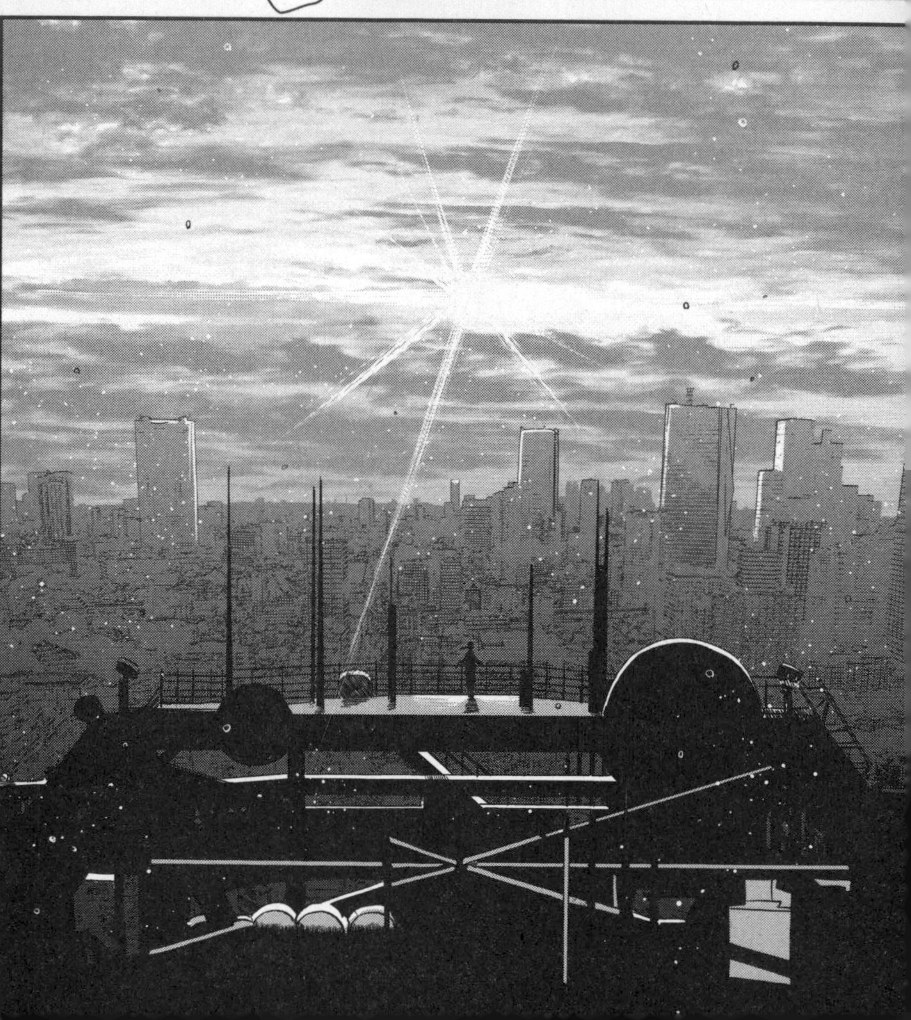

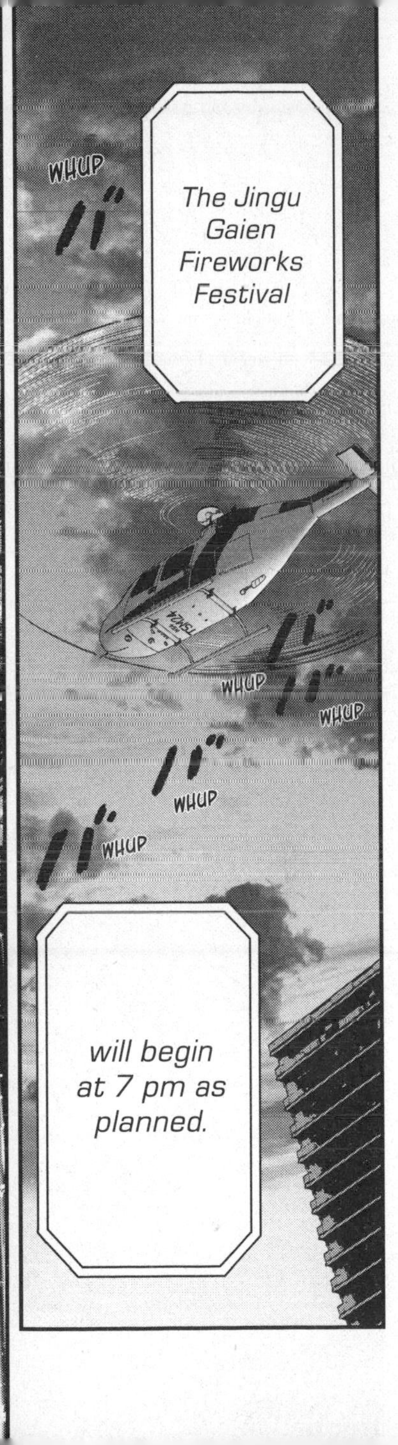
WHUP
The Jingu Gaien Fireworks Festival
WHUP
WHUP
WHUP
WHUP
will begin at 7 pm as planned.

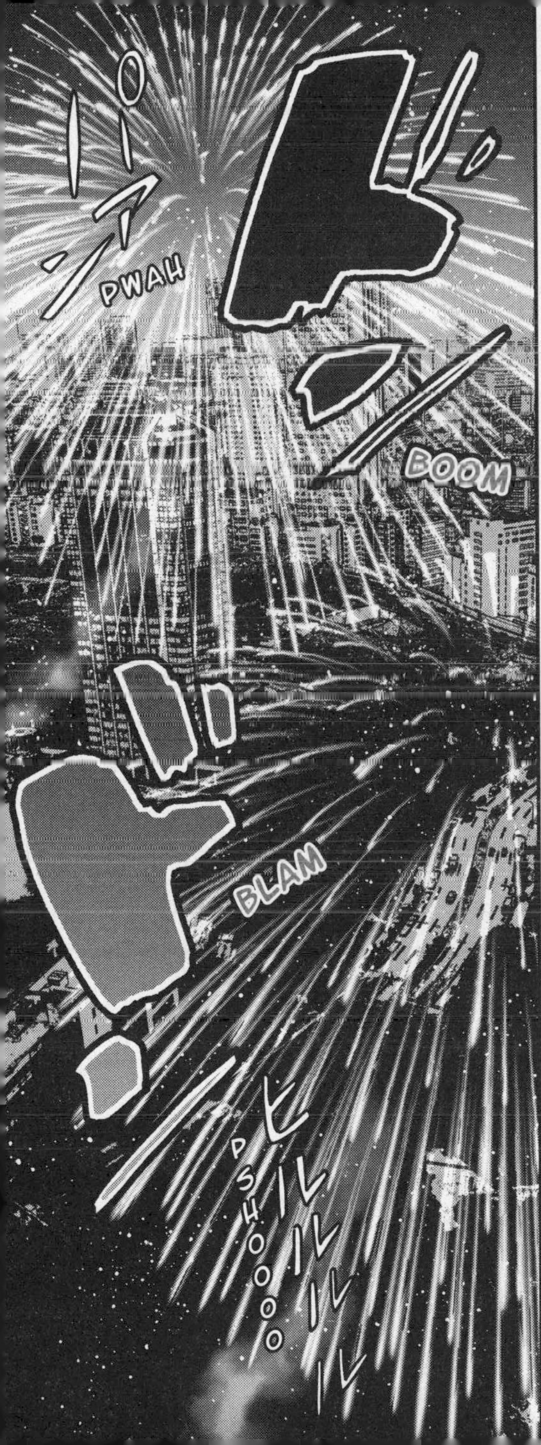
PWAH
BOOM
BLAM
PSHOOOO

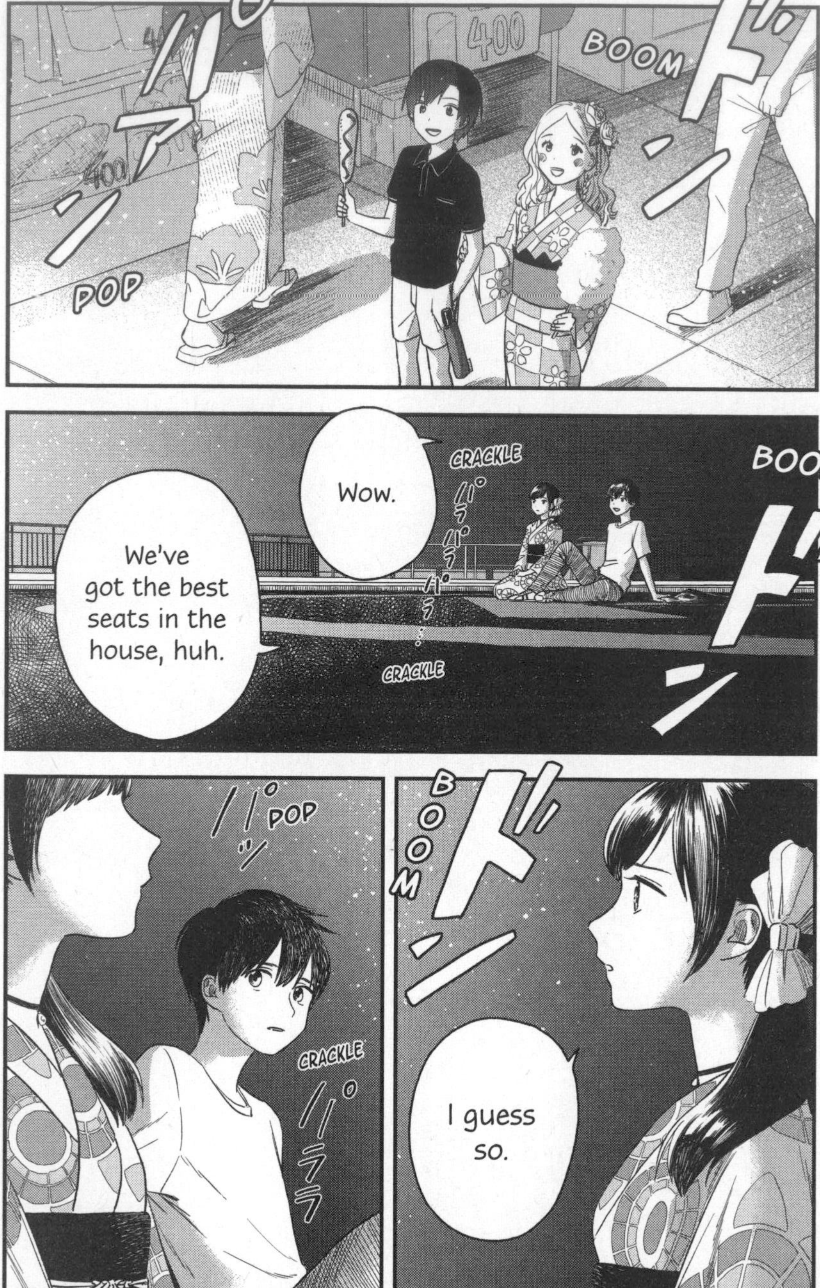
BOOM
ドン
パァン
POP
BOOM
ドン
Wow.
CRACKLE
パラパラパラ…
CRACKLE
We've got the best seats in the house, huh.
BOOM
ドン
I guess so.
POP
パッ
CRACKLE
パラ

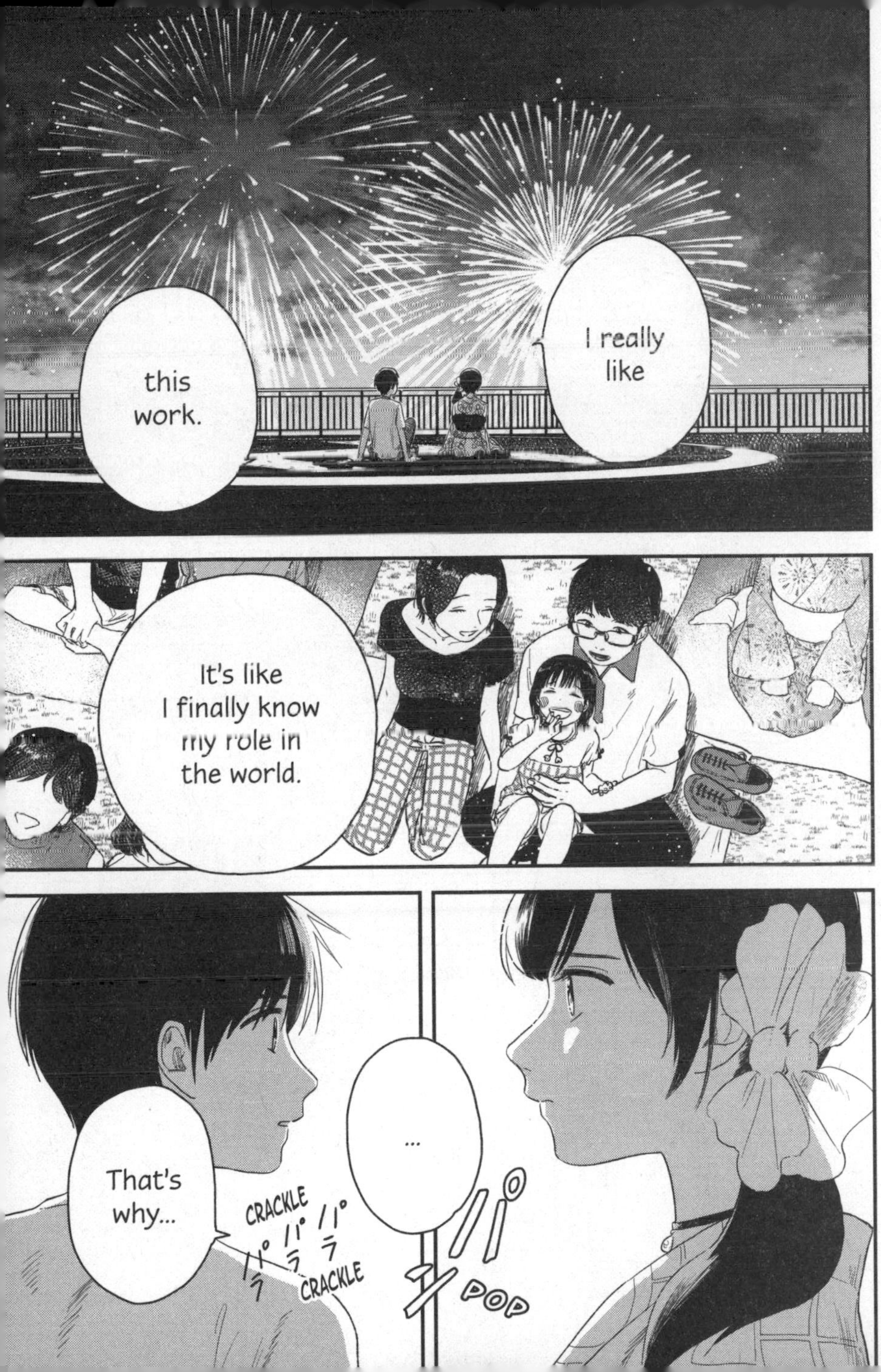
I really like
this work.
It's like I finally know my role in the world.
パ
POP
...
That's why...
CRACKLE
パラパラ
CRACKLE

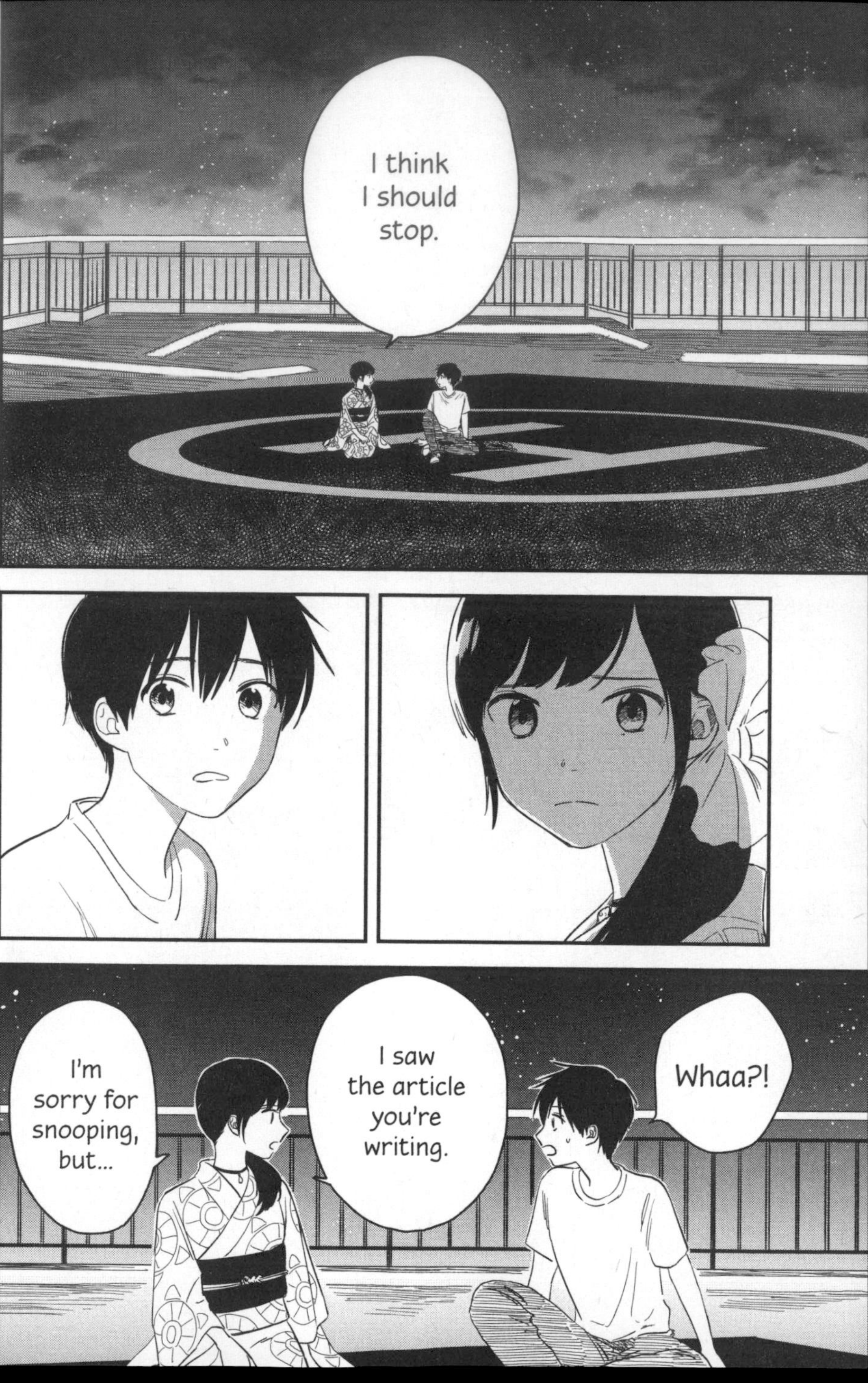
I think I should stop.
I'm sorry for snooping, but...
I saw the article you're writing.
Whaa?!

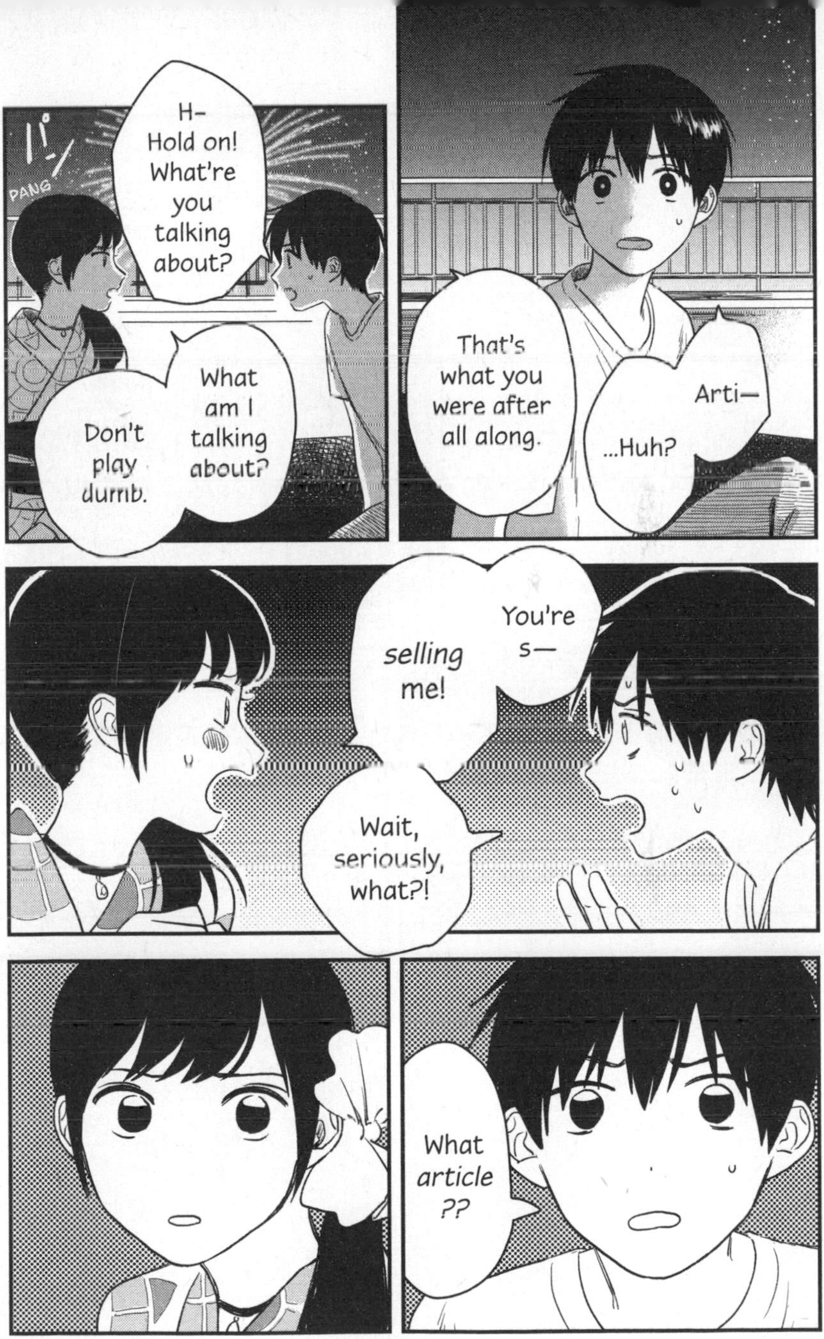
Arti—
...Huh?
That's what you were after all along.
H- Hold on! What're you talking about?
パン
PANG
What am I talking about?
Don't play dumb.
You're s—
selling me!
Wait, seriously, what?!
What article ??

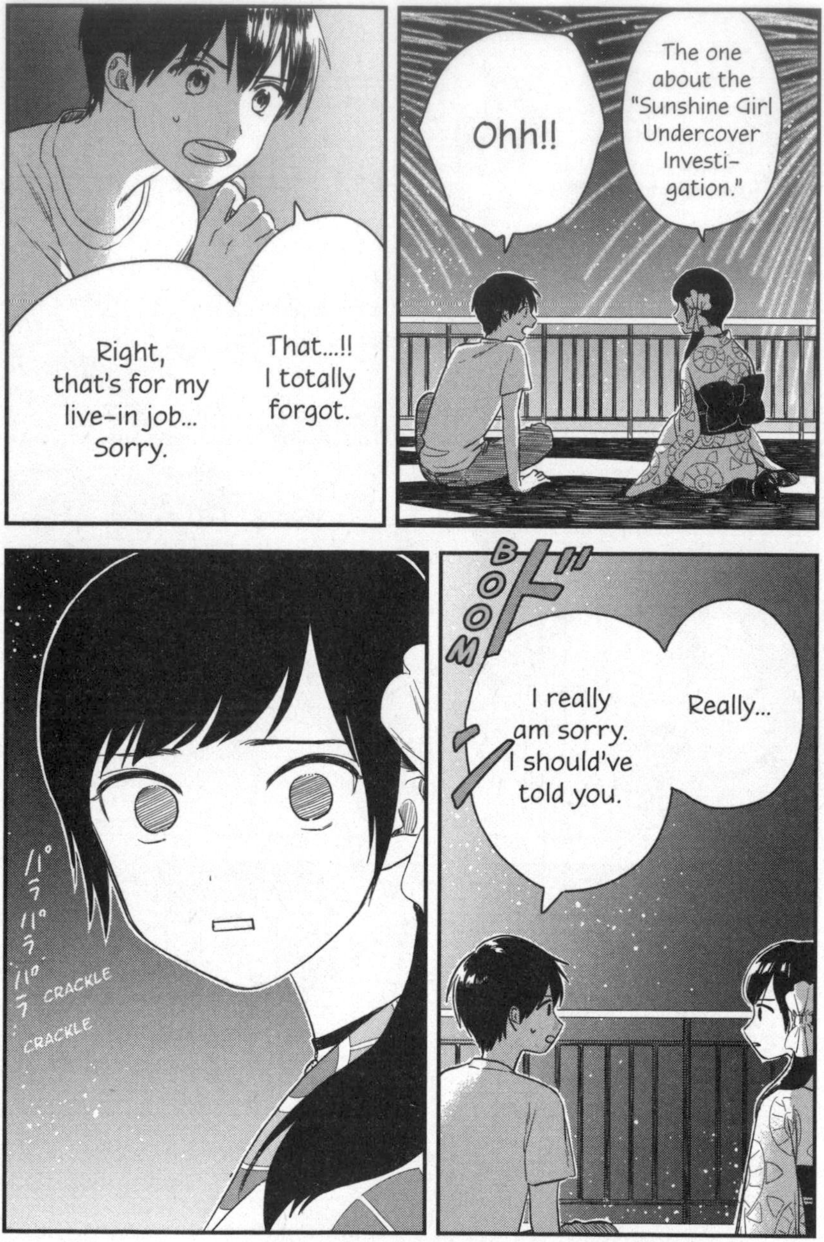
The one about the "Sunshine Girl Undercover Investi-gation."
Ohh!!
That...!! I totally forgot.
Right, that's for my live-in job... Sorry.
BOOM
Really...
I really am sorry. I should've told you.
パラパラパラ
CRACKLE
CRACKLE

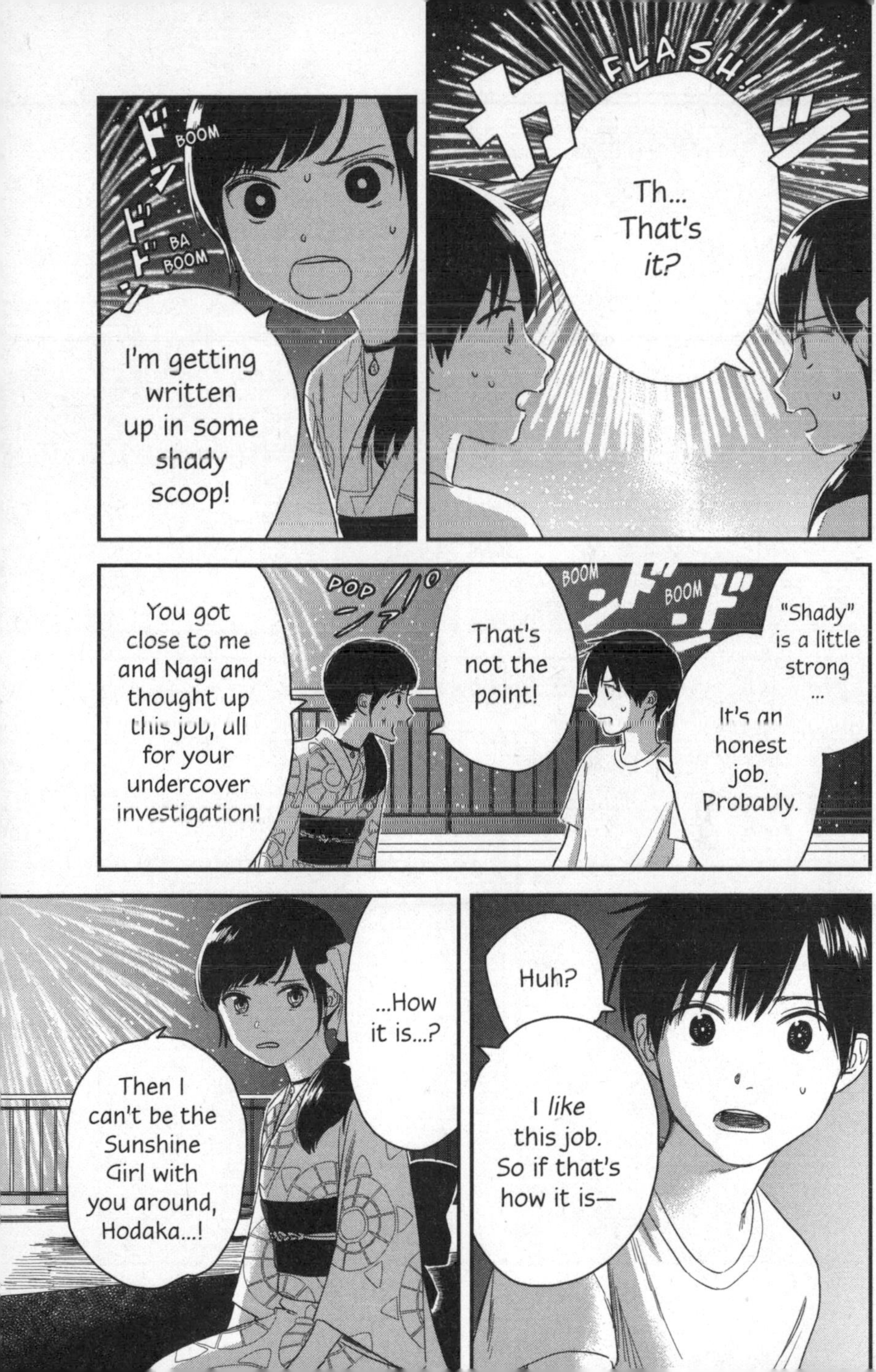
FLASH!
Th... That's *it?*
BOOM
BA BOOM
I'm getting written up in some shady scoop!
BOOM
BOOM
"Shady" is a little strong ...
It's an honest job. Probably.
That's not the point!
POP
You got close to me and Nagi and thought up this job, all for your undercover investigation!
Huh?
I *like* this job. So if that's how it is—
...How it is...?
Then I can't be the Sunshine Girl with you around, Hodaka...!

it's starting to...

Besides...

...

Miss Hina?

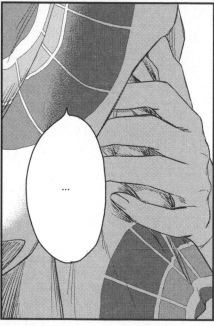

...

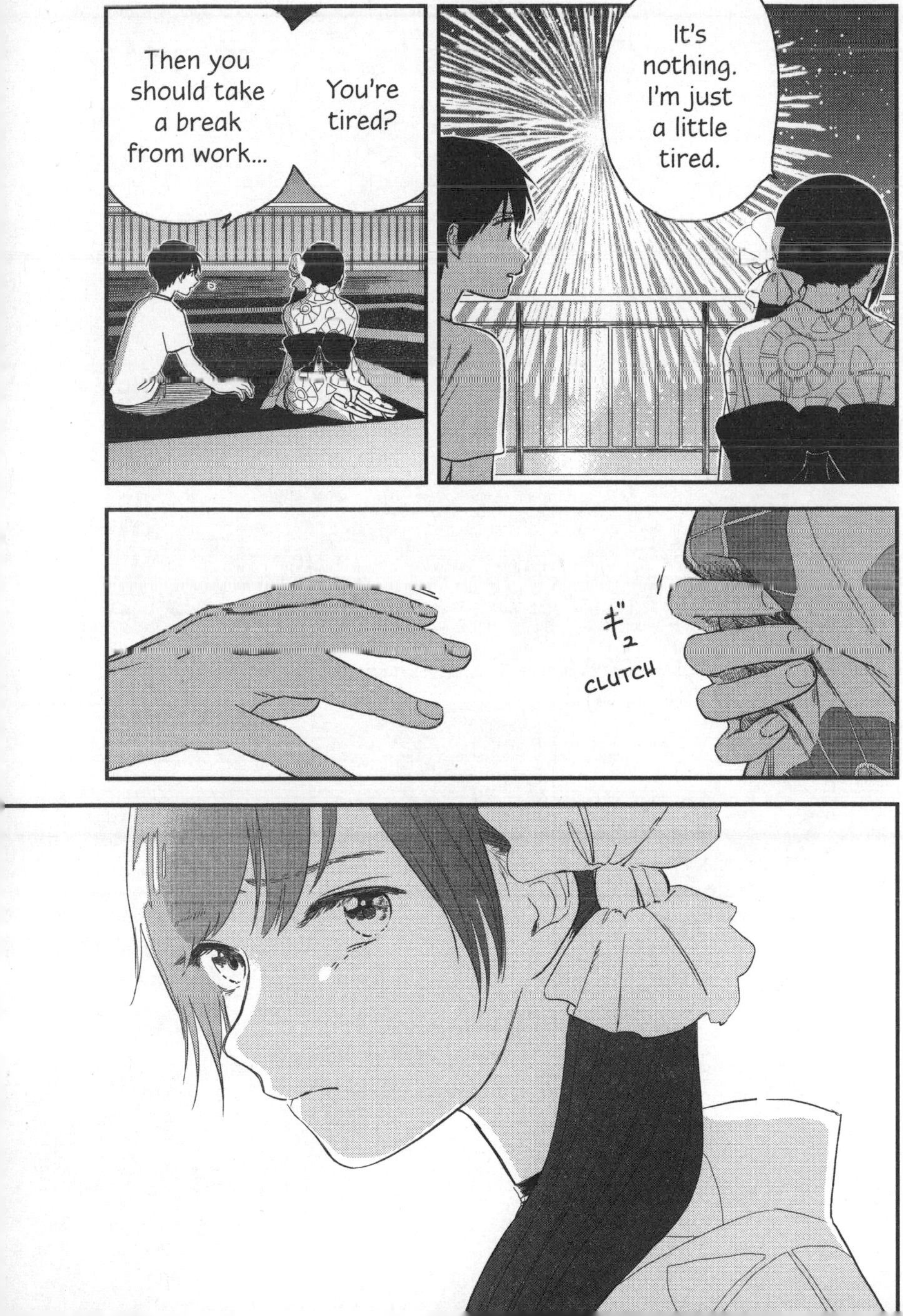
It's nothing. I'm just a little tired.
You're tired?
Then you should take a break from work...
ギュ
CLUTCH

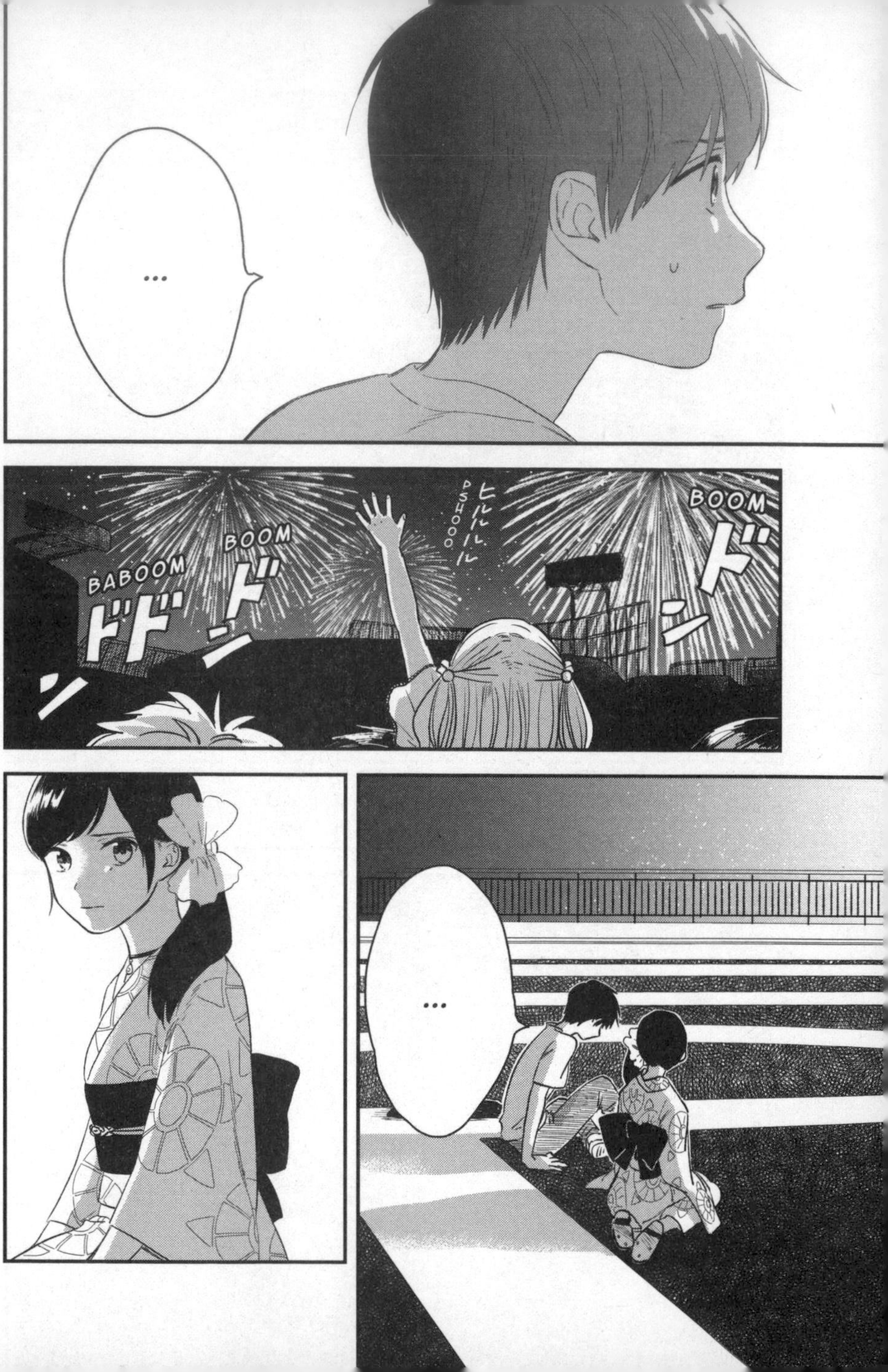
...
BOOM
ドン
ヒルルルル
PSHOOO
BOOM
ドーン
BABOOM
ドドン
...

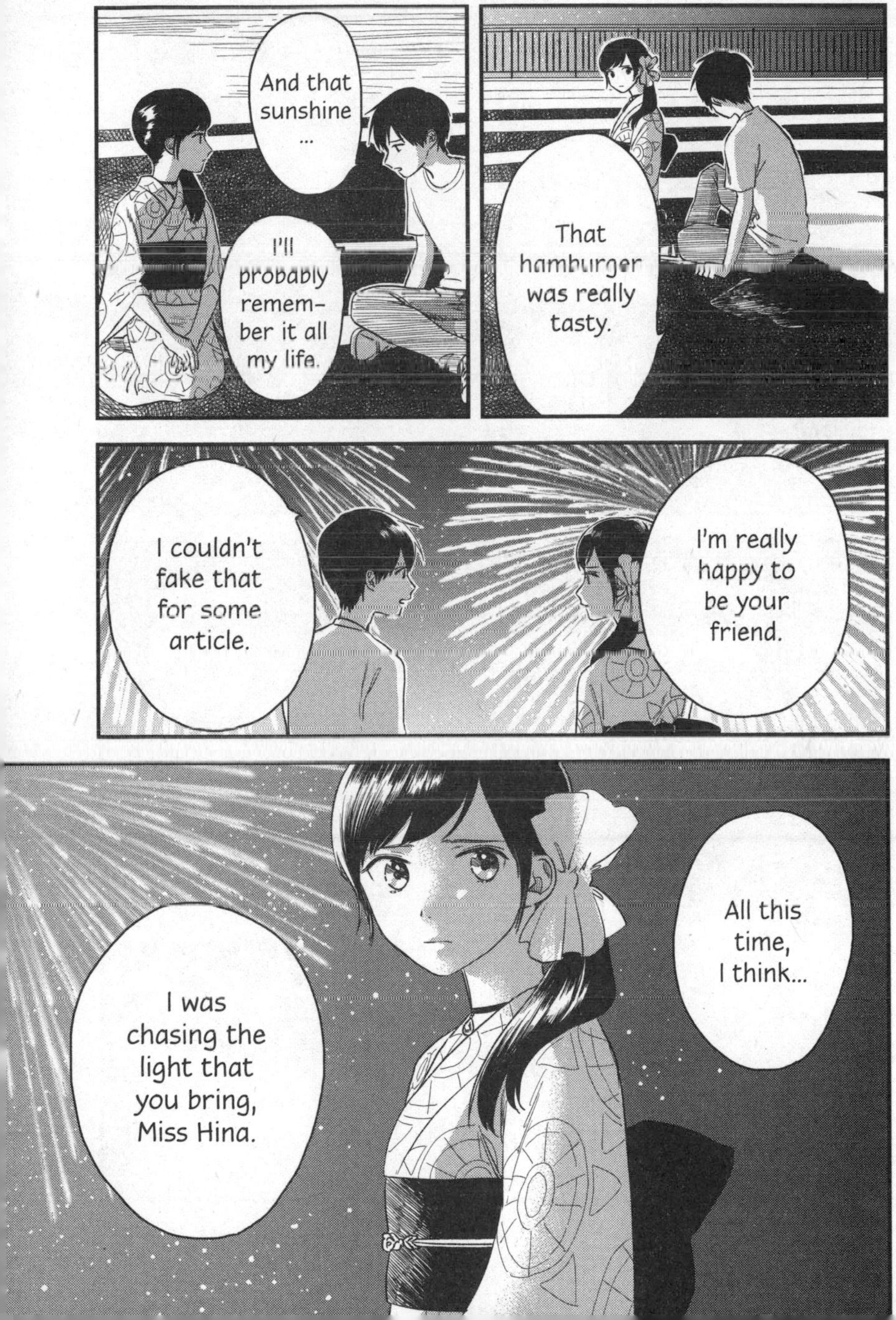
That hamburger was really tasty.
And that sunshine ...
I'll probably remem-ber it all my life.
I'm really happy to be your friend.
I couldn't fake that for some article.
All this time, I think...
I was chasing the light that you bring, Miss Hina.

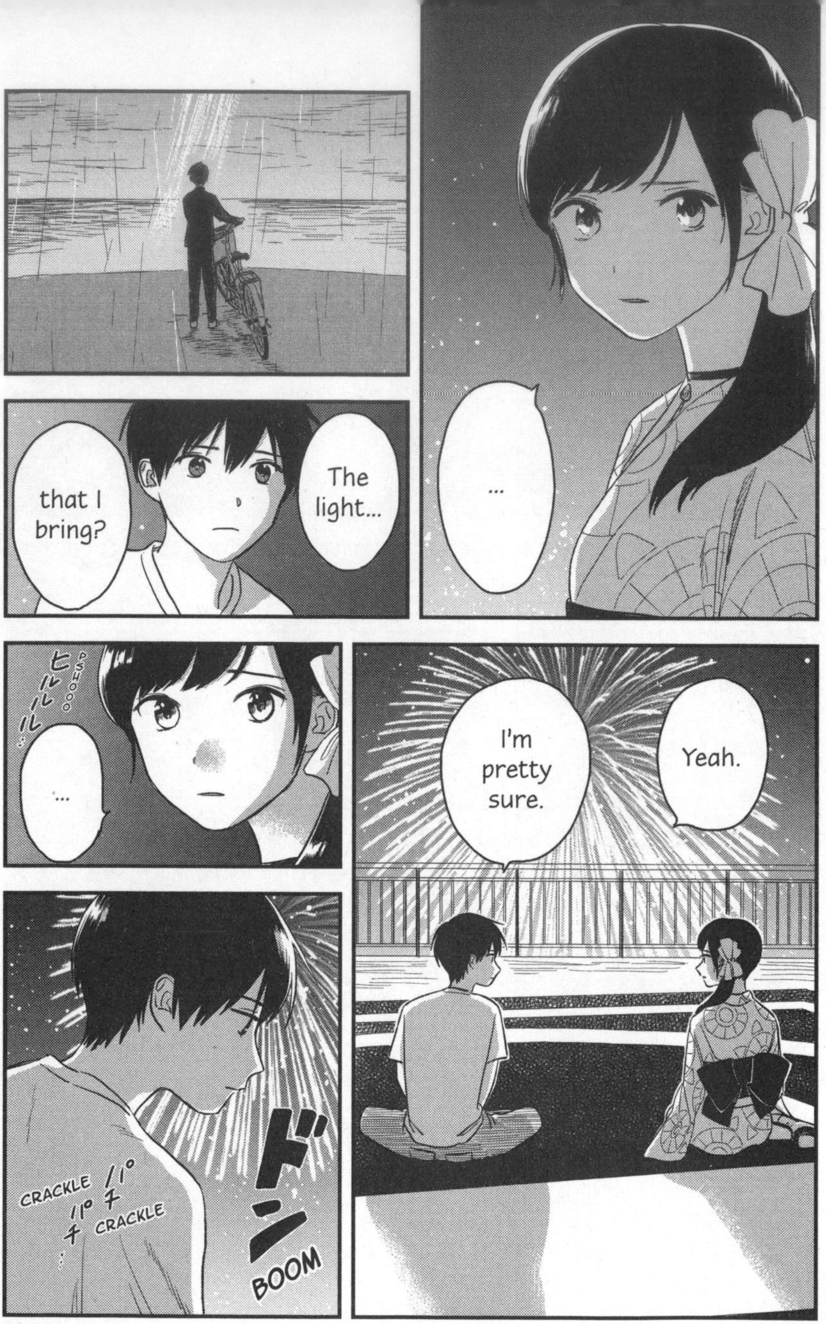
...
The light...
that I bring?
Yeah.
I'm pretty sure.
ヒュルルル…
PSHOOO
...
ドン
BOOM
パチパチ…
CRACKLE
CRACKLE

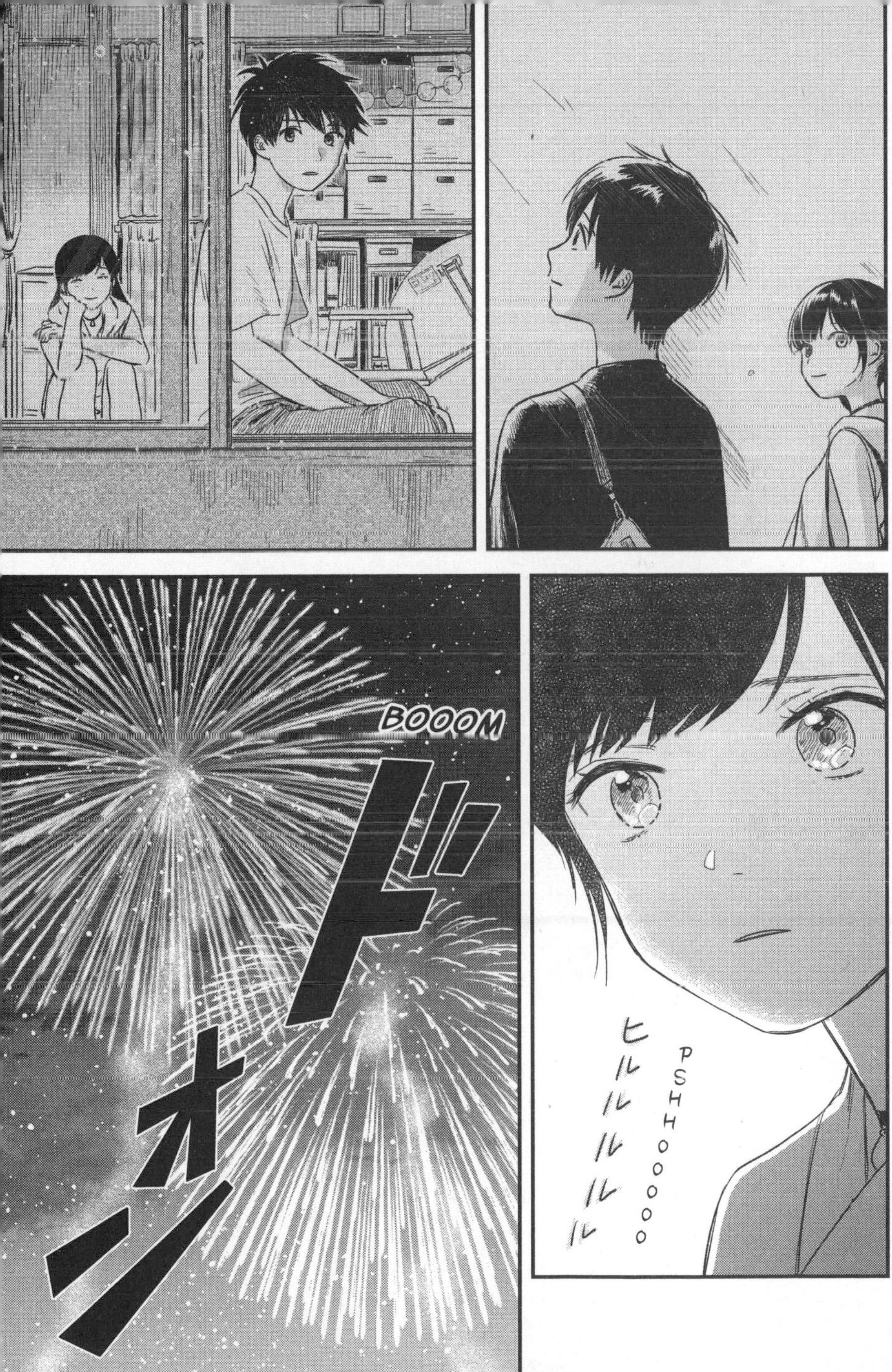
PSHHOOOOO
ヒルルルルル
BOOOM
ドオン

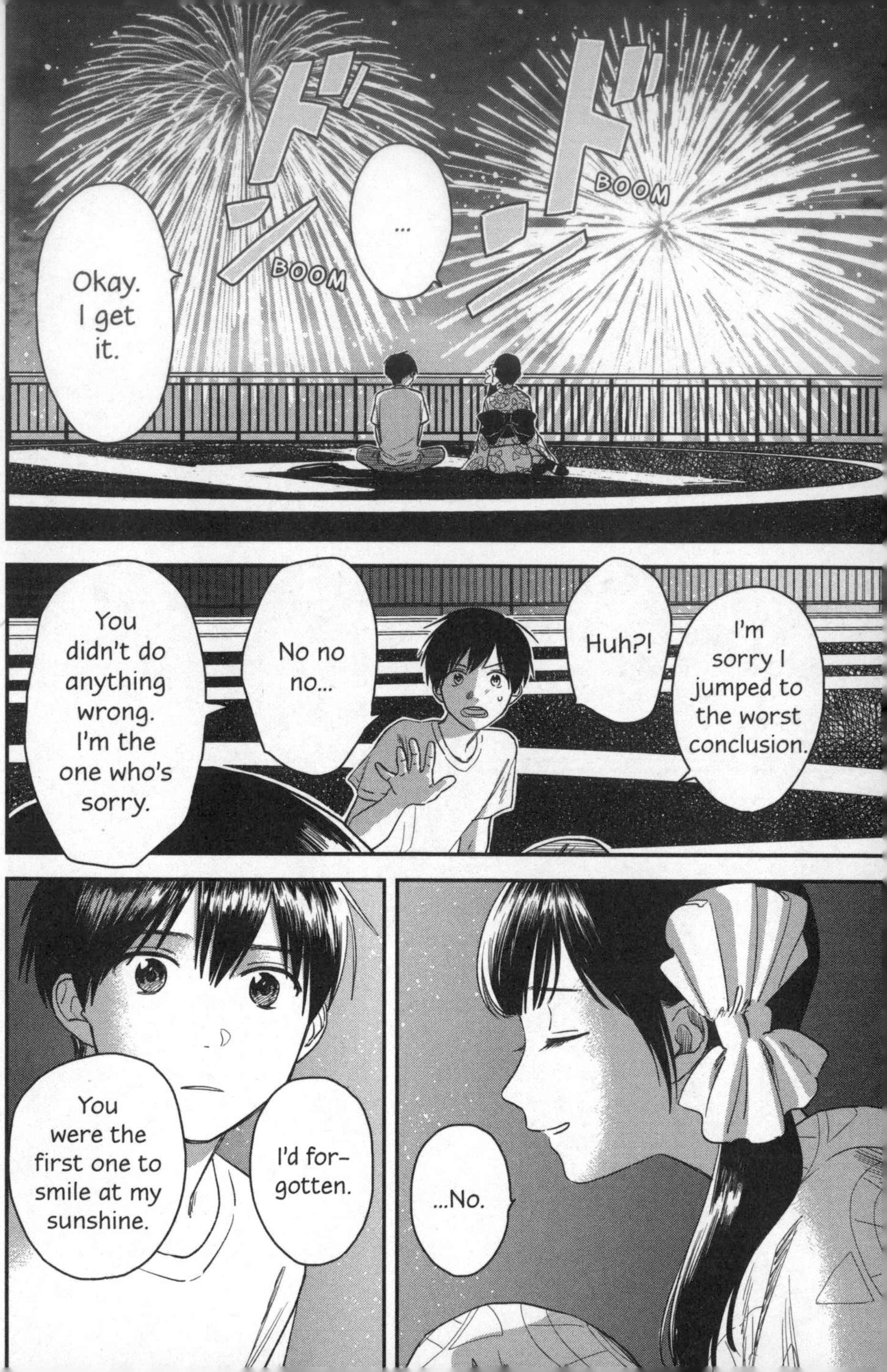
BOOM
...
BOOM
Okay. I get it.
I'm sorry I jumped to the worst conclusion.
Huh?!
No no no...
You didn't do anything wrong. I'm the one who's sorry.
...No.
I'd for-gotten.
You were the first one to smile at my sunshine.

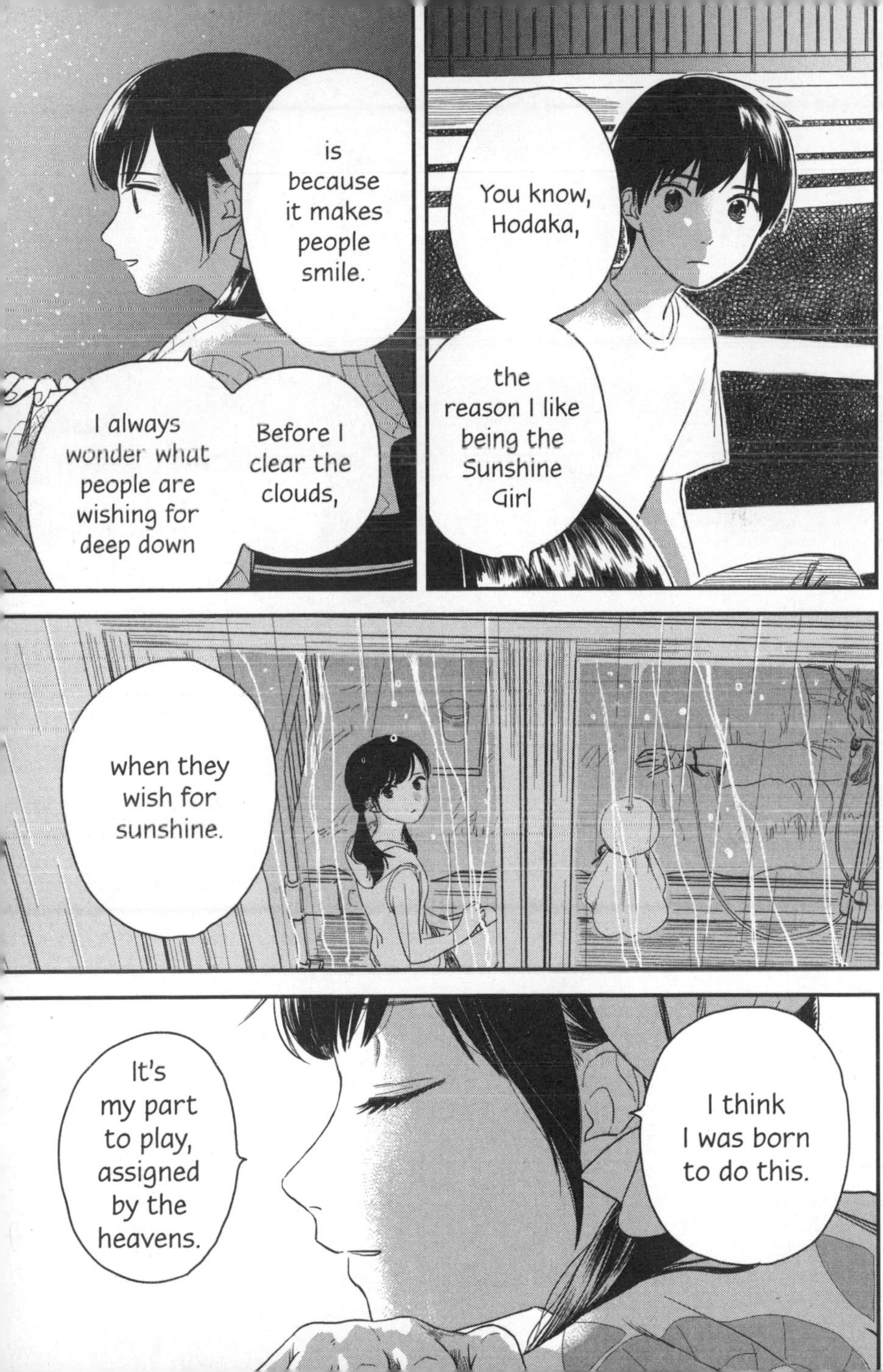
You know, Hodaka,
the reason I like being the Sunshine Girl
is because it makes people smile.
Before I clear the clouds,
I always wonder what people are wishing for deep down
when they wish for sunshine.
I think I was born to do this.
It's my part to play, assigned by the heavens.

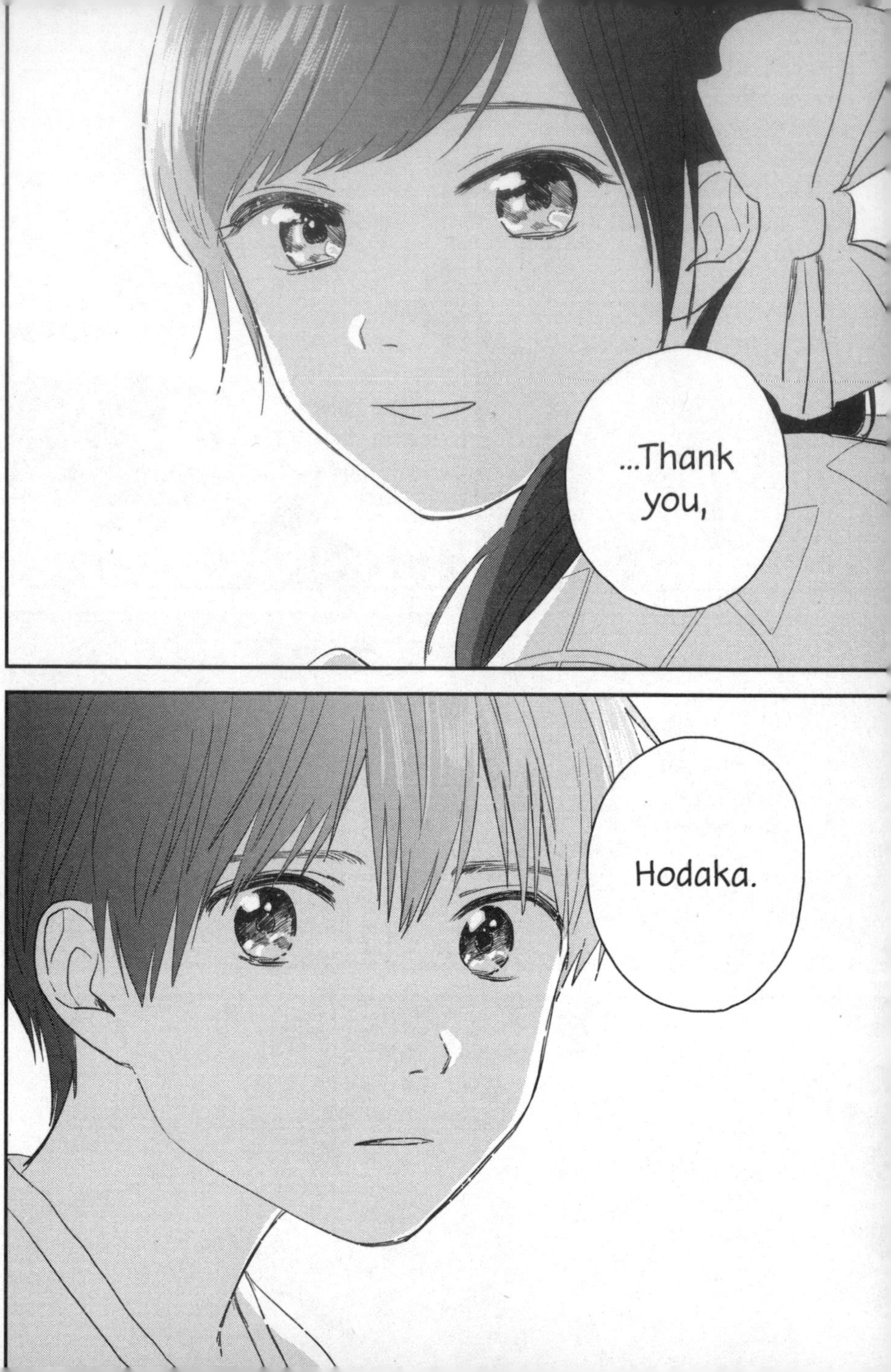
...Thank you,
Hodaka.

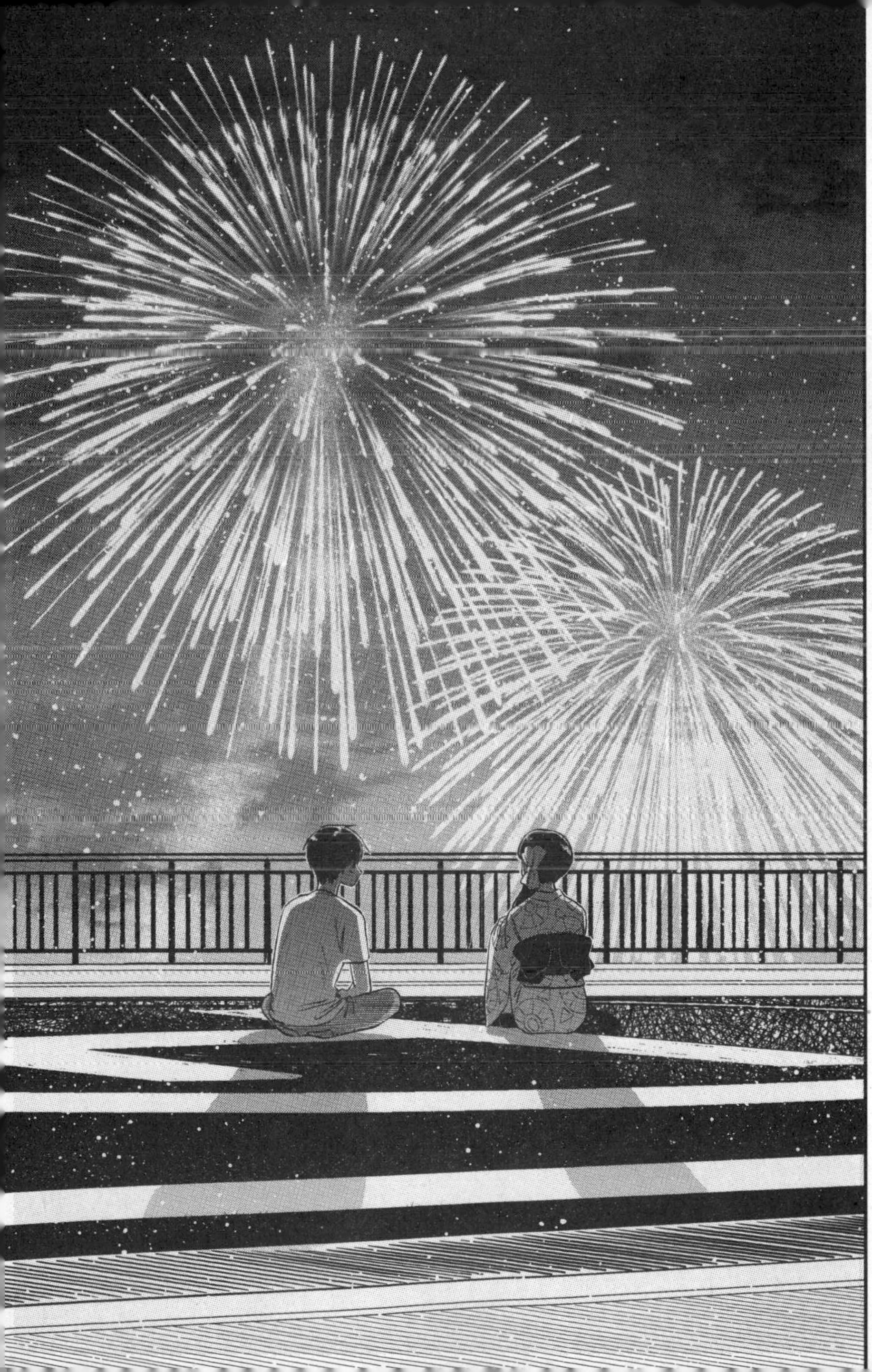

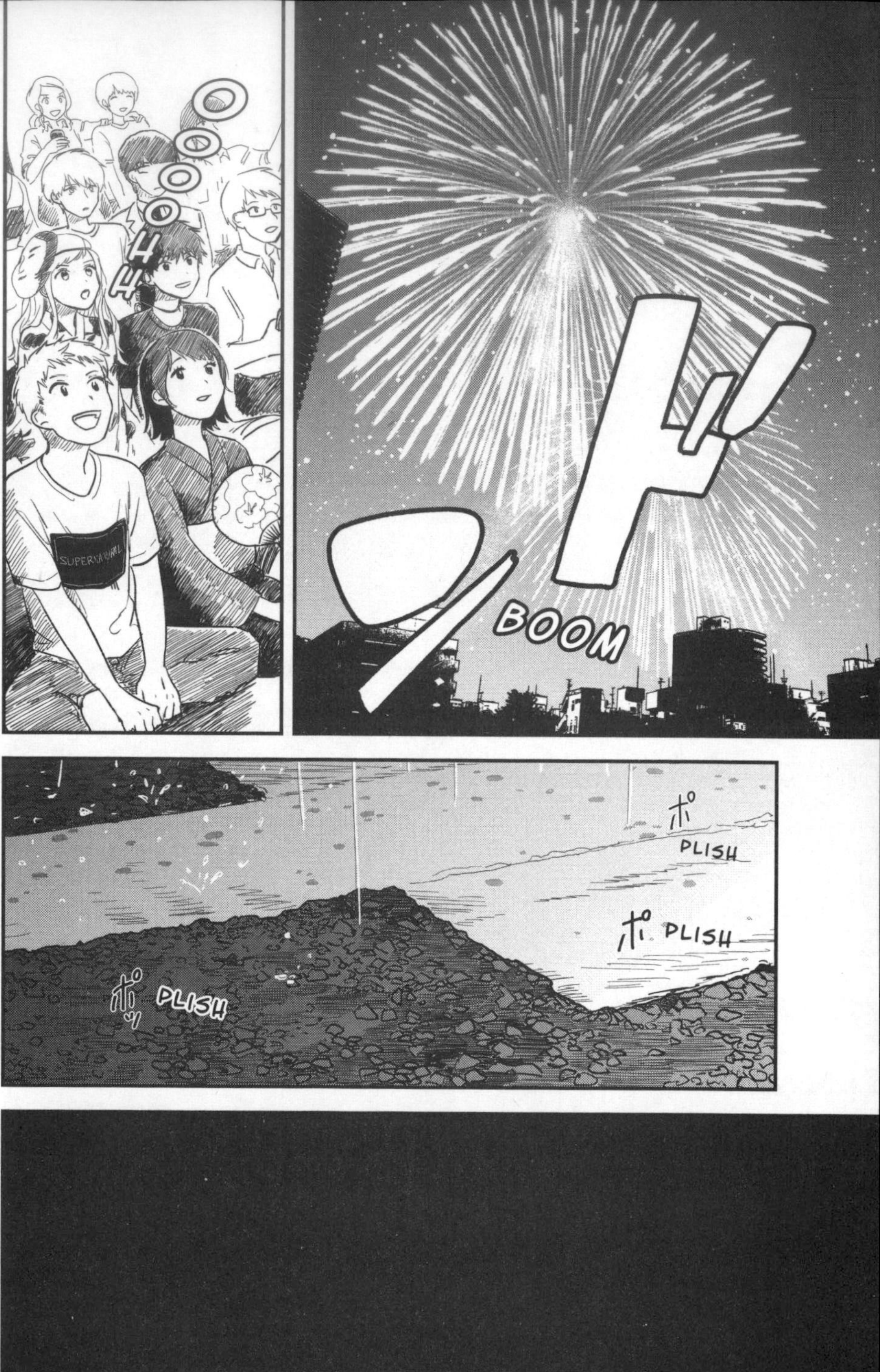
BOOM
OOOOHHH
PLISH
PLISH
PLISH

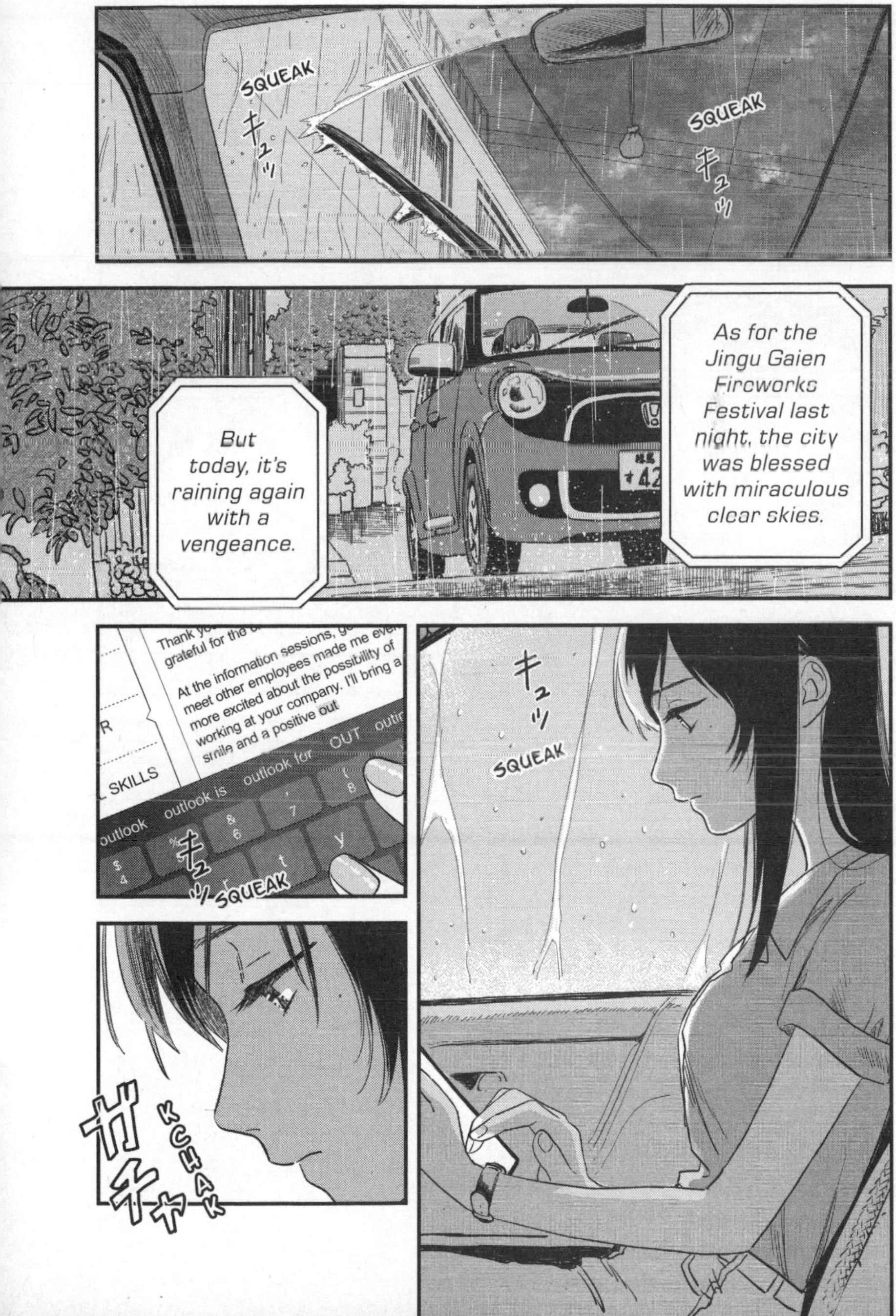
SQUEAK
キュッ
SQUEAK
キュッ
As for the Jingu Gaien Fireworks Festival last night, the city was blessed with miraculous clear skies.
But today, it's raining again with a vengeance.
キュッ
SQUEAK
At the information sessions,
meet other employees made me even
more excited about the possibility of
working at your company. I'll bring a
smile and a positive out
outlook for
OUT
outlook is
outlook
SKILLS
キュッ
SQUEAK
ガチャ
KCHAK

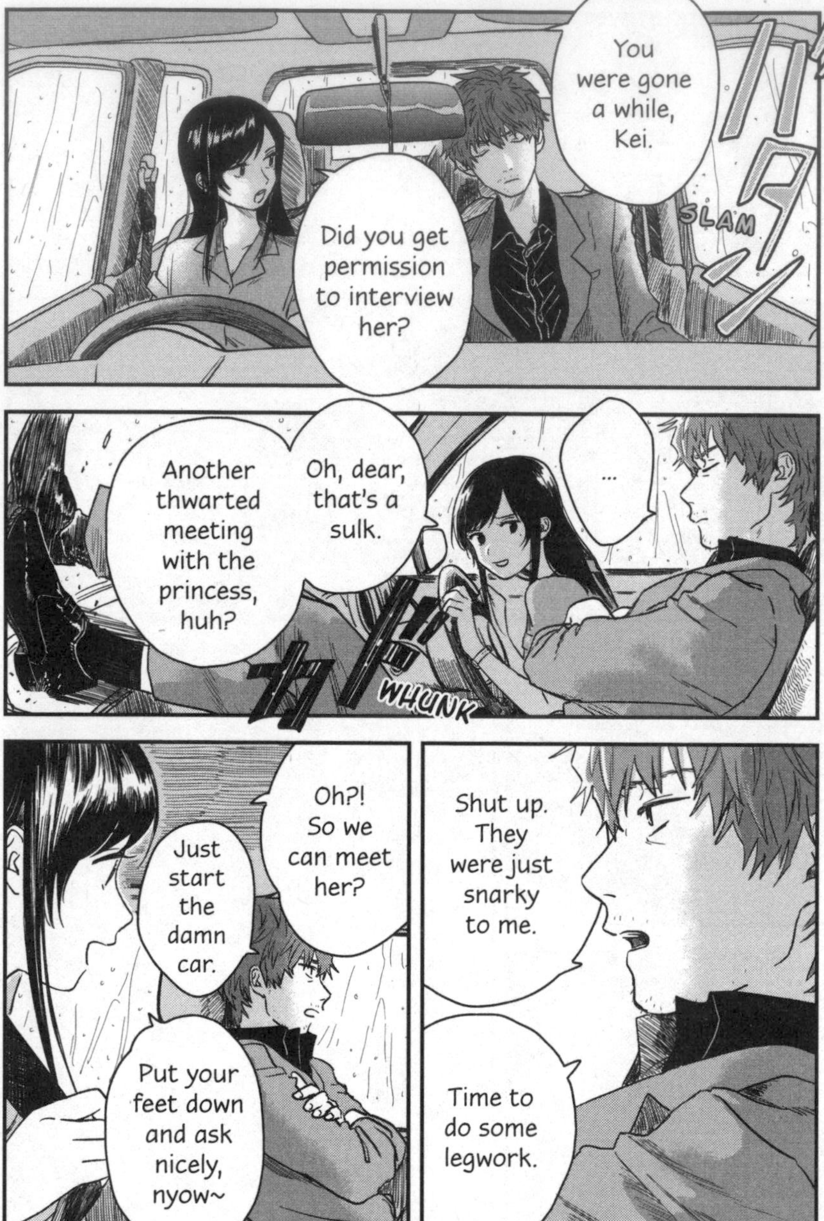
You were gone a while, Kei.
SLAM
Did you get permission to interview her?
...
Oh, dear, that's a sulk.
Another thwarted meeting with the princess, huh?
WHUNK
Shut up. They were just snarky to me.
Time to do some legwork.
Oh?! So we can meet her?
Just start the damn car.
Put your feet down and ask nicely, nyow~

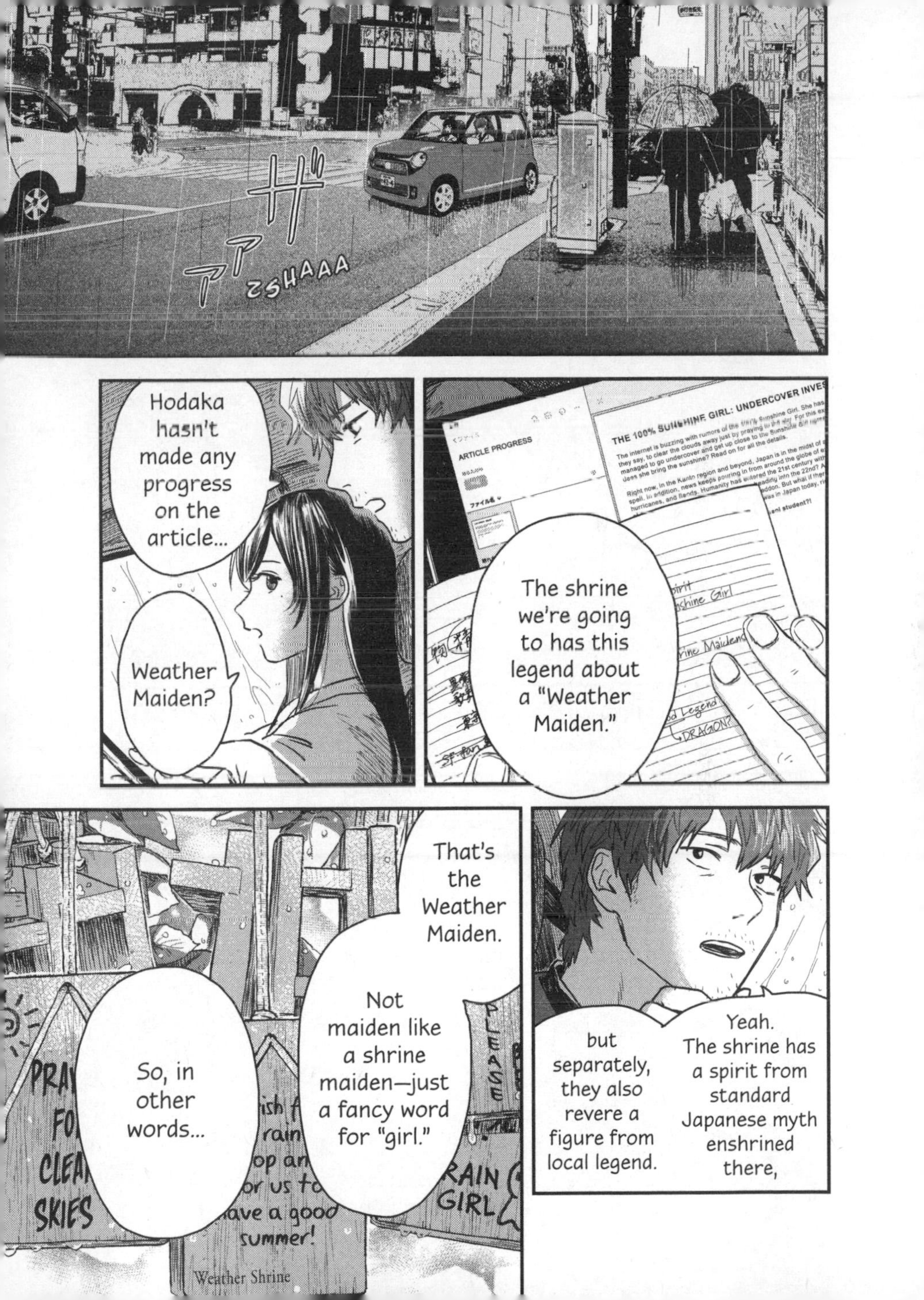

ZSHAAA
ARTICLE PROGRESS
The shrine we're going to has this legend about a "Weather Maiden."
DRAGON?
Hodaka hasn't made any progress on the article...
Weather Maiden?
Yeah. The shrine has a spirit from standard Japanese myth enshrined there,
but separately, they also revere a figure from local legend.
That's the Weather Maiden.
Not maiden like a shrine maiden—just a fancy word for "girl."
So, in other words...
PLEASE
RAIN GIRL
SKIES
summer!
Weather Shrine

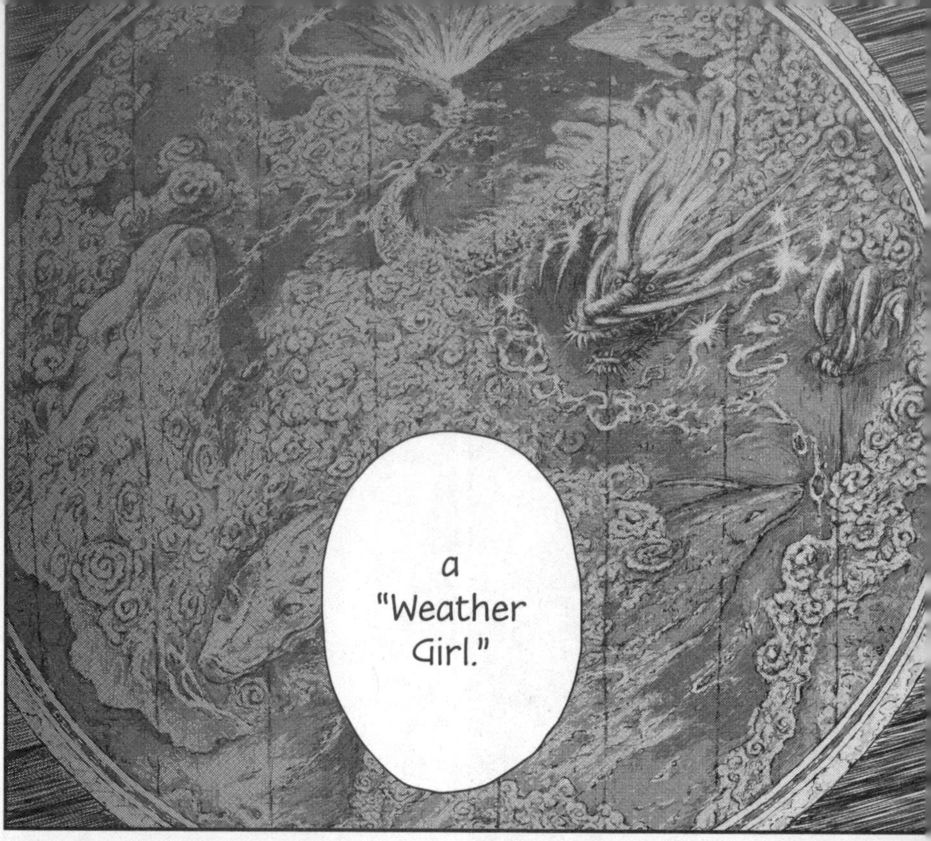
a "Weather Girl."
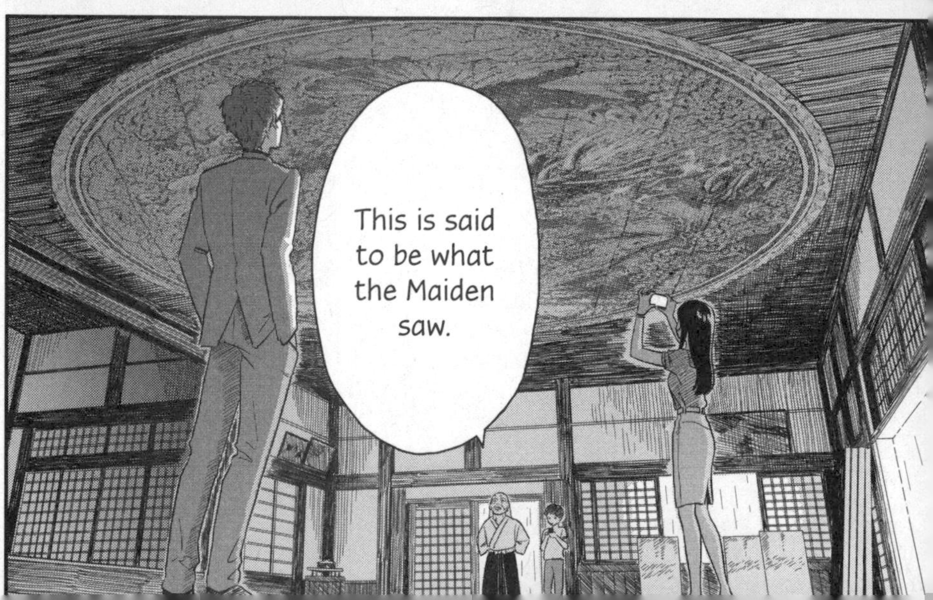
This is said to be what the Maiden saw.

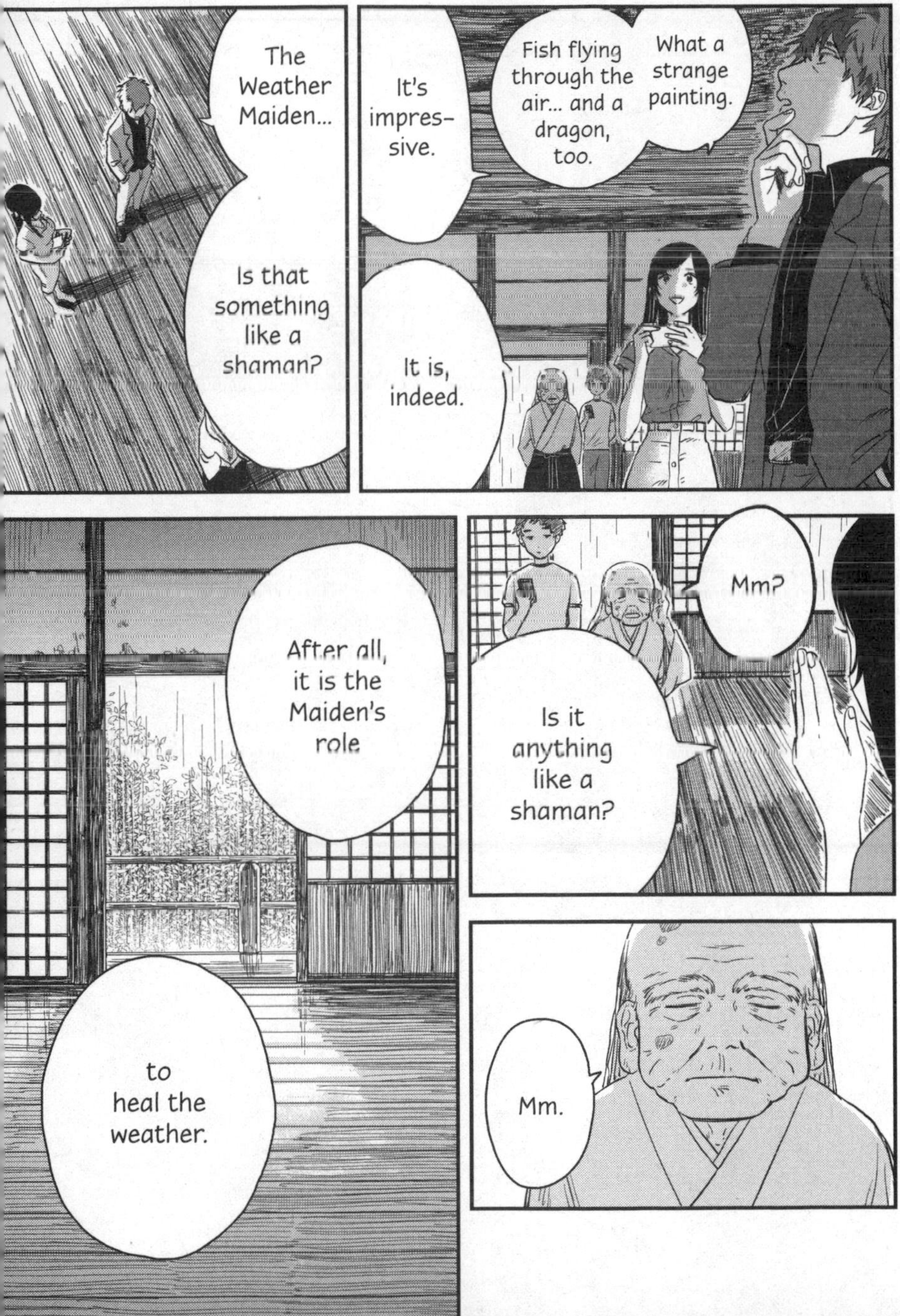
What a strange painting.
Fish flying through the air... and a dragon, too.
It's impres-sive.
It is, indeed.
The Weather Maiden...
Is that something like a shaman?
Mm?
Is it anything like a shaman?
Mm.
After all, it is the Maiden's role
to heal the weather.

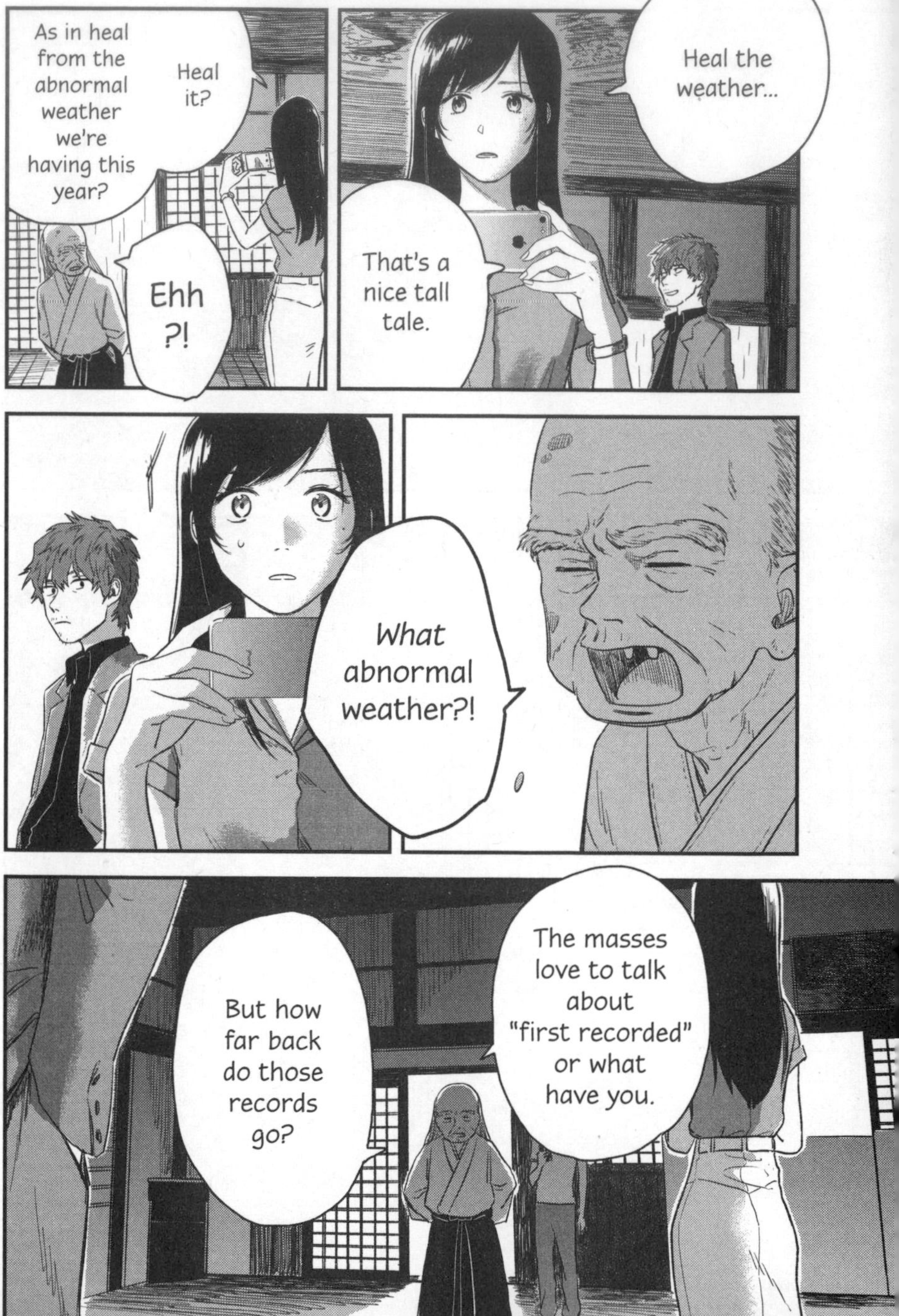
Heal the weather...
That's a nice tall tale.
Heal it?
As in heal from the abnormal weather we're having this year?
Ehh ?!
What abnormal weather?!
The masses love to talk about "first recorded" or what have you.
But how far back do those records go?

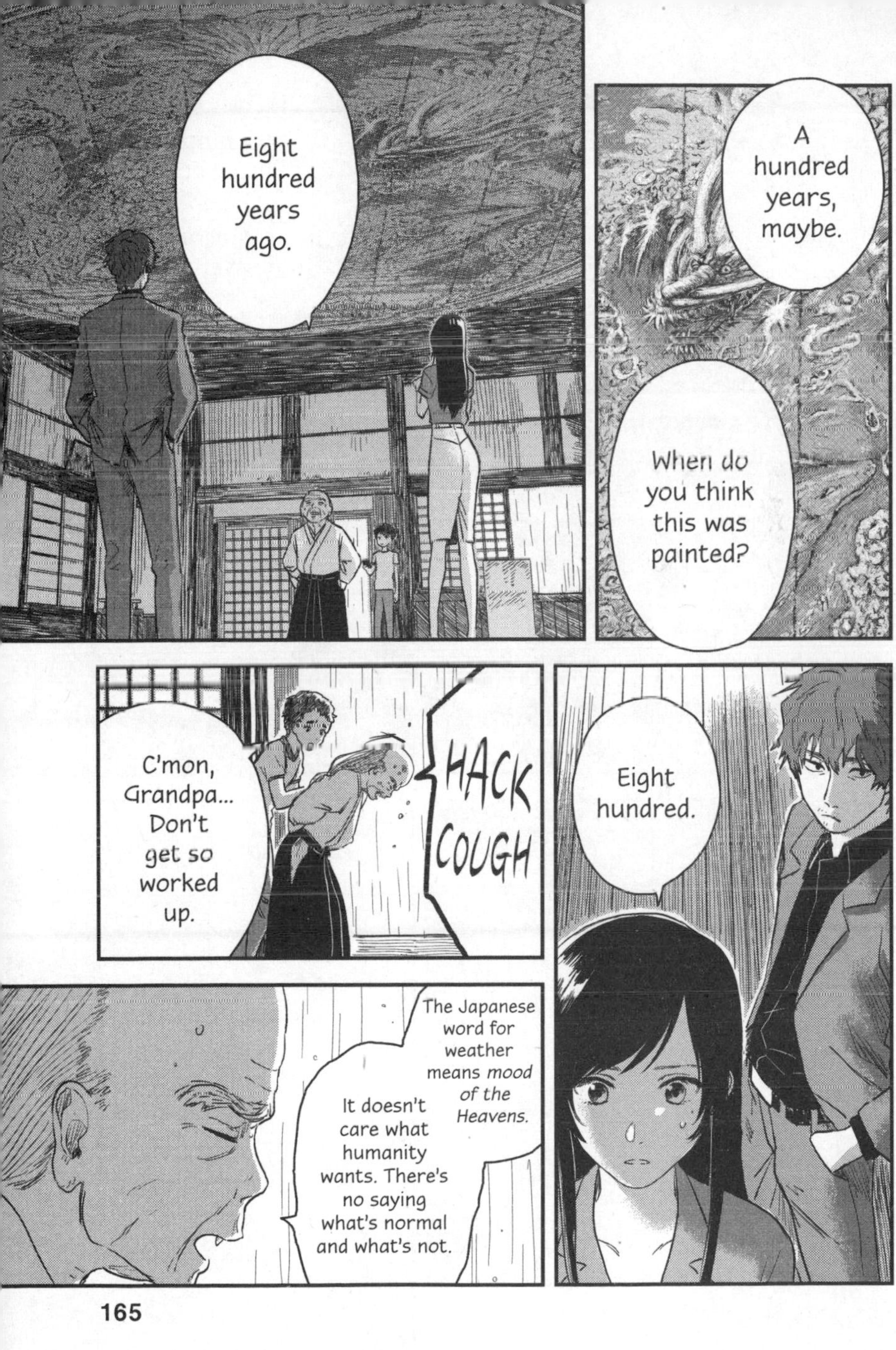
A hundred years, maybe.
When do you think this was painted?
Eight hundred years ago.
Eight hundred.
HACK COUGH
C'mon, Grandpa... Don't get so worked up.
The Japanese word for weather means *mood of the Heavens.*
It doesn't care what humanity wants. There's no saying what's normal and what's not.

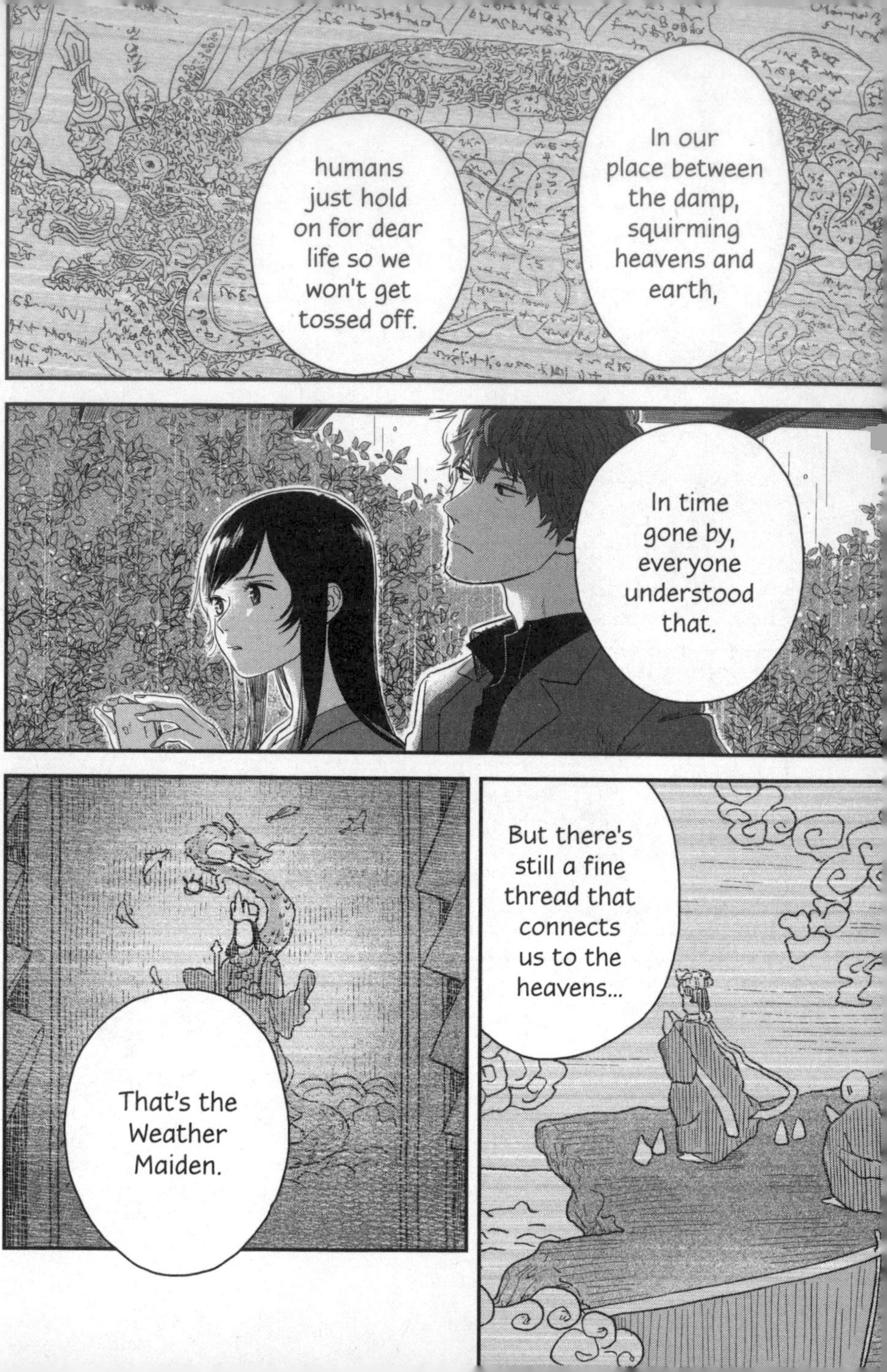
In our place between the damp, squirming heavens and earth,
humans just hold on for dear life so we won't get tossed off.
In time gone by, everyone understood that.
But there's still a fine thread that connects us to the heavens...
That's the Weather Maiden.

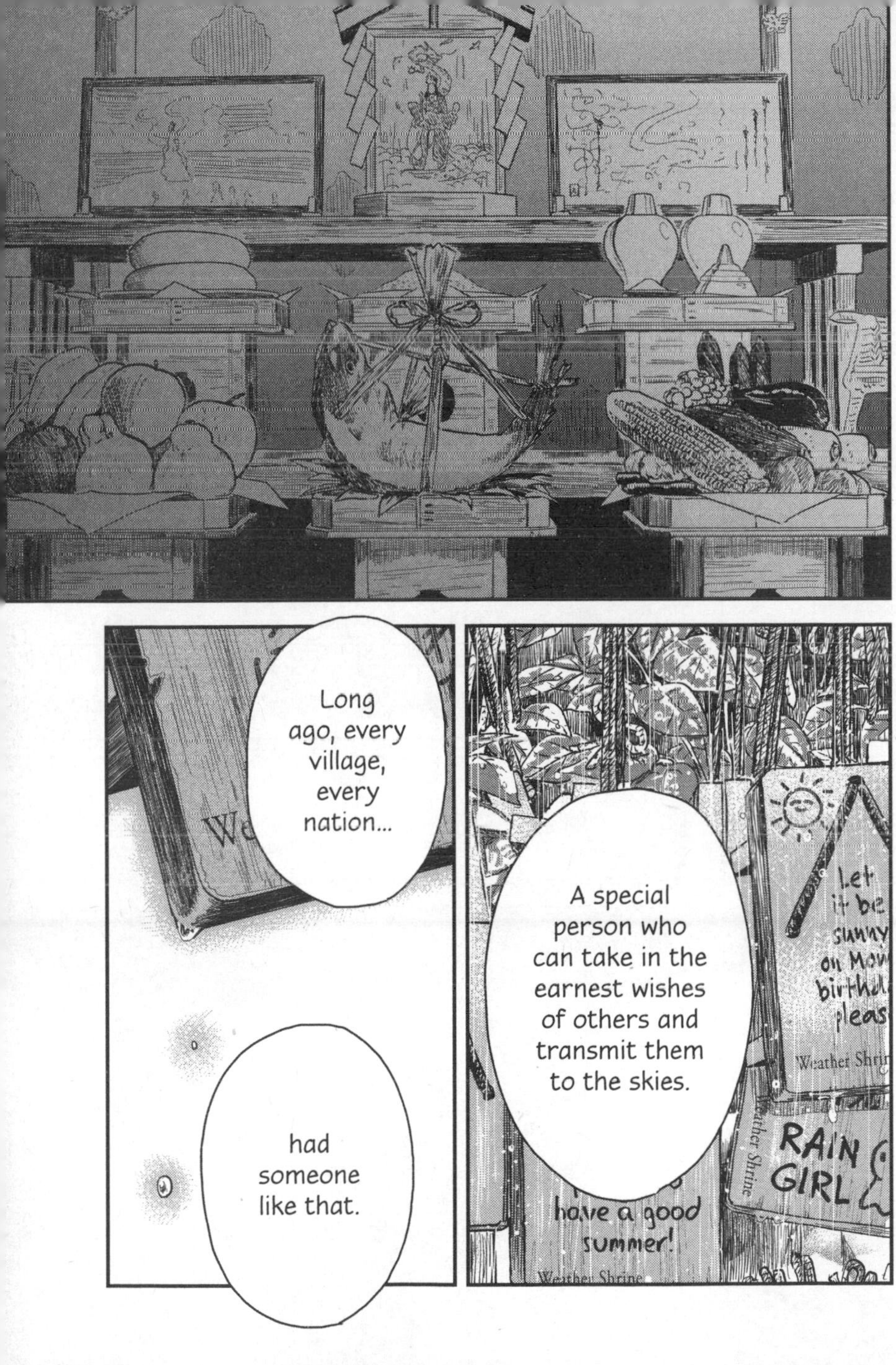
A special person who can take in the earnest wishes of others and transmit them to the skies.
Weather Shrine
RAIN GIRL
have a good summer!
Long ago, every village, every nation...
had someone like that.

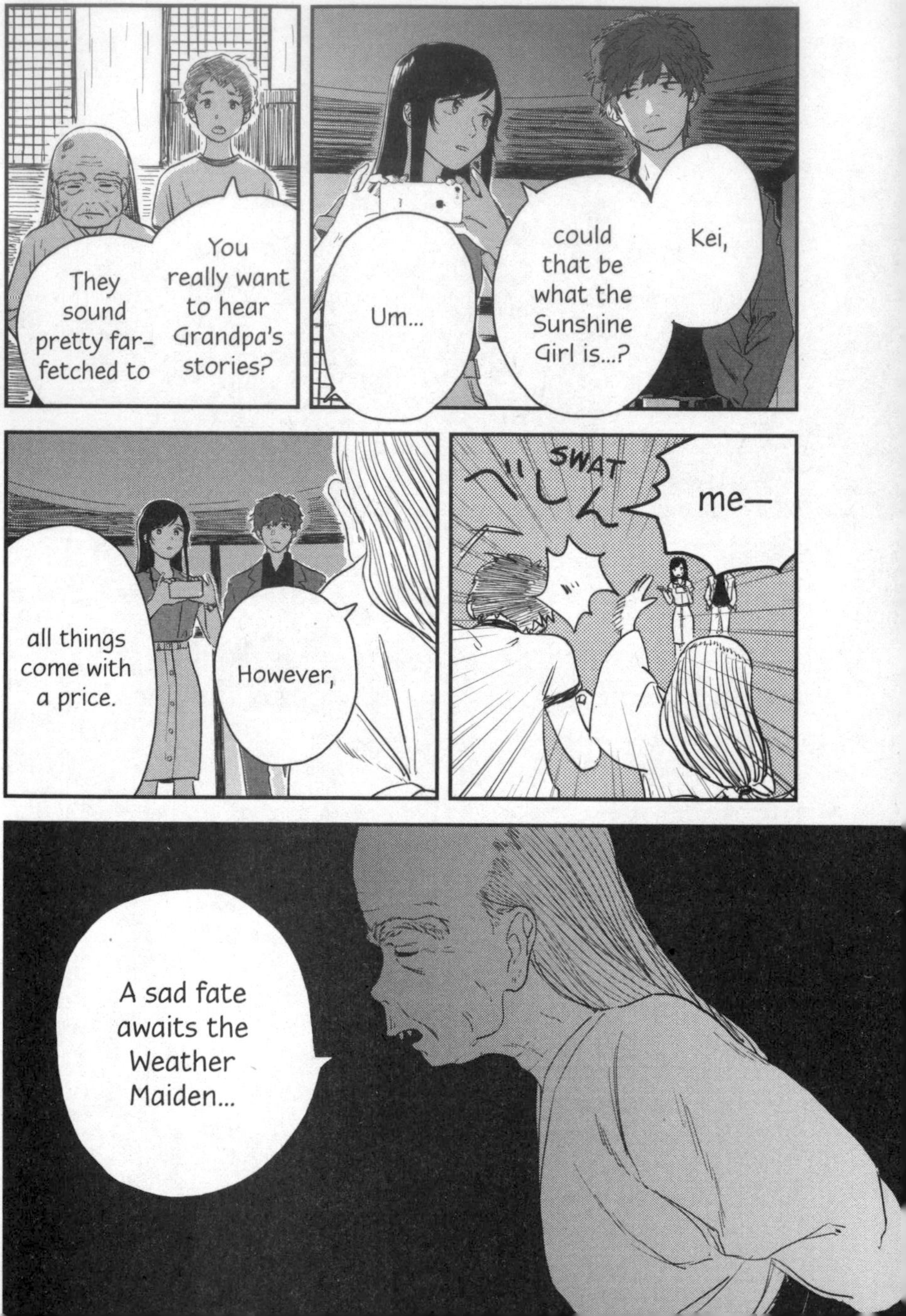
Kei,
could that be what the Sunshine Girl is...?
Um...
You really want to hear Grandpa's stories?
They sound pretty far-fetched to
SWAT
me—
However,
all things come with a price.
A sad fate awaits the Weather Maiden...

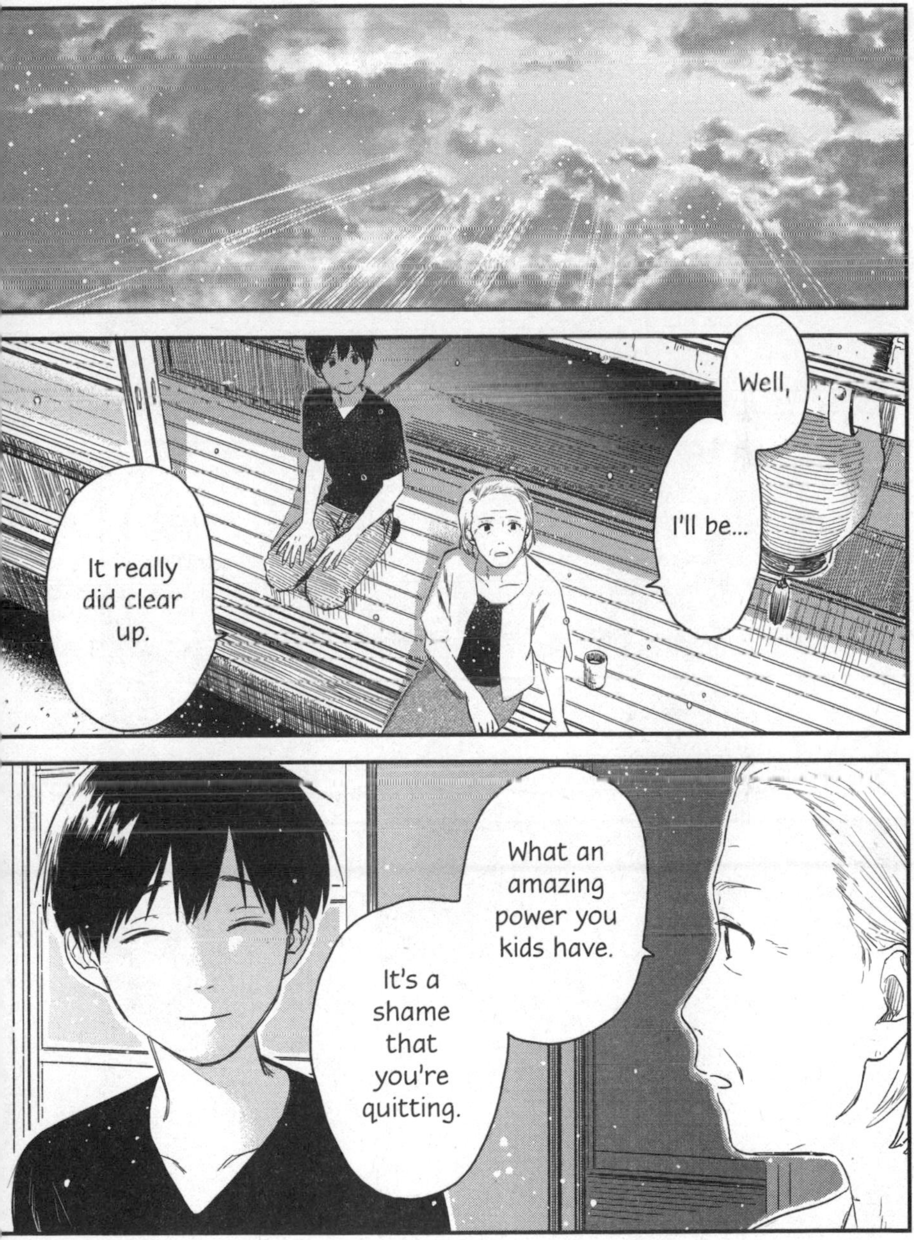
Well, I'll be...
It really did clear up.
What an amazing power you kids have.
It's a shame that you're quitting.

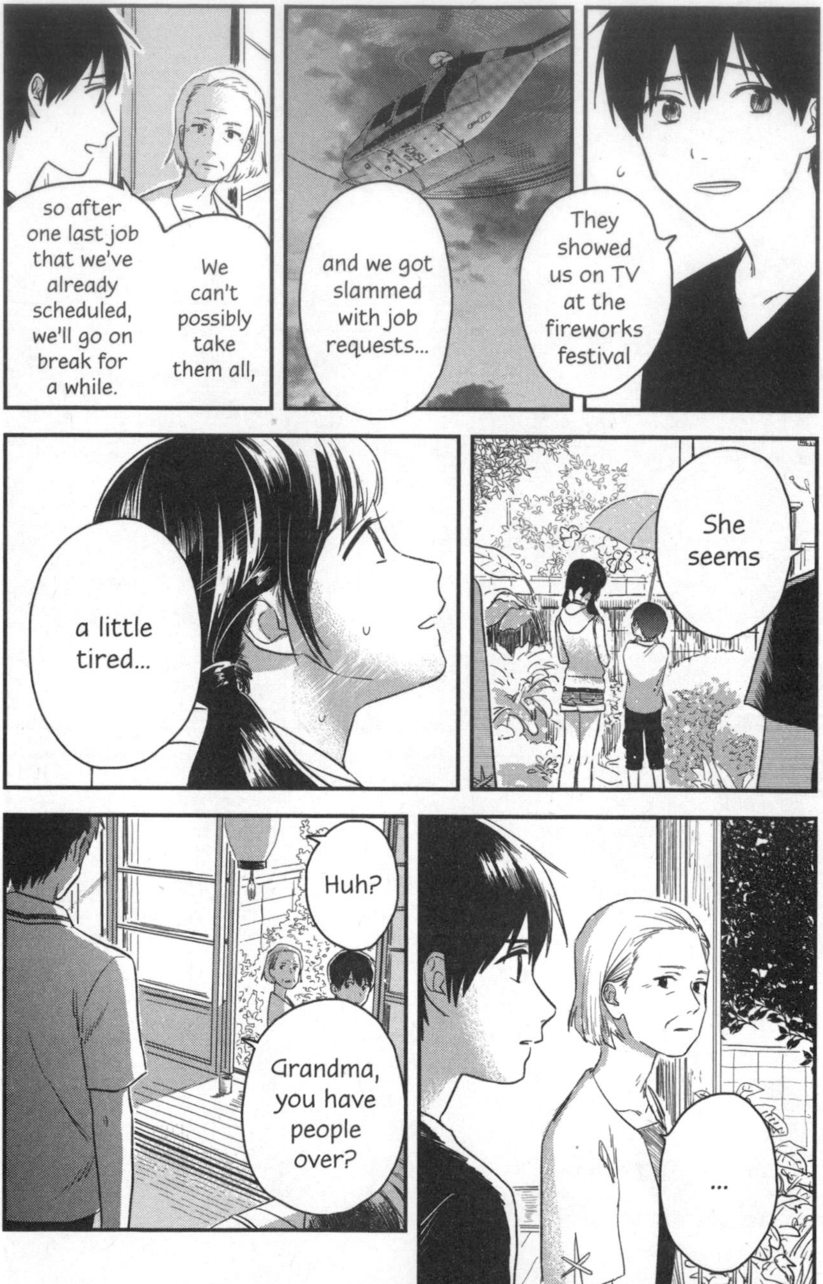
They showed us on TV at the fireworks festival
and we got slammed with job requests...
We can't possibly take them all,
so after one last job that we've already scheduled, we'll go on break for a while.
She seems
a little tired...
...
Huh?
Grandma, you have people over?

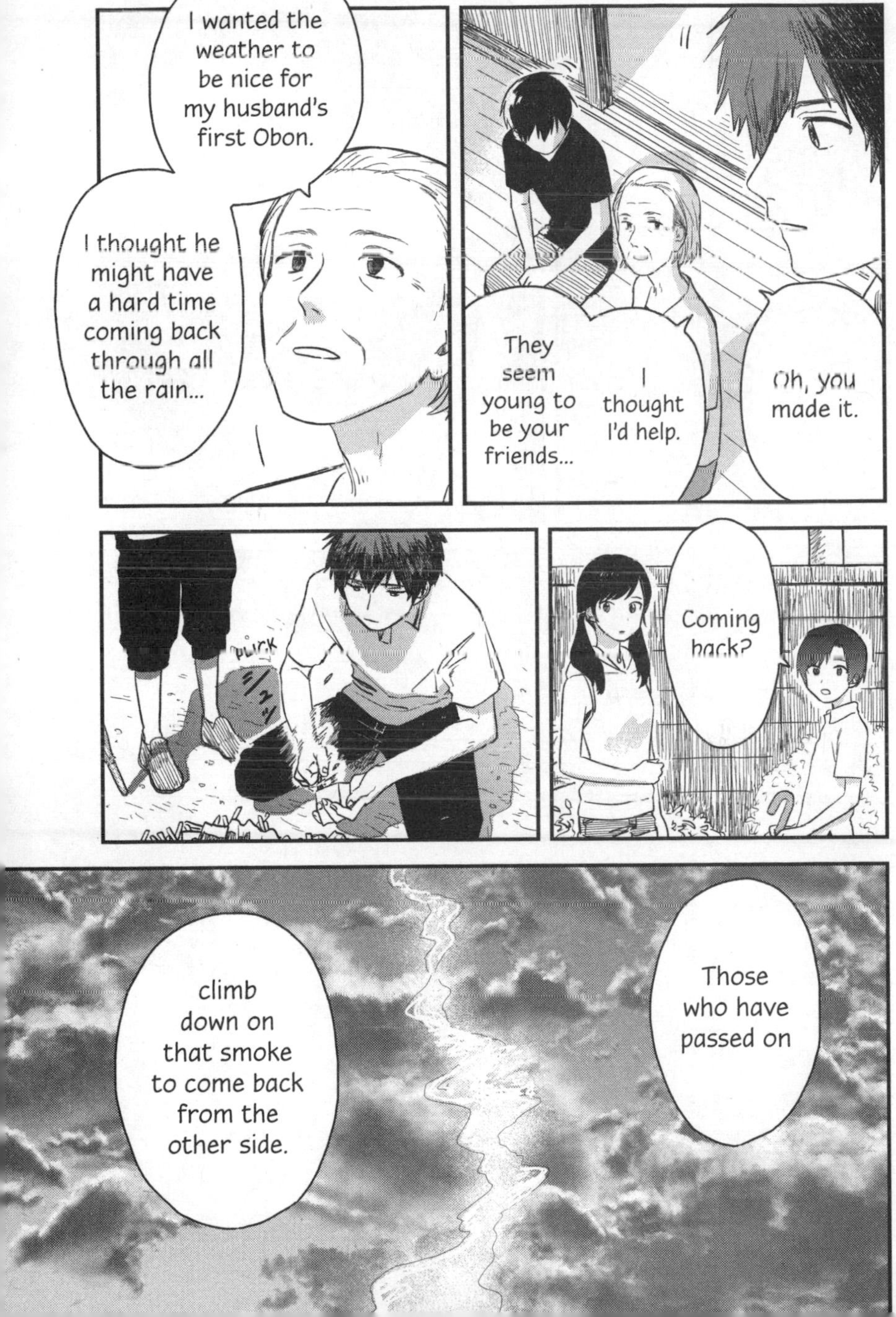
Oh, you made it.
I thought I'd help.
They seem young to be your friends...
I wanted the weather to be nice for my husband's first Obon.
I thought he might have a hard time coming back through all the rain...
Coming back?
FLICK
Those who have passed on
climb down on that smoke to come back from the other side.

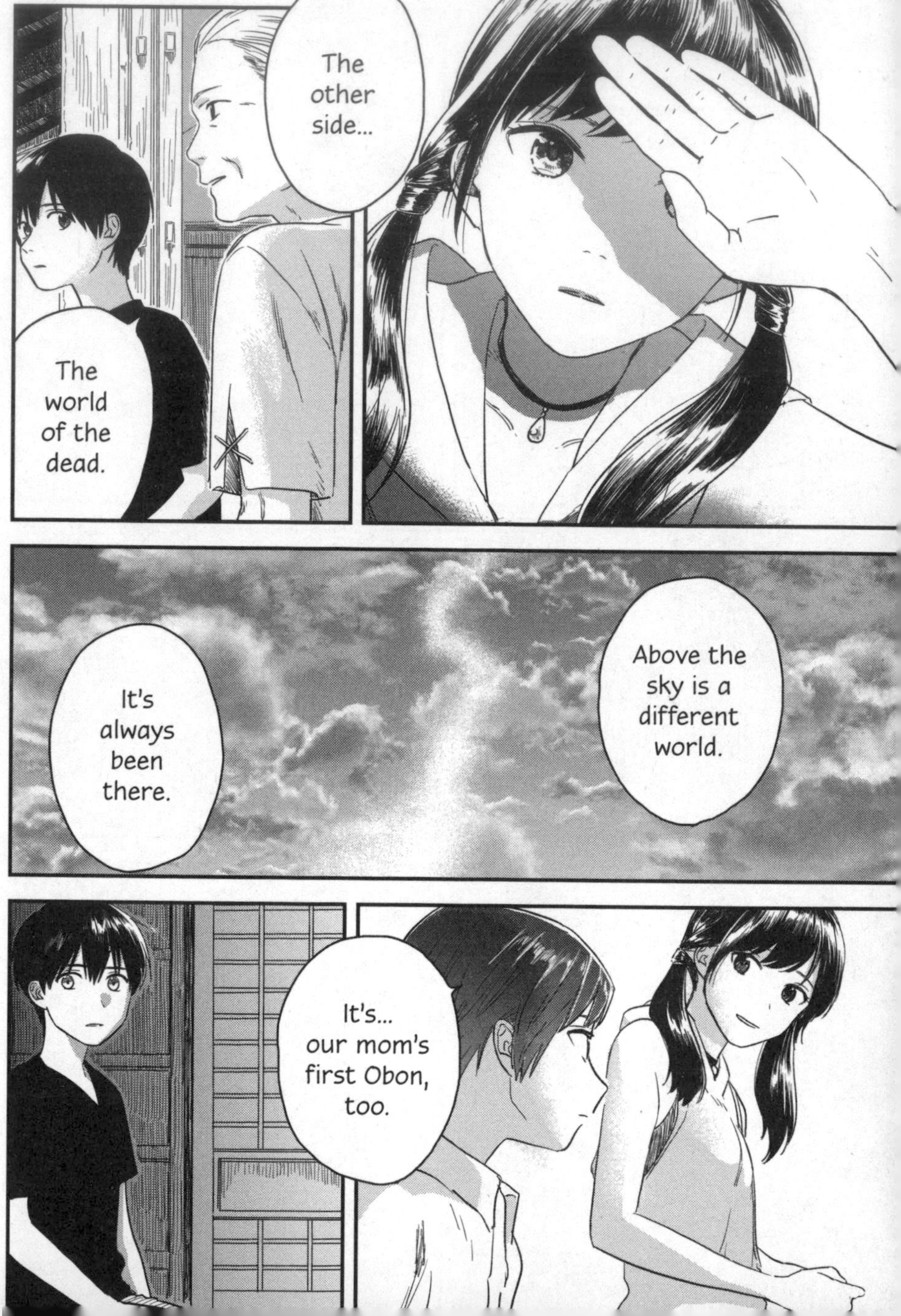
The other side...
The world of the dead.
Above the sky is a different world.
It's always been there.
It's... our mom's first Obon, too.

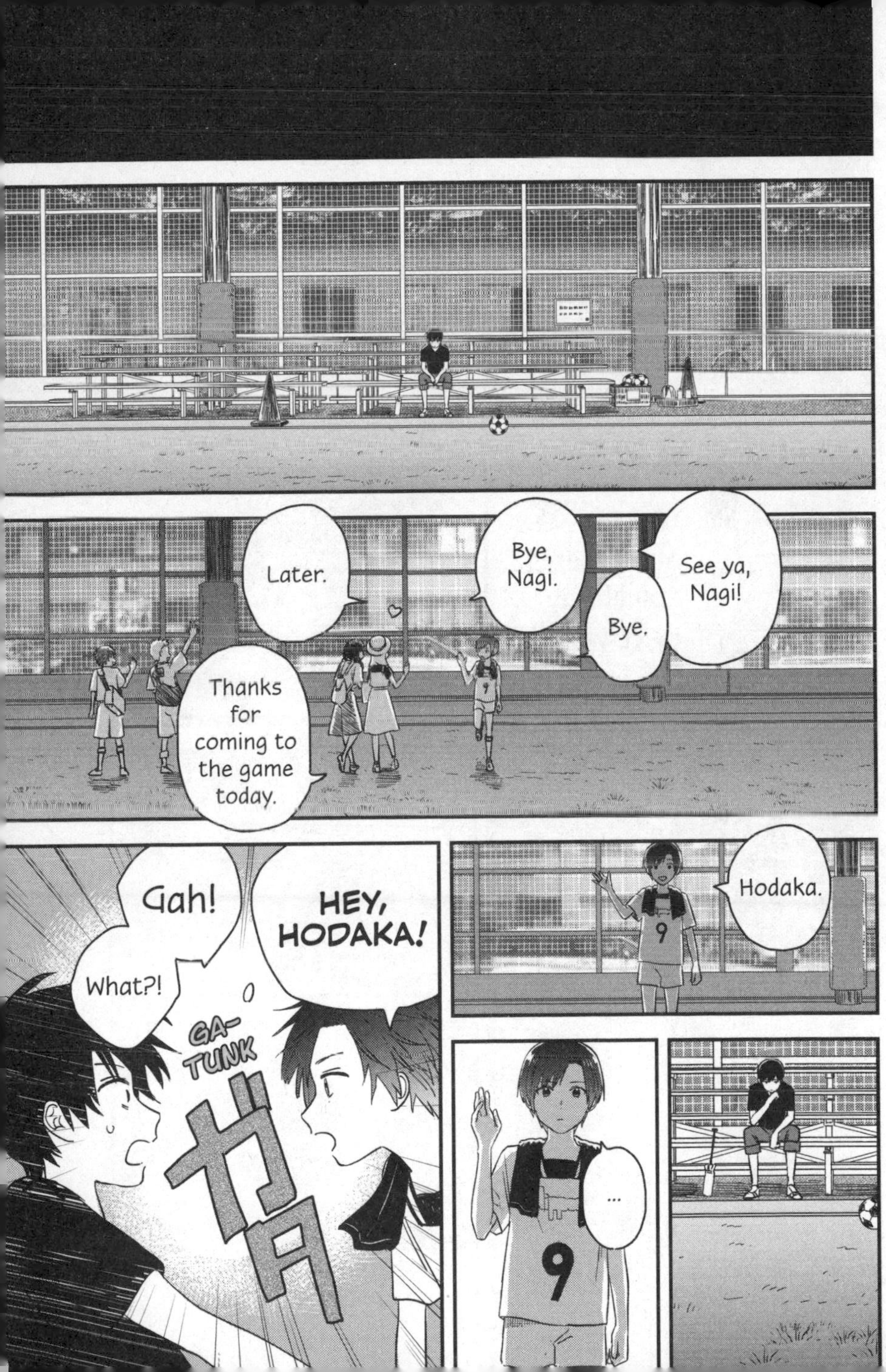
See ya, Nagi!
Bye.
Bye, Nagi.
Later.
Thanks for coming to the game today.
Hodaka.
...
HEY, HODAKA!
Gah!
What?!
GA-TUNK

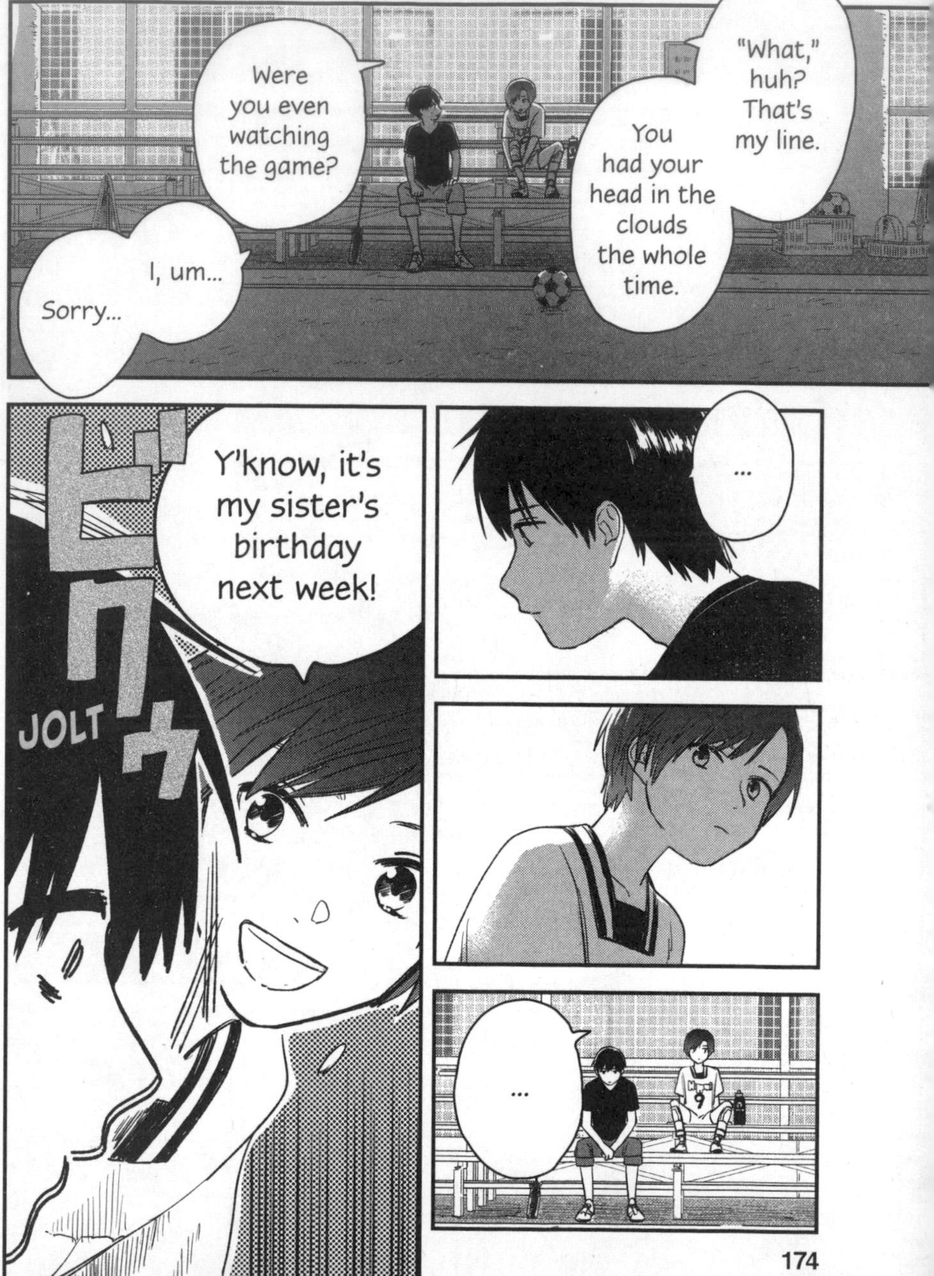
"What," huh? That's my line.
You had your head in the clouds the whole time.
Were you even watching the game?
I, um... Sorry...
...
...
ビクゥ
JOLT
Y'know, it's my sister's birthday next week!

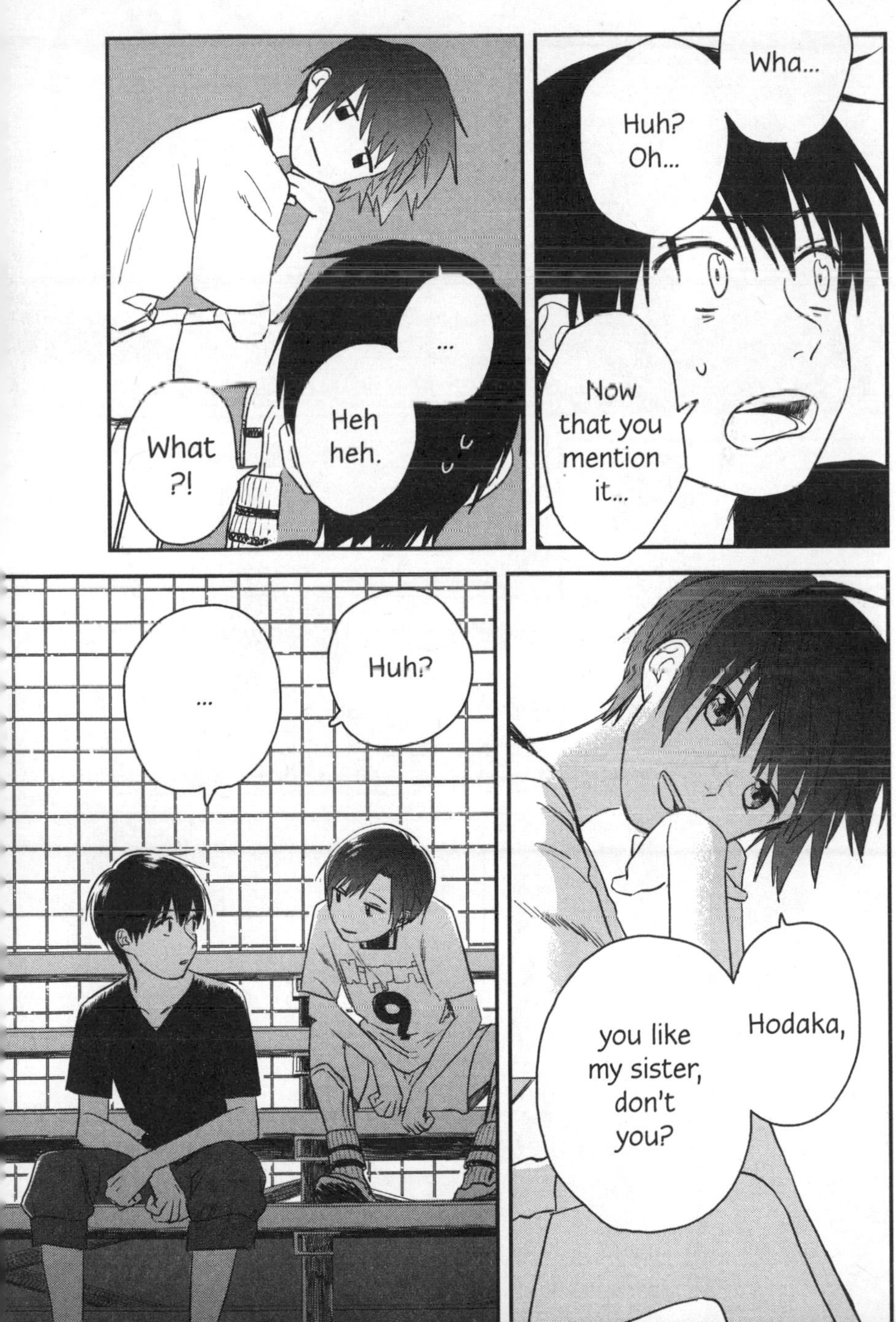
Wha...
Huh? Oh...
Now that you mention it...
...
Heh heh.
What?!
Hodaka,
you like my sister, don't you?
Huh?
...

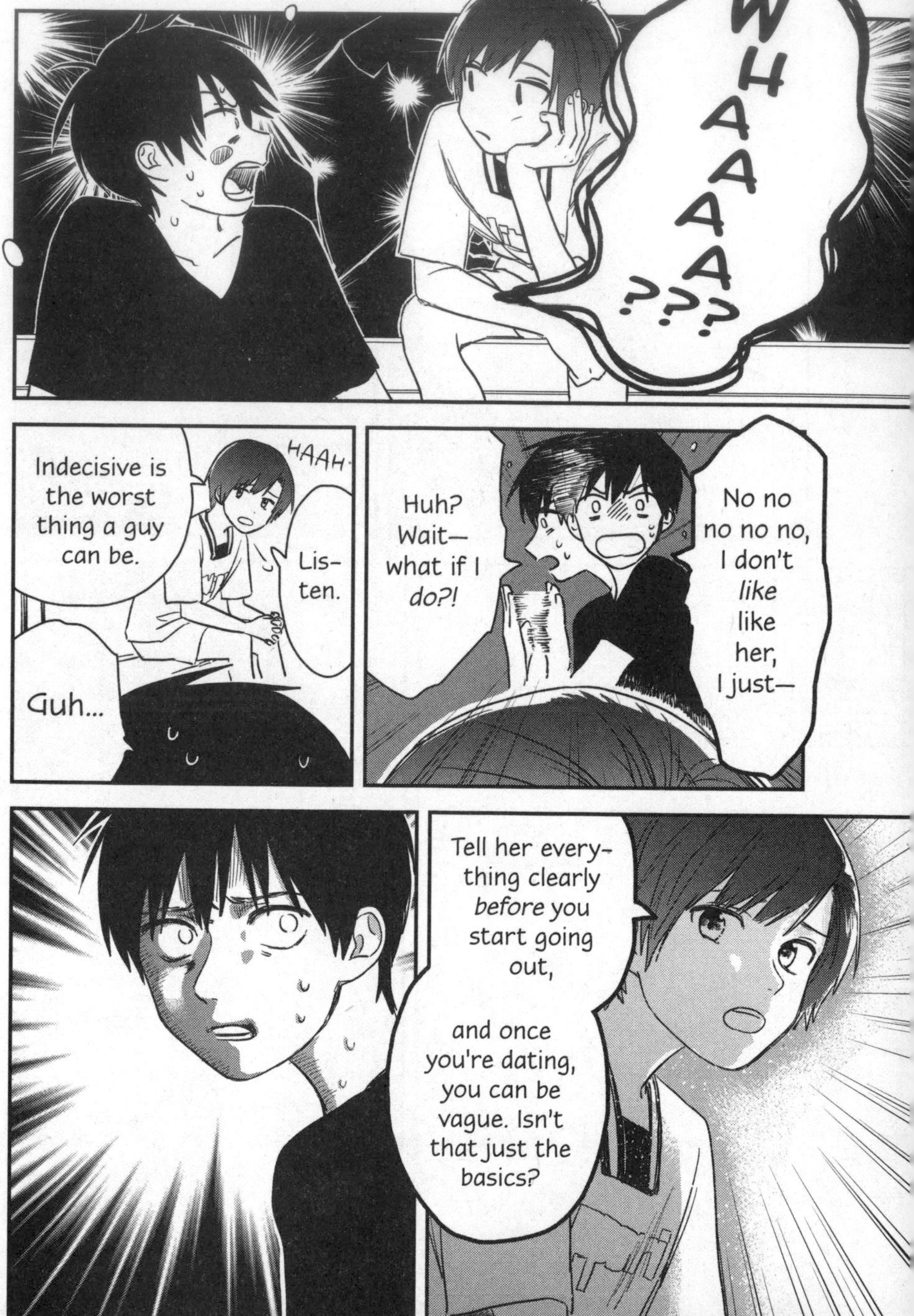
WHAAAAA???
No no no no no, I don't like like her, I just—
Huh? Wait—what if I do?!
HAAAH
Indecisive is the worst thing a guy can be.
Lis-ten.
Guh...
Tell her every-thing clearly before you start going out,
and once you're dating, you can be vague. Isn't that just the basics?

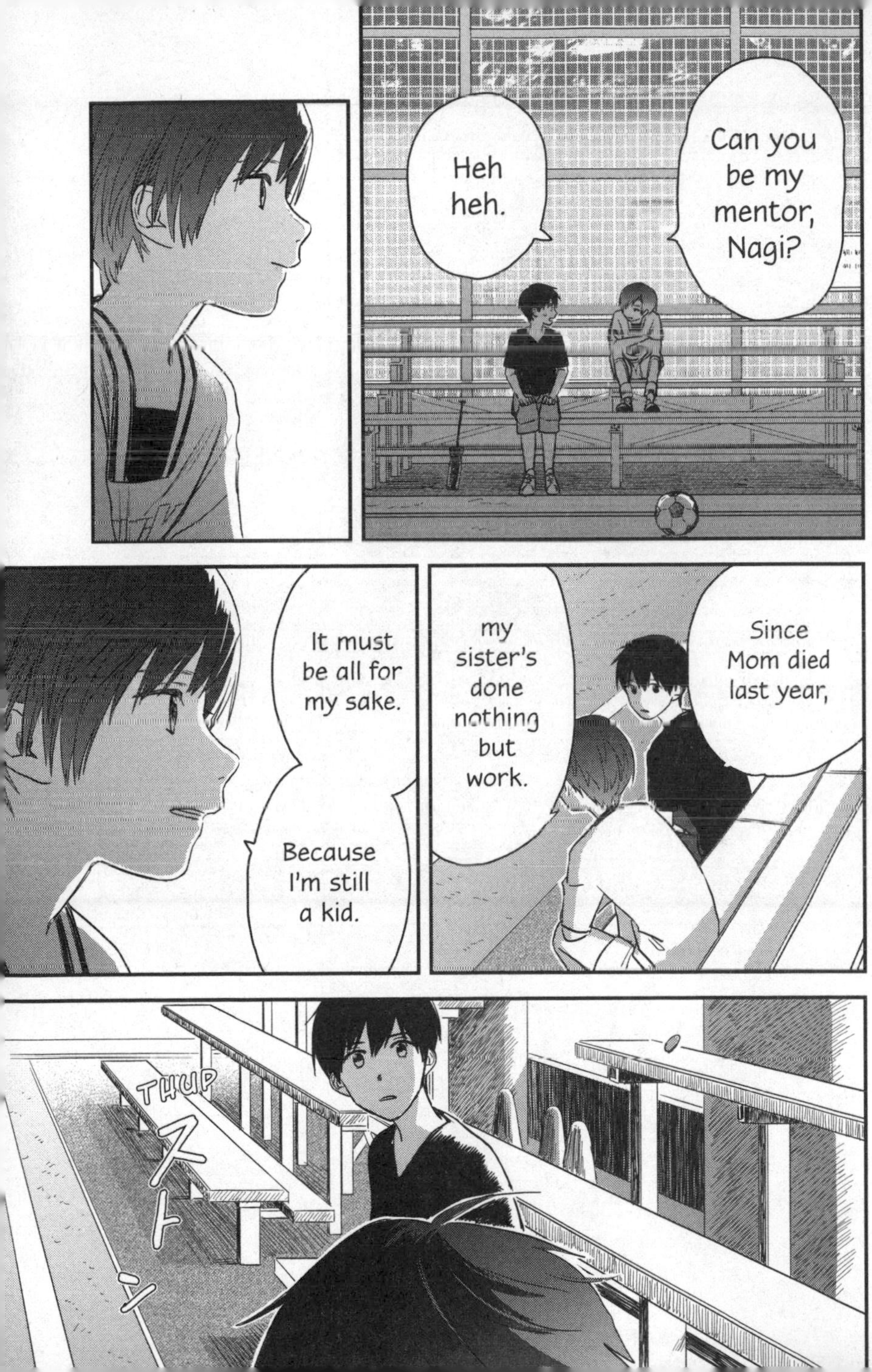
Can you be my mentor, Nagi?
Heh heh.
Since Mom died last year,
my sister's done nothing but work.
It must be all for my sake.
Because I'm still a kid.
THUP
ストン

So I want my sister to enjoy her life more, like a normal girl.

Well...

I'm not totally sure you're the right guy, Hodaka, but here you are.

BUMP

Gotta get her a present, right? Hmm.

JR 新宿駅

JR Shinjuku Station

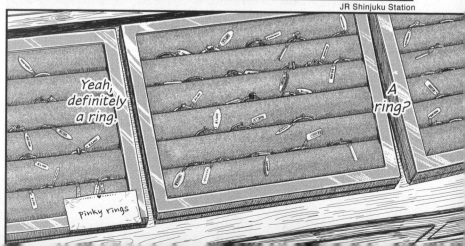

Yeah, definitely a ring.

A ring?

pinky rings

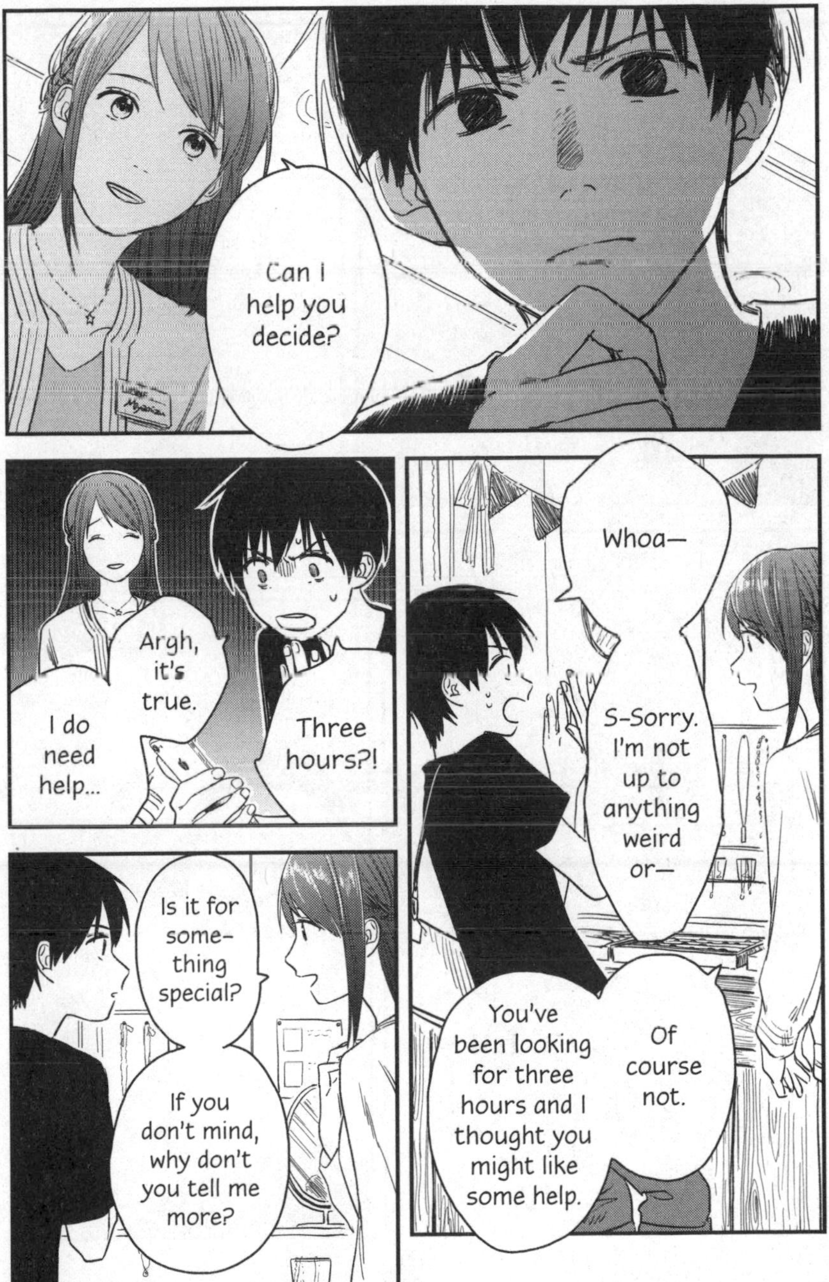
Can I help you decide?
Whoa—
S-Sorry. I'm not up to anything weird or—
Of course not.
You've been looking for three hours and I thought you might like some help.
Three hours?!
Argh, it's true.
I do need help...
Is it for some-thing special?
If you don't mind, why don't you tell me more?

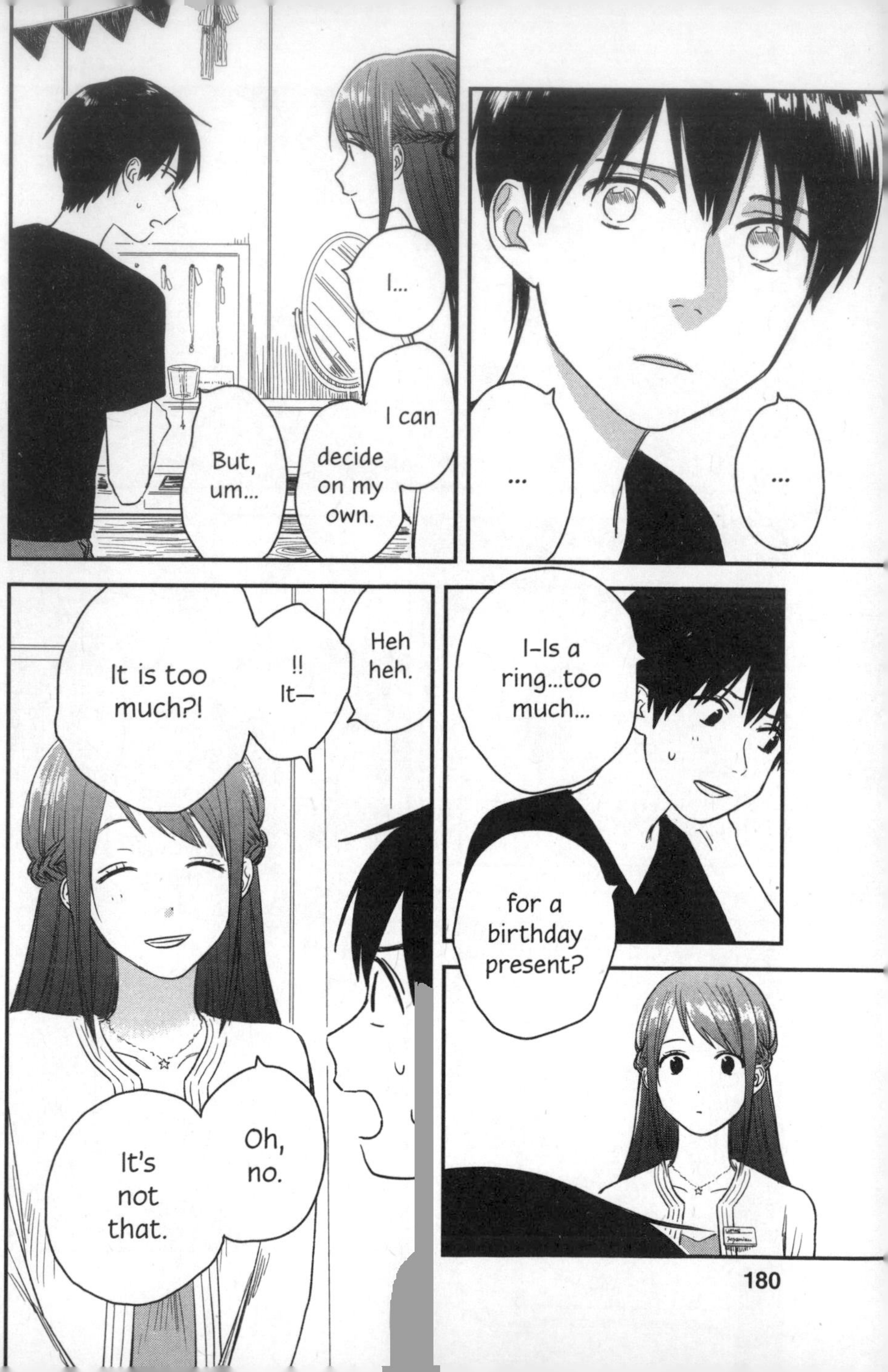
...
...
I...
I can decide on my own.
But, um...
I-Is a ring...too much...
for a birthday present?
Heh heh.
!! It—
It is too much?!
Oh, no.
It's not that.

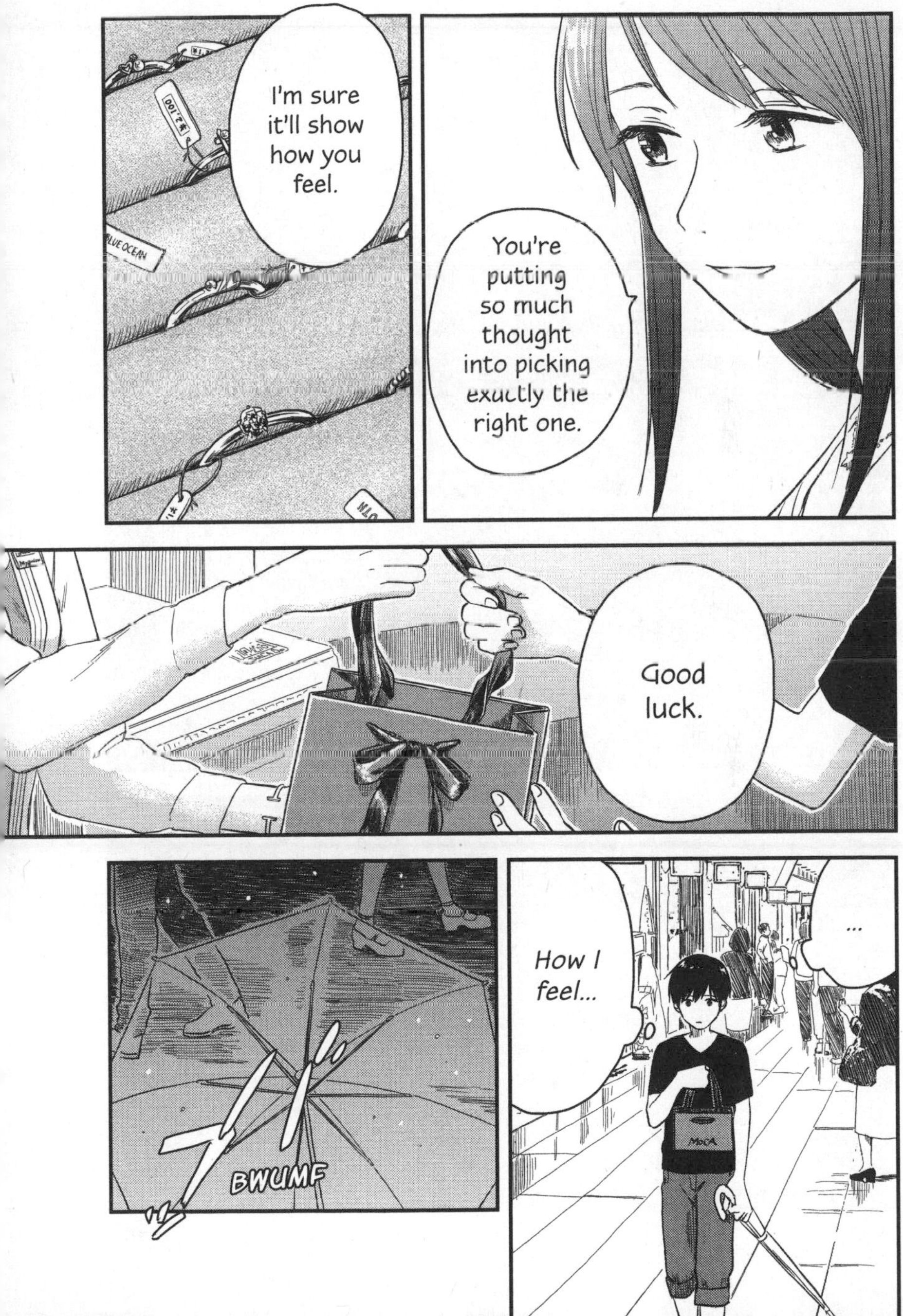
You're putting so much thought into picking exactly the right one.
I'm sure it'll show how you feel.
BLUE OCEAN
Good luck.
...
How I feel...
BWUMF

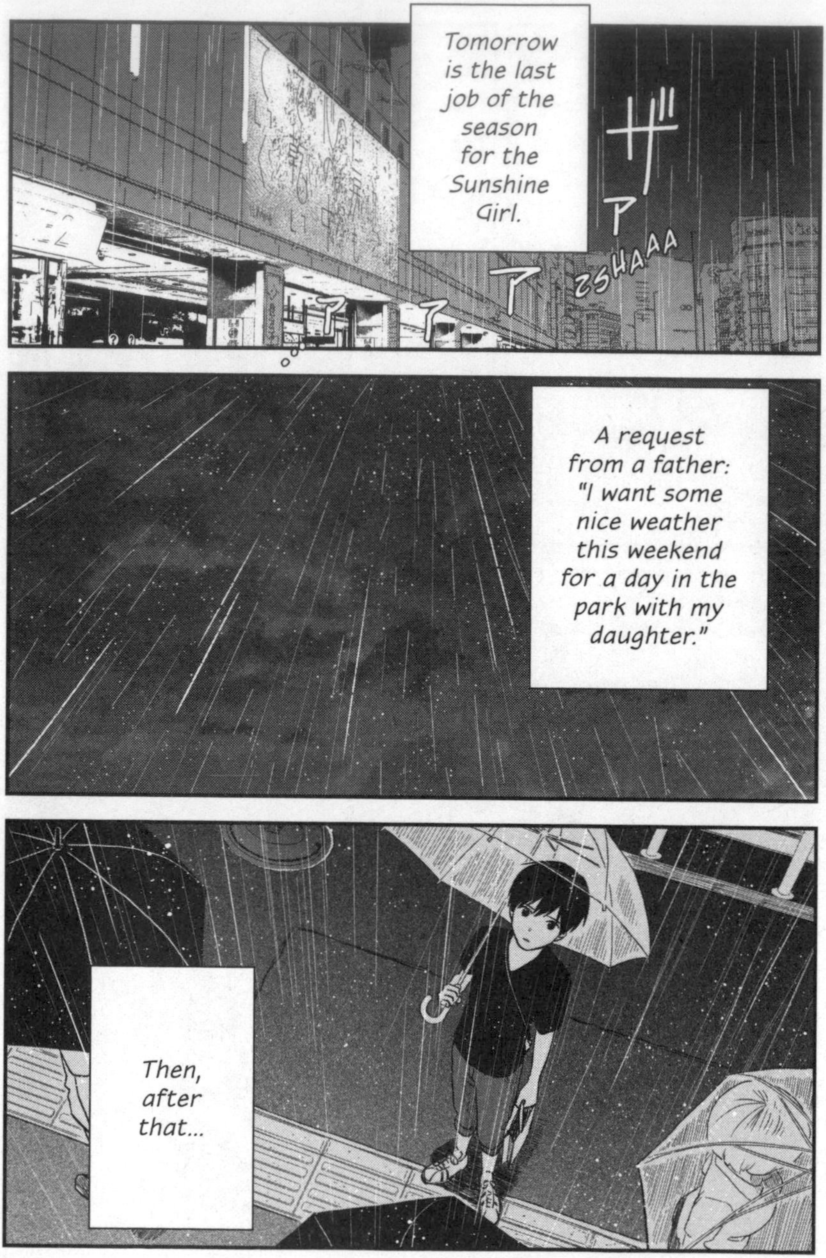
Tomorrow is the last job of the season for the Sunshine Girl.
ザアアアア
ZSHAAA
A request from a father: "I want some nice weather this weekend for a day in the park with my daughter."
Then, after that...

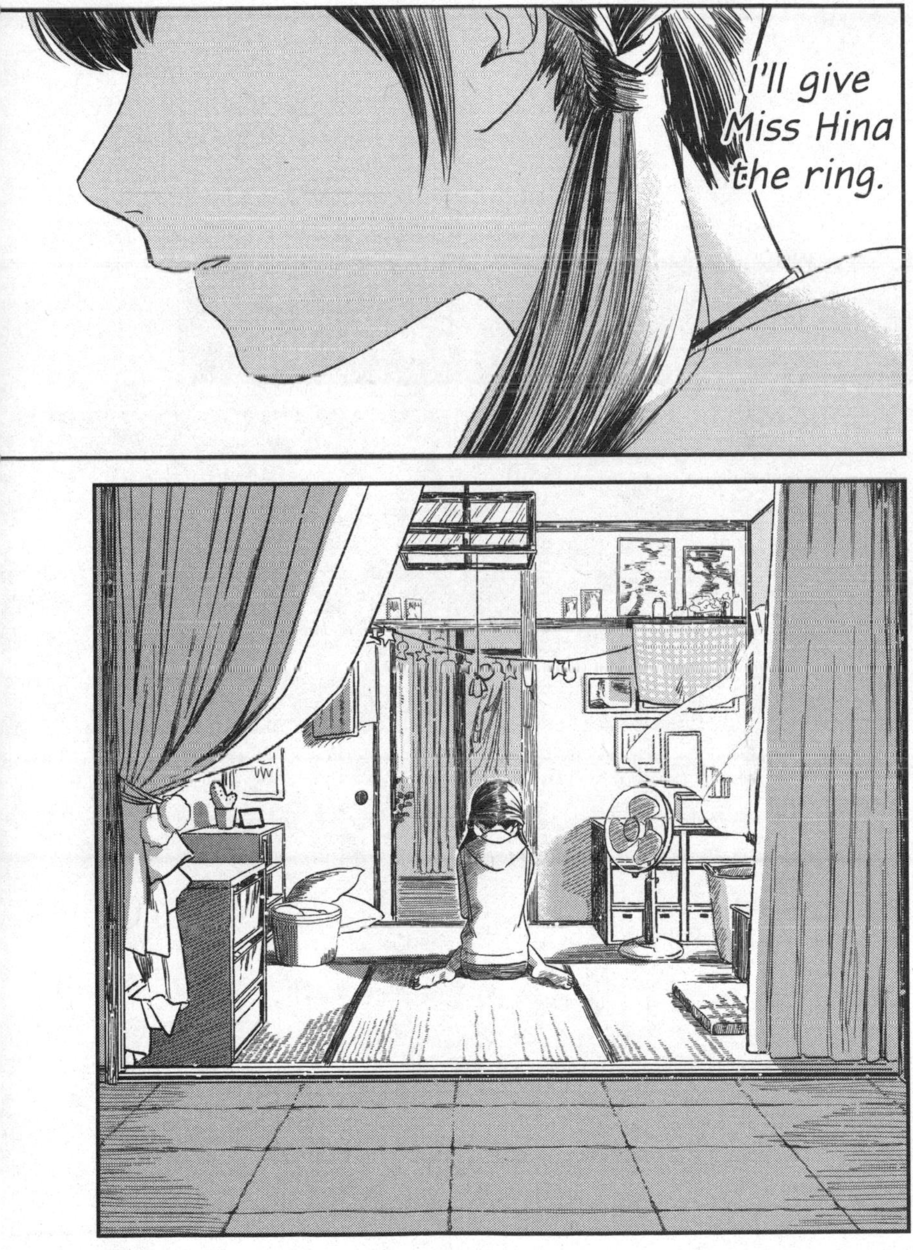
I'll give
Miss Hina
the ring.

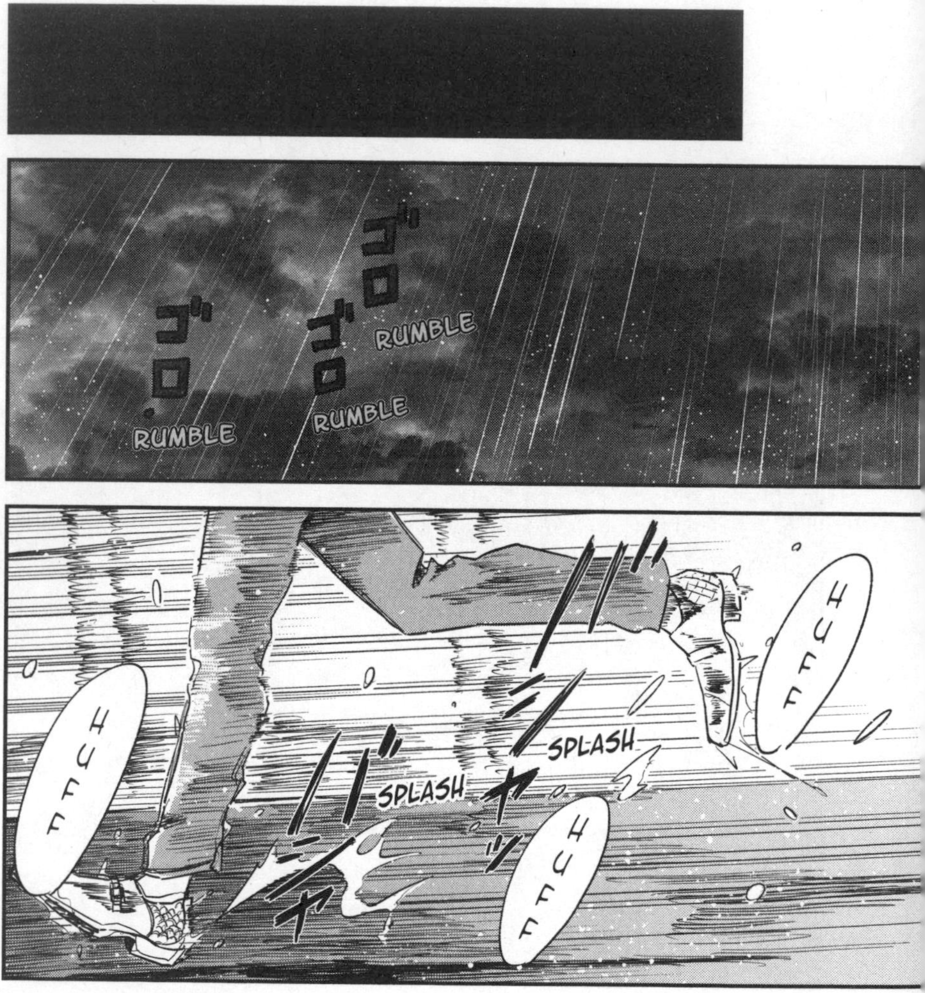
ゴロ
RUMBLE
ゴロ
RUMBLE
ゴロ
RUMBLE
HUFF
SPLASH
SPLASH
HUFF
HUFF

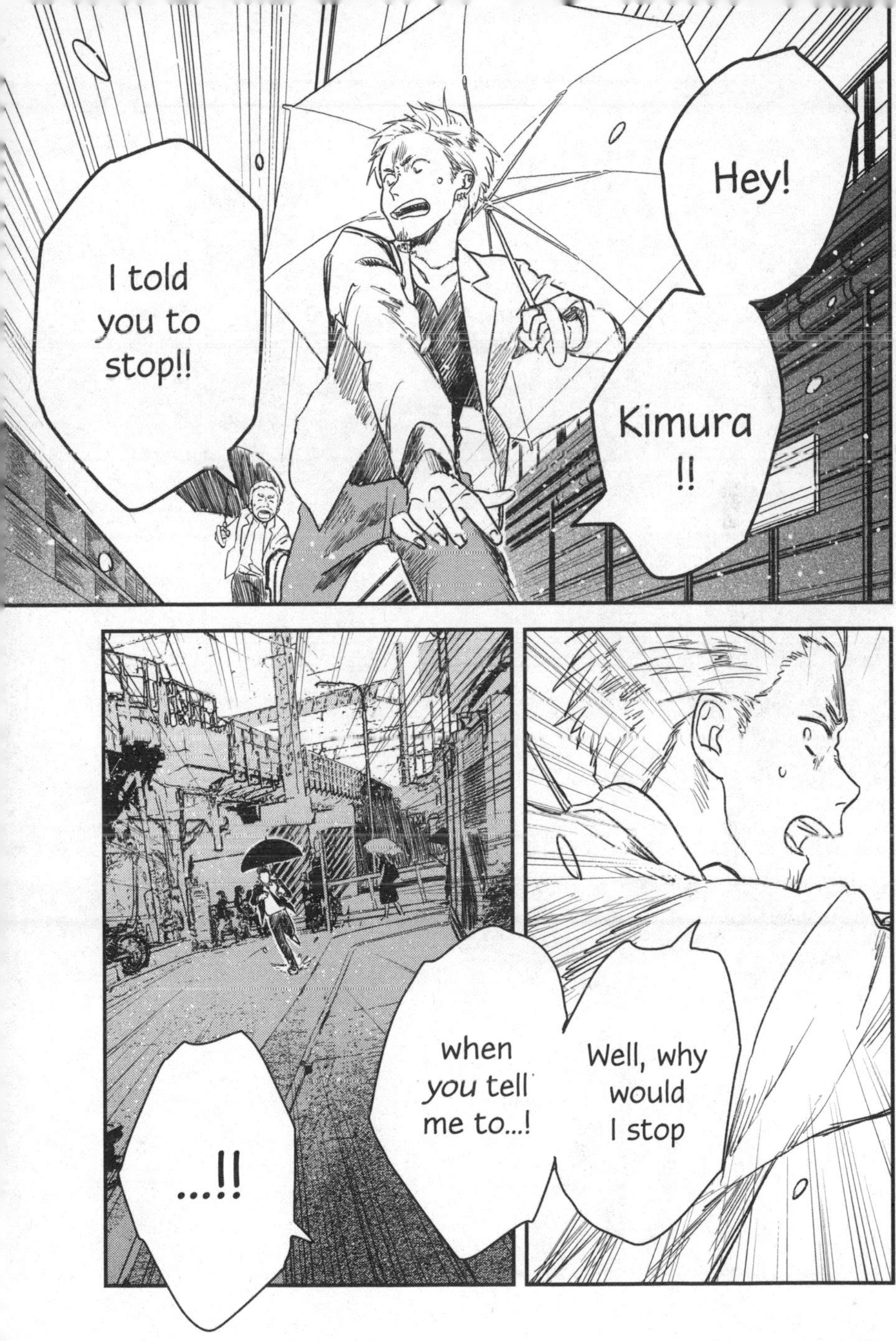
Hey!
Kimura !!
I told you to stop!!
Well, why would I stop
when *you* tell me to...!
...!!

HUFF
HUFF
HUFF
Er...
SIIIIIGH
Um, officer, I swear I didn't know
she was under-age...
...Huh...?

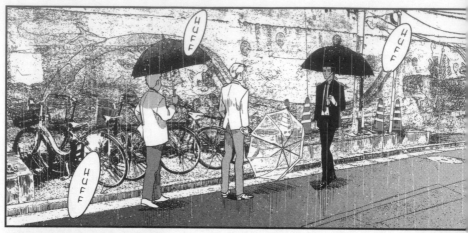

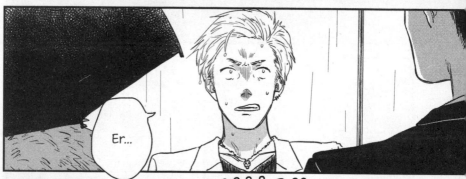

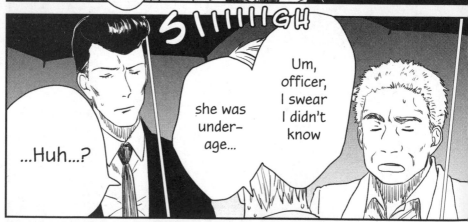

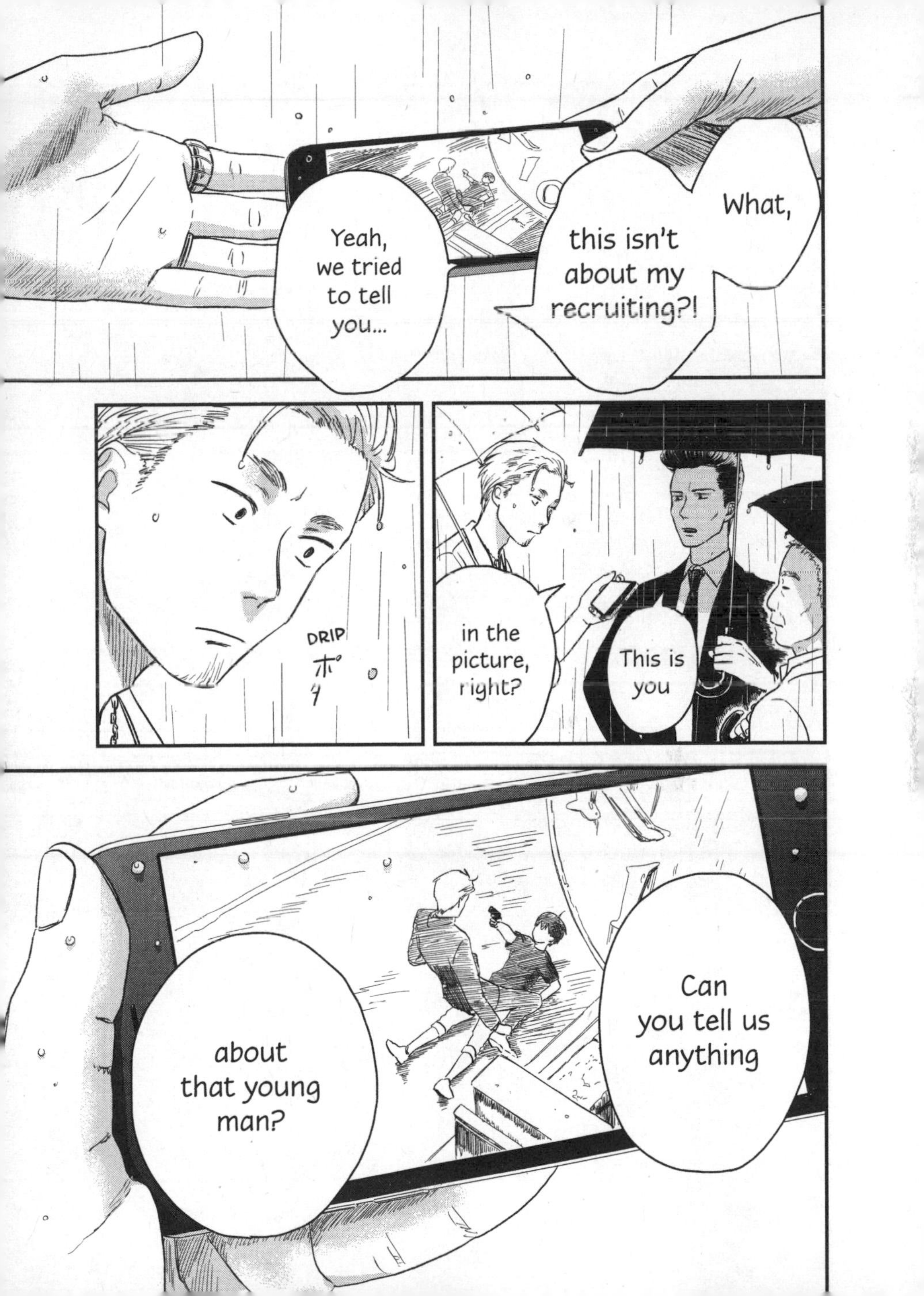
What, this isn't about my recruiting?!
Yeah, we tried to tell you...
This is you
in the picture, right?
DRIP
Can you tell us anything
about that young man?

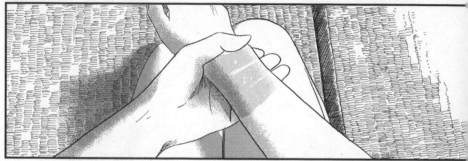

Weathering With You Volume 1 - END

Special Issue

Thursday's Child has Far to Go

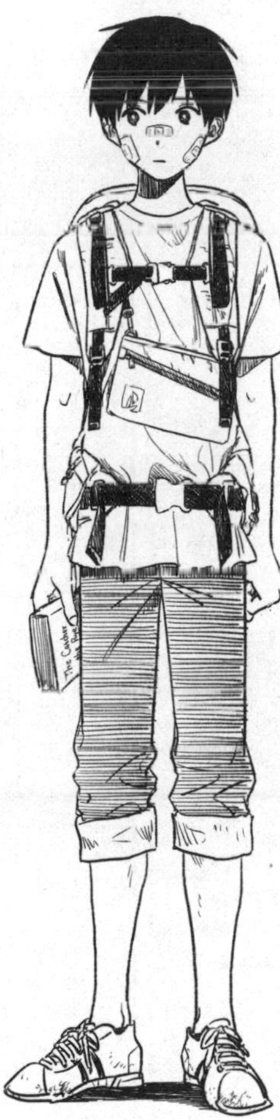

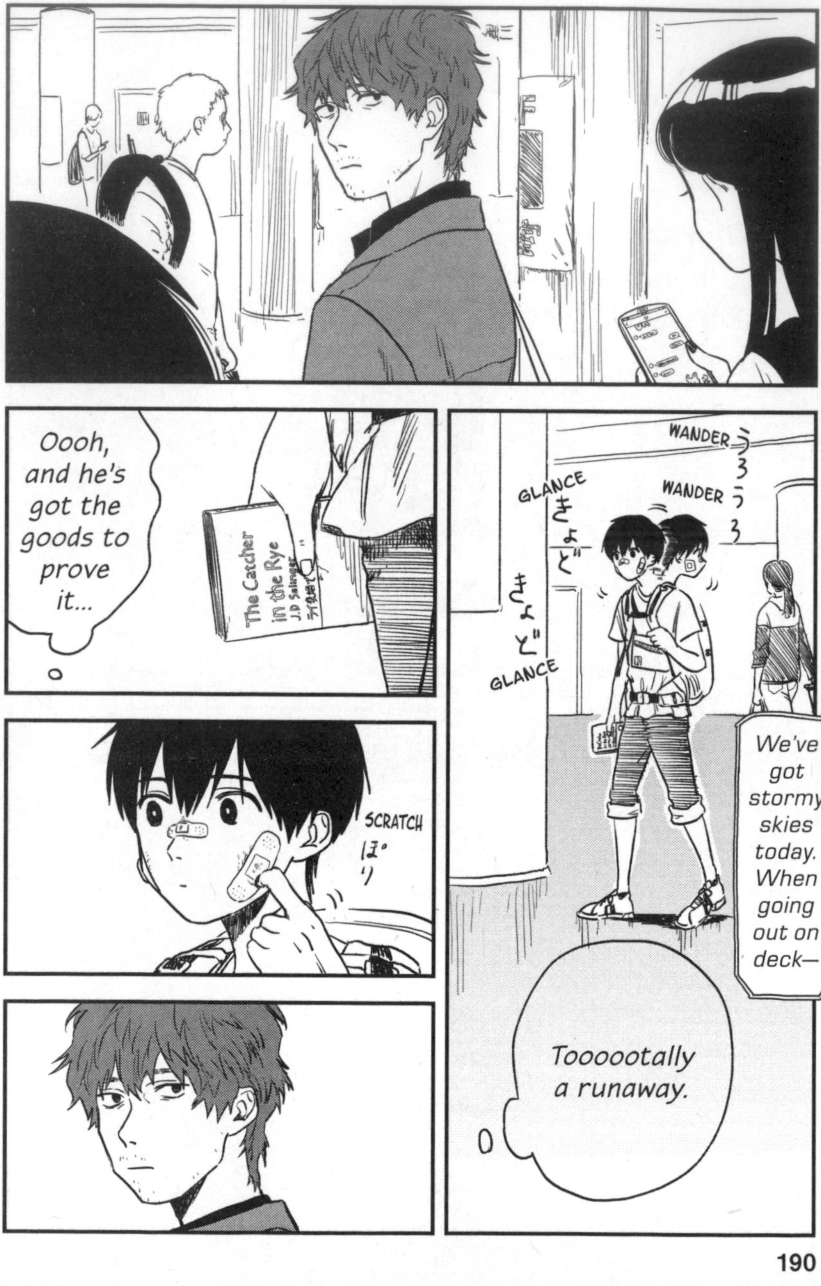
WANDER うろ
WANDER うろ
GLANCE きょど
GLANCE きょど
We've got stormy skies today. When going out on deck—
Toooootally a runaway.
Oooh, and he's got the goods to prove it...
The Catcher in the Rye
J.D Salinger
SCRATCH ぽり

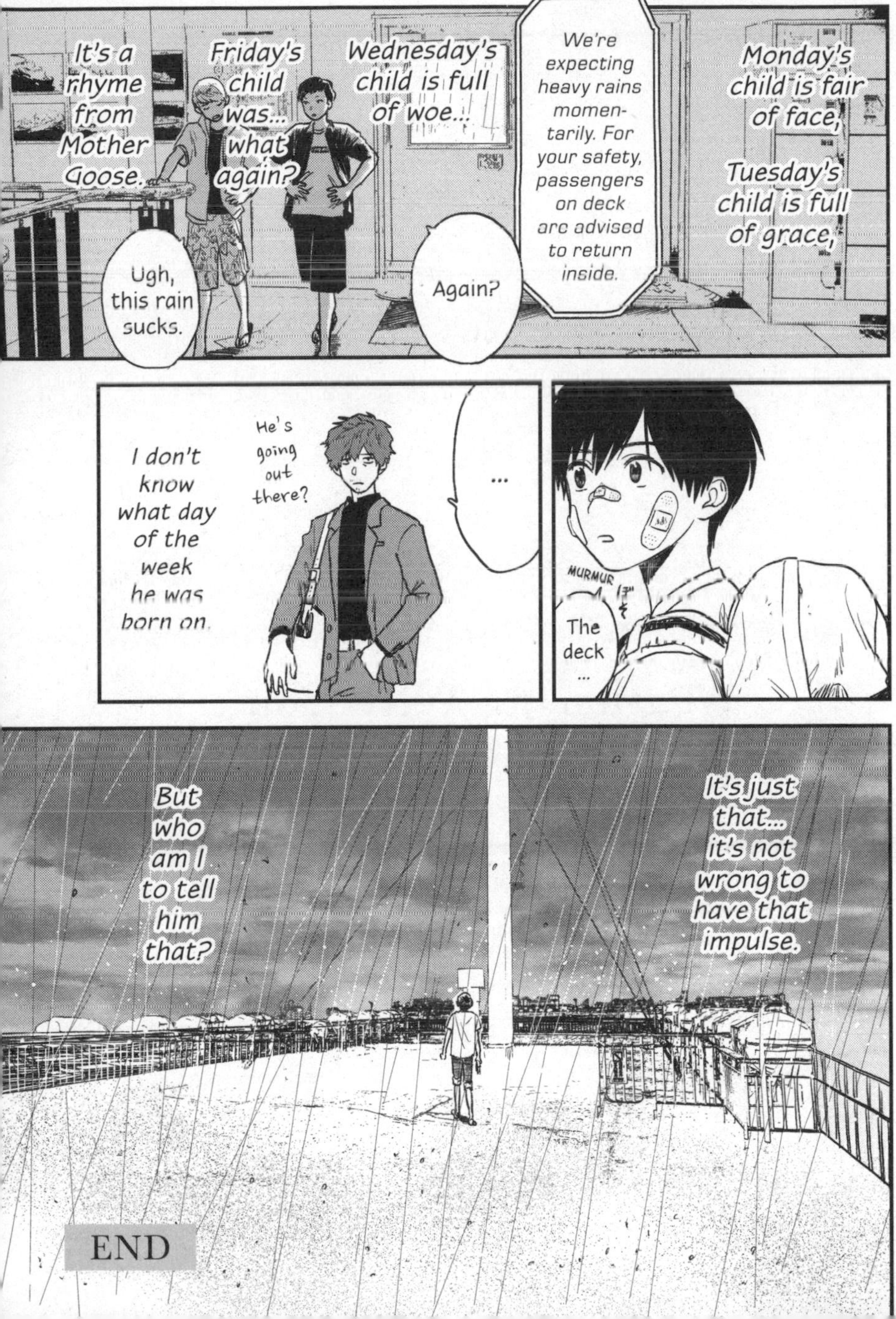
Monday's child is fair of face,
Tuesday's child is full of grace,
We're expecting heavy rains momentarily. For your safety, passengers on deck arc advised to return inside.
Wednesday's child is full of woe...
Again?
Friday's child was... what again?
Ugh, this rain sucks.
It's a rhyme from Mother Goose.
MURMUR
The deck ...
...
He's going out there?
I don't know what day of the week he was born on.
It's just that... it's not wrong to have that impulse.
But who am I to tell him that?
END

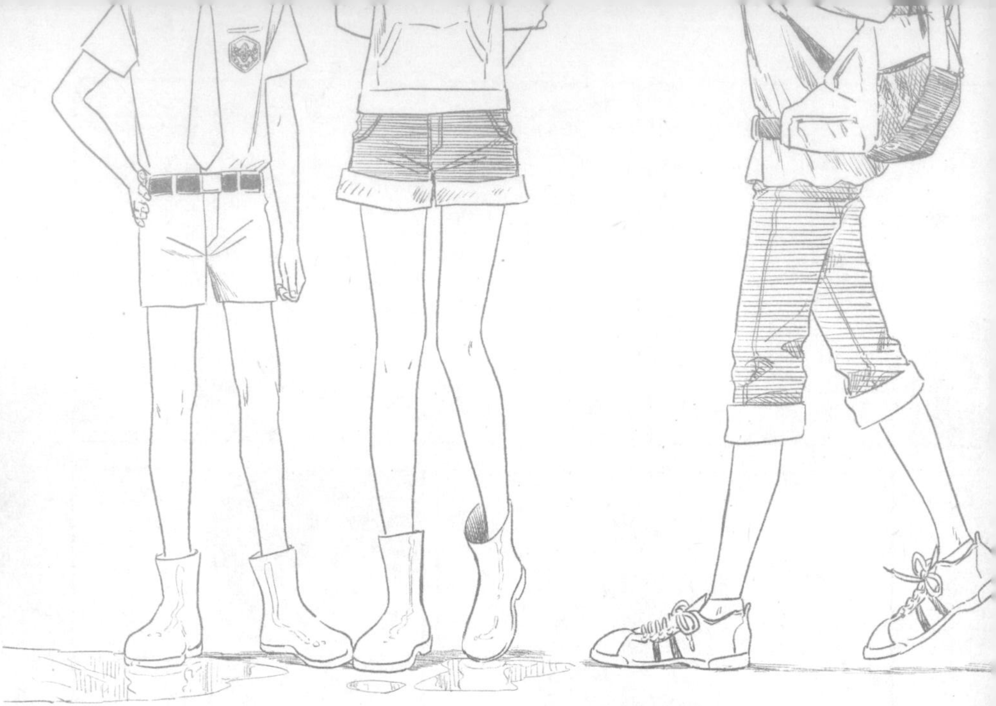

Weathering With You

Translation Notes

p. 31 "Hostess Bar"
A bar where female staff are paid to serve alcohol and engage in conversations with their (primarily male) customers. A common feature of East Asian nightlife.

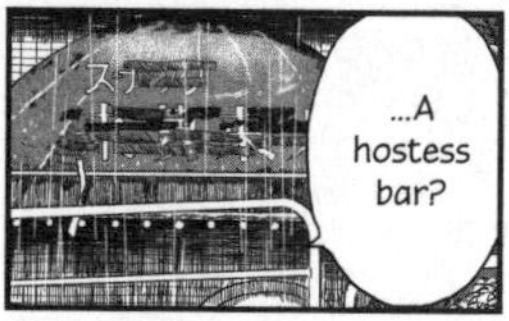
...A hostess bar?

p. 109 "Yakiniku"
Literally "grilled meat." Sounds tasty!

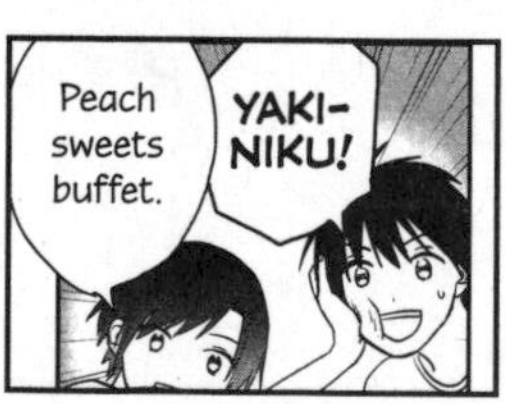
YAKI-NIKU!
Peach sweets buffet.

Notes contintued on the next page!

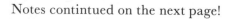

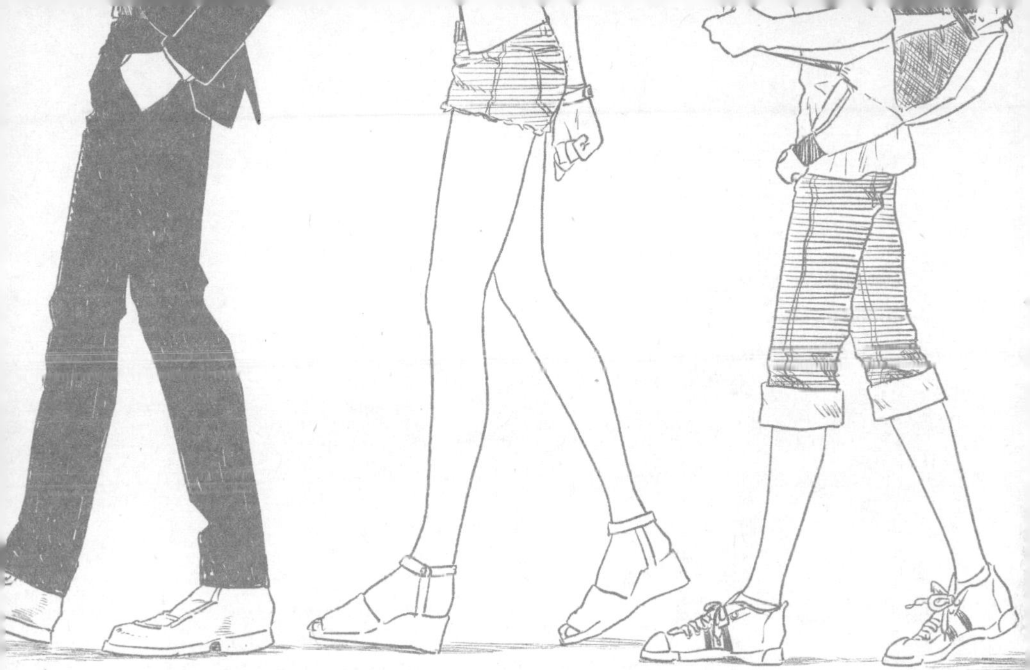

Weathering With You

Translation Notes CONTINUED

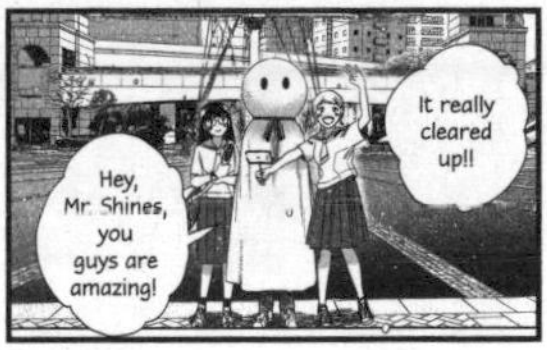
It really cleared up!!
Hey, Mr. Shines, you guys are amazing!

p. 111 “Mr. Shines”
In the scene to the left, Hodaka dresses up as Mr. Shines, a life-sized “*teru teru bōzu.*” Literally meaning “shine shine monk,” the small white charms are believed to stop rain and guarantee sunshine. If you turn to page 92, you can see that Hodaka hung many *teru teru bōzu* on Hina’s umbrella for luck!

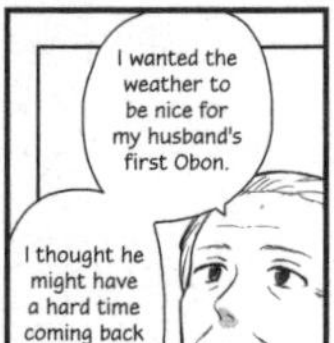
I wanted the weather to be nice for my husband's first Obon.
I thought he might have a hard time coming back through all the rain...

p. 171 “Obon”
Also known as “Obon Festival,” it is a Buddhist custom in which people honor their ancestors and invite them back home. Generally observed from August 13-15.

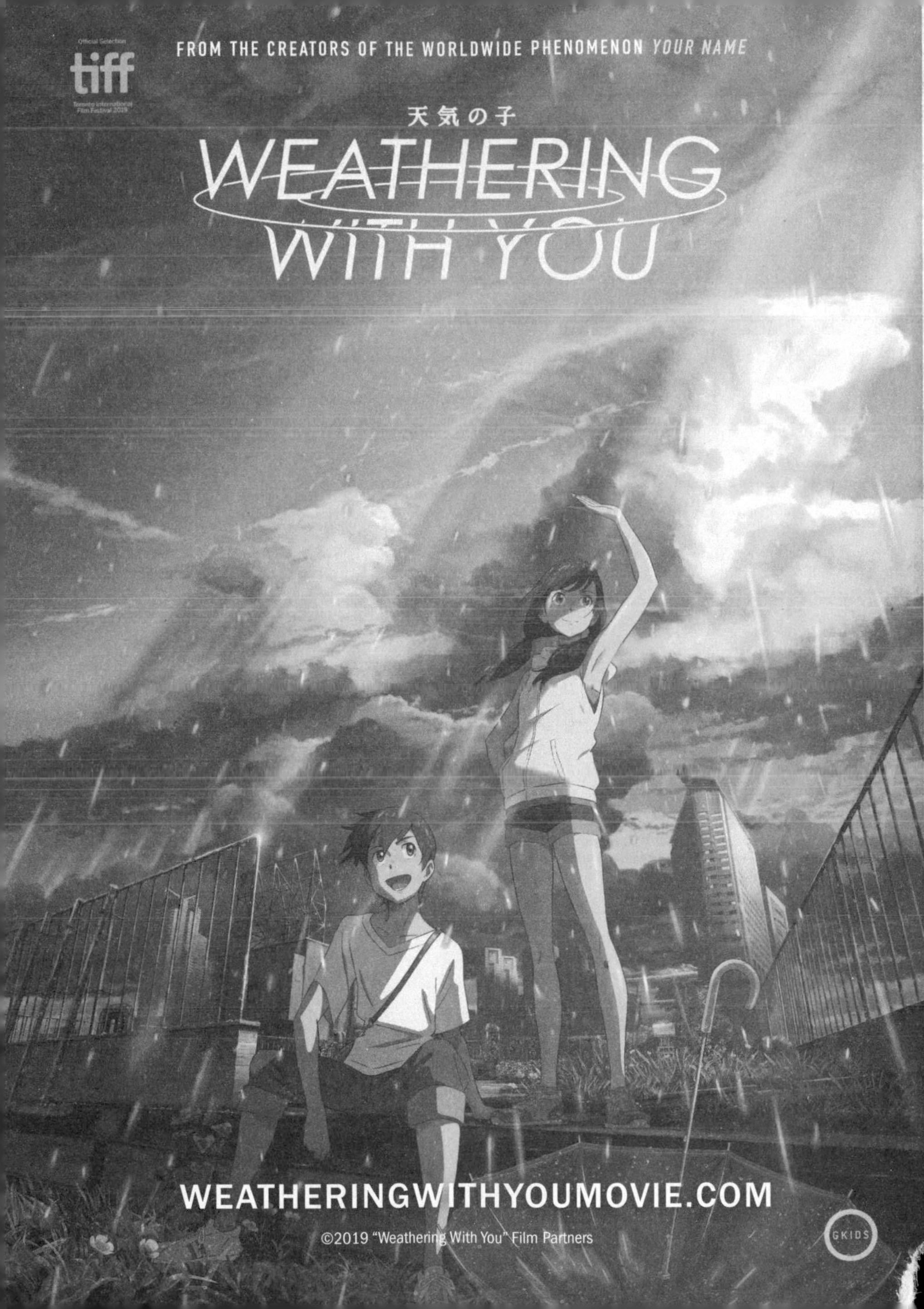
Official Selection
tiff
Toronto International Film Festival 2019
FROM THE CREATORS OF THE WORLDWIDE PHENOMENON *YOUR NAME*
天気の子
WEATHERING WITH YOU
WEATHERINGWITHYOUMOVIE.COM
©2019 "Weathering With You" Film Partners
GKIDS

Weathering With You 1

A Vertical Comics Edition

Editing: Kristi Fernandez
Translation: Melissa Tanaka
Production: Risa Cho
Lorina Mapa

First published in Japan in 2019 by Kodansha, Ltd., Tokyo
Publication rights for this English edition arranged through Kodansha, Ltd., Tokyo
English language version produced by Vertical Comics, an imprint of Kodansha USA Publishing, LLC

Translation provided by Vertical Comics, 2020
Published by Kodansha USA Publishing, LLC, New York

Originally published in Japanese as *Tenki no Ko 1* by Kodansha, Ltd., 2019
Tenki no Ko first serialized in *Afternoon*, Kodansha, Ltd., 2019-2020

This is a work of fiction.

ISBN: 978-1-949980-83-7

Manufactured in the United States of America

First Edition

Fourth Printing

Kodansha USA Publishing, LLC
451 Park Avenue South
7th Floor
New York, NY 10016
www.kodansha.us

Vertical books are distributed through Penguin-Random House Publisher Services.